CH00765560

"This is a significant, well-annotated exhibition of the
1960s consciousness experiments mere months befor
Odorisio, the astute editor of the recent magisterial *N*
a new wave of scholarly contemplatives who explore Merton's strategic inner work to
transcend himself in service and witness to the global communities of those who pray.
Odorisio lays out evidence of Merton's having lost his 'self' forward through deeper
inner experiences of solitude and community. Merton beacons hope that all divisions
of our true and false selves will disappear at last into a universal matrix of love."

—Jonathan Montaldo, *Bridges to Contemplative Living with Thomas Merton*

"Merton was at his best in informal settings. This newly published material provides
examples: two sets of talks to monastics and two collections of letters both in his
ipsissima verba. Edited with intelligence, warmth, and clear documentation, the book
makes some of his last, most important teaching on prayer widely available. It is an
important contribution to Merton primary sources."

—Bonnie Thurston, author of *Shaped by the End You Live For: Thomas Merton's
Monastic Spirituality*

"What a marvelous, unexpected gift! These series of informal talks to a cherished
community of Cistercian women and later to a small group of their invited guests,
along with related materials, sparkle and inspire with Thomas Merton's characteristic
insight, humor, and wisdom. Expertly introduced and edited by David Odorisio, this
volume presents Merton at the top of his form and fills a gap we didn't even know
existed in the literary record of the final months of his life."

—Patrick F. O'Connell, editor, *Thomas Merton: Selected Essays*

"As one of the participants of the [October] 1968 Redwoods Conferences, I can sum up
the atmosphere of those days in one word: electrified—and this in every respect . . . even
the most mundane exchange seemed to be charged with high voltage. *Thomas Merton in
California* gives readers the privilege to sense for themselves the formidable creative charge
of those encounters as if they were there. What higher praise could there be for this book?"

—David Steindl-Rast, OSB, monk, author, co-founder of grateful.org

"With fresh, astute editing, Odorisio offers us a powerful entry into Merton's post-
Vatican II thinking about human consciousness that reveals Merton's deep sense of
play, spiritual honesty, and belief in the 'cosmic community of creatures.' These 1968
Redwood Conferences and letters to Mother Myriam Dardenne, OCSO, that created
an 'alleluia experience' for Merton are now, for the first time, available to contemporary
readers. Promise yourself a thorough and engaging reading."

—Monica Weis, SSJ, professor emerita of English, Nazareth University

"With *Thomas Merton in California*, expertly edited by David M. Odorisio, we have the mature Merton of 1968 speaking on prayer, spirituality, and interfaith dialogue, along with other areas of concern for him at that time. Merton's previously unavailable talks to the community at Our Lady of the Redwoods from May and October 1968 will appeal to seekers everywhere as he tells the sisters, quite simply yet profoundly, 'The great thing is prayer. Prayer itself . . . if you want a life of prayer, the way to get it is by praying.' These talks, given just days before his departure for Asia and weeks before his untimely death, show Merton's deep rootedness in the monastic tradition and his Catholic faith, while still being open to other faith traditions and becoming, as he tells the sisters, 'as good a Buddhist as I can.'"

—Paul M. Pearson, director, Thomas Merton Center

"The young man who thought of himself as a contemplative in Greenwich Village now comes full circle after decades of monastic life to the crucible of contemporary culture and thought in Northern California, not only with his dear friends at Redwoods Monastery, but in his jaunts into San Francisco, jazz clubs, and Beat bookstores. The conferences contained here are more like conversations that Merton initiates, and you can almost hear the restless Trappist breathless with excitement about the future, particularly his own. To read *Thomas Merton in California* is more like listening in, not only to his dizzyingly wide-ranging erudition but on candid descriptions of his own daily life as a solitary that do well to shatter the romantic illusions of hermit life. A profoundly intimate and fascinating glimpse into one of the greatest minds and most important voices of the twentieth century."

—Cyprian Consiglio, OSB Cam, author of *Prayer in the Cave of the Heart* and *Spirit, Soul, Body*

"Here we hear Merton in his own voice—candid, uncensored, heartfelt—as he explores human consciousness through lenses of Christian, Hindu, Sufi, and Zen mysticism. We owe David M. Odorisio a debt of gratitude for his artfully-crafted introduction to the landscape and spirit of Redwoods, judiciously edited transcriptions of Merton's talks and letters, and informative yet unobtrusive annotation. This book is a treasure— informative and inspiring! It will touch readers' minds and hearts!"

—Christine M. Bochen, professor emerita of religious studies at Nazareth University, Rochester, New York

Thomas Merton in California

The Redwoods Conferences and Letters

edited by David M. Odorisio

foreword by Kathy DeVico, OCSO

preface by Douglas E. Christie

LITURGICAL PRESS
Collegeville, Minnesota

litpress.org

Cover design by Brice Hemmer

1   2   3   4   5   6   7   8   9

Library of Congress Cataloging-in-Publication Data

Names: Odorisio, David M., editor.
Title: Thomas Merton in California : the Redwoods conferences and letters / edited by David M. Odorisio.
Description: Collegeville, Minnesota : Liturgical Press, [2024] | Includes index. | Summary: "In May and October of 1968, Thomas Merton offered two extended conferences at Our Lady of the Redwoods Abbey, a Cistercian women's community in Northern California. It is comprised of previously unpublished letters and over twenty-six hours of conference talks"— Provided by publisher.
Identifiers: LCCN 2023030058 (print) | LCCN 2023030059 (ebook) | ISBN 9798400800313 (trade paperback) | ISBN 9798400800320 (epub) | ISBN 9798400800337 (pdf)
Subjects: LCSH: Merton, Thomas, 1915-1968. | BISAC: RELIGION / Monasticism | RELIGION / Christianity / Catholic
Classification: LCC BX4705.M542 T497 2024 (print) | LCC BX4705.M542 (ebook) | DDC 271/.12502—dc23/eng/20231017
LC record available at https://lccn.loc.gov/2023030058
LC ebook record available at https://lccn.loc.gov/2023030059

To the Sisters of Redwoods Monastery—
past, present, and future

and

For Jonathan
"Go in peace, for we have sworn friendship with each other
in the name of the Lord."
1 Samuel 20:42

Contents

Foreword

The material in this book came out of two visits that Thomas Merton made to Our Lady of the Redwoods Abbey in 1968. The first visit was in May when Merton spoke to the monastic community, having been asked by the abbess, Mother Myriam Dardenne, to give the sisters their annual retreat. The second visit was in October just before Merton was flying to Asia, where he was to give a talk in Bangkok and where his untimely death occurred. The context of this second visit was a gathering of religious women and men who were interested in contemplative prayer, specifically how to deepen in this prayer form.

Why Redwoods? What was the background that preceded these two important encounters at Redwoods Monastery? To answer these questions, we need to return to the foundation of the abbey. Redwoods was founded in stages; three groups each of four sisters came at different times over the course of a year, and by different modes of travel. The first group of four sisters included the founding abbess, Mother Myriam, and three other sisters. Because they were coming from Belgium, a European culture, they wanted to get an experience, even if ever so brief, of monastic life lived in the United States. Thus, on their journey to the West Coast they visited several monasteries.

This first group of four left their monastery of Our Lady of Nazareth on October 9, 1962, just as the Second Vatican Council was beginning. They traveled by boat, taking the *Rotterdam* from the Netherlands to Ellis Island in New York. They visited Mount Saint Mary's Abbey in Wrentham, Massachusetts, Saint Joseph's Abbey in Spencer, Massachusetts, Holy Cross Abbey in Berryville, Virginia, and finally, Gethsemani Abbey in Kentucky. The visit to Gethsemani was providential. One evening they had supper with a monk named Fr. Louis. At the beginning they were not aware that this monk was "Thomas Merton." Nonetheless, the relation began from this initial encounter. Merton was fascinated by the mysticism of the Low Countries, and this awakened his interest in the new foundation. As their correspondence shows, this meeting over a meal was the beginning of a relationship that grew over time, especially between Mother Myriam and Merton.

By 1968, Gethsemani had a new abbot who allowed Merton to take several outside commitments. Merton accepted the invitation from Mother Myriam to come to Redwoods. The talks that ensued in both May and October were recorded. Reels and reels of recordings were stored in the archives of Redwoods, untouched until this time. A friend of the monastery had these old reels transferred onto CDs, as well as digitized. In the summer of 2021, another providential encounter occurred, when David Odorisio visited Redwoods. It became immediately clear that David had the expertise, the spiritual depth, and editorial skills and sensitivity to transcribe this material and put it into book form. I have nothing but praise for David and trust in his integrity. He obviously has a deep connection with Merton and his passion has been evident each step of the way.

About the material itself: the literary style does not make for an easy read. What do I mean? The talks are not written out conferences. Merton prepared his talks ahead of time and had voluminous notes; however, the presentation format is dialogical. The participants are encouraged to interrupt and ask their questions or offer their comments during each session. The weakness of this approach is that often a certain depth is missing in the topics that Merton is speaking about. What is clear, however, is that Merton was at home with the community. There is abundant laughter throughout his presentations, and one gets a tangible sense of the relaxed nature of these meetings. Merton's impromptu manner reveals his human side, which brings a balance to his intellectual and theological depth. The relaxed atmosphere also allows Merton to have a sense of freedom, where he could be himself and not worry about having his words critiqued by outside reviewers.

What stands out in his talks was how informed he was of other religions: Sufism, Native American rituals, and Hinduism, especially the various forms of yoga. Merton's interest in other religions was prophetic for Catholicism, and his trip to Asia was the final statement of his openness to other religions. He was in many ways a forerunner of monastic interreligious dialogue. He remained clearly rooted in Christ. His whole theological and anthropological approach came out of his life in Christ. His study of these other religions, including Buddhism, only deepened his monastic life and left us a source of rich religious and spiritual teaching. Added to this was how the wisdom and theological underpinnings of these other religions served to deepen his own Christianity.

Obviously, Merton scholars will be very interested in this material since it was so close to Merton's death. However, I would encourage those readers who are not scholars to imagine themselves as part of these retreat gatherings, anxious to hear what Merton has to say about contemplative prayer, about how God is manifested in our humanity. The following excerpt from the beginning of his conferences in May surely draws the reader into this interactive gathering of monastic and spiritual seekers. It speaks of the human person's capacity for God (*capax Dei*), the capacity to embody the life of Christ, the gospel horizon where God's love is the force of healing, transformation, and forgiveness. This stunning statement puts in bas-relief the immediate and end goal of the spiritual life:

> The fundamental, deepest thing that man has found is himself, his true self. Which is in God. Because in finding his true self, he finds God. He finds the root; he finds the ground. And that is because man is a very peculiar kind of being. Man is the being in whose consciousness God manifests Himself. In a certain sense, man is delegated by God to be God's consciousness of Himself in a creature. Man has the vocation to be conscious as creature of his Ground in God, and in such an intimate way that when man confesses and witnesses to his rootedness in God, it is God Himself who is confessing and witnessing this.[1]

The historical period in which Merton offered these words is not so different from the times in which we find ourselves today. May these conferences as a whole offer a hopeful reminder of our common vocation and of the ultimate rootedness of our "Ground in God."

Sr. Kathy DeVico, Abbess, OCSO
Our Lady of the Redwoods Abbey
Whitethorn, California
January 26, 2023
Solemnity of the Founders of Citeaux

1. Merton is, of course, expressing himself in the language of his time.

Preface

Thomas Merton at Redwoods

It is not uncommon for readers of Thomas Merton's works to describe feeling a sense of personal connection to his writing, as if he is speaking directly to them. This was one of his gifts as a writer: to write with such intimacy, openness, and honesty that readers felt challenged to consider their own personal involvement with the questions he was raising in his work, and to ask what might be at stake for them. Certainly, this has been true for me. Reading this remarkable collection of talks given at Redwoods Monastery in 1968, I felt again the power of his distinctive voice and his capacity to articulate with clarity and depth some of our most urgent spiritual and existential questions. For me personally, these talks also resonate with a sense of recognition born of a deep familiarity with this place and long friendship with this particular monastic community.

I first visited Redwoods Monastery in the Fall of 1977, less than ten years after Merton's time there. Recently graduated from college, I was hungry for an experience of silence and solitude that, until then, I had mostly encountered in the pages of books. Some of these books were written by Thomas Merton—*The Seven Storey Mountain, New Seeds of Contemplation,* and *Conjectures of a Guilty Bystander,* among others—whose work I had devoured as an undergraduate at the University of California at Santa Cruz. Merton's work, along with other, more ancient writing in the contemplative tradition toward which Merton's writing had pointed me—including the *Sayings of the Desert Fathers and Mothers,* the *Showings* of Julian of Norwich, and Teresa of Avila's *The Interior Castle*—opened up within me an awareness of a depth dimension to Christian spiritual experience that was at the time almost completely unknown to me, but which subsequently became an important and necessary part of my own life path.

Still, I had little sense at the time of the actual context of these writings, specifically the monastic context. What was a monastery exactly? And what did it mean to live as part of a monastic community? At the time, I could not really say. And while Merton's writings suggested that Christian monastic life and culture was very much alive and well in mid-twentieth century America, it came as something of a surprise to me to learn that it was actually possible to visit and stay in a monastery — or that there was a Cistercian monastery within driving (or hitch-hiking) distance of where I currently lived. I decided I needed to see for myself. So that fall, I set off on a six-month monastic pilgrimage that would take me to monastic houses in Wales, France, Italy, Greece, and finally to Saint Catherine's Monastery at the foot of Mount Sinai. I was searching for something, something I could not easily name, but that was moving me to enter and spend time in the silence and stillness of these monastic spaces.

Redwoods Monastery was the first place I stopped. That I was there at all owed much to a remarkable piece of writing I had encountered a couple of years earlier. It was entitled "Thomas Merton, Man of Prayer," by David Steindl-Rast, and was part of a collection of essays about Merton edited by Brother Patrick Hart. Most of these essays offered perspectives on Merton's contributions to this or that dimension of monastic thought and practice. Steindl-Rast's essay was different. It was in large part a transcription of a talk on prayer Merton had given to the community at Redwoods Monastery in 1968. And it was riveting—lucid, informal, free-flowing, and marked by a sense of simplicity, freedom, and openness that I found so moving.

I must have registered on some level that these were notes from a talk. But at the time what struck me most was the atmosphere of the piece, steeped in silence and attention, skeptical of the value of words, returning always to the fundamental reality of prayer. "Nothing that anyone says will be that important," Merton notes at the beginning. "The great thing is prayer. Prayer itself. If you want a life of prayer, the way to get it is by praying." I remember smiling when I read this. Smiling and perhaps wincing a little at how little I had yet incorporated the truth of this idea into my own life. After all, I was not really looking for a theory of prayer, or a guide to prayer. No, I wanted a *life* of prayer. And yet so much of my own behavior, my reading, thinking, reflecting, only served to distance me from what I most deeply wanted. Here was a reminder—both reassuring and challenging—of the call to return always to what the gospels call "the one thing necessary." Not as something to strive towards or construct, but simply to *realize*. "In prayer we discover what we already have," he observed. "You start where you are and you deepen what you already have and you realize that you are already there. We already have everything, but we don't know it and we don't experience it. Everything has been given to us in Christ. All we need is to experience what we already possess."

We already have everything. These words ring with as much power and truth today as they did in 1968, when Merton uttered them amidst that circle of friends at Redwoods Monastery. And they suggest something about the importance and beauty of this new collection of the talks Merton gave at Redwoods Monastery that year, transcribed and edited with great skill and care by David Odorisio, and made available to us here for the first time. Some may wonder whether we need yet another posthumous publication of Thomas Merton's writings more than fifty years after his death; but there is something distinctive and compelling about these talks that make them deserving of our close and careful attention.

One reason for this, perhaps the most immediate, is the insight these talks give us into Merton's thinking during the last year of his life. One of the first and earliest glimpses we had of this period of Merton's life came with the publication of *Woods, Shore, Desert,* a slim, chiseled selection from Merton's journals, published in 1982, that captured his felt sense of what it was like for him to travel to California and New Mexico in 1968, including his thoughts about the possibility of settling somewhere in the West upon his return from Asia. A fuller picture of this period of his life emerged in 1998 with the publication of the seventh volume of his journals, *The Other Side of the Mountain,* which helped to situate his time in California as a crucial axis point between his long years as a monk of Gethsemani Abbey in Kentucky and his final journey to Asia.

With the appearance of this collection of Merton's Redwoods talks, we have an opportunity to take an even closer look into this important last chapter of his life and to gain access, in a way that is quite distinct from the literary form of his journals or from his correspondence during this time, to how his thinking was unfolding in "real time" at a critical juncture of his life. Here in this rich and intimate dialogical space, he was often thinking out loud, testing ideas, pushing himself to understand better what it might mean to strip contemplative thought and practice down to its essentials. He was also clearly enjoying himself.

Readers will certainly notice this sense of enjoyment on almost every page; the word "laughter"—placed in brackets by the editor—appears frequently and is just one indication of how often the proceedings slowed or even halted so that those gathered could catch up with the intended or unintended humor provoked by Merton's often wry or whimsical observations. The talks themselves take up a number of serious subjects—the state of contemporary monastic life; prayer, freedom, and doubt; alienation; mystical consciousness; interreligious dialogue; and social and environmental concerns. But the climate of the talks was open, informal, exploratory, and marked by a deep sense of play. This also means that the discourse is not infrequently free-form and occasionally diffuse, retaining the distinctive, rambling charm of the original conversations but sometimes requiring patience and understanding from the reader. Still, I would suggest that much of the value to be found in these talks, and the thought that emerges from them, is rooted in this playful, open climate of inquiry.

Even so, one might well ask how much there is to be gained from listening in on these conversations among monks, nuns, and others gathered in this monastic space at a specific moment in time in the spring and fall of 1968. Is there anything original or important about the content of the talks themselves? How much can we really learn in the year 2023 from reflections on, say "Modern Consciousness," or "The Origins of Modern Consciousness," rooted in the very specific intellectual and cultural assumptions of the 1960s? Or rather, how much of this material can we reasonably expect will still speak to us in this moment? That is, I think, a fair question, and one that I found myself asking from time to time as I read through this manuscript. Other readers may also find themselves struggling with this. Even so, as my earlier comments regarding the talk entitled here "Life in Prayer" suggest, many of the questions posed in these conferences remain very much alive for us today. And the honesty and depth with which Merton and his interlocutors engage these questions is both refreshing and encouraging.

Often while reading this work, I found myself captivated, as I have been so many times before in reading Merton's work, by his deeply personal and inimitable *style* of thinking, by the freedom, openness, and spontaneity that have always characterized his best writing and which are on such vivid display here. One does not have to agree with the particular ideas he presents in this or that conference to appreciate the care and attention and sense of spiritual honesty he brings to his inquiry. These have always been characteristic features of Thomas Merton's best writing and thinking. Here, they are enhanced and deepened by the dialogical character of these conferences; often he is responding to particular questions of those who were present at these gatherings, questions almost always arising from a sense of real existential urgency.

So too with Merton's responses. In this sense, the depth of "spirit" in the exchanges between Merton and his interlocutors often counts for as much as the particular ideas being expressed. Listening in on these exchanges during a historical moment when political and cultural differences (in society and in the church) sometimes make it feel almost impossible for us to communicate with one another openly and in a spirit of genuine dialogue, these conferences help remind us of what is still possible.

More than fifty years on, the Redwoods Monastery community continues to follow the ancient Christian monastic way with depth and integrity. Merton sensed these qualities during the time he spent with the community in 1968 and commented on it often. And this is something about these conferences that is also worth lifting up and appreciating: they are not only of a particular time but also of a specific place. These talks took place not just anywhere, but here in this women's Cistercian monastery, founded in the early 1960s by sisters from Belgium, and which slowly, over time, became inculturated within the redwood forests of Northern California.

It is difficult to miss the spirit of the place in these conferences. It shines through in so many ways—in the distinctive ecological character of the place that so often informs the mood and feeling of the conversation that unfolds here; in the courage and openness of this vibrant community of women who play an essential role in this work of shared inquiry; and in the silence infusing and grounding everything. As readers and seekers, we are invited to listen carefully and attentively—to the silence, to words and thought arising from it, and to the deep currents of Spirit moving through it. Perhaps we can add our own voices to a conversation that is, after all, continuing to unfold among us.

Douglas E. Christie
Los Angeles, California

Introduction

"The Nocturnal Balconies of California"

–Thomas Merton on the Lost Coast

David M. Odorisio

I dream every night of the west.   —*Thomas Merton*[1]

To visit the Abbey of Our Lady of the Redwoods is to enter an ancient silence—not only the silence of the monastic cloister, but a more primeval silence, composed of, or rather emanating from, the forests, rivers, and towering redwood trees that make up California's "Lost Coast." Situated at the southern terminus of the Mattole River watershed in Mendocino County, Redwoods Monastery serves as a locus of not only monastic, but also ecological consciousness.[2] At approximately eighty miles in length,

1. Journal entry of May 22, 1968 (*The Other Side of the Mountain: The End of the Journey. The Journals of Thomas Merton, vol. 7: 1967–1968*, ed. Patrick Hart [New York: HarperCollins, 1998], 110).

2. The Mattole River is a vast and "remote watershed that exists without the protection of large public designations. . . . Before the middle of the twentieth century, the Mattole watershed was one of the most productive stretches of old-growth redwood forest in the region. By 1987, in thirty years the timber industry had mowed more than 90 percent of the watershed's forest . . . the river is now the site of a major, citizen-led restoration effort" (Obi Kaufman, *The Coasts of California* [Berkeley, CA: Heyday, 2022], 135). Merton would witness this destruction firsthand in 1968: "The redwood lands appear. . . . from the air you

California's Lost Coast is "the longest stretch of undeveloped coastline in America."[3] Within this expanse of isolated wilderness, Redwoods Monastery lies in proximity to one particular section of the coastline, the Sinkyone Wilderness State Park.[4] This twenty-mile now-protected coastal landscape was particularly important to the eremitical wanderings of Trappist monk and spiritual author Thomas Merton (1915-1968), and became the imaginal locus of his increasing search for solitude along the Northern California coast. Home to Needle Rock and Bear Harbor, Merton would poetically infuse these remote wilderness spaces with a contemplative *eros* that revealed his heart's desire to return and even relocate to these windswept shores and bluffs—a song of praise echoing across "the nocturnal balconies of California" that Merton presciently envisaged in his journal en route to Redwoods Monastery.[5]

Redwoods Monastery: A Place In-Between

In the fall of 1962, just as Vatican II was getting started in Rome, four sisters from the Cistercian community of Our Lady of Nazareth in Brecht, Belgium, boarded the transatlantic ocean liner "Rotterdam." The sisters, still wearing full habits and veils, were bound for Northern California to found a new Cistercian community.[6]

---

can see . . . where the hillsides have been slashed into, ravaged, sacked, stripped, eroded with no hope of regrowth of these marvelous trees" (*Other Side of the Mountain*, 96). On the restoration—and contemplative beauty—of the wild salmon returning to Redwoods Monastery's Thompson Creek, see Douglas E. Christie, *The Blue Sapphire of the Mind: Notes for a Contemplative Ecology* (Oxford: Oxford University Press, 2013), 141–43, 261–62.

3. Excluding Alaska. Kaufman adds, "Having proven impenetrable by roads, the craggy, steep terrain passingly resembles an exaggerated version of Big Sur's popular coastline, several hundred miles south." The average rainfall along the Lost Coast is over 100 inches a year (*The Coasts of California*, 275).

4. Redwoods Monastery is eight miles by road, or three miles "as the crow flies" from the Sinkyone Wilderness. For an Indigenous history of this region, including the devastating account of Sally Bell, lone survivor of the Needle Rock massacre in the 1850s, see Douglas E. Christie, *The Insurmountable Darkness of Love: Mysticism, Loss, and the Common Life* (Oxford: Oxford University Press, 2022), 84–85, and 253–54, fn. 5.

5. "Nocturnal balconies" was inspired by a French phrase ("les balcons nocturnes") from a book on the history of the Abbey of Port Royal that captured Merton's imagination (*Other Side of the Mountain*, 92, fn. 4).

6. www.redwoodsabbey.org/our-history.

Thus begins the "origin story" of Redwoods Monastery. Sisters Cecilia, Placida, Veronique, along with founding abbess, Myriam Dardenne, would embark from Holland on October 9, 1962, and arrive in New York seven days later. The fledgling community made visits to Cistercian houses at Berryville,[7] Wrentham (the only women's community at that time), Spencer, and Gethsemani, where the charismatic Dardenne would first meet Thomas Merton.[8] This began a correspondence that would last from 1962 until Merton's untimely death in 1968, and result in his two visits to Redwoods Monastery in May and October of that same year.

The sisters arrived at their location on October 31, 1962—a 240-acre former logging site, just south of Whitethorn, California. The land was donated by art director and architect, Bob Usher, which he fittingly named "Green Pastures."[9] Dardenne describes her initial encounter with the land in stunning and poetic terms:

> The clearings breathed in the midst of what is left of the Redwoods forest. The place is solitary: the land felt to us like the end of the world, one of the last frontiers of the West. . . . The isolation, the solitude were real . . . What we most connected with, in our wilderness, was the primitive Citeaux.[10]

The following year, in February and June of 1963, nine additional sisters arrived. With the help of monks from New Clairvaux in Vina, California,

---

7. Cistercian Abbot General, Dom Gabriel Sortais, described Holy Cross Abbey in Berryville, Virginia, to Mother Myriam as "the mystical garden of monasticism" due to the monastic renewal then-underway (Christine M. Bochen with Victor A. Kramer, "A Journey into Wholeness: An Interview about Thomas Merton with Myriam Dardenne at Redwoods Monastery," *The Merton Annual* 14 [2001]: 38).

8. Dardenne described Merton as "shy, very shy . . . he could be a taxicab driver, I thought" (Bochen, "'A Journey into Wholeness,'" 39). Dardenne also details Merton's immediate and supportive interest in the new foundation of Redwoods Monastery (40–41).

9. *Redwoods Monastery Newsletter* (Fall 2012), 4. Usher (1901–1990) received an auditory "locution" in 1959 that he was to "Give the property to God," and approached the Cistercians of New Clairvaux Abbey regarding the gift. During travels in Europe, Usher met Sortais in Rome, and offered the property to the Order (4). Usher spent the last twenty years of his life at New Clairvaux Abbey in Vina, CA.

10. Bochen, "'A Journey into Wholeness,'" 37–38. Dardenne's reference here is to the original Cistercian foundation in Citeaux, France, made by Robert of Molesme in 1098.

land was cleared and more permanent buildings erected. The monastery and chapel were blessed in 1967—one year prior to Merton's visits in 1968.

For the past fifty-five years, the recorded conferences that Merton offered at Redwoods Monastery during each of these visits remained untranscribed and unavailable to the public. Mother Myriam attempted her own transcriptions—including limited mimeographed distribution—and initiated correspondence with James Laughlin, a trustee of the Merton Legacy Trust and founder of New Directions Publishing, regarding the possibility of publication.[11] According to Sharon Duggan, Redwoods Monastery General Counsel:

> Myriam was intently focused on this recorded material and spent years talking, writing, and sharing about it. It was always her desire to see them transcribed and made available. Somewhere around 1996, Myriam had the reel-to-reel tapes put on cassettes. At that point, she worked on trying to get them transcribed. . . . At some point, she did get help from professional transcriber(s).[12]

Results, however, were limited, and while Mother Myriam continued to speak publicly about Merton's Redwoods conferences through presentations and interviews, publication remained elusive and deferred.[13]

---

11. See unpublished letters from Laughlin to Dardenne (February 4, 1969), and Dardenne to Laughlin (February 17, 1970; Redwoods Monastery Archive). There is an additional letter from Laughlin to Sr. Mary Aquin Chester, IHM (February 20, 1969), regarding the distribution of mimeographed copies of the October conferences, which Sr. Mary appears to have edited (see Dardenne to Laughlin, February 17, 1970). Dardenne outlines her vision for the proposed volume as follows: "This is the way I plan to proceed: In a first part . . . I would give some personal reflections about Thomas Merton . . . our first encounter at Gethsemani in 1962, our rare correspondence over the following years, his stays at Redwoods . . . and finally his sudden end. . . . In the second part of the book, Tom would speak himself" (letter to Laughlin, February 17, 1970).

12. Sharon Duggan, personal correspondence (June 25, 2022).

13. In 1998, Dardenne participated in the panel discussion, "Women Who Knew Merton," at Bellarmine University, and was a plenary speaker at the Seventh General Meeting of the International Thomas Merton Society in 2001 (Bochen, " 'A Journey into Wholeness,' " 33). See also Dardenne's contributions to the 1980 symposium, "The Monk as Universal Archetype" (in Raimundo Panikkar, *Blessed Simplicity: The Monk as Universal Archetype* [New York: Seabury Press, 1982], 178–94).

Until now. Merton's Redwoods conferences are presented here in their totality, and for the first time made available to the public. Comprising just over twenty-six hours of previously unpublished material, this volume constitutes the largest remaining uncatalogued repository of Merton's legacy. Offered on two occasions in the final year of his life, these conferences include Merton's contemplative insights on the spiritual life, prayer, and identity—topics familiar to longtime Merton readers— as well as unique comparative reflections on traditions as diverse as Hinduism, yoga, Sufism, Zen, and Indigenous rites of passage, and new material on the origins and development of modern consciousness. The May 1968 conferences additionally offer a unique window into the cloister and concerns of the times, through dialogue with members of the Redwoods monastic community, as well as, in October 1968, extended discussion with visiting members of contemplative communities across the U.S.—including a young Br. David Steindl-Rast. Over a half-century after Merton originally offered these conferences, this material is now made publicly available through the generosity of Redwoods Monastery and the Merton Legacy Trust.

Thomas Merton on the Lost Coast

Who can see such trees and bear to be away from them? I must go back.
It is not right that I should die under lesser trees.[14]

The Sinkyone Wilderness cut a deep and lasting impression upon Merton. Readers of his journals are fortunate to have both his immediate impressions of the Lost Coast, as well as post-trip reflections. Writing on location, in an entry dated May 13, 1968, Merton's naturalistic and poetic depiction of his surrounding environment is at its best and worth quoting at length:

> I am on the Pacific shore—perhaps fifty miles south of Cape Mendocino. Wide open, deserted hillside frequent[ed] only by sheep and swallows, sun and wind. No people for miles either way. Breakers on the black sand. Crying gulls fly down and land neatly on their

---

14. Merton, May 30, 1968 (*Other Side of the Mountain*, 112).

own shadows. I am halfway between Needle Rock, where there is an abandoned house and Bear Harbor, where there is another abandoned house—three miles between them. No human habitation in sight. . . . North, toward Shelter Cove, a manufactory of clouds where the wind piles up smoky moisture along the steep flanks of the mountains. Their tops are completely hidden. Back inland, in the Mattole Valley at the convent, it is probably raining. South, bare twin pyramids. And down at the shore, a point of rock on which there is a silent immobile convocation of seabirds, perhaps pelicans. Far out at sea, a long low coastal vessel seems to get nowhere. It hangs in an isolated patch of light like something in eternity.[15]

Merton's impressions of the natural beauty of the coast remained with him. Writing in his journal upon his return to Gethsemani in May 1968, Merton practically gushes:

Northern California was unforgettable. I want very much to go back. Especially to Bear Harbor, the isolated cove on the Pacific shore where the Jones house is and which, I think, can be rented: the barrier, the reef, the eucalyptus trees, the steep slopes crowned by fir, the cove full of drift-redwood logs—black sand, black stones, and restless sea—the whole show, those deserted pyramids, the hollow full of wild iris, the steep road overhanging the sea, Needle Rock. I seem to remember every vale of that shore.[16]

He was enthralled. To Merton, "The country which is nowhere is the real home; only it seems that the Pacific Shore at Needle Rock is more nowhere than this, and Bear Harbor is more nowhere still," and later states, "My desolate shore is Mendocino. I must return."[17]

---

15. May 13, 1968 (*Other Side of the Mountain*, 97).

16. May 21, 1968 (*Other Side of the Mountain*, 117). In a journal entry rivaling Thoreau, Merton depicts a hollow just inland from Bear Harbor: "A small loud stream, many quail. The calm ocean . . . very blue through the trees. Calla lilies growing wild. A very active flycatcher. The sun shines through his wings as through a Japanese fan. . . . Many ferns. . . . Wild fox gloves by the stream just where it sings loudest" (May 14, 1968; *Other Side of the Mountain*, 99).

17. May 30, 1968 (*Other Side of the Mountain*, 110).

As Merton reminisces and reflects upon his time at Redwoods, it is clear how his memories intertwine both the Redwoods community and the coast:

> I went out first the second day (Wednesday [May] 8th) driven by the postulant Carole, in her Volkswagen. The mist, the immense drop of the slope down to the invisible sea. . . . The bare pines where the slope had burnt. . . . The ranch, far below, by the surf, and finally the abandoned house, the barn, the dead tree at Needle Rock. . . . I walked barefoot in the sand until after three hours. . . . and as I walked in the surf a sudden big wave soaked me up to the thighs and I did not dry all afternoon. . . . Friday I drove out with Gracie Jones . . . and this time climbed high up on the slope. It was a bright day and the sea was calm, and I looked out over the glittering blue water, realizing more and more that this was where I really belonged. I shall never forget it. I need the sound of those waves, that desolation, that emptiness.[18]

Merton admits, "I need the silence and the emptying. Radical change in my ideas out there."[19] It is perhaps to this end that he remarks after seeing his photographs of the California coast (developed and enlarged by John Howard Griffin), and which serve as a fitting summary of the reflexive—daresay, mystical—significance of the place:

> The Agfa film brought out the great *Yang-Yin* of sea rock mist, diffused light and half hidden mountain—an interior landscape, yet there. In other words, what is written within me is there, "Thou art that."[20]

---

18. May 21, 1968 (*Other Side of the Mountain*, 119–20).

19. *Other Side of the Mountain*, 120.

20. May 22, 1968 (*Other Side of the Mountain*, OSM, 110). "Thou art that," is a reference to the Sanskrit phrase *tat tvam asi*, repeated throughout the ancient Indian *Upanisads* to denote the inherent intimacy—and non-duality—between the *atman* or personal spirit, and the transcendent or universal *Brahman*.

The Search for Solitude—and Community:
Thomas Merton at Redwoods Monastery

The long low monastery—its significance in the mist.[21]

I call to mind Dominique and her alleluias, and the shore.
They sustain me.[22]

While time on the Pacific shore may have further inclined Merton's ear to his ever-deepening pursuit of solitude, his relationships with the members of the Redwoods Monastery community, including participation in the liturgy, were central to his visit. Writing from New Mexico at Christ in the Desert Monastery on May 17, Merton reflects:

> The liturgy at the Redwoods was excellent. I enjoyed the daily con-celebration with Father Roger, with the nuns coming up to stand around close to the altar at the end of the offertory and one of them extinguishing the candles as they retired after communion.[23]

And twice notes, "The alleluia antiphon for Terce . . . composed by Sister Dominique, stays with me and is associated with the monastery"[24]; and "The voices and chants of the nuns very good. I cannot forget the Alleluia for Terce. . . . A lovely melody all involved in my memories of the Pacific."[25]

Perhaps it was this immersion into a contemplative community of women that impressed upon Merton the most. Depicting their liturgical and monastic garb, Merton remarks:

> Beauty of these Flemish nuns and of the American nuns too. More beautiful in their simple blue and gray dresses without veils than in the affected and voluminous Cistercian habits—the cowl and choker. But they wear light cowls in choir and can wear such veils as they please. Some, like the chantress, a dignified mantilla.[26]

---

21. May 30, 1968 (*Other Side of the Mountain*, 111).
22. September 3, 1968 (*Other Side of the Mountain*, 164).
23. *Other Side of the Mountain*, 105.
24. *Other Side of the Mountain*, 105.
25. May 21, 1968 (*Other Side of the Mountain*, 119).
26. May 14, 1968 (*Other Side of the Mountain*, 98).

Describing feeling "very related to those bright and open nuns,"[27] Merton would upon his return compose a near-litany to the Redwoods community:

> And are you there, my dears? Still under the big trees, going about your ways and your tasks, up the steep slope to the roomy wooden place where the chasubles are woven—Sister Gerarda on a bicycle to the guest quarters, Sister William to bake hosts . . . warm Sister Veronica in the kitchen, Sister Katryn to be an obscure descendent of Eckhart's Sister Katrei. . . .[28] Sister Dominique, the impulsive, the blue-dressed, the full of melodies, who drove me in the car to the store to buy Levis . . . gentle Sister Leslie from Vassar and blue-eyed Sister Diane from Arizona interested in Ashrams and Sister Shalom and Sister Cecilia, who came later to the party—and Mother Myriam, the Abbess, was responsible for this wonderful place. Which ones have I forgotten besides the two postulants . . . Carole with the Volkswagen and . . . Portia from San Francisco?[29]

Of course, the community's animals were included in Merton's observational hymns of praise as well:

> Fr. Roger's dog Yogi, which belonged to Sr. Diane before she entered. Yogi liking to go for walks, running from the guest house, expressing delight, chasing the cats away from his food.[30]

One can imagine that, surrounded by the *communitas* of such caring and attentive female figures, Merton might have felt nurtured and contented in a manner that had long eluded him; encountering at Redwoods Monastery an embodied, lived reality of what had previously remained feminine mythopoesis.[31]

---

27. *Other Side of the Mountain*, 122.

28. Merton adds: "Sister Katryn and Sister Christofora were the ones who seemed to respond the most knowingly whenever Eckhart was mentioned." This is a reference to Eckhart's "Sister Catherine" Treatise (see Bernard McGinn, *Meister Eckhart: Teacher and Preacher* [Mahwah, NJ: Paulist Press, 1986], 349–87).

29. May 30, 1968 (*Other Side of the Mountain*, 110).

30. May 21, 1968 (*Other Side of the Mountain*, 119). See also May 30, 1968: "Yogi and the cats. He fought them over his meat. He let them have his milk. Yogi used to belong to Diane. She asked about Ashrams, Diane!" (*Other Side of the Mountain*, 111).

31. Of course, Merton's very embodied and lived relationship with "M." preceded his visit to Redwoods (see Christine Bochen's "Introduction" to *Learning to Love: The Journals*

The Correspondence: Thomas Merton and Myriam Dardenne

While the cast of characters grows as Merton's relationship to the community deepens, the correspondence between Merton and Mother Myriam preceding and following his visits to Redwoods Monastery cannot be overlooked as they set an important context and background for the conferences as a whole. Contained in this volume is the entirety of the extant letters between Merton and Dardenne, spanning the eight years from their initial meeting at the Abbey of Gethsemani in 1962, to just a few days before Merton's death in Bangkok, Thailand, on December 10, 1968. The correspondence, which reaches over thirty pages, includes several previously unpublished pieces from Merton, as well as the entirety of Mother Myriam's letters, published here for the first time. In addition to revealing their unique spirits and personalities, the letters also read like a primer in post-Vatican II theology, ecclesial politics, and monastic renewal. Capturing these various movements of the Spirit, Merton and Dardenne's exchange demonstrates the sense of openness and possibility—as well as caution—regarding the liturgical innovations, monastic reform movements, and growing interest in contemplative and charismatic prayer within late 1960s U.S. Catholic religious communities.

Central to these cultural movements of the Spirit lies the impetus for the October conference and a major turn in the Merton-Dardenne correspondence: the House of Prayer movement. Briefly defined as a late 1960s turn toward charismatic renewal following a post-Vatican II resurgence of interest in prayer—including the creation of spaces dedicated to it—the Immaculate Heart of Mary community at Monroe, Michigan, decided to host a conference dedicated to the topic. Merton corresponded with several Servants of the Immaculate Heart of Mary (IHM) sisters throughout March and July 1968, first regarding an invitation to the Monroe meeting,

---

of Thomas Merton, Vol. 6: 1966–1967 [New York: HarperCollins, 1997], xiii–xxiv; and James Wiseman, "Learning to Love and Learning the Price: Thomas Merton and the Challenge of Celibacy," *The Merton Annual* 12 [1999]: 85–102). This is not to minimize the importance of Merton's previous—and deeply significant—imaginal encounters with archetypal feminine figures, e.g., in his poem-sequence "Hagia Sophia"; his dreams of "Proverb" and the "Chinese Princess"; and devotional drawings of various female faces (see Jonathan Montaldo, "A Gallery of Women's Faces and Dreams of Women From the Drawings and Journals of Thomas Merton," *The Merton Annual* 14 [2001]: 155–72).

and subsequently, in regard to Merton's proposed gathering at Redwoods Monastery.[32] Following the Monroe conference, Mother Myriam writes enthusiastically to Merton:

> I had my prejudices in going, but now, I regret that you were not present. The Spirit was speaking. To me, this genuine desire for prayer and the contemplative attitude in apostolic-"active" groups speaks worlds of newness for the Christian religious life of the future.[33]

Since Merton was not able to attend at Monroe, the compromise, to host a follow-up conference at Redwoods in October 1968, evidences Merton's commitment to matters of religious renewal, not only among contemplative orders, but also among more actively engaged communities.[34]

An additional, pivotal theme, that arises both in Merton's correspondence with Dardenne, as well as throughout the letters included in Part II, is Merton's continued quest to secure a potential hermitage location on the California coast in proximity to Redwoods Monastery. Back at Gethsemani, Merton writes in a journal passage dated May 24, 1968:

> Lonely for the Pacific and the Redwoods. A sense that somehow when I was there I was unutterably happy—and maybe I was. Certainly, every minute I was there, especially by the sea, I felt I was at home—as if I had come a very long way to where I really belonged. . . . In the end, I think I came to the best decision when I was out there: to try to get permission to spend Lent at least at Bear Harbor, but to maintain my "stability" here.[35]

32. See Merton's July 11, 1968, letter to Dardenne: "[Mother Benedicta Brennan, IHM] knows of my idea and is eager to have a meeting at Redwoods" (p. 400, below).

33. August 28, 1968.

34. See also Merton's conferences given to religious sisters upon his return from California in May 1968, published as *The Springs of Contemplation: A Retreat at the Abbey of Gethsemani*, ed. Jane Marie Richardson (New York: Farrar, Straus and Giroux, 1992), 127–274.

35. *Other Side of the Mountain*, 122. See also May 28: "I must not kid myself about this. But it would certainly be very good to live alone in the cove at Bear Harbor and come in once a week to give the nuns a talk and pick up supplies" (*Other Side of the Mountain*, 123). Merton wrote on May 14: "I told them I wanted to ask my Abbot's permission to

True to form, however, a few weeks pass only for Merton to remark in a journal entry of June 4: "Useless nostalgia for Needle Rock, Bear Harbor, the Redwoods!"[36] He is quick to counter by July 19:

> More than anything I want to find a really quiet, isolated place—
> —where no one knows I am (I want to disappear).
> —where I can get down to the thing I really want and need to do.
> —from which, if necessary, I can come out to help others (e.g. at the Redwoods). . . .
> —maybe this can be a step towards the hermit colony Fr. Flavian wants.[37]

Merton finally concedes on a more tempered note, journaling on July 29, two months prior to his departure for Alaska and then Redwoods: "In eight weeks I am to leave here. And who knows—I may not come back. Not that I expect anything to go wrong—though it might—but I might conceivably settle in California to start the hermit thing Fr. Flavian spoke of: it depends."[38]

By October, however, and following his trip to the remote Alaskan coast and wilderness,[39] Merton's enthusiasm shifts as he writes from Redwoods Monastery to his abbot Flavian Burns:

> I can say without hesitation that the California coast is hopeless as regards solitude. Everywhere there is a land boom in progress and speculators are opening up new developments on every side. They can't lose, the population is increasing so fast people are going to have to build all over the place. Even at Bear Harbor which I liked so much last May, the bulldozers are active and they are opening up a lot of roads that will obviously be for housing sometime. It is just a question of time before this whole place will be spoiled.[40]

---

spend Lent in the abandoned house at Needle Rock. Sister Dominique said they would all fight one another for the chance to bring me supplies" (*Other Side of the Mountain*, 98).

36. *Other Side of the Mountain*, 125.

37. *Other Side of the Mountain*, 142.

38. *Other Side of the Mountain*, 147–48. On the idea of a "hermit colony," see Merton's letters to Flavian Burns, included in Part II of this volume.

39. For Merton's Alaska journals, letters, and conferences, see *Thomas Merton in Alaska*, ed. Robert E. Daggy (New York: New Directions, 1989).

40. October 9, 1968 (*The School of Charity: Letters on Religious Renewal and Spiritual Direction*, ed. Patrick Hart [New York: Farrar, Straus and Giroux, 1990], 402).

Writing only a few days later, however, and again from Redwoods, Merton composes a more balanced response:

> I am very fond of this place. It is a shame California is developing so much, for there are fine solitary places all around here. Even if developments continue, there are good places in the woods near the convent which could be well protected. I am seriously thinking of the possibility of settling near here and my new Abbot, would, I think be favorable.[41]

Merton's correspondence with Myriam Dardenne, as well as his California letters as a whole, weave a narrative tapestry that synthesizes Merton's increased longing for solitude along the isolated and breathtaking California coast with his continued need for community and meaningful personal relationships. However, with his invitation to attend the Meeting of Monastic Superiors in Bangkok (along with the subsequent contacts and connections that followed), Merton's horizons increasingly expand toward Asia.

Ultimately, Merton's vision focuses not only on securing land for a hermitage along the coast, but also of equal importance, a location in proximity to Redwoods Monastery itself, which serves as a central point from which Merton lands—and departs—for Asia. In this sense, Redwoods Monastery, the conferences he participates in, and his own "California dreaming" each demonstrate and develop themes central to what readers find in the final year of Merton's life: the desire for increased solitude in remote wilderness places; an ongoing personal *kenosis* ("self-emptying"); and an evolving ecumenical and interreligious "universal consciousness."[42] The continued exploration of such uncharted internal and external geographies drives Merton onwards towards Asia—the "home" he had never before been.[43]

---

41. October 11, 1968, to Dom Jacques Winandy (*School of Charity*, 403).

42. "The task of the solitary person and the hermit is to realize . . . in a very special way, a universal consciousness" (*Thomas Merton: Preview of the Asian Journey*, ed. Walter Capps [New York: Crossroad, 1989], 69; see also David M. Odorisio, "'Yes to Everyone': Thomas Merton's Radical Ecumenism and Inter-Monastic Mysticism of the Ground," *The Merton Seasonal* 46.4 [2021]: 3–11).

43. *Other Side of the Mountain*, 205.

The Redwoods Conferences: May and October 1968

May 1968

In an April 28 letter to Myriam Dardenne, Merton outlines his vision for the May visit:

> What I'd like to do would be to have a couple of good sessions each day, mainly dialogue [or] seminar. . . . . The subject I'd like to pursue . . . is "the modern religious consciousness"—which means wondering if such a thing exists . . . and if so what kind of shapes does it take on? This would be against the traditional backgrounds of religious consciousness in Zen, Sufism, the 12th century Cistercians, St. Benedict, Desert Fathers.[44]

Merton states that he is "coming not with answers but with questions," and offers the "imperative that we monks and nuns devote ourselves to some search in this area," which, he specifically notes, "is ours to explore."[45] The topics that Merton lists in his letter are later mirrored in a brief outline, penned en route to California:

> Nazareth, Beguines, mystics of the Rhineland, beginning of the modern consciousness. . . . Contemplative mystique. Feminine mystique. Theology of vows. Monastic life as an eschatological sign. Risk and hope. . . . Ecclesiastical power. Power prevents renewal. Power prevents real change. Garments of skin in the Greek Fathers. Hindu Kosas, then modern consciousness. Montaigne, Descartes, Pascal, Sufis, and Zen.[46]

Merton would later affirm, "[a] lot of good discussion" took place, and that "Mother Myriam especially very smart. All the community excellent."[47]

---

44. *School of Charity*, 378.

45. *School of Charity*, 378.

46. *Other Side of the Mountain*, 93. Merton later summarizes, "I gave talks on 'the veils,' on Karma Yoga, Bhakti Yoga, the 'contemplative mystique,' the 'feminine mystique' (a curse), and then on Sufism. In the room with big windows looking on a tiny yard with a sort of Zen garden in it" (*Other Side of the Mountain*, 119).

47. *Other Side of the Mountain*, 119.

Merton's primary focus in the May conferences is outlining an historical genealogy of the origins of modern Western consciousness. A vast and wide-ranging topic, Merton focuses on the evolution of post-Enlightenment secularism and offers several comparative religious contrasts as evidence of additional "types" of "consciousnesses" available to persons today. Regarding the post-Cartesian "[p]rimacy of the conscious subject," Merton remarks in his journal, " 'Convince yourself that you exist!' Baloney!"[48] To Merton, a type of "karma yoga" is needed to counter modern alienation, where work serves "as narcotic" and needs differentiation "from healthy and free work."[49] The Hindu yoga tradition, particularly classic karma yoga texts (for example, the *Bhagavad Gita* and the *Astavakra Gita*), become central to recovering from what Merton calls the "Computer Karma" of "American civilization."[50] Additional interreligious topics on Hinduism, including talks on the *Upanishads*, karma and bhakti yoga, and the Hindu stages of life (*asramas*), as well as conferences on Sufi spirituality, including extended reflections on Ibn Arabi and mystical exegesis in the Quran, each orient around questions of contemplative *praxis* and the intentional cultivation of such specific aspects of religious consciousness—often treated as corollary (and even cure) to the rampant individualism and subsequent alienation of the modern American "I."

Writing to Flavian Burns from California, Merton describes the general structure of the conferences, along with his initial impressions of Redwoods Monastery:

> This place here is ideal. . . . Perfect for retreat. Complete isolation and silence. And the woods are magnificent. I have the whole day to myself until Vespers, after which I work for two hours in a long conference [and] dialogue. Yesterday I was more entirely alone and in silence even than at Gethsemani for a good part of the day. . . .

---

48. *Other Side of the Mountain*, 96.

49. *Other Side of the Mountain*, 103; see also *Springs of Contemplation*, 213–19.

50. *Other Side of the Mountain*, 103; see the introduction as well as essays on these specific topics and texts in *Merton and Hinduism: The Yoga of the Heart*, ed. David M. Odorisio (Louisville, KY: Fons Vitae, 2021).

The community here is very alive, very simple, and very real. I think you'd love this place as I do.[51]

Merton finished the conferences on Sunday, May 12, and spent the subsequent two days on the coast, where he first discovers Bear Harbor on May 14.[52] Writing again to his abbot: "Finished the talks to the nuns on Sunday and am now on retreat: which means the whole day in complete solitude over by the Pacific. Not a soul there, only seabirds and sheep."[53] On May 16, Merton leaves Redwoods Monastery with Mother Myriam and Sr. Katryn for San Francisco, passing through Garberville, the Eel River Valley, Willits, Ukiah, Cloverdale, and Santa Rosa. In the North Beach neighborhood of San Francisco, Merton meets up with Beat poet and City Lights publisher, Lawrence Ferlinghetti, and ends up sleeping in the City Lights publication office before departing for Albuquerque and Christ in the Desert Monastery in New Mexico.[54]

October 1968

Prior to this volume, the sole first-person published account including material from the October conferences has been Br. David Steindl-Rast's 1974 essay, "Man of Prayer."[55] As mentioned previously, the impetus for the October gathering was convening several prominent voices in contemplative renewal and Catholic charismatic prayer, specifically in regard to the House of Prayer movement. As Merton notes in a journal entry dated October 11:

Today begins a three-day conference—on contemplative life, houses of prayer, etc. "Organized" . . . at request of Mother Benedicta of

---

51. May 8, 1968 (*School of Charity*, 379–80).

52. *Other Side of the Mountain*, 120.

53. *School of Charity*, 380. And later, "I had the days to myself mostly, and all the work was in the evenings: Vespers at 3:30, then from 4 to 6 a conference . . . then more after supper, the late session being more informal" (May 21, 1968; *Other Side of the Mountain*, 119).

54. *Other Side of the Mountain*, 120. Christ in the Desert is located near Abiquiu, NM, approximately 60 miles north of Santa Fe, in the Chama Canyon (see *Other Side of the Mountain*, 105–8).

55. In *Thomas Merton/Monk: A Monastic Tribute*, ed. Patrick Hart (New York: Sheed & Ward, 1974), 79–89.

the IHMs of Monroe, Michigan. Last evening Mother Myriam and
I casually wondered what to do. Decided I was after all to give some
talks about something and start the usual discussions.[56]

Attendees arrived at Redwoods Monastery from around the U.S.,
including "Two [Sister Adorers of the Precious Blood] from Alaska—
Mother Rita Mary and Sr. Mary," along with Passionist priest, Fr. Ed
Hennessey; Sr. Anne E. (Mary Aquin) Chester, IHM; Mother Margaret
(Benedicta) Brennan, IMH; Sr. Marie Goldstein, RSHM; Sr. Jane Marie
Richardson from Loretto in Kentucky, and Br. David from Mount Saviour
Monastery in New York.[57] In a journal entry dated October 13, Merton
summarizes the conference proceedings:

> The three-day (2-½ day) workshop at Redwoods seems to have gone
> well—and was quickly over. On the first day (Friday) torrents of rain
> all day. The next day dark and misty; today bright again. The confer-
> ence this morning was in the old chapel (library) and then after Mass
> we had a fine lunch in the community room, a short talk finally and
> then I went and threw things pell-mell into my bags and we left.[58]

Merton would fly to Bangkok on Tuesday from San Francisco International airport. Redwoods Monastery would become his final foothold in
the U.S., while the California coast would offer Merton his visual finale
of North American soil: "Muir Woods, Bodega Bay, Point Reyes, and
then two tiny rock islands. And then nothing. Only blue sea."[59] Thomas
Merton was gone—his legacy not to be forgotten.

---

56. *Other Side of the Mountain*, 200.

57. It is difficult to ascertain the entirety of those in attendance, which additionally
included certain unidentified members of the Redwoods community, and surprise drop-in
visitors who might have attended only select portions of the conferences. In her memoir
of the House of Prayer movement, Ann E. Chester affirms several of the aforementioned
attendees as well as names "a former novice from Gethsemane [*sic*] who happened to be
at Redwoods" (*My Journey in the House of Prayer* [Monroe, MI: Pathways Press, 1991],
13; see also the photograph of Merton at Redwoods that appears on p. 13).

58. *Other Side of the Mountain*, 201.

59. *Other Side of the Mountain*, 205; the "two tiny rock islands" being potentially the
Farallon Islands.

A Portrait on the Pacific: Thomas Merton and Gracie Jones

"Looking down from the steep height, I saw Gracie, very small, very far, carrying her blanket from the dead tree to the car."[60] In a post-trip journal entry of May 30, 1968, Merton recalls his time on the Lost Coast with Gracie Jones, a young African American Marin County mother, who had reached out to Mother Myriam regarding a personal retreat at Redwoods Monastery. The date of her arrival at the monastery just happened to coincide with Merton's visit. Offering to drive him to Needle Rock, Jones was so moved by their serendipitous encounter—and coastal excursion—that she later published an essay, "Four Days with Merton," in her local San Rafael, California, newspaper, which is included in this volume as an Appendix. Jones was deeply disturbed by the racism in her community, and in the U.S. as a whole, and planned to write a book, *The Negro and the Catholic Church*, for which Merton agreed to write a Preface. Jones also took several color photographs of Merton, some of the last depicting him before his departure for Asia. As Merton would later recall, summarizing his time in California: "Gracie Jones sent some pictures of the Redwoods and of the shore at Needle Rock. I remember those extraordinary days."[61]

Speaking Across Time: From California's "Nocturnal Balconies" to Today

Even in the midst of his lifelong search for solitude, Thomas Merton was a person who cultivated deep and lasting personal relationships. His time in California and at Redwoods Monastery was indicative of this. Whether through his initial support of the Redwoods foundation, ongoing correspondence with Mother Myriam, and conferences offered at Redwoods in May and October 1968, Merton's relationships with the Redwoods Monastery community as whole—sisters, retreatants, and neighbors[62]—demonstrated a gregarious and fraternal acceptance of those who came into his welcoming orbit. Equally, Mother Myriam and the Redwoods

---

60. *Other Side of the Mountain*, 113.

61. *Other Side of the Mountain*, 129.

62. Merton was friendly with Redwoods neighbor, Al Groth (see, e.g., *Other Side of the Mountain*, 119), and corresponded with Frank Jones following his May visit regarding renting his property at Bear Harbor (see p. 420, below).

community supported and encouraged Merton; not only in his pursuit of potential hermitage sites along the Lost Coast, but also as he prepared for his Asian journey. It was to Redwoods Monastery that Merton—*gratia Dei*—was called, and it was the Redwoods community, including the land surrounding it, that nurtured his soul under those tall trees, and nourished his spirit along the wild and majestic California coast. Redwoods Monastery was Thomas Merton's final North American "station," as the Sufis would call it—a stopping point that constituted a vital-yet-impermanent segment of the long arc and spiritual trajectory of his fatefully abbreviated life.

The impact and importance of Redwoods Monastery on Merton's growth and development, as witnessed through his relationships with Myriam Dardenne, the Redwoods community, and the breathtaking natural order of the California coast is not to be underestimated, and is revealed here, in Merton's own voice, for the first time.

Mapping Thomas Merton in California

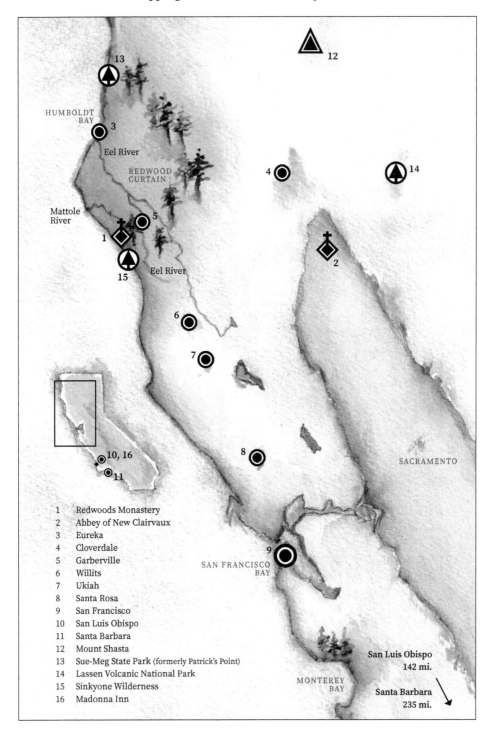

HUMBOLDT
BAY

Eel River

REDWOOD
CURTAIN

Mattole
River

Eel River

SACRAMENTO

SAN FRANCISCO
BAY

1   Redwoods Monastery
2   Abbey of New Clairvaux
3   Eureka
4   Cloverdale
5   Garberville
6   Willits
7   Ukiah
8   Santa Rosa
9   San Francisco
10   San Luis Obispo
11   Santa Barbara
12   Mount Shasta
13   Sue-Meg State Park (formerly Patrick's Point)
14   Lassen Volcanic National Park
15   Sinkyone Wilderness
16   Madonna Inn

San Luis Obispo
142 mi.

Santa Barbara
235 mi.

MONTEREY
BAY

Artwork and design by Patrick Walling

On the Road with Thomas Merton

The California Itinerary in His Own Words[1]

May 1968

May 6
Louisville to Chicago
Chicago to San Francisco

We are all secrets. But now, where there are suggested gaps, one can divine rocks and snow. . . . Reading the calligraphy of snow on a mountainside as if my own ancestors were hailing me.

We bump. We burst into secrets. (94)

[A] sense of recovering something of myself that has been long lost. . . . [T]his is a different land, a different country. (95)

San Francisco to Eureka

Distant presences of Lassen peak and Mount Shasta, especially Shasta . . . like great silent Mexican gods, white and solemn. . . . The redwood lands appear. Even from the air you can see that the trees are huge. . . . We land in Eureka. . . . Vast sea, like lead, with a cold steady, humid wind blowing off it . . . almost as if there were no town at all. (96)

Merton is picked up at the Eureka airport by Sister Leslie and Father Roger of Redwoods Monastery. They travel south by car from Eureka to Redwoods Monastery in Whitethorn.

---

1. All citations are from the final volume of Merton's published journals, *The Other Side of the Mountain: The End of the Journey*, vol. 7: 1967–1968, ed. Patrick Hart (New York: HarperCollins, 1998). Page numbers follow each passage.

Driving down through the redwoods was indescribably beautiful along Eel River. There is one long stretch where the big trees have been protected and saved—like a completely primeval forest. . . . A most moving place—like a cathedral. (96)

May 7–14
Our Lady of the Redwoods Monastery
Merton delivers conferences to the Redwoods community and visits Needle Rock and Bear Harbor.

May 13
I am on the Pacific shore—perhaps fifty miles south of Cape Mendocino. Wide open, deserted hillside frequent[ed] only by sheep and swallows, sun and wind. . . . Breakers on the black sand. Crying gulls fly down and land neatly on their own shadows. I am halfway between Needle Rock, where there is an abandoned house and Bear Harbor, where there is another abandoned house—three miles between them. No human habitation in sight on all the miles of shore line either way. . . . North, toward Shelter Cove, a manufactory of clouds where the wind piles up smoky moisture along the steep flanks of the mountains. . . . Back inland, in the Mattole Valley at the convent, it is probably raining. South, bare twin pyramids. . . . Far out at sea, a long low coastal vessel seems to get nowhere. It hangs in an isolated patch of light like something in eternity. (97)

May 15
Merton departs Redwoods Monastery by car with Mother Myriam, Sister Katryn, and Redwoods Monastery neighbor Al Groth. They travel south to San Francisco, including dinner in North Beach, and for Merton, an evening with Lawrence Ferlinghetti.

Eel River Valley. Redwoods. Redwood tourist traps, but also real groves. . . . [L]unch at Ukiah. . . . At Santa Rosa. . . . The fine wide ranches, low white houses, eucalyptus, pepper wood pine, fruit trees. We crossed the Golden Gate Bridge in bright sunlight, the whole city clear.

Downtown San Francisco. . . . I called Ferlinghetti . . . went to City Lights. . . . I went off with him to an Espresso place on Grant Avenue, the Trieste, where a young musician told of some visions he had had. Good visions. . . . I stayed overnight . . . at City Lights publications offices. A bedroom with a mattress on the floor, a guitar and a tape recorder and a window opening on a fire escape—a block from Telegraph Hill. (101-2)

May 16
Merton departs San Francisco for Christ in the Desert Monastery, Abiquiu, New Mexico

I said goodbye to Mother Myriam and Sister Katryn at the airport in San Francisco. Her plane left two hours after mine for New York and Brussels and for the General Chapter of Abbesses at Citeaux. (104)

October 1968

October 2
Merton arrives in San Francisco from Anchorage, Alaska; stays at the International Inn in San Francisco.

October 3
Merton departs San Francisco by plane for Santa Barbara; speaks at the Center for Democratic Institutions at the invitation of W. H. "Ping" Ferry.[2]

October 4
In the morning, Merton concelebrates Mass with Hugh McKiernon at La Casa de Maria, Retreat Center of the IHM Sisters in Santa Barbara, then travels north by car with the Ferrys along Highway 101 from Santa Barbara to San Francisco. Stops at the Mount Madonna Inn near San Luis Obispo. In San Francisco, Merton dines with poet Czeslaw Milosz and others.

A feeling of oversaturation with talk, food, drink, movement, sensations. The Madonna Inn on the road (U.S. 101) outside San Luis Obispo

---

2. For a published transcription of Merton's talk, see Walter Capps, ed., *Thomas Merton: Preview of the Asian Journey* (New York: Crossroad, 1989). Selections of Merton's correspondence with Ferry are included below (pp. 417–20).

exemplifies the madness of it. A totally extravagant creation, a Disneyland motel. . . . Arrived [in San Francisco] fairly tired, had dinner with Paul Jacobs and his wife, and Czeslaw Milosz and his wife at the Yen Ching—excellent North Chinese food. (199)

October 5
Then we drove off around the Embarcadero [in San Francisco], over the Golden Gate Bridge, stopped a little at Muir Woods, then on up Route 1. Pleasant little towns, winding road, eucalyptus trees, hills, shore. We came fairly late in the afternoon to Mendocino [where they spend the night]. (200)

October 6
Our Lady of the Redwoods Monastery
We spent most of the morning on the country road that goes along the ridge above Bear Harbor. Finally found Bear Harbor—and was shocked to see it was being torn up by bulldozers—roads are being cut and Jones seems to be trying to open up the same sort of development as is taking place at Shelter Cove. Everything on this coast is in movement. . . . There is little or no hope of the real kind of solitude I look for. (200)

Merton arrives at Redwoods Monastery the evening of October 6; spends much of the week preparing for his Asian journey (medical shots and finalizing his Darjeeling talk) and visits Patrick's Point with the Ferrys.

October 10
I was able to take my lunch to Needle Rock and spend the afternoon there. Quiet, empty, even the sheep ranch is now vacated. . . . When I arrived there was a layer of mist hanging about half way down the mountain—casting metallic blue shadows on the sea far out. And near shore the water was green and ultramarine—long quiet rollers furling themselves in orderly succession and crashing on the beach. Hundreds of birds—pelicans—cormorants patrolling the water. Scores of young brown gulls. And then sea lions rising for air and swimming under the rollers just before they'd break. . . . I can still think of nowhere I would rather settle than at that ranch—if it could stay more or less as it is. (201)

October 11–13
Conferences
After midnight, in the rain, [the participants] all arrived from the plane at Eureka—headlights, muffled voices, doors opening and closing. A Passionist shares my bathroom. . . . Most of the others are nuns. Two from Alaska. . . . On the first day (Friday) torrents of rain all day. The next day dark and misty; today [Sunday] bright again. (200)

October 13
Merton finishes the final conference and then returns south by car to San Francisco with Redwoods postulant Portia Webster and Sr. Marie Goldstein, RSHM, with stops in Ukiah and Sausalito. Stays at the Clift Hotel in San Francisco.

Got into the hotel, big room—not as quiet as might be with traffic on Geary—turned on the radio and there was Ella Fitzgerald singing. (201)

October 14
San Francisco
Lesson: not to travel with so many books. I bought more . . . unable to resist the bookstores in San Francisco. . . . said Tierce standing on a fire escape looking out over the Bay, the Bay Bridge, the island, the ships. (205)

October 15
Merton departs San Francisco for Honolulu, Hawaii, en route to Bangkok, Thailand.

We tilted east over the shining city. There was no mist this morning. All the big buildings went by. The green parks. The big red bridge over the Golden Gate. Muir Woods, Bodega Bay, Point Reyes, and then two tiny rock islands. And then nothing. Only blue sea. (205)

Typewriter, City Lights Office, San Francisco

Coast Live Oak, Redwoods Monastery

Redwoods: Trees and Sisters

Father Roger Among the Redwoods

*Photographs by Thomas Merton used with permission of the Merton Legacy Trust
and Thomas Merton Center at Bellarmine University*

Part I

THE REDWOODS
CONFERENCES

May 1968

Redwoods Monastery Church Exterior
(Used with Permission, Redwoods Monastery Archives)

Chapter One

Modern Consciousness

The conference recording begins with a brief dialogue between Merton and members of the Redwoods community.[1]

Sr. Cecilia: One should concretely experience what surrender to Christ is. And what solitude is, which, in each man's life must have a rightful place.

Comment: But in the monk's and nun's life, solitude plays a [role] in a special, conscious way, and the two live this [solitude] consciously. To live it out, [it has] to be expressed in concrete circumstances.

Merton: Like here [at Redwoods Monastery]. It's true, because here you've got better circumstances for solitude and for our life than anywhere that I know about. While perhaps Mepkin is nice, too; I don't know. You have fewer snakes in Mepkin [laughter].[2] But it really is. You are most blessed, and I really hope that nothing will ever get in the way of you fulfilling what you came here to do, because you really have a beautiful thing here.

There's a special quality in our life and that's what I want to talk about. A quality of life which we are called to keep alive in the world. Not only a quality of Christian life, but even a quality of human life. As you were

---

1. According to Dardenne's notes, Merton was not initially in favor of the conferences being recorded. Merton must have changed his mind, as the recordings, and subsequently this volume, begin mid-discussion, which explains why there is no formal opening (Sharon Duggan, personal communication, June 25, 2022).

2. Mepkin Abbey, Trappist monastery near Monck's Corner, South Carolina, founded in 1949.

saying today, there has to be a real, human quality; and it depends on us to keep it alive.

I'm going to hope for quite a bit of dialogue with you, but I will talk a bit at the beginning of each session, because we have long sessions, and I do have a certain amount of material that you probably wouldn't get in any other way. It's going to be all kinds of strange things from all directions, so I'll pull in everything that I can.

It's a question of maintaining this special quality of depth in our life, in the context of the modern world in which we live. We need to understand what is meant when people are talking about modern consciousness, and when they talk about a religious consciousness—[especially when] they say that the two things don't go together. The ones who preach this as dogma are mostly Catholics [laughs]: "The worst possible thing that you can do is have a contemplative vocation, because that is almost the next thing to being damned." And it's very close, because you're involved in that terrible thing, "interiority," which is *subjective*.[3] But we have to consider all these things.

I'm going to talk about modern consciousness. Who knows what modern consciousness is? Here we all are, we're all modern people, and we've all got a modern consciousness of one sort or another; and yet, I don't think any of us have won any prizes on modern consciousness. Who has the modern consciousness, and who hasn't? Well, in the course of these talks, I think I might drag in things from all directions. Some things, for example, on the origins of modern consciousness—things from Montaigne, from people like Descartes, and from Pascal. Pascal fits both modern and religious [consciousness] in a certain way. Things from Sartre, who is a kind of spokesman of a certain type of modern consciousness; bring him in. But I also want to talk about the religious consciousness, and I want to talk about it against the background of real, solid, traditional experience going back millennia, and that will bring in Hinduism, and Islam, and Buddhism—a little bit of everything from that area, too. There is, as an absolute fact of human life and experience, a

---

3. Merton is jokingly referring to pre-Vatican II attitudes towards contemplation; particularly, suspicion around "mysticism," prevalent in the wake of the "Quietism" crisis in the seventeenth century (see Bernard McGinn, *The Crisis of Mysticism: Quietism in Seventeenth-Century Spain, Italy, and France* [New York: Herder & Herder, 2021], 301–12).

great heritage of profound religious consciousness, and people called to the kind of life that we're called to will obviously be convinced in some way or other that this is perhaps the greatest dimension of human life.

The fundamental, deepest thing that man has found is himself, his true self. Which is in God. Because in finding his true self, he finds God. He finds the root; he finds the ground. And that is because man is a very peculiar kind of being. Man is the being in whose consciousness God manifests Himself. In a certain sense, man is delegated by God to be God's consciousness of Himself in a creature. Man has the vocation to be conscious as creature of his Ground in God, and in such an intimate way that when man confesses and witnesses to his rootedness in God, it is God Himself who is confessing and witnessing this. Now, this is a staggering truth, and this is apparently the kind of truth that modern man is not prepared to accept. Yet he is, in a certain way, because there is something in man that seems to drive people to look for this kind of rootedness.

Let's face the fact that the Catholic contemplative life is at the moment under a strong attack from progressive Catholics. The real enemy, as far as we're concerned, is not the Marxist. Marxists have, on occasion—the ones who are hip to what's going on—will quite sincerely profess great admiration for the values of the [contemplative life]; for example, people like St. Teresa [of Avila]. Now, they find that there's something there. She's got something that they haven't got, and that's something that they're interested in.

And then you've got Simone de Beauvoir, who was very close to Sartre, as everybody knows. She's got a very interesting thing on woman and on what's happened to woman, and a defense of woman, and how the Catholic Church has really given woman the works, and woman has had a very bad treatment from the Catholic Church. But she will say, "All right, but," as she gets around to the Catholic mystics, and says, "Well, most of them are pathological." Then she says, "But St. Teresa, now there was somebody who really made it." And John of the Cross; she'll bring in John of the Cross and the relationship between Teresa and John of the Cross. She says this was a great thing; these were two people who—even though they were Catholics [laughter]—they really had something; they really broke through to something deep.

Well, on the other hand, you will find people regularly appearing in the *National Catholic Reporter*, and asking, "Can a cloistered life be

Christian?" I mean, can cloistered nuns be saved, without leaving? This is one of the great current questions in the *NCR*: is a cloistered nun a Christian at all? And then there are all sorts of arguments about how they can't really be Christians; they're poor deluded people, and so forth. We were replying rather weakly and ambiguously. We were coming back with the same old thing, "Well, we're praying for the world." Well, that doesn't cut any ice anymore. Of course, we do not really have to justify ourselves in their eyes. That's not necessarily our job. But we do have to face the fact that it does raise doubts in our own hearts. And it's good for us to doubt. We should doubt. And we should question our vocation. St. Bernard questioned his vocation: *Bernarde ad quid venisti*? He said, "What are you here for?" He questioned our vocation.

So, you develop in life as to frequently question your vocation seriously, and it has to be questioned. It has to be, because otherwise it doesn't grow. And I could go on record here as being one of the group that can say: the people who think that you should be constantly going back to your novitiate all through your religious life—that's very nice from a certain point of view, but it cannot possibly mean that you just constantly go back to the person that you were. You may go back to the same kind of enthusiasm of a different situation, but you cannot once again become that person. I would not, under any circumstances, want to be the person that I was in Gethsemani in 1942 [laughter]. If I were, I'd probably need a straitjacket [laughter]. You do develop, and things change.

But we do have to take stock of our lives. We have to take stock of this whole question of the contemplative life. The word "contemplative" itself is a very difficult concept to deal with anymore as a real description of our life. Why? Because it has a bad heritage. "Contemplative" is a Platonic word, and the thing that's really bad about it, is not that "contemplative equals solitude," or "contemplative equals silence," but "contemplative" suggests something that is very misleading in all descriptions of our kind of life. It suggests a subject-object division. A contemplative is a subject contemplating an object.

Now, you find right away that one of the basic things that we have to discover in our life is that God is not an object. God is a subject. If you contemplate God as an object in our life—this may be a very interesting and profitable exercise—but it is not really what we are called to do, because we are called not just to look at God, but to live in Him, and He in us, and we in Him, in such a way that He is the subject of our subject. He is the "is-ness" of our "is." The "is-ness" of our existence, or however you want to put it.

This idea of contemplation also suggests an intellectual exercise, and of course, where it really goes back to is the Platonic heritage of the contemplation of Ideas. Ideal realities. Well, that's just not for us. That's what we don't do, as a matter of fact. We're not concentrated on ideals. Of course, this suggests a certain philosophical context. A context of philosophical idealism, which implies a sharp cleavage between matter and spirit, and matter and body and soul, and this split gets all the way through everything. This is contrary to modern consciousness. Why? Because modern consciousness, if you go back to people like Descartes, who got it going, is mortally ill with that split. [We have been] trying to recover [from this] at all costs.

You've got people like Freud, for example, who has done modern man a great service in exorcising this split. The body-soul split has had to go, because you can't live that way anymore. It might have been profitable at a time when people lived very close to, or [were] very involved in matter. Medieval people were very earthy people, and they could afford to be idealistic.

I'm always getting into fights with people, who will occasionally send a big barrage of objections down to me at Gethsemani, saying, "What are you doing out there; you condemn God's good creation."[4] Well, I would like to point out that I think [the contemplative life] is much more in contact with—I mean, there's a lot of God's good creation around here, and look what they've done to it. We like the redwoods and they sell the redwoods. I mean, all you've got to do is travel around here [to see that] the people who are maintaining that the contemplative life is abstract, immoral, and out of touch with creation, are the [same] ones that are ravaging these sections of the hills, and tearing everything down and tearing it apart—in such a way that it'll never grow back. That doesn't, to me, reflect a great respect for God's good creation. But for them, God's good creation is New York [City]. There's nothing wrong with New York, either [laughter], but it does have some aspects that are not exactly purely divine, you know [laughter]. It has a side where you regret the concrete and you'd like to see a little more of God's good creation. The air is not quite as fresh as it is right here.

4. See, e.g., the correspondence between Merton and theologian Rosemary Radford Ruether, *At Home in the World: The Letters of Thomas Merton and Rosemary Radford Ruether*, ed. Mary Tardiff (Maryknoll, NY: Orbis, 1995).

This just occurred to me: I think at this point we could digress a little and think of the heritage of this particular monastery community here. This goes back to Flemish mystical communities of the twelfth and thirteenth centuries, which were radical. This was a great radical movement, a movement of radical Christianity, [which] spread through the Rhineland and the Low Countries, and other parts of Europe, too, at the same time, and it was really radical. It had a tremendous effect in forming the modern consciousness, because it was tied in with [Meister] Eckhart and people like that. Eckhart is certainly a great man—although he may be wrong on some points—but certainly terrific. Those of you [here] who are Americans and who don't come from the Old Country, recognize that you are in the heritage of Eckhart, and people like the Beguines and the Flemish mystics, who were very radical people—and very free people. A heritage of freedom.[5]

Incidentally, that is one of the things that I would say is very important for us: the capacity to witness to the solidity and authenticity of our life by a kind of freedom. There has to be a certain freedom in our life.

Let me read something from Freud as we go along here. This is almost the last sentence of a very beautiful book by Freud. It's a book I think that everybody should read, [called] *Civilization and its Discontents*.[6] It's a very good book for us. It's fine for our kind of life, because it does have a great deal to say about the whole business of the world. Freud puts his finger on something that is very, very crucial for us. It's the idea of alienation.[7]

This book, incidentally, is the one that has a great deal to say about the death instinct and the aggressive instinct. Freud emphasizes the polarity in human life between Eros and Thanatos, between love and the destructive instinct. It's a prophetic book. It's absolutely prophetic, because what he is saying, is that the destructive instinct is the one that's going to cause

5. Redwoods Monastery was founded from the Flemish Cistercian community of Our Lady of Nazareth in Belgium, which traces its origins to the thirteenth century and its first prioress, Beatrice of Nazareth (1200–1268). Merton is tracing the historical connection and "mystical genealogy" from Nazareth through to the present day.

6. First published in 1930. Historian Peter Gay summarizes Freud's late essay as "a fertile and original meditation on the irreparable conflict between the individual and his institutional surroundings" (*The Freud Reader* [New York: Norton, 1989], 722). Merton mentions reading "the last half" of the book in a journal entry of April 18, 1968, and describes it as "truly prophetic" (*Other Side of the Mountain*, 82).

7. At this point, one of the sisters enters the room and Merton responds, "Nice to see you. Find yourself a seat. We're just about to quote Freud, so you came just at the right time," with much laughter from the group.

the trouble—it already is—and that this death instinct and this aggressive instinct is the thing that is gradually growing. He foresees [this] at the end of the book, [where] he says that man can destroy himself. This is before they had the atomic bomb. Freud saw this, and in this situation, what does he say? He ends up with this terrific sentence, which I think describes our vocation. He says: "It is vouchsafed to a few, with hardly any effort, to save from the whirlpool of their own emotions the deepest truths, to which we others have to force our way, ceaselessly groping amid torturing uncertainties."[8] Well, both of these can apply to us. There should be in our communities a few people that you occasionally run into, who are able to, by virtue of a great simplicity, to save from the whirlpool of their own emotions the deepest truths. This sense that Freud had of the reality of these powerful forces conflicting within us, and at the same time of the possibility of saving from this whirlpool the deepest truths. Whether or not you can do that easily, you've got to [try]. If you can't do it easily, then you have to be like the rest of us, and we have to do it the hard way. Freud includes himself, and I include myself, and I think that's the way we are. We [often] have to force our way, ceaselessly groping amidst torturing uncertainties.[9]

I think that is something that we really have to remember, because the real key to renewal in our life is the acceptance of this fact, and the thing that's blocking renewal is an unconscious resistance against this. There is a kind of conservatism, which is very well meant, but which attempts to create a life in which there are no torturing uncertainties. It attempts to suppress the uncertainties and the risks that go with doing something different. And that is deadly. That is the real bad thing about conservatism: that it refuses to allow a struggle to take place. There is a necessary struggle that has to take place, and there is a refusal to let it take place, and in an age when you've had people like Freud, this is no longer permissible. It has to be understood that this struggle has to be faced, and in this struggle, we do not triumph with great power, but we ceaselessly grope.

The liberty that the Cistercian asks for is the liberty to grope amidst torturing uncertainties, and not to be told that the uncertainties don't

---

8. Sigmund Freud, *Civilization and Its Discontents* (New York: Norton, 2010), 94.

9. See also Merton's "A Letter on the Contemplative Life," where he writes, "My brother, perhaps in my solitude I have become as it were an explorer for you, a searcher in realms which you are not able to visit—except perhaps in the company of your psychiatrist" (August 21, 1967) in *The Monastic Journey*, ed. Patrick Hart (Kalamazoo, MI: Cistercian Publications, 1992), 171. I am grateful to Jonathan Montaldo for pointing me in the direction of this quote.

exist. The thing that reduces us to despair, is when people come in vested with great authority, and tell us that the uncertainties don't exist. This is simply not acceptable. It's not possible to tell people this. There's no way of telling them, but they have to face the fact, that they cannot, by a *fiat* of their authority, cross these uncertainties out—because they're our life. It is in these uncertainties that the real stuff of life comes up.

At this point, I could recommend another book, and this is a very good one. I started to speak to you about it yesterday when we were driving in, and then we saw another bunch of bigger and better redwoods [laughter], and I was completely unable to speak. This is a Persian psychoanalyst who is working in Washington, and he is equally well-versed in the various schools of psychoanalysis, and in Persian Sufism, which is this [Islamic] mystical school of contemplation. He has written a very good book. The title is *Final Integration in the Adult Personality*,[10] and his point in this book is that psychoanalysis is not going far enough; that it only attempts to get a person adjusted to a society which is sick anyway, and that the real vocation of psychoanalysis, which it cannot achieve by itself—it needs a higher discipline, like Sufism, or some [other] religious-mystical discipline—is to liberate man; not just to adjust man to society, but to take him beyond society. And that the real "final integration" of the human being is not when he becomes integrated into society, but when he has integrated *out of it.* That is to say, when he is strong enough to function without being dominated by social norms; he has his own norms.

Now, this is, purely and simply, the New Testament; particularly what has been forgotten about the New Testament. This is the heart of the New Testament, which says you become a follower of Christ; you are no longer a follower of Caesar; you are no longer a follower of the Sanhedrin; and you don't need the temple. You don't need any of these things; you have the Spirit, and you follow the Spirit. But first, one has to have the Spirit, and then block out any kind of unhealthy Gnosticism, in which some-

---

10. A. Reza Arasteh, *Final Integration in the Adult Personality* (Leiden: Brill, 1965). For Merton's review of this work, see his essay, "Final Integration: Toward a 'Monastic Therapy,'" in *Contemplation in a World of Action* (New York: Doubleday, 1973), 219–31. Merton corresponded with Arasteh from 1965–1968, selections of which are included in *The Hidden Ground of Love: The Letters of Thomas Merton on Religious Experience and Social Concerns*, ed. William H. Shannon (New York: Farrar, Straus and Giroux, 1985), 40–43.

body says, "I have got the Spirit and get out of my way." You've got the Church; you have the community. The Spirit is given to the community. The Spirit is given to each one and to all. It is the community—the loving community called together to seek God's love and will in their common life in Christ. And then the community can also admit that maybe this individual has the Spirit in some form that nobody else understands: "Okay, we'll try it out, but . . ."

And that applies, for example, to the hermit life in our life. Obviously, the sanction for being a hermit in a Cistercian community comes from the community. You don't just go and twist the arm of the superior. That's the way it worked out for me at Gethsemani, and I feel very good about it, because everybody was behind it. They all said, "Sure, that's what he ought to do," and the Abbot got his council, and the council voted on it unanimously, and they all said, "Go ahead," and so it was fine. But supposing you get situations where somebody does this and nobody can see it—it's a different sort of thing. And this has been taken over by officials and by Curial machinery, and so it is no longer really the Spirit. I mean, the Holy Spirit may have to rubber stamp this after it's done—[the Spirit] must have a sore arm from doing this after the last six centuries or so—but it shouldn't be that way. It should be a question of a real liberty of the person beyond social norms, and beyond laws.

So, this means a development of consciousness—a deeper kind of consciousness. A person should have a solid awareness of the Spirit guiding him beyond the level of a certain accepted norm. And right now, I would say that there is in this country a tremendous sense of need for this among young people. There is a sweeping movement that looks like charism. It may or may not be, but there is a need for a charismatic [movement], or upheaval, in this country. People sense this in all directions. They feel that the country is just rotten and that it's collapsing; that if it goes on with what it regards as efficient and right—and all this computerized existence that they're living—the thing's going to blow up. That it has no future with this, and that there has to be something else, and they're groping for something. I don't know what they're finding, but they're groping anyway. There is this need for a totally different kind of life, and the feeling that if you get integrated fully and completely into the kind of society that we have officially in this country, you just get into a machine that's simply going over the falls. You get involved in something like this

Vietnam business, which is just absolutely impossible, and then you buy one part of it and you're caught with the whole thing, and then you can't let go of one piece of it without letting go of the whole works.

This is again getting close to our kind of situation; because with the monks, very often you'll find entire communities of profoundly contemplative people praying madly for the success of the war in Vietnam because they don't know any better. How can you have a charismatic community if it is taken in completely by the official interpretation of things given by an establishment which is morally dubious? Then we're told not to concern ourselves with these things. If we don't concern ourselves with these things in some way, then we just simply accept an official answer that we have not examined. This is a real problem for us. You constantly run into this; it's a dilemma for us.

People say, "Oh, if you take an interest in the Vietnam War, you're betraying your contemplative vocation," and I say, "If you *don't* take an interest in the Vietnam War, you're betraying your contemplative vocation" —because where it is, is in this. A curious thing about this: I have a very good friend who's a Buddhist monk[11] and who's been in this country for some time, and has been going around trying to persuade people to see the war over there as his Buddhist people see it. He's not a politician; he's actually one of the most brilliant intellectuals in Vietnam, and one of the best poets in Vietnam, and a very fine person. He's taught Buddhist psychology at Columbia. His monastery was in Huế. So, these two monasteries, one Catholic and one Buddhist, were both destroyed by the Americans in the big fight in Huế recently, and the Benedictines were scattered all over the place, and this man's monks were scattered all over; and his spiritual master was killed, and he said that none of the master's disciples were able to be there for his burial.[12] What's curious is that we're all in the same boat. How absurd would it be, to be a Benedictine back here, supporting the war effort, which just simply results in the extermi-

---

11. This is a reference to Thich Nhat Hanh (1926–2022), whose safety Merton advocated for in his 1966 essay, "Nhat Hanh is My Brother" (in *Faith and Violence: Christian Teaching and Christian Practice* [Notre Dame: University of Notre Dame Press, 1968], 106–9).

12. There appears to be no corroborating evidence to support Merton's claims regarding the destruction of either Tu Hieu (the "Root Temple" of Thich Nhat Hanh), or the Benedictine Thien An Abbey. For a history of Thien An, see: www.thevietnamese.org/2020/10/thien-an-abbey-45-years-under-the-governments-fist (accessed July 5, 2023).

nation of our kind of people [i.e., monastics]; no matter what side you're on, you just get exterminated.

This is something that we have to face. We have to be informed about these things, because the judgment of God on the world is manifest in these things in some obscure kind of way. If we don't know about this, we are missing the boat. On the other hand, we also can't get involved in these really stupid arguments that go on about it. I was involved in one of these things recently myself. There was a fellow in Kentucky who decided that he was going to refuse induction in the draft, and he had also had several other raw deals, and they decided they were going to put him in jail. So, he went down to refuse induction, and I gave a letter in support of him, and this got in the Catholic papers. There was a considerable amount of correspondence about this, including one man in Louisville who said that he was too old to burn his draft card, but by golly he was going to burn my books! [laughter] So, he had a book-burning party or something like that, and there was a great deal of fury about, "That priest! How can he say such things?" You can get into some very stupid arguments, and there's really no point. But we really do have to know what these things are about.

You talk about consciousness, the modern consciousness, the religious consciousness. Today, this is a whole new question from what it used to be, say, in the Middle Ages. In the Middle Ages, theoretically, you didn't even stop to consider what kind of a consciousness you were going to develop. Maybe you might think over whether you would be a soldier or a priest, but basically, they all developed the same kind of consciousness.

Today, we live in a culture where you've got a consciousness supermarket, and you've got every possibility, theoretically. If you really want to, you can develop anything that you like. You can try anything. So, it is important to take this into account: that there are choices, and we have to know what the choices are. For example, speaking again about this Buddhist monk, one of the reasons why he and I get along very well is because he and I have very much the same kind of consciousness. We experience life in the same way. I experience life much more like him than I do some of the other monks at Gethsemani, or some of the people who are in business in Louisville, for example. There are people in Louisville that I know that I can't talk to. There's nothing to say except, "It's a nice day," or something like that. There's no communication possible, except on a completely superficial level, because they have a totally different kind of consciousness.

That's a key word for us. Our life is one in which we develop a certain kind of consciousness. And there are choices, too, but strictly speaking, we should be oriented towards a kind of consciousness which cuts across religious frontiers. In other words, we will normally be closer to the Zen Buddhist than we might be to a good Catholic businessman; or, we will be closer to the Hindu, who really has deepened his religious disciplines, than we will be to somebody much closer to us—perhaps even our own parents, in some cases.

But, once again, we run into a problem, because in our life there is a tendency to inhibit and narrow things down in this particular way. There's a tendency to force an official kind of exteriorized consciousness where it's all predigested for you. Of course, we don't have the same problem that we used to have when the *Spiritual Directory* had to be read at certain moments of the day, and in the novitiate. We were simply brainwashed by this particular kind of spirituality. We don't have that today. But there is a kind of "official" feeling in the Order that there's a right way for a Cistercian to behave, and you shouldn't get too deep into some of these things. You've always had a certain type of person in our Order who is immediately suspicious of anybody who's too interested in prayer. In the old days it was very acceptable at Gethsemani to make a big deal of running around visiting altars—which is all right, it doesn't do any harm. If a man spent 15 minutes—or he spent a whole two hours—visiting altars, or crucifixes and statues of the Blessed Mother in the cemetery. If he spent two hours doing that, fine. If he spent the same two hours just sitting in a pew by himself, there's something radically wrong with it. That was the sort of thing we used to be up against. Of course, there were reasons for it, because very often people did go wrong with that, and they got wrong ideas.

People who did that, rightly or wrongly, were looking for something. What was it? Were they right or wrong? Was there something, some other way in which they could have found this? Was this a temporary thing, and then was there some other dimension in which it could be found later on? These are crucial questions for us, because if people in our monasteries are not really developing, and developing in their own way, then we've got problems. We have trouble. But it's so difficult for anybody to know what is his own way, or her own way, to develop. Again, it gets back to these torturing uncertainties. We do have to grope and experiment, and people have to make mistakes, but once a mistake is made, then put the pieces back together again and start over. Whereas, in some monasteries there is a tendency, as soon as there's any kind of a mistake, to throw everything out the window and sweep everything under the rug, and make like it didn't happen [laughter]. "Mistakes are just not possible. Mistakes don't happen in our life."

You've got lots of people that have been in Gethsemani, for example, that are scattered all over the country with great wounds, and nobody's ever going to bind these wounds up. At one time, they weren't even allowed to come back for a certain period. They couldn't even come back and talk to their friends. This is just an official way of handling things. It doesn't really respond to what is a real human reality.[13]

On the other hand, as I was going to say a minute ago, you've got a lot of noncommitted people. I'm going to read you a letter from one of the poets that contributes to my magazine, which is personal, but it's not secret or anything. There are a lot of people who feel guilty about seeking or about deepening a religious consciousness, with the idea that this is just a way of getting peace, of pacifying yourself. I'll just read this text without commenting on it first, and talk about it afterwards. It probably goes back to a reaction against the "happiness pill" approach to religion which was so prevalent in the 1950s. In this country there were a lot of popular preachers at that time—Norman Vincent Peale[14] and people like that—who were giving everybody the impression that all they had to do was embrace religion and they would have no more problems. They were even telling people, "Don't go to these psychoanalysts; all you need is an act of faith. Then it's all fixed." This was going great for about ten years there in the '50s, and of course it fell through when they found out they made an act of faith and still had the same trouble [laughter].

People seem to have felt since then that if you go after this religion thing, it's somehow dishonest. From a certain point of view, the way they're looking at it, it is true, if one does this in the wrong way.

---

13. See Merton's poem, "Gethsemani, May '66," with its opening line: "Many have gone away injured / From the house of God" (*Eighteen Poems* [New York: New Directions, 1985], published in limited edition and now out of print).

14. Norman Vincent Peale (1898–1993) was an influential—if controversial—American minister and popularizer of the notion of "positive thinking," made famous through his best-selling book *The Power of Positive Thinking: A Practical Guide to Mastering the Problems of Everyday Living* (New York: Prentice Hall, 1952).

I'll just read this from this very interesting person, who is, as a matter of fact, married. All the people who write for this little magazine of mine[15] turn out be very much the same kind of people [laughter]. They are all living somewhere in Arkansas, or in the Canadian Rockies, or Mexico. They're all monks of a kind. They're quiet people living way off in the country on some little farm, just with their [family]. Usually they're married, or there with their husband and two or three children. They're quite poor and they don't want to get rich.

She's one of these. She lives in Arkansas, and is a very good poet. In fact, a tremendous poet.[16] She's sent me a manuscript of a book of poetry that I think is just fabulous, and it is basically a very religious book of poetry; the religious content of it is mostly Mexican Indian religion. Mayan religion. She has traveled a lot in Mexico, and she knows a great deal about the Mexican myths and traditions; she's made a wonderful poetic use of them, applying them to man's emotional complex. She's got stuff about tigers, about things that are going on inside of her. Very fine.

But then she writes this, which is a great contrast to her poetry, on the question of inner peace: "It's possible, perhaps. How can we find peace? How can we find a God? It seems selfish for me to think of God." In other words, it's a self-indulgence, and in a sense, she's right; when she's thinking of it in terms of this Norman Vincent Peale thing, or anything that could help outside the human effort. "I can't see beyond humanity. To work for all of us, for any of us to work for many things: to work for peace, to work for understanding, to work to find life, and to see life, and to do whatever we can do about it; to train ourselves to do things we can see, see to do. What I think you are saying, too"—well, yes and no—"But to me it is to work as though no God existed. To work as though there were nothing but the devil. Because the thought of a God gives some sense of peace, but if you think there is only a little man carrying a time load in this world, and all of us are little men carrying a time load strapped to our backs, we surely are going to do something about it."

---

15. Merton is referring to his literary magazine *Monks Pond* which ran over four issues throughout 1968; reprinted as *Monks Pond: Thomas Merton's "Little Magazine,"* ed. Robert E. Daggy (Lexington, KY: University Press of Kentucky, 1989).

16. This is a reference to American poet Besmilr Brigham (1913–2000); see *Monks Pond*, 71–72, 108, 148–52, 222–26, 345.

Well, I don't know. I'm not saying that she's right or wrong; I'm just reading this as an example of the way so many people feel: that this whole religion business is radically dishonest. They feel that what happens if you bring in the idea of God, and if you surrender to God, and you do the will of God, you're simply evading the issue of—the key word here being—"a little man carrying a time load in this world." You're not carrying your own burden. From a certain point of view, that is a good statement, because religion is not for that. We're not supposed to evade carrying our cross, but that is, as a matter of fact, very often what it can be. To what extent do we assume that, once we have made our surrender to God, that He really hasn't got a right to give us any more troubles? Or, if He does give us troubles, He's just squeezing us a little bit to make us pray more, but really it can't last very long. Well, maybe that's nothing to do with it?

This is an important point. We're going to run into this again in Sartre, because this is one of Sartre's big statements—not just about Christians, but about the whole of society—that he rejects. It's what he considers a dishonest business of pushing it all off onto some abstract being, rather than concretely bearing your own burden. That, I think, is something that we're going to have to come to grips with, and this will come up as we go through here, because once again, in the conservative repression of any kind of change and progress, they're really defending this dishonest attitude. What it really boils down to is a kind of justification, not by faith, but by the institution and by the setup. It's the old story of, "If you just do what you're told, and just keep the Rule the way you're told, everything will be all right; stop complaining." And that's not true. The Book of Job is about that. Job's friends argued from morning to night: "Job, if you had just done this. The reason why you got troubles is you missed something along the line; there was something you ought to have done that you just didn't do." We may have to carry a great burden.

As a matter of fact, the idea of the existence of God is neither here nor there in this whole question. This is one of the big problems of discussing this thing with modern man. Camus comes up with this: the problem of suffering, what about it? And it all ultimately becomes an apologetic question: can God exist if you suffer? And to get involved in that is to get involved in a vicious circle; it has no end, because it's not the question.

What she is saying, then, from this point of view, is right. God is not there to justify or to explain, or to take care of suffering in one way or the other. That's not it. He will help us suffer if we have to suffer—and we [will] have [to], no questions asked. And it is not a question of whether it's right for me to suffer, or right for me not to suffer. If I have to suffer, I have to suffer, and it has to be faced. It's not something to be telling people the reason they suffer is because they're not a Catholic, or the reason you suffer is because you're a sinner; or because you've done this, or you've done that. This is the thing with Job's friends. Those days are over for religion. Religion cannot explain or justify anything in the eyes of people who have these questions.

The only thing that I can do for somebody like this, is just simply be her brother; often, that's all she wants, it's so simple. To push it further, if she is in a jam and if I can help her, I help her. I don't come along with a big sign saying, "This help is coming to you at the courtesy of the Catholic Church" [laughter]. It's just simply that I'm her brother.

That's why I'm editing this little magazine that has nothing about religion in it. It is in the form of a community. If I insisted on talking to these people about abstract religion; if I said, "Now, wait a minute, I'm not going to publish your poem unless you assure me that you are going to bear your cross with more nobility in the future" [laughter]—that's got nothing to do with it; whereas, being a brother has everything to do with it. It's that simple, because that's the way Christ did it, and that is the way we should do it. But if, as communities in this Order, we're going to do this, we're going to have to be a little bit different. Down in our place, you get into the bookstore, and there are signs saying, "Don't do this" and "Keep out of there," and "Excommunication"; and, of course, I've been excommunicated—I got excommunicated again today. I got inside the valley up there [inside the cloister] [laughter].

This is the real problem of the monastic life. We have to be able to be a community in which the community is not made by "the wall"; because it's a lie to say that just within the wall all are brothers, and outside the wall are not brothers. There has to be an interrelationship. Certainly, there has to be a special relationship between those who have the same commitment, but they should also have relationships with people outside, who, to some extent, can come in.

Take, for example, the question of married people and religious community life. It was Holy Saturday and I was sitting outside in my hermitage with my shoes off, having a nice time—lying in the sun and waiting for evening to go to the Vigil service—and out comes a pickup truck with three people in it: one of my ex-novices; two, his wife; and three, their baby [laughter]. They roll up to the hermitage and all pile out, and we all sit on the grass and talk for a couple of hours.

He wasn't even allowed to come near the place under the old Abbot. Under the new Abbot, he just came, and it was, "Oh, hello, glad to see you." He's got a little farm in Indiana. He's living a quiet life on his farm with his wife and kid, and he said, "I've often been thinking of just getting a little farm near here." He spoke of a place that he and I both knew back in the hills where there had been a previous hermit who went way back in our time. We had a hermit about 50 years ago. He was back over there, and it was this farm next to that. Here's this person who used to be there, and wants to come back with his wife and just be around the place, but he can't. Whereas another former novice of mine, who is this poet in Nicaragua,[17] who's got a community going on an island down there—he's a secular priest, but he's got permission from the bishop to run a little monastic community. One of his men was in seminary with him and was going to join the community, and then he decided he wanted to get married. So, he went and got married—went back to Columbia, where he married this girl, and came back to the community. He's not living in the community, but he and his wife are living near the community and they're part of it. They help with it, and his wife also does a little work— there's several families living on the same island, and she does work with the children there.[18]

This is a perfectly good monastic formula. Why not? People can be marginal members of the community; people who have a claim on the community, who have been in it and for some reason left, and then remain, to some extent, part of it.

That kind of thing is what makes our life more relevant, and it implies a different kind of consciousness. It is not simply to purify one's own

17. Merton is referring here to Ernesto Cardenal (1925–2020). Merton and Cardenal corresponded from 1959 until Merton's death in 1968. Their letters are collected in *From the Monastery to the World: The Letters of Thomas Merton and Ernesto Cardenal*, trans. and ed. Jessie Sandoval (Berkeley: Counterpoint, 2017).

18. This is a reference to poet William Agudelo; see *From the Monastery to the World*, 211, 226–27, 232–33, 237.

soul, and to get more virtues, and to be really polished up—like a nice car, really cleaned up—so if and when you're called back to the factory, you're a real presentable model [laughter].

On the contrary, there is a consciousness of certain levels of depth and dimension in life, which are at the same time very simple, and not necessarily able to be put into words; but which are worked out in human, personal relationships. Then, when the relationships are set up, the consciousness follows; rather than the other way around: you develop a certain kind of consciousness and then everybody likes you, and if you don't feel happy, it's because you feel you're not worthy, and then people don't like you because you're not worthy, so that you have to be worthy, and blah, blah, blah. The whole idea of "being worthy," the consciousness of being "worthy," is a very deceptive thing. It is a worm in the apple of religion—of the religious consciousness. The person who is religious in order to be worthy of love creates a hard problem, and that is, in a certain sense, what these people feel. It's what Sartre really feels, although Sartre is a tough man, and he's got all sorts of rough ideas; but I think he really feels this about religious people. When we get around to him, we'll see that.

I don't know how the time's going, but I think I've talked enough now; I think we ought to stop a bit and have some discussion.

A question is raised regarding Merton's earlier comments about the cloistered life being "unchristian" in its separation from "the world."

The argument is that the very instinct to enter a cloister is "unchristian," because it means turning one's back on the world. Of course, the problem is that it's only a half truth. I think the real problem with this particular type of critic is that it's a rather superficial assumption that he makes. He's got it all nice and neat. Do you know that book *Animal Farm* by George Orwell?[19] Well, this is a book where the animals on a farm had a revolution and it was all taken over by the pigs [laughter]. The pigs decide to teach the other animals a simple way of distinguishing right and wrong. It was a revolution against the people, against man. So, the pigs, in order to instruct these other less smart animals, put up a big sign giving the

---

19. Eric Arthur Blair (1903–1950), aka "George Orwell." His satirical novel, *Animal Farm*, was originally published in 1945.

principle: "Four Legs Good. Two Legs Bad." Anything with two legs, a human being, was bad; anything with four legs, an animal, was good. Real simple.

I think it's the same kind of argument that's going on now about the contemplative life: "In the City, Good. Out of the City, Bad." Anybody who has any desire to be alone, bad. Anybody who desires to be with other people all the time, good. But this doesn't prove anything. I think what we have to do is answer the argument by being Christians in the cloister. Then, if they are convinced by that, all right; if they're not, too bad. We've done our part. But we do have to ask ourselves the same question: are we living our cloistered life in a Christian way, or is it an evasion? And when it's formulated in a certain way, it's an evasion. The problem that we're up against, once again, is that very often there's a "conservative" way, which is an evasion. It's not Christian if it's followed through in all its implications because it implies the same argument from our side: "In the cloister, good; out of the cloister, bad." Everything that happens in the cloister, good; everything that happens outside the cloister, bad. Anybody who is in the world is a sinner; anybody who is in the cloister is a saint. We know that's not true.

That's the way it goes. You've got the habit on, you've got your rosary, you're there on time, and that's it. I think one of the things that is very important in our renewal is that we are now experiencing [Martin] Luther's questions—and it's a good thing that we do. The one thing I always used to say to groups of Protestant ministers when they would come to Gethsemani: I would tell them, "Nobody here can be a monk *really* unless he has gone through Luther's experience." Because Luther had to discover that you were not justified by monastic "good works"—you had to be justified by faith.

The next thing I want to take up is the question of the mystique of religious women, which is a big problem today. We'll take that up after supper.

Mother Myriam comments on the idea of the cloister, as it was originally conceived for women's communities, as "unchristian."

The question of the growth of convent life has two sides. When you go back to the Church Fathers, [the idea] was [actually] an emancipation of woman. The cloister was a place of freedom where the woman was no longer the possession of a husband. In late Roman society, to be a wife was no joke—it was a tough life. The woman who became a virgin consecrated to Christ was emancipated; it was the only form of feminine emancipation that was possible at that time. Then it became an institutionalized thing. Of course, it took some time for it to get that way.[20]

Question: What are the angles that we could look at to justify our contemplative life?

Well, it goes back to, for example, the Freud quote. A contemplative life is justified if it enables people to come more honestly to grips with themselves. We are, to some extent, opposed to the world; but what is it in the world that we are opposed to? The fact that they have a good time? No. The fact that the world is, to a great extent, artificial. The thing that I want to talk about most is this idea of alienation. Worldly society is essentially an alienated society. I'll have another talk to define that—a society in which a person is not his own. Now, if the cloistered life is just another form of alienation, it is not justified. That's the point. But if the cloistered life is freedom—if a person entering the cloister ceases to be alienated—then it is justified. This brings out the whole problem that we're going to be up against in [monastic] renewal. Renewal means fighting alienation—and we can do it—because all of the people that I know that have really bitten into cloistered life are very individual people. For good or for bad—but they're all individual people. They've got their thing and they're going to do it.[21]

I think for us, we simply have to be ourselves, and the justification of our life is if we honestly feel that in spite of everything, we have managed to be ourselves. Then it's all right for us. I can certainly say that myself. I've had a struggle and all that, but they really haven't stopped me being

20. See Merton's essay "Virginity and Humanism in the Western Fathers," in *Mystics and Zen Masters* (New York: Farrar, Straus and Giroux, 1967), 113–27.

21. As an example, Merton tells the story of Fr. Stephen Pitra, "unofficial" gardener at Gethsemani. For Merton's homage to him, see his late poem, "Elegy for a Trappist," in *The Collected Poems of Thomas Merton* (New York: New Directions, 1977), 631–32. See also Merton's journal entry dated October 13, 1966 (*Learning to Love: The Journals of Thomas Merton, vol. 6: 1966-1967*, ed. Christine M. Bochen [San Francisco: HarperCollins, 1997], 147–48).

myself. On the other hand, they've let me. They really have, and ultimately, if I am not authentic enough, maybe it's my fault—but I can't really say that I've been blocked all that much. I've been blocked in some ways, but they can't block you. They can't really do anything to you. Just off the record, I found this out over years with things like censorship—Dom Gabriel [Sortais]—the fights that I've had with that man. There was this thing on peace that I was doing, that came out in *Seeds of Destruction*, a big long section on peace.[22]

First, I wrote three short essays for the basis of this one long thing, and they were approved and allowed to appear in magazines—good. Then they were to come out as a book. So, I put them together and I said, "May I publish these three articles, previously in a magazine. I want to put them in a book." "No. You've written enough about peace. The bishops are the ones who are supposed to talk about peace." Okay, fine. I won't publish. Then the publisher gets after me. He says, "What's the idea? Where are those articles?" I said, "I can't publish them." Meanwhile, Dom Gabriel dies. The publisher writes to the new censor, and he says, "No, we can't. He shouldn't be writing about peace." The publisher says, "I need these!" Then Dom Ignace [Gillet] says, "Well, you can write, but you better make certain changes. You've got to rewrite it." So, I rewrote it three times as long and everything that I said before that I wasn't allowed to say, I said— and I said *more*. Then Dom Ignace said, "Very good, fine, you may now publish this" [laughter]. So, the total result was you just got out more. Very often it is true that when they block you, maybe it's better. Maybe there's a better time. Maybe there's a better way.

A question is raised regarding different forms of consciousness; differing levels of awareness among members of religious communities.

In a community, [different forms of consciousness] should be complimentary. When a community is really doing what it should, we should help one another to deepen our consciousness. That's not always what happens, but it should be. Ideally speaking, we should be helping one another to be mystics—of course, how can you do that? But that's what

---

22. "The Christian in World Crisis," in *Seeds of Destruction* (New York: Farrar, Straus and Giroux, 1964), 93–184.

we should be doing. That's what Cistercian monasteries are for. That's what Nazareth was for in the days of Blessed Beatrice [of Nazareth]. Of course, that formula got highly corrupted—by the time we all entered it had become, "You help your brother become a mystic by the chapter of faults." That's where you help him become a mystic—slap him down.

But we should be helping one another—let's put it in simpler words—to love. We help one another to love more, and you help people to love, not by saying "love," but *by loving*. That's the justification of our life: if there is love, it's justified, and it should not be just a little in-growing love. It should be a love that reaches out to everybody.

Comment: You said that we have to help each other deepen our consciousness; to go further, and even to direct that consciousness in the same direction, and that without these same kinds of consciousness there is no communication possible.

For us, we're all going in the same direction, and we should be helping one another to love and experience a love that is in God—not only to love, but to experience the meaning of love in the Grounded-ness of love in God and in Christ.

I meant to say, a monastic community should be made up, to a certain extent, of like-minded people.

Yes, not by conformity, and it should be of one mind and one heart in Christ; but that presupposes differences in unity, and difference overall. We are all called for one thing, which is to become conscious of God, but there's where you get the problem in these contemplative "communities," where everybody is an individual contemplative. There, "consciousness of God" means not consciousness of brother or sister—"I have to be conscious of God and shut everybody else out and get rid of these people." The idea that "when you don't see anybody, then you're more conscious of God," is an illusion. Of course, there are times when you have to be alone, but we help one another by respecting one another's need for solitude, and also by reciprocally sacrificing solitude when it's needed for community. It's a constant, dynamic action going on.

One of the real essential things of consciousness that should be common is the consciousness of this dynamism of love in the community. That is the thing that helps everybody grow. If everybody is commonly conscious of a dynamism of love working in the community, and if at certain moments they're all conscious of it together, then that's fulfilling [the authentic purpose of community]. But if nobody's ever conscious of this, you can't blame it on an abstract community, because the community is made up of people. If nobody's ever conscious of love acting dynamically, well what's the matter with *them*? Don't you think that is pretty fundamental for Cistercians?

Question: Do you see the eremitical vocation as a flowering out of the community?

Any love that a hermit has for God is also a part of the community's love. He owes much to the community. It's because the community has love in it, that he is able to go out and love God. For us as Cistercians, I think that there is no other formula. The hermit life in Cistercian communities is always an exception, and always is a function of the community. Of course, this has advantages and disadvantages. I think that the best formula is the way we have it [at Gethsemani], because you're right on the property. You're right close to the monastery. It seems to me for Cistercians it's the best model, because you're right there, and they all do some work for the community. Everybody does something. And you're right there: if my electricity goes wrong, the community electrician comes up. It's not much different from having a private room, really, but it should always remain exceptional. We're getting people now that are trying to enter [the community] on the grounds that they will one day become hermits, which is absolutely wrong. It's quite interesting that our new abbot is himself one of the hermits. Our new abbot was a hermit and the old one went to be a hermit [laughter]. So, there's a charism there!

Chapter Two

Alienation and the Feminine Mystique

This is something that I'm not supposed to talk about. It's something I don't really know about, actually. It's this whole business of women in the Church, and I want to try to work together around the idea of a mystique about women. It's also a mystique about the contemplative life. The two tend to go together because you've got cloistered women.[1]

Before I get into that, I want to talk about alienation,[2] which is important because that's what leads into this [idea of "mystique"]. Alienation is one of the key ideas in Marx, and then Freud got into it, too. It's important, because this has been forced upon large numbers of people by the kind of society that we live in. An alienated person is one who is forced to live according to somebody else's idea. In this country, [the Black community] has traditionally had to conform to an idea that just wasn't right. It was the white man's explanation of the [Black experience]. The worst kind of alienation is not the kind where you are aware about being alienated, but when you accept somebody else's idea; when somebody else's idea of you becomes your own idea of yourself, and yet your own life keeps telling you that this can't be true. You're not like this. That is what an alienated existence is.

---

1. Compare to the chapter entitled, "The Feminine Mystique," in *The Springs of Contemplation: A Retreat at the Abbey of Gethsemani* (New York: Farrar, Straus and Giroux, 1992), 161–76. Merton delivered these talks to a gathering of contemplative nuns in May 1968 upon his return from Redwoods Monastery and there are a number of similarities.

2. See also Merton's essay, "Why Alienation Is for Everybody," in *The Literary Essays of Thomas Merton* (New York: New Directions, 1981), 381–84.

Marx's idea is more about economic alienation; that the workman does the work and somebody else takes the profit. The profit doesn't go to the workman; the workman gets a bare subsistence wage. The workman is producing a surplus value which somebody else is getting, and therefore his work isn't his own anymore, and he's living somebody else's life. This has changed since then and the workman is getting a little bit better deal.

The argument that I'm following is that women tend to be alienated in society, which is essentially a masculine society. Now, you tell me, because I don't know; but I read a book on this and I found it fairly convincing,[3] and there's a certain amount of evidence that women in the Church have a tough time. It's quite clear that women are, more or less, kept in a minor role in the Church. Obviously, the mere fact, for example, of the problems that the Sisters in this country have—the active orders—Sister Luke, and the IHMs, and people like that.[4] They're granted certain rights by Rome to arrange their life as they see fit, and then when they do it, they're told not to. Obviously, a person in that kind of position is somehow being mistreated and oppressed.

This raises the question. Certainly, women are unfairly treated in the Church. This, I think, people are beginning to realize. But the right people aren't beginning to admit it yet. I'm not going to talk about this, because this is something that everybody knows, but what's behind it? What about the mentality that's behind it? And how does that affect us in the cloistered life? Or in the contemplative life? I think there's a relationship: first of all, because so many contemplatives are women; and secondly, because with

3. Merton mentions feminist theologian Mary Daly in *Springs of Contemplation*, 163; see also his comments below (p. 68).

4. Sister Mary Luke Tobin, SL (1908–2006), one of the few women religious invited to participate in Vatican II. She was a friend and regular correspondent with Merton (see Bonnie Thurston and Mary Swain, eds. *Hidden in the Same Mystery: Thomas Merton and Loretto* [Louisville, KY: Fons Vitae, 2010]). Regarding the Servants of the Immaculate Heart of Mary (IHM): this is most likely a reference to the Immaculate Heart Community in Los Angeles, who, in 1967, were ordered by the Archbishop of Los Angeles, Cardinal James McIntyre, to end renewal in their order or cease teaching in all diocesan schools. In 1969, 327 members of the community formally requested dispensation from their vows, and in 1970, 220 former IHM sisters formed their own ecumenical community (www.immaculateheartcommunity.org/ihc-history; accessed November 10, 2021). See also Anita Caspary, *Witness to Integrity: The Crisis of the Immaculate Heart Community of California* (Collegeville, MN: Liturgical Press, 2003) and the film, *Rebel Hearts* (2021).

regard to the contemplative life and with regard to women, you've got a mystique on both sides.

What's a "mystique"? A mystique ties in with alienation. A mystique is an idea which has been given too much reality. For example, the mystique of "woman," which is not necessarily the reality of woman, but it's an idea about woman, and is substituted for what woman really is. If it is true, this could be a very serious problem. I never realized it before. Maybe you haven't. I don't know. Maybe you have.

But certainly, the mystique of the contemplative life is a big problem. For example, the mystique of a contemplative life is this idea of a contemplative who has nothing to do with the world. A perfectly abstracted person who is dealing only with God and has no interest in the world; forgotten everything. Has no care for parents; never writes letters home anymore.

When people, for example, automatically sit down and say, "The first way to solve our problems is to define a 'monk.'" They're thinking in terms of a mystique because, unconsciously, they know that a mystique is something that you can use very efficiently; because if you can get something down on paper and then try to get people to agree that that's what they're supposed to be—you've got them. No matter what they do, you've got them. And if you happen to be one of those that helped make the definition, then you have it worse than anybody else; you agreed, you're one of them! I don't know whether women have cooperated in the formation of a mystique of women or not. I think to some extent they may have, but it could be a real bad thing.

What is this mystique of women? [Here] I'm following, for example, Gertrud von Le Fort.[5] I myself used to buy this pretty much: woman as an ideal.[6] The point is that this really doesn't benefit women at all. The real point behind this is you idealize woman, and then you can humiliate her at the same time. You're probably already sparked; you probably know this, but I haven't thought about this being a man. It's an idealization of femininity, *the* feminine; there is something mysterious and powerful

---

5. Baroness Gertrud von Le Fort (1876–1971), German essayist, author, and poet.

6. Merton's relationship with women has been well-documented and commented upon; see Christine Bochen's "Introduction" to *Learning to Love*, xiii–xxiv; and James Wiseman, "Learning to Love and Learning the Price: Thomas Merton and the Challenge of Celibacy" (*The Merton Annual* 12 [1999]: 85–102).

about *the* feminine. "The feminine" is something that's mysterious, and it's silent and hidden, receptive, open, passive, obedient, docile [laughter].[7] What do you think the feminine mystique is? Can you add anything to it?

Comment: First of all, I would think that this mystique of women is not only made by women, but also by men.

It is principally by men.

In religious life, all the Rules, cloister, etc., have been made by men. I don't know if there is a sociological [analysis] or if it is possible to study that through history to see which is the reflection of women as becoming related to men or vice versa—probably both.[8]

I think they both cooperated there.

Mother Myriam: But it was also [embedded in] the culture, so that it might be only today that intelligent men and women can begin to get out of that and to see each other as persons. That's the key. I like very much, psychologically speaking, the position of Karl Stern,[9] who really exposes beautifully the gravity of the 1960s—this is the whole Jungian approach to the human person, that both men and women have a feminine and a masculine side.[10]

7. Merton is, tongue-in-cheek, naming various projections onto "the feminine," which, interestingly, mirror several of William James' classic characterizations of "mystical experience" in his *Varieties of Religious Experience* (e.g., "passivity"); see Grace Jantzen, *Power, Gender and Christian Mysticism* (Cambridge: Cambridge University Press, 1995), 1–25.

8. On the circumscription of the bodies of women religious in the Middle Ages, see Jantzen, *Power, Gender and Christian Mysticism*, 196–207.

9. Karl Stern (1906–1975), influential psychiatrist, Roman Catholic convert, and author of *The Flight from Woman* (New York: Farrar, Straus and Giroux, 1965). See Merton's letter to Stern, dated February 1962 (*Witness to Freedom: Letters in Times of Crisis*, ed. William H. Shannon [New York: Farrar, Straus and Giroux, 1994], 34).

10. C. G. Jung termed the inner feminine aspect *anima* and the inner masculine *animus* (see, e.g., *Aion: Researches into the Phenomenology of the Self* [Princeton: Princeton University Press, 1959], chap. 3). See also Robert Waldron, *Thomas Merton in Search of His Soul: A Jungian Perspective* (Notre Dame: Ave Maria Press, 1991), chap. 6; and Christine Bochen and Victor A. Kramer, "'A Journey into Wholeness': An Interview about Thomas Merton with Myriam Dardenne at Redwoods Monastery," *The Merton Annual* 14 (2001): 53–54.

Both [Stern and Jung] say that, in men and women, you have a different quantity of femininity and of masculinity; otherwise, a man could never be a contemplative or a woman could never have an executive position. Of course, there is a biological difference; our hormones are different, etc., so we are different. But I think that we have to discover each other as persons.

Exactly. What happens with the feminine mystique is an exaltation of a feminine nature, which doesn't really exist. You don't have a masculine nature and feminine nature—you've got human nature. And the two components of human nature may vary in each, but it's the person that matters. Where this thing goes wrong is when a man falls in love; if he falls in love with the femininity of somebody, this is baloney. But that's what everybody does.[11] There is a real sentimentality in the feminine mystique of the U.S.A., which is related to an idealization of the mother. But it's an idealization; it has no real meaning as far as giving woman a real place in anything. It's [also] a subjection: an idealized sentimental subjection to a mother figure.[12] And the American male is a very complicated thing, too, because he's scared of woman to begin with. But the situation being what it is, we have got a real problem in this country because it affects everything. Women are half the population, and if the whole idea of what a woman is, and what relationships between men and women are supposed to be is so fouled up, it's a problem that affects everything. I think it's one of the big problems.

Comment: It really makes you sick to see what's on TV, and when you see magazines for girls in college, where all that is told there is how to be attractive to get the male, to get married. That's the whole [point].

You're not a person. And then you get relationships between a man and [a] woman that are almost never personal; and there's a pseudo-personal element that gets into it. It's always "pseudo." There must be a pile of real hate involved in some of this business.

---

11. Merton is referring here to the psychology of romantic love from a Jungian perspective; for a popular approach, see Robert A. Johnson, *Owning Your Own Shadow: Understanding the Dark Side of the Psyche* (New York: HarperCollins, 1993), chap. 2.

12. Compare to *Springs of Contemplation*, 170–71.

Mother Myriam: I speak now with my eyes on Europeans. I don't know too much of American society, but it would seem to be that the pseudo-image of the woman is so much overdone; that the man is in an inferiority situation and that he has to compensate.

The thing has become so unreal that it's terribly difficult for people to really love one another in a situation like that; because they're always coping with these phantasms. When a person is so dominated by the phantasm, this is the real alienation. One of the real sources is commercial; the fact that people stand to make money out of this. Of course, in Europe, it's a more long-standing institution, and it's always been in better taste. It's [also] been more subdued, and it's been in stereotyped forms. But here it is constantly being reinvented. This is the great art of America, to constantly reinvent this myth every month, when the new magazines come out, you have a slightly new picture.

There are all sorts of little things that we can develop in terms of this consciousness. The practical thing that I would suggest is this: I think that a contemplative of a certain type should be a person who can read these things. I can pick up an ad and really read it; because it's most instructive. When you do this, you're free. If you really have the intelligence and the detachment, and the sense to pick up these things and to see what's really said—and to see the implications. You learn an enormous amount.

One of the things that I'm doing now is what they call "found poetry." You find something that is not intended to be a poem, but you see it as a poem and it becomes a poem.[13] You take out the part that you like. I've been doing a great deal of that with ads; ironic satirical stuff from ads. There's just piles of material. You learn a great deal about what's happening. There's so much subliminal stuff going on; there's a great deal of subconscious stuff that's in the air of which it is good to be conscious. It's healthy to be aware of these sick things that are subconscious. Contemplatives are like trees that clear the air at night. Instead of simply going through routines of prayer that are prescribed by somebody else, and living up to an idea that somebody else has given us; [it is better] to be

---

13. For an example, see Merton's journal entry of September 18, 1968, composed at the Convent of the Precious Blood, Eagle River, Alaska, and titled, "Mosaic: Alaska Papers and Funnies" (*Other Side of the Mountain*, 183–85).

independently aware of these things ourselves and to be able to notice them, if not say anything about them, and to be able to laugh at them.

Just as there is a mystique of woman, there's a mystique of the contemplative. Take an Abbot General, for example, who is necessarily on the road all the time. And everywhere he goes, he's preaching the value of stability: "The monk who never goes anywhere" [laughter]. This is purely hypothetical.[14] This is how a contemplative mystique is formed. You've got ideas that nobody can live by. And they'll be maintained efficiently with everybody offering incense to this idea and claiming to believe in it. So, in the end, what you've got are ideas that nobody really believes in.

Now what happens when you've got a reform or renewal coming in? If you just simply renew the contemplative mystique, all you do is try to renew those ideas. You realize that people have ceased to believe in them and you try to make them credible. That's the renewal. And it's doomed to failure. This can't be done. Of course, you can't blame these people because it's an official disease. And it's the simple way to do it on an artificial basis. But as long as everything comes down from the head office—this is common to everybody in Rome, because as everybody knows, the people in the Curia are formulating all kinds of abstract ideas that they don't actually care about; but they're enforcing them on other people. A renewal is not possible in such terms as that—but how does one get that across? Does one have to tell anybody that? I don't know, maybe it's just sufficient to realize it. It would be nice to get it across. Maybe sometime I'll try and write an article about it. These things can be said in a nice way.

But I really think it's a characteristic problem of our society, which has gotten into the religious life. It's in everything and it's in our life, too. And, once again, you ask, "How is our life justified?" If our life is built on this, it's not justified. If we are able to be free from these things, then it is justified. What we have to do with our life is to be free from these things. For example, a great deal of the trouble with Superiors. This is another

---

14. Merton's point with this hypothetical is the superior who is not "practicing what s/he preaches" and the subsequent example this sets in monastic communities. There is of course ancient precedent for this, e.g., Bernard of Clairvaux, who was more often than not on the road, preaching and conducting ecclesial business, rather than in his own monastery (see Brian Patrick McGuire, *Bernard of Clairvaux: An Inner Life* [Ithaca: Cornell University Press, 2020]).

unconscious psychological thing that people go through. It's a thing that kids go through if they're fighting with their parents. The rebellion against parents tended to deliberately be ineffective. It was rough up to a point, but it was self-defeating. Instead of really rebelling, the child merely invited punishment and got punished. This is more an old-time formula, because now what happens is the child invites punishment and doesn't get punished, and that creates a further problem. There has to be a real rebellion or nothing. In the old days, there was a tendency to rebel just enough to get punished. Then you had established a communication with the "old man." We tend to do that too in religion. We want a reaction: "At least let's get a reaction out of the Holy Office, even if it's 'No'!" So, we create a stink and then something comes back "No," and then we can have something to be mad about. But it is better to start with another kind of freedom, which is freedom from the ideas of these people. This is where we have to be free. We have to be free from their thinking. And then once we're free from their thinking, we don't have to operate within the framework of that thinking.

Comment: We should move positively ahead—not against. There is so much energy lost in that struggle.

That's the sort of thing that has to be done everywhere. The youth have to do it, the nuns have to do it, the monks have to do it. Everybody has to be free in this sense. And somebody has to give them a chance to be free. They have to be told that this is where it is, or reminded, or helped. I think that's the hardest thing in religion: to channel this energy in the right direction.

Wouldn't it perhaps be stated as: people have to be awake and aware of themselves as individuals, regardless of the community or how large the community is, whether it's one or twenty?

As persons in a community there is a sort of reciprocity. A person becomes more a person if he's really working with other people. If he's accepted by others as a person and he's accepting them as a person. But he's got to be a person himself. That's one of the big things, because who is this "self"? We've got our idea of it, and then you've got the Asian idea, which is much deeper.

When you're living in the system, which is built on a false mystique, then you have to move completely outside that system to be free.

You can be in it, if you're in it, and not of it. It's our Lord's formula about the world.

It seems that the system could almost force you in some way to be—

It will. It's in this area today that martyrdom is valid and can be demanded. In the Roman times, it was so simple: here is the god of something or other, and you just offered the incense.

This is, after all, the creative tension of life.[15]

Yes. This is the world in the sense of *The Gospel of John*[16]—the world that is evil, the world that cripples people; the world that maims people, destroys them for its own purposes—it is the world of alienation. And everybody who wants to be a Christian has to rebel against that world and has to help other people rebel against it, and has to be free. It's a revolution. A revolution on a psychological or cultural plane, but we are, in that sense, revolutionaries. A monk who is not a revolutionary in that sense is wasting his time. That's all we're for.

That's the modern interpretation of St. Benedict's thing to be "alien to the ways of the world."[17] Since the world alienates me from myself, then to become myself, I have to become alien to the world, in this sense. Then, and only then, can I do what the progressive Christian demands of me; that is, return to the world with something to give it.

---

15. Again, these comments are each from various unidentified speakers.

16. E.g., John 17:11, 14-18.

17. See Merton's comments in his essay, "Dialogue and Renewal": "There is no question . . . that the monk lives as one who is basically alien to the ways of the world (*a saeculi actibus se facere alienum*). So says St. Benedict . . . " (in *Contemplation in a World of Action* [New York: Doubleday, 1973], 108). Merton is citing the *Rule of Saint Benedict* 4.20-21: "Your way of acting should be different from the world's way; the love of Christ must come before all else" (in Timothy Fry, ed., *RB 1980: Rule of Saint Benedict in Latin and English* [Collegeville, MN: Liturgical Press, 1981], 182, 183).

That's the negative point. The positive point is that as religious we should be people who have the capacity to relate to one another amidst sexual differences as persons, completely. That is the function of chastity. That's what the vow of chastity is about. It's that you can relate to a person of the other sex exactly as a person; without any concern regarding sexuality as a different nature and becoming obsessed with the difference of the other person. This implies a whole new deepening of our anthropology as Christians. An anthropology that means women as well as men, and an anthropology that sees the real complementarity that has to be worked out on this personal level. I think that's where contemplatives have a great deal to do.

That would perhaps be something that a meeting like this would make us aware of—the possibility of the contemplative life taking on this kind of a relationship instead of the completely artificial thing where nuns are all boxed up in their little boxes and the Abbots are all out there making rules for all the nuns on how to keep the little boxes all closed.

Is there anything more on this feminine mystique and this contemplative mystique? One of the Superiors of this little cloister that the active Franciscans have, said this is a particular problem of these cloistered houses in active Orders; that they are judged in terms of a contemplative mystique.[18]

We sense that too—that people expect us to live according to their image.

It's a very unreasonable image and it's a very unfair treatment, too. One of the things that they expect of us is that we've got to be infallible. That's the whole purpose perhaps behind all this strictness: to put people in a position where they can't possibly do anything wrong; to make sure that at least there's somebody in the Church that isn't doing anything wrong—and now everything's all right. That's [then] called "the sanctity

18. Most likely a reference to Sr. Elaine M. Bane, OSF, of the Allegany, New York, Franciscan community at St. Bonaventure College, who had developed a *ritiro* for her convent and was instrumental in organizing the retreats for contemplative superiors that Merton held at Gethsemani in December 1967 and May 1968, later published as *Springs of Contemplation*. Merton's correspondence with Bane appears in *The School of Charity: Letters on Religious Renewal and Spiritual Direction*, ed. Patrick Hart (New York: Farrar, Straus and Giroux, 1990), 144–46, 296–97, 339–40, 352–53, 357, 366.

of the Church." You've got certain people who are locked up in cold storage. This is the "cold storage" idea of religious consecration; and then this makes everybody else feel a little bit better. It's rationalized in terms of [Religious Sisters as] "victim souls," for example.

That is the thing that we're up against. It takes a lot of resisting sometimes. At Gethsemani we've got it worse than anybody else because we've got the biggest image; and it's partly my fault! [laughter] If I could burn those earlier books [laughter].

But this is really something that we have to be aware of. No mystique. We have to be realistic about everything: about the life, about people, and about everything that we do. Only on those conditions can we really go on.

The thing that I really want to talk about is Sufism. This was more just preparing the ground. That's where I want to go from here. I think I'll take that up tomorrow. But this concept of the self is terribly important. We are struggling with a debased concept of the self. It's debased to some extent by popular psychology, and of course, again, by advertising. It's a question of who you identify with; and if they can get you to identify with the person who has certain fears and certain needs—they've got you. And that is what's happened to everybody.

It's very strong even with us who are trying to be free. Just think of how people are dominated in this country by the need to be loved—in a superficial way; not real love, but the need to be accepted and appreciated. You can't begin unless you're free to some extent from that. Yet, who can be free? Because it's a real tyranny. Consequently, there's so much time wasted just doing things to placate other people unnecessarily—and then we think this is virtue.

It wouldn't be so bad if we weren't ambivalent about it. Because when we do these things on a certain level, on a deeper level, there is a more real self, which is being deprived of its real rights and is kicking. We suffer from this, and we attribute the suffering to something else. One of the big problems in our life is the consciousness that we are not the real person that we should be, but we transfer this to another level. This is where the mystique comes in. You transfer a real need for a deeper consciousness. You identify with a mystique and then play some little games. This is a dreadful thing. The whole thing gets sterilized.

So maybe we ought to get down to some of these Hindu ideas. I'll take the Hindu thing tomorrow a little bit, just one aspect of it, and then some of the Sufi material along with that. Then at the same time, pointing out ways in which this modern consciousness developed. But the whole aim is to be free from this kind of domination.

You mean being free beyond manipulation?

Yes. Being free, where your less-real selves cannot be used by the people who know how to use them.

Like where Jesus said, "Nobody can take my life away, but I give it of myself."[19]

Yes, exactly. Real autonomy, where a person's acts proceed from the real self. If the most real ground of self is not myself only, but God, then such a person is really manifesting God in the world.

---

19. John 10:18: "No one has taken it away from me, but I lay it down on my own. I have authority to lay it down, and I have authority to take it back. This commandment I received from My Father."

Chapter Three

The Feminine Mystique, Millennial Consciousness, and Ecological Conscience

Merton opens the second day of conferences with the following prayer:
Oh Lord, You have put Your wisdom in every religion.
Teach us, as we think of the Asian religions, to find a truth there
that we need to learn that will bring us closer to You.

I'm going to talk about Hinduism, but I'm first going to go over some unfinished business from the day before. What's happened to the relation between man and woman? Before, we were saying a kind of disintegration and dissociation has happened in the formation of this European and American culture to which we belong. This European and American culture, in which we are in, and in which we are involved, is in difficulties. One of the reasons why is because men and women are not confronting one another as persons. On the contrary, we are confronting one another in various roles.

One of the main roles is the role of "nun." That has become so much a role; that is to say, you fit into it. It's a real easy category, and the whole thing is arranged in such a way that it's very easy to fit into it as a category and to get lost in it as a category. Very often people are content to settle for a role and a category rather than to have to be a person; and sometimes, the religious life is made easy for that kind of evasion. One of the things we're struggling with now, in so many cases, is it has been that, and that's one of the causes of trouble for people.

When a person is settled into a thing like that, he is content to have organized evasion; yet, when all of a sudden, it's shaken up a little bit and the organized prop is taken away—then you're in trouble. What do you do? Of course, it's extremely painful in situations where the props are taken away and yet you're not really able to do anything anyway; it's no longer an organized evasion, but it's no longer anything else. This is extremely difficult for a lot of people. I think it's one of the main reasons why so many people are leaving [religious life]—because it's intolerable. It's no longer what it was, and nothing has been put in its place. Nobody is giving them any real notion of how to be a person.

There's [also] the vicious circle of the mass media business on the nun. In a certain sense, it's so easy to let *Time* and *Life* tell you what kind of nun is really the "in" kind of nun. A lot of people go to mass media. Somebody writes an article for the *Post*, and then somebody reads that, and then they use that against somebody they don't agree with. It's a vicious circle of nonsense all the way around. It's all nonsense.

What it really does get to, as I was saying last night, is a question of what the religious life for monks and nuns should mean; as an opportunity to confront one another in a way "which is qualitatively different from that of the past." A new quality of relationship between men and women in religious life, and of course, outside of it, too. For that, however, there has to be [outside] contact, and they're scared to death of that, because that is part of the renewal. It is necessary for monks and nuns to confront one another and to see one another as persons, and to share one another's ideas. Until that's done, there's going to be something lacking. It has to be done.

How are we going to do it? I don't know, but it has to be there in some way or other. This author is a woman called Mary Daly.[1] Talking about nuns, she makes it quite clear—and I think it's true—that the Church has more and more tended to give the nun the role of embodying the "eternal feminine." Of course, the veil is the thing. This is what the veil is for, and this is what the grille is for. This is what all these things are for. That is why this is such a problem; even if people don't realize it.

The real idea of the cloister is freedom from interference by men; rather than just simply, "Keep these guys out. We want to run our own place"

---

1. Mary Daly (1928-2010), radical feminist theologian who taught at Boston College for over three decades and authored numerous influential books, including *The Church and the Second Sex* (Boston: Beacon Press, 1968), of which Merton might be citing and referencing here. Merton quotes Daly in the preceding paragraph.

[laughter]. Then you also had many who, in the religious state as nuns, realized that there was something about all the things that they did have, which symbolized not femininity, but the dignity of the person; which is what the consecration of the nun really amounts to. It's not a consecration of a quasi-feminine nature of femininity, but of personality. Personality in a woman, but personality above all. That's very important. What we have to do is, as we said before, make everything about the life of a nun in a convent manifest the person, rather than this femininity pitch and this femininity symbol. What nuns have to be is persons, and that may mean going exactly the opposite of what had to be done before.[2] It may [have to] be a totally different process. Everything that we have or what we wear, what we do, has to imply some kind of a reasonable choice on this whole point of, "Is it a symbol that I have accepted bondage as a woman? Or is it a symbol that I have accepted freedom as a bride of Christ?" That's what everybody has to help with, but that's what the "official" people are trying not to do.

All these things have become barriers to communication. Now, it has to be the opposite: a sign that I have a personality that I do not lose when I enter into communication with somebody else. For example, the way the cloister, the way enclosure, is treated; the way it was treated with us—and still is to some extent. They didn't say it in so many words, but the argument was, "Once you leave the enclosure, you've lost your identity"—because your identity is to be a person within an enclosure. Therefore, once you're outside the enclosure, you no longer have any identity as a monk. You're a non-person. I would say, "Let me show you if I'm not a person when I get out of this enclosure." But that's what they're afraid of. Of course, what they don't have is for you to be a person with an identity that does not depend on these external things.

Well, let's consider that the femininity thing is finished and we are now in the new era; we're in the Kingdom now. We're in the eschatological Kingdom as far as this whole business of femininity goes. In Christ, there

2. From the mid-1960s onward, Merton was deeply influenced by the philosophy of "personalism" as demonstrated here and throughout the Redwoods conferences. On the significant influence of French Catholic philosopher Jacques Maritain on Merton's understanding of personalism, see Anne E. Carr, *A Search for Wisdom and Spirit: Thomas Merton's Theology of the Self* (Notre Dame: University of Notre Dame Press, 1988), 123, 133.

are no longer people categorized according to sex, age, race, status—anything like that. We are free from this.

Now we go on to one other point that I wanted to fit in somewhere and might as well just fit it in here. There is a deep connection between conscience and consciousness, and since we are in such a crucial situation today in the world, I thought up a distinction between two kinds of conscience. I think you can really reduce almost everything that goes on in public life and in the Church to one or the other of these, in certain ways. It's a very sketchy sort of thing. It's bad to try to reduce everything to two categories; but nevertheless, I think that you do see a division growing up in regard to how certain thinkers and philosophers are giving out the leading ideas. They tend to go in one of these two directions. Here, conscience and consciousness go together. *Consciousness* in the sense of an awareness of an attitude towards the world, and *conscience* in the sense of a basis for decision about what to do with the world. These two attitudes, I call the *ecological conscience* and the *millennial consciousness*.[3] This will require a little bit of explanation, but I think it's a useful division.

Millennial consciousness is something that is very deep in our history. This is the kind of consciousness which is based in Christianity, Judaism, and in the Bible. There is a spontaneous, instinctive reaction to events, and to what happened, and what the world is about by saying, "We are on the verge of the millennium. There is a great age just about to begin and we are just reaching it." And, being on the verge of this great change, something has to be done; a decision has to be made. There's a right decision and there's a wrong decision, and it's very important to make the right one, because those who make the wrong one, they're going to be destroyed. Those who make the right one will be saved.

With this goes, more or less, that the right decision implies a destruction of the past. Now, where you find this, obviously, is in Communism. The revolutionary consciousness is a millennial constant. "We are just on the point. History is now making a turning point, and if you want to

---

3. Merton develops these themes in a February 16, 1968, letter to Barbara Hubbard (*Witness to Freedom*, 74–75). See also Gordon Oyer, *Signs of Hope: Thomas Merton's Letters on Peace, Race, and Ecology* (New York: Orbis, 2021), 231–32. I am grateful to Paul M. Pearson for bringing this material to my attention.

get around the corner in the right way, you have to come with us. There is one party that has the answer, and that answer means the destruction of capitalist society and the institution of socialist society. This is the answer." It's all very simple; once you've got this thing lined up, you just follow the instructions on the bottle and the rest goes.

Another very interesting form of it is in what they call the "Cargo Cults,"[4] which most people have never heard of, but they're very important. This is a tremendously important movement in places like New Guinea and Polynesia, and also the South Sea islands, and also in Africa, in a different form, and all over the place. You see it everywhere in different forms. In a Cargo Cult, say, in New Guinea, native people are confronted with white people who come in with an enormous amount of equipment, and this is, to them, a terrific shock. Here come these totally different people and they have a totally different way of living, and they have all this material. They say to themselves, "Why is it that these people have all these things and we haven't?" Along with that, "Why don't they give us some of these things? If they've got so much, why don't they give us some?" They look back into their own past, and [seeing] their own society is based on reciprocity, they say, "These fellows come in here, they take away all our land, and then we work on the land, and they don't give us anything for doing it. Why don't they give us some of the things that they've got since we're working for them?" On the other hand, the white man is saying, "Well, these people are so stupid, you can't give them anything, and you might as well just give them peanuts because they're ignorant and they're inferior."

This is a real crisis for them, and in order to handle this crisis, they look into their past and they say, "What's the fault? Where did things go wrong?" They say, "Maybe this old religion we have wasn't so good?" Then they get the idea that Christianity is what brings the Cargo. By the 'thirties—there's been a real history of this in the 1930s—they all were exemplary Christians, and Christianity was flourishing in the missions

---

4. See Merton's essay, "Cargo Cults of the South Pacifica," in *Love and Living* (New York: Farrar, Straus and Giroux, 1979), 80–94. See also Merton's journal entry of February 26, 1968: "The more I read of Cargo cults the more I am excited by the material: it seems to be tremendously important and significant for our time. It opens new perspectives in *everything*" (*Other Side of the Mountain*, 59).

there, but they were all waiting for something. They were exemplary Christians for five years, ten years. Then a lot of unrest started going through the people, and they said, "We've been exemplary Christians and he hasn't told us yet." The missionary says, "Tell you what?" "You know, tell us, give us the answer; the real answer—what we became Christians for: how do you get the Cargo?" He says, "Get away from here! What do you think this is?" Then they say, "These people have cheated us. They have not told us the full story and they're not giving us the full information; we've got to discover it for ourselves." So, they began observing what people did: the white man sat at a desk and wrote out a note and gave it to somebody, and then somebody passed it on to somebody else, and there you are: there's this boatload of stuff. So, they would institute a new religion in which the rituals were imitations of things that the white man was doing.[5]

For example, they would have a meal around the table with lots of flowers. They thought that the flowers had something to do with bringing the Cargo. The police said, "This flower business is very suspicious," and they would immediately arrest anybody who had flowers on the table. Then they said, "Ah, we've really got the answer. This must be it since the police are so excited." So, they would have flowers hidden in closets, and then the police would come and search for all the flowers and you would get these ridiculous things going on.[6] You get a vicious circle of these idiot policemen and these [local] people chasing each other around like this with these mad ideas until you've got a psychosis going all through.

They would all go raring off into the jungle and clear a whole part of jungle, put up an airstrip, and then sit by it and wait for a plane to come. Then the white men would hear they'd put up another airstrip in the jungle; they'd all go rush out there and arrest everybody for putting up an airstrip. The whole thing was completely insane. But these cults went on and on like this. It's an example of the millennial consciousness. The idea that we're on the threshold: a crucial thing is going to happen and you've got to know the right thing to do. But the right thing to do is positive and negative. The negative means the old thing has to be thrown out. One of the things that these people did at one point was that if they had anything belonging to their past, even native money or shell money, they'd throw it all in the bay; kill all the livestock, destroy everything they had, because

5. "Cargo Cults," 81–82.
6. "Cargo Cults," 82.

they had been told that this was a condition for the new. That then they would soon have free goods, and that the boat has already arrived on the next island—just kill all the livestock and tomorrow, it'll be here. Tragic things happening like this.[7]

That's an example of the millennial consciousness; but now, you find that this is everywhere. This is a modern madness, which is universal. People are willing to do anything: "I'll do the craziest thing if somebody will tell them that this is going to bring about the millennium. This is the thing that you have to do." They will go through the same kind of routine. Black Power is something like this—to some extent. There is a little of this in Black Power.[8] Evidently there's something of this in this "Cultural Revolution" in China. It's the same kind of thing that's in Communism.[9] It's also a little bit in the renewal of the Catholic Church. For a lot of people, renewal in the Catholic Church is a glorified Cargo Cult. They're going through the same routine as these people with the Cargo Cult.[10]

This is a temptation to Christians because it also seems to be eschatological, but it's a false eschatological consciousness. It appears to be eschatological, but it isn't. The true eschatological consciousness is of the Kingdom and the final fulfillment; but the real fulfillment is an ecological conscience, which means to say, what an ecology *is*. It is the awareness of a cosmic community of creatures; that we are members of a larger than human community on earth. We're in it with all the animals, and we're in it with all the plants, and we're in it with the elements, and the water, and the earth. This consciousness, instead of going like the other one [millennial], is constantly saying, "Now, wait a minute, you cannot afford to destroy even a bug without stopping and thinking what you're doing"; because what we have is good.

You don't destroy what we have in order to get something that we haven't got that's going to be so wonderful—it's what we have is wonderful. You cannot afford to be destroying any of it without a tremendously important reason. This is the consciousness which unfortunately is losing

7. "Cargo Cults," 82–83.

8. "Black power, in its extreme forms, seeks to discredit all compromise, all old ways of seeing and doing" ("Cargo Cults," 84).

9. "This is what is happening in modern China, where it is held that the only beliefs of value are those of Mao Tse-tung and young revolutionaries are constantly engaging in systematic attacks on everything old" ("Cargo Cults," 84).

10. See "Cargo Cults," 86.

out, because you can't get anywhere with it. Fortunately, there are a few people around—a minority of people have this—but it's an enormous struggle. You have to struggle for every tree.

In Kentucky, it's the same thing. You've got this frightful situation, this really demonic situation, where the people living back in the Kentucky hills were absolutely robbed a hundred years ago. These simple people were told to move into the hills from Virginia and places like that. They didn't know what it was all about. They would get out in the hills and have a little bit of land and begin farming. Then somebody would come along: first, the lumber interests came in and said, "We're going to pay you so much for the trees on your land," and give him some ridiculous sum; then give him a contract, strip the land of lumber, and then disappear. Then the mining interests come along and say, "In case you don't know, we own the mineral rights here." Nobody's sold it to them, they just got the mineral rights somehow or other; there was some trick to it. The fellow bought the land and had not thought of buying the mineral rights, too.

When these mining interests have the mineral rights to a person's property, the person is finished, because they can come in and have not only a right to put a mine wherever they want to, they can come in and they can bulldoze the whole thing completely. They can take the surface off it. They can even bulldoze your house down. You could have a good lawsuit if they did; but if you have no money, what are you going to do against a company that comes along? There was a woman in Kentucky who finally laid down in front of the bulldozers and refused to let them go through. They arrested her, put her in jail, and the bulldozer completed the job.

To resist something like that takes an enormous amount of effort, and very often it's useless, but it has to be done. Of course, what Catholic moral theologian ever gave an instant of thought to this kind of thing? This was one of the real problems: questions of air pollution and water pollution. Here, you can still drink from a creek; but in Kentucky, nobody would dare drink from a creek. I have a well behind my house; I can't drink the water from the well. I have to get purified water from the monastery. This is in the debt of the country. There's a real problem.

The ecological conscience is something that I think is very relevant for us, for our kind of life: for contemplatives, for monks and nuns. We should be very much aware of being a member of a community of living beings, which we respect. This doesn't mean to say that you never kill a fly, but you've got to be careful.

This spring, I noticed there were flies in the hermitage, so I would spray the hermitage. I came back, and outside of the hermitage I found a dead fly catcher. A fly outside of the hermitage had got some of this [spray] that came out through the window, and the fly catcher ate it and died. You have to think about these things.

This kind of consciousness is essential to anyone who is open to the quality of existence, and the consciousness and depth that we are thinking of. Living in a community like this, you're very aware of it. You would be more aware of it than most people, but all of us should be aware of this. For example, at Gethsemani, one of the oldest problems you've got there is preventing people from cutting down trees that don't need to be cut down. I remember once planting a tree at a certain point in the monastery, and it was to provide shade for when you came out of the place where you'd change for work. One day, I walked up the path and somebody was just getting ready to go for it! I almost maimed him! [laughter]

I think it's good to have books along these lines. I don't know if this is in the batch of articles [I sent you]. Is there one called "The Wild Places"?[11] Good. Well, that's about this [topic], and refers to a good book about people like John Muir.

Comment: And Rachel Carson?

Rachel Carson, certainly. Her book, *Silent Spring*, should be known and practiced, and there are many others.[12] There's a very interesting man

11. In a journal entry of February 25, 1968, Merton writes, "Yesterday I wrote a short piece on Wilderness (the Nash book). . . . Importance of the 'ecological conscience'" (*Other Side of the Mountain*, 58). Merton's essay, "The Wild Places," first appeared in *The Catholic Worker* (June, 1968), and is a review of Roderick Nash's *Wilderness and the American Mind* (New Haven: Yale University Press, 1967). As Patrick F. O'Connell writes, the "essay is the most extensive presentation of Merton's developing ecological awareness in the final years of his life" (in Thomas Merton, *Selected Essays*, ed. Patrick F. O'Connell [New York: Orbis Books, 2013], 442).

12. Rachel Carson (1907–1964), influential American conservationist whose 1962 book *Silent Spring* (New York: Houghton Mifflin) brought widespread attention to the unregulated use of pesticides in the agricultural industry. The public reaction to her book led to numerous policy changes including an agricultural ban on DDT usage and ultimately the creation of the Environmental Protection Agency (EPA). Merton's appreciative 1963 letter to Carson, written in response to *Silent Spring*, is included in *Witness to Freedom*,

called Aldo Leopold who is not very much published.[13] He's the one that actually invented this term "ecological conscience." He really has developed the idea. It is absolutely crucial for now. The people who have this kind of conscience are at least contributing to the survival of the world. The others are endangering it. The others are a menace, absolutely. I've yet to see a Cardinal coming out on the ecological side, but they'll easily come out on the millennial one. You know, "Bomb Vietnam back into the Stone Age."[14] It wasn't a Cardinal that said that, but it was close enough. Another bishop preached a sermon before the President and said, "What we are doing in Vietnam is difficult, but it's a work of love."

Have you got any discussion on this? Then we'll go on with Hinduism. Any questions?

We can be aware of this ecological need, but what positively can we do?

I think probably it makes sense to get tied up with one of the organizations that's constantly writing in to people. It's the only way you can do anything in this particular realm in this country. The Sierra Club or The Wilderness Society, or something like that. Not everybody in the community has to be doing it; but at a crucial point, you need to write a letter to that Congressman and stop him, just when he's about to give his vote for cutting all the redwoods from here to Seattle.

You have to know the key people; you have to know who they are, and you have to know who to write to. I do belong to The Wilderness Society, and they send you information. They tell you where the pinch is coming next—where they're going to put up a dam next, or where they're

---

70–72. See also Monica Weis, *The Environmental Vision of Thomas Merton* (Lexington, KY: University Press of Kentucky, 2011).

13. Aldo Leopold (1887–1948), conservationist, philosopher, educator, and author of *A Sand County Almanac* (Oxford: Oxford University Press, 1949), is best known for his concept of a "land ethic," which "calls for an ethical, caring relationship between people and nature" (https://www.aldoleopold.org/about/aldo-leopold. Accessed November 8, 2021). Merton references Leopold in "The Wild Places" and cites him there—as here—as originating the phrase "ecological conscience."

14. A statement attributed to Air Force Gen. Curtis LeMay (1906–90); see Curtis E. LeMay with MacKinley Kantor, *Mission with LeMay: My Story* (Garden City, NY: Doubleday), 565.

just going to destroy. What happens is, in one decade, Congress will set aside an area as a wilderness area that's not to be touched. Then, lo and behold, ten years later, they'll turn around and approve a dam, which is going to flood half of it.

They're just dealing with bigger payoffs.

Yes, exactly. The company that will be putting in a dam—an electric company or something like that—will give these guys plenty of money, and before you know it, this is going through, and then all of the conservationists come rushing in at the last minute and try and stop the thing, and it gets to be pretty hard to stop. But that's the way it is all along the lines. With the redwoods, you've got these big lumber companies; they get out of paying taxes because they're giving money to bribing these people.[15]

15. The concluding discussion is mostly inaudible due to the sound fading in and out. The content centers generally around the topic of what practical steps can be taken within the context of ecological awareness, and for individuals and communities to do what they can in the face of ecological crises.

Chapter Four

Psychological Aspects of Religious Life and Karma Yoga[1]

Now, getting back to religion: do you have any further questions? You've got the background of this psychology course. What about that?[2]

Comment: Well, I myself would be interested in what you would say on sadness.

Oh, back on the sadness thing?

Yes, in a religious manner.

Well, what did I say? [laughter]

The connection with perfection, and the seed of a deep sadness.

The need to do things as perfectly as possible. Well, what is sadness? Sadness is a kind of death. It's a little death. It's a little psychological death. It's not a real death, but what happens is: something clicks in our psychology, which in a very small way kills us. It doesn't kill us very much, but it kills

---

1. This tape begins where the section on ecological conscience ends; however, there is a gap in the recording which begins mid-topic with the discussion of the psychology of sadness here.

2. This is perhaps a reference to a course taken by, or offered for, members of the Redwoods community.

us a little bit. When it does that, our vitality is lessened, and we don't want to respond. There's a negation; we negate life in ourselves. We say, "Oh, it's not worth it." A lot of things come into it. This is a very complicated thing.

Sadness is, to some extent, self-punishment. Perhaps one of the big things in the machinery [of sadness] is that if I have in the back of my mind the idea that something ought to be very perfect—if I do something, it should be very perfect—and then I do something that's not so perfect; then I punish myself. Now, I punish myself by making myself sad.

Self-punishment is a very important concept. Why? Psychologically, we have a little self-punishment mechanism built into our psychology from childhood, and that is called the introjection of parental authority.[3] What happens is, when I'm a little child and I don't have my own judgment, papa spanks me a few times, and then I get into my machinery—not in a moral sense, but an instinctive reaction—which, as soon as I get around to doing the same thing that I got spanked for, instead of him having to spank me, I spank myself. I spank myself mentally.

Mother Myriam: I would also think that this is a kind of resentment towards oneself that one cannot get rid of. We turn in. We are caught in this cyclone.

Oh yes. The word for that is self-hate.

And so, we are paralyzed using those [negative self-beliefs] in our practice. It kills your creative dynamism. It's a sin against life.

That's right. The real thing that is really bad about this, is that we like to do this. Ultimately, what goes on is not really that we want to, but there is a choice. It's an instinctive preference. It's not voluntary. It's not conscious. But there is an unconscious preference for this masochistic suffering, and this is very prevalent. As she said, it may be bad in [professed] religious, but it's awfully bad in outside people, too.

I say that, too. She said that anxiety and sadness actually can be high in religious, but it can be cultural, too.

---

3. Merton read deeply in psychoanalytic psychology, where the concept of "introjection" originates. See Merton's Working Notebook 9 for his reading notes on psychoanalysis, archived at the Thomas Merton Center at Bellarmine University.

It's higher outside, in a way, because just looking at somewhere like Gethsemani—certainly, there are people that are sad, but it's nowhere near as bad as some of the people I know in Louisville, for example. There's one man I know in Louisville—who's a psychiatrist incidentally—and oh, does he go into these dreadful depressions.[4] When it's like that, it gets into everybody else, too. There are certain people that when they're that depressed, they affect other people. In a certain way, they punish other people by being [depressed], because what happens is—well you know what happens—sulking is a favorite sport of religious [laughter].

You punish yourself and you punish somebody else, too. I want to do something or other perfectly, and then I don't, and Sister so-and-so smiled [laughter]. I say, "Well, okay. It's partly your fault." Then I get real mean, close up to her, and radiate resistance. It's the old business of, you're walking around the community, "Today, I do not smile at anybody. Today, I'm not friends with anyone." Then everybody is, "Well, today is her day to be in that mood" [laughter].

This is standard in all religious life. It's punishment. To get at the root of that, what we have to do, is to see that we don't need to punish ourselves for failing, because it's irrational. The perfection that we wanted to obtain was not rationally to be expected. There's no point in taking it further down the line and saying, "Be patient." It's too late to say, "Be patient," because the cause has been placed, and when you place the cause, the effect follows.

Comment: We are also trying at times to make the other responsible for where we are, as a way of getting attention, and pulling the other to get us out of our consciousness of childish tricky ways. It is really a phenomenon that we should analyze.

It is good to analyze all the effects, but what's important is to see where the cause really is, and where the cause really is, is in expecting for ourselves results which are not rational to expect. Why do we do that? I would say there's the real problem; that's what we have to really get at.

We are set up at every moment expecting certain things that we want as a result of our action. These are things built into our motives. A lot of it goes back to motivation, "Why am I doing such-and-such a thing?" The big problem is that most of our motivation is unconscious—really, most

---

4. A reference to Merton's friend Dr. James Wygal.

of it. It's like the iceberg. There's a little bit above, but there's an enormous amount under the water. This unconscious motivation is something that goes back to acts that we don't remember, and things that have happened; a residue of all these things.

We should be able to run the thing backwards and help one another, instead of punishing one another for our own motives not coming through; to be able to help one another. Humor is one of the best things. Laughing most of these things off is about the best thing you can do with it—and keeping a realistic spirit going in the community.

Once you've got a totally unrealistic spirit behind everything, it's impossible to avoid these things. Like the old spirit of most of our monasteries, which made this depression inevitable all the time. Another thing is the feeling of helplessness; but tied in again is, "I want to do a thing perfectly," and then I feel that I'm helpless to do it perfectly. Then I really punish myself for that—punish myself for being helpless. Maybe a lot of it is due to the fact that we were pushed into these helpless situations. There's a certain built-in helplessness in living life in a certain way. There's no question about it. I was very conscious over a long period at Gethsemani that there was a systematic imposition of helplessness on the monks. There were certain occasions where you were made to feel your utter helplessness. Often, this was rubbed in. Then they wondered why people got nasty. A person doesn't like to feel helpless.

That's the kind of thing you get with this authoritarian routine in the Order. The authoritarian types, they want to make you feel helpless and remind you of the fact that you have no recourse. Of course, they've got their problems, too. That's what's happening, for example, where people are trying to assert their rights and these other people—they're insecure, too. When they're scared, they have to reassure themselves by laying down the law and [saying], "Beyond this point, you can't move. I'm telling you."[5] Then, if they can do that successfully, they feel a little better. But they're looking for their version of perfection, too.

The thing is: what do we want out of life? What am I really doing this for? That's the thing. Why do I do anything that I do?[6]

---

5. Merton strikes the table with each word to emphasize his point here.

6. The tape unfortunately ends here mid-discussion and abruptly begins again with the topic of karma yoga in the following section.

Let's develop the karma yoga thing a little bit more positively here.[7] The way the Hindu would spell it out would be this: where the trouble is, is that I am taking myself too seriously as the one who is doing this. "I am the doer. I am the doer, the actor, and the enjoyer." The Hindus would say that if you start from that point of view in any way, you've had it. You're in the mess. You're in the mangle from then on. The way they would approach it, and the way the Sufis of Islam would approach it, and the way I think certain Christian mystics would approach it in the past, is that, first of all, all that I am is an instrument of God, and all I want to be is an instrument of God. Whether I do good or bad, I am still, in a certain sense, an instrument of God, because everything that happens, it's done by God. This is pushing it a little extreme, but this is the Muslim way of living, the Islamic way of looking at it. If I am perfectly content with my role as an instrument of God, all this disappears. I do what I can. I try to please God, and if I try to please God, I please God. If I try to be an instrument of God, I am an instrument of God. If I fail, He will take care of the results. If I do something wrong, I try to do it to please him. If I didn't, then I'm sorry.

But then you get the old business of being too upset over faults. We're bound to fail sometimes. Sometimes we have to fail. Sometimes it's God's will that we fail, in a certain sense. One of the things that we have to say is that there are certain mistakes that we make, that we have to make, because if we don't, we won't learn. These mistakes, in a certain sense, are part of God's will for us. And when we make them, then we're sorry, that's too bad, but it had to be and that shows me who I am, and what I am. So, I accept it. On top of this, there is this basic thing, which I think is a positive and important thing: it's gratitude for being used as an instrument, no matter what the result is.

---

7. Compare Merton's remarks here to his conference on karma yoga included in *Merton and Hinduism: The Yoga of the Heart*, ed. David M. Odorisio (Louisville, KY: Fons Vitae, 2021), 363–71. Merton's comments orient around the definition of karma yoga as renouncing attachment to the fruits of one's actions as outlined in the classic Indian text *The Bhagavad Gita*.

This is what I would recommend, personally, as a religious answer: the awareness that I am an instrument of God, and gratitude that He uses me as an instrument, even though I failed. Even if I'm a bad instrument, I want to be a better one; but he has chosen me as an instrument. What a thing. How marvelous this is. That my action, by love, and by faith, falls into the pattern of God's action, and its only part of a greater thing. I make a mistake. Good Lord, is the world going to end because I didn't do the thing perfectly right? This, I think, is the real religious answer. What we have to cultivate is this awareness that we're not all alone in this. That it's not "I"—that "I'm" doing this alone. "I alone do this," or "I alone enjoy this," and "I alone have the fruits of the action." It's not "I" alone. It is God, and it is part of the whole universe. Everything that happens is part of this whole. This, I think, is where you get peace. Only on the basis of something like this is there real peace.

One thing that [karma yogis] add on is that when a person acts in this particular kind of way, this action without self-seeking becomes a blessing to the world: "I should be grateful not only that I am an instrument of God, but the fact that in accepting this, I am bringing blessing into the world by having a kind of peace and contentment in myself." I'm radiating this to the rest of the world.

This is the exact opposite of the other thing. The other machinery is: "I alone am acting. I'm doing this, and I want this result, and [if] I don't get this result, I'm going to punish myself, and I'm going to punish the world. Because I'm mad at the whole thing, and I don't want it to be the way it is." Turn it around and you've got: "God is acting; I am His instrument. I will do what I can [and] if I fail, He will make it better. If I fail, it's good for me to fail, but it won't harm His ends. I am glad that He chooses me, that He acts through me. I'm grateful, and this is a blessing to the world."

Incidentally, in all the Asian religions, there is a systematic practice of benevolence towards all creatures; towards the rest of the universe. There's a sense of trying to act in such a way that when you complete an action, you share the fruits with everybody. You want all beings to be happy. You want all beings to be delivered. This is one of the basic Buddhist vows.[8]

---

8. Merton is referencing the Bodhisattva Vow, a fundamental precept that all committed Buddhist practitioners make whether lay or monastic to forsake paradise (*nirvana*) until all sentient beings have become liberated from the cycle of suffering and rebirth (*samsara*). The classic text outlining this path is Shantideva's eighth-century *Bodhicaryāvatāra*, translated as *The Way of the Bodhisattva* (Boston: Shambhala, 2006).

Comment: It's something about salvation for sentient beings.

Yes, and the Buddhist vows not only to fulfill the whole Dharma, but not to quit until every sentient being is delivered. That's one of the Buddhist methods of meditation. As you sit in the midst of nature, you simply wish well to all the creatures that are around us: all the creatures you don't see; all the little bugs and all the little mice; the squirrels. You wish them well. You wish them all to be saved along with you.

This is part of karma yoga. When you're working, you do your own little part in the universe. You are sweeping the floor, or digging the garden, or cutting wood—anything that you have to do. This is your part in this great, big, concert of action, which is directed by God, and your part is ordered to the wellbeing of everything. It's your little part of love, and you, as an instrument of God, will that through you, God's love should reach out to all creatures. You can't obviously go around and pat each little creature on the head, and say, "I love you, little creature." You just do your work, and then this goes out to everybody. I would say that's the basic idea of karma yoga, and I think it's very important for us to really get that, and to combat sadness and discouragement.

You can get into a vicious circle of psychology. Psychology doesn't do the whole thing. Psychology just gives you the beginning, and if you get into a vicious circle, you can just do the same thing over and over again, because instead of saying, "All right, my actions shouldn't be perfect, but my motives should be perfect"; or, "My psychology should be perfect"; or, "I shouldn't have anything wrong with [myself], I shouldn't have any complexes." But I have, and that's part of the thing. Psychological problems and heritage are part of one's karma, and this is something you have to live with. Suppose I have some kind of a neurosis. Okay, that's something I have to live with.

Incidentally, what is the time? [laughter] Oh, we have plenty of time. This is a good time to talk about Morita Therapy.[9] Have you ever heard

---

9. Compare to *Springs of Contemplation*, 185–89. Remarking on his own version of Morita Therapy, Merton states: "This to me is absolutely the most helpful thing I can think of. It's what I did when I was out in California. I had every day free until evening, when we worked for about three hours. I had four days on the Pacific shore with no one in sight and nothing but water around. Doing absolutely nothing except sitting there watching the waves come in and the clouds piling up over the hills" (*Springs of Contemplation*, 189).

of that? It's a form of psychotherapy used in Zen Buddhism. Have you heard of it?

Comment: No.

It has been written about. It's quite interesting. This is not a therapy for every kind of psychic trouble, but for a certain kind of psychic trouble— the kind that ordinary people would get [laughter]. You don't have to be nuts to have it. It's [for] when you become so hung up on something, and so uptight about something, that you feel there's certain ordinary things in life that you ought to be able to do, and you just can't handle them anymore. It's just too much [laughter]. It's some silly thing, which is just: "No" [laughter]. There's a joke that the difference between a neurotic and a psychotic is that a psychotic thinks that two and two is five, and he's perfectly happy, but a neurotic knows that two and two is four, and can't stand it [laughter]. This is where a person can't face some silly little thing; they can't sleep, can't eat, and then gets headaches, and—

Comment: Ulcers . . .

—ulcers, and worries. Ordinary things. Finally, they may get settled; they become hallucinated in a mild way. What does Morita Therapy do with this? This is quite interesting. This is based on Zen practice. A Japanese psychotherapist who knew Zen devised this way of therapy.[10] No analysis, no Oedipus complex, nothing [laughter]. No "what did your daddy do to you when you were three"—none of it. You just take the person and you put them in a room. It's a four-or-five-week thing. You've heard of it?

Comment: I've heard of this.

You have heard of it, then. Well, what you do is, you take the person, put them in a room. No books, nothing. You put them in a room, and say, "Go ahead. You've got symptoms? Have your symptoms." A Buddhist nun had this and she was seeing snakes. The doctor says, "Go ahead. See snakes." He put her in a room: "Don't do anything. Just stay in bed and see snakes." She says, "What do I do if I see the snakes?" The doctor says,

10. Shoma Morita, MD (1874–1938).

"Count them. Tell me what they look like. Tell me how they behave. Tell me what color they are. Observe them closely and tell me all about them."

He leaves her in the room, and two or three days later, he comes back and says, "How are the snakes?" She says, "Oh, when I started to look at them, they disappeared" [laughter]. The point is that this ties in very much with the idea of consciousness. Now that's the first week. The first week, they're completely left to face this whole business, and simply to experience what they experience. Then after about a week, they're tired of that. They've had enough, and they're ready for a little more action. Then, the second week, they can go out and do light work; they can work in the garden to pull weeds and things like that.

What they have to do is experience very concretely what they're doing. When they're pulling the weeds, they should experience that they're pulling weeds: they see little animals; watch the little animals; watch the little bugs; and be aware, completely aware, of what they are doing. If necessary, they can come back and report, write a diary: "I saw a little black and white bug today that went like this." There are four or five of them in this thing together in the second week, and they get together and meet. They talk about the bugs and things: "I saw this leaf." Gradually, they begin to start talking real sense: "I enjoyed it so much this afternoon. It was such fun. There was a great big bug like this." Then the third week, it just goes on progressively. They do bigger work, and more running around; then, if during this time their symptoms come back, they should experience them, but as symptoms. "The things that I saw: I saw these little animals, and also, I had a symptom." Then, if the Buddhist nun saw the snake again, she would definitely experience the snake as unreal and the bug as real.

Also, at the same time, she would experience the fact that there's nothing particularly wrong with having a symptom; that everybody experiences these things to some extent, but they just don't get so hung up. Then a person can feel bad about something and it doesn't really matter that much. You can feel bad about it, but then so what? You don't have to worry about it that much. Then, when they experience those things in that way, they experience them in the way that everybody else [does]. Most people, if something bothers you, it doesn't have to bother you that much. So, that's the whole story.

The worst thing that you can do with somebody like that is, "Oh, it's nothing." Because the person experiences it as something very serious. If somebody experiences something as really critical, and somebody else says, "Oh, it's nothing," then they're put in a real quandary. It's a real tough position to be in, because they question their whole identity. What are they going to do? How are they going to account for the fact that they experience this terrible thing, which somebody else says, "It's just nothing."

What happens in this particular setup is that the person's experience is recognized. The doctor says, "I know you experienced that. I understand. I know exactly how you feel. You're seeing snakes; therefore, I think it would be very good if you just concentrated on seeing snakes for a while to fully experience it." Then, the whole thing falls back into place. This ties in with what we were talking about before, in that we never come to grips with the kind of illusions that are the normal illusions that everybody has, and one of these is the illusion that what I do has to be perfect. Or, what I do has to be very good; or what I do has to be very satisfying; or what I do has to have this or that result.

This is exactly the same as seeing a snake—only everybody does it—and since it's acceptable and built into society, it's not regarded as an illusion; it's regarded as reality. I would say, therefore, that it's very important for us, in our kind of life, to be unmasking these illusions, instead of creating a different set of them. You take a person from outside, and you take away some of the outside illusions, and then we substitute some others that we've got, and that's what passed for religious training at one point in the past. You simply give a person a whole new set of stereotypes and statements about the way life is, and they're all like seeing snakes.

You convince a person that when you do something in such and such a way that it's perfect. Then you make it so hard that it's almost impossible to do it, but then the people believe this. That's not it. Certainly, a monastery should be a place in which we learn to come to grips with not only fears that are purely idiosyncratic—purely the matter of an individual—but also the ones that are circulating in society. That's another freedom. We should strive to be somewhat free from these things, but we can't be absolutely free from them. Every time I say something like this, it's possible to take it and put it in the wrong context.

If I say "freedom," then I must be free, and then, instead of saying, "Every act I do must be perfect," or, "Every act I do must be free." Well, it's the same problem. The freedom consists in not having to be perfectly free. Of course, this is why Zen keeps saying all these funny things. Zen keeps making all these weird statements, because you say something and then you contradict it immediately, in order to make sure that there's not a hang up involved. Then you are free. In all these Asian [systems] we get the feeling [that] they take you way out into outer space, [but] they always end up by bringing you right back here.

The thing that we should always feel—and this is the thing I always wonder about when talking about these things—when you talk, and talk, and talk. You never know when somebody's going to leave with the idea that these are impossible things that they [now] have to do. All [Zen] would say about it, is that there's nothing strange about any of this. It's all right here. In a certain sense, we're doing it right now. We're practicing—

Comment: I don't follow.

If you want to practice karma yoga—we're doing it now. If what we're doing here and now is purely and simply, "here and now," and we're not expecting to leave here and do something fabulous, then what we're doing here is simply an action of God. We have to have this faith. What is happening here is not that we are people who are learning from some source, some trick source somewhere, some new way of getting in good with God, and then maybe tomorrow something is going to happen that will make us much better. What is happening now is an act of God. All the things that are involved in what's going on now; there's been a chain of causes placed by God.

For example, Mother [Myriam] invited me here, and one thing led to another, and now here we are. Definitely a chain of events, set in motion by God, for purposes of God. We're all doing this for no other reason than that it makes us cooperate with God. If we're doing that, we're practicing karma yoga right now. If we're content with that, we're practicing karma yoga well. If we're not worried about whether it's perfect, we're doing okay, and there's nothing to worry about.

If we become self-conscious of the fact, then the thing to do is to remember how it feels to be doing a thing in a simple way, and then do it again, the next time there's an opportunity. That's all. Ultimately, there's so much talking, there's so many words, and there's so many ideas given out that we have to be very careful that it doesn't get to be just merely a flow of words. Then we have to realize that while the words are flowing, we are also acting, and to remember that what happens is not to remember the words, but to remember whatever came through to us as the result of our participation in what was going on.

Again, that's what's happened. It happens all the time in all the things that we do, and that kind of thing gives us some sense of what they really mean by "karma yoga." As soon as you say the word "yoga," it's dangerous. It's one of those words, which, if you say it, immediately creates the wrong impression. Why? Well, it's "mysterious," it's "Oriental," and there's all sorts of "strange" things involved in it. But no, it's just life. It's simply living.

Well, I think I'll leave that one there. I think I've more or less covered it. I got one or two other notes here, but you've probably got some more questions. For example, there is such a thing as work becoming a narcotic. A kind of a narcosis of work, which is very American. Everybody knows dozens of business men who systematically work late at the office because they can't stand to go home. Because when they go home, they realize that the whole thing is flopping, it's not working out, and maybe there's a real reason, maybe there isn't. Perhaps a lot of it comes from an illusion of a perfect—think of the married people that are simply being driven nuts by the illusions that they have about what married life is supposed to be all about. It's dreadful what some of those people must suffer, because again, they're constantly being needled with these ideas that married life has to be something utterly, perfectly balanced, and everybody is so wise and so smart, and this wonderful reciprocity. They have a lot of troubles—and you're never supposed to have any troubles, really. If you have troubles, then is something the matter?

I'm sure that there are lots of people outside [the monastery] who could be very happily married for long periods—for a whole lifetime—and their marriage breaks up in two years, because they're harassed by these crazy ideas. I think I've exhausted that subject.

Comment: It seems to me that there is a tendency to stress the world too much [today] and to lose a healthy perception—to stress the efficiency of being and living, and the efficiency of being productive, but also as your only profession: that who you are is what you do. Today, the emphasis tends to be that we're [oriented more towards] social action and solidarity with others, and [in order for it] to be effective, we lose too much [in our ascetic and monastic life] of this "karma yoga."

That's another dimension of it. I think that we ought to be much more conscious than we are of the fact that in [religious or monastic] renewal, there's a whole set of obsessions at work. It's worth your life to say things like this, but I'll say it among friends, that a lot of this progressive stuff is really obsession. There's too much obsessive concern with things that are, say, fashionable in a way—fashionable isn't the right word—but the social action thing. This obsessive need to justify our existence by showing how we contribute to the advancement of society.

It really is the sense of the Church's guilt in the face of Communism—and not a mature sense of guilt. It's this feeling that because Communism is being so successful, apparently, and we're not, that maybe they've got something that we ought to have. That we ought to get onto this trick that they've got, and we're falling over ourselves to prove that we're really concerned about helping everybody. Of course, we should help. It's good that the Church should help people, but we don't have to go out and work in factories. You don't have to feel [that] because we're not working in factories, we're not real monks.

Comment: We don't have to, but we might need to.

Yes, if we wanted to, perhaps.

We might have to if we can't make a living here. I don't mind at all for social reasons, but we might have to because the economy [has caused] us to.

That's true, but that's another matter. There is a false feeling among monks now—because of the worker-priests, which is a perfectly good thing—it has become a fashionable question in monasticism to say, "Well, now, a monk should be somebody who's working in a factory, and a twentieth-century monk who is *not* working in a factory is *not* an authentic monk." This is very prevalent in certain places. People now have guilt feelings about not working in a factory. [Alongside that is] the feeling that you're not entitled to live in the [rural] country, for example. You have people who feel that way. You've got to be in the city.

Mother Myriam: That's true. I'm going to say, personally, I have this feeling less now about this beautiful property.

But it is a problem.

Comment: Of course, I realize that in the whole mess of man, this type of life has meaning, and you can't be everything to everybody.

This is something we really have to study, because it is a real problem, and it has to be worked out. It can't be evaded. I think that we have to take into consideration many more elements than we do. One of them is: how true is it to say that you should not be here in this beautiful place?

Mother Myriam: It's my karma yoga [laughter].

How true is it? What's the basis for that? Yes?

Fr. Roger:[11] You spoke about two kinds of yoga: one is karma yoga and the other one?

Of love [bhakti]. I'll do that tomorrow, because it's a big subject. It's on the same level with [karma yoga]. The two go together, to some extent, and bhakti yoga is actually the closest thing to the kind of spirituality that we tend to think of as Christian. The real Christian "love of God" spirituality. I'll talk about that tomorrow, because it is a whole subject in itself.

But this would then be further established?

Oh yes. It's not karma yoga. It's different, because karma yoga is for the person who simply works.

Does it presuppose karma yoga?

No, you don't necessarily have to go from karma yoga to bhakti yoga. These yogas are for different temperaments. Karma yoga is really for the active person; since everybody is to some extent active, karma yoga is for everybody. But karma yoga as a life profession is for the one who has to work.

---

11. Roger de Ganck, OCSO (1908–2000), monk, priest, and scholar of thirteenth-century Cistercian women's monasticism, served as chaplain, first at the Abbey of Our Lady of Nazareth, Brecht, Belgium, and then at Redwoods Monastery until his death in 2000. A selection of Merton's letters to Fr. Roger are included below (pp. 422–23).

Especially for the layman who has to work for a living and has to maintain a family. This is the formula for the householder with a family to be a saint.

But they are not necessarily to become married people. Would they have to go through this monastic life you spoke of first?

No. Karma yoga is for married people.

As well as monks too, then?

Monks too.

This counts as karma yoga?

Anybody who has any kind of an active life practices karma yoga, but the state of the layman is ideally the state of karma yoga; not the state of the monk. The state of the monk is ideally the state of the *sannyasin* who has renounced everything. Karma yoga is perfectly compatible with owning property, and with managing a business. It's compatible with a non-monastic life, but it's compatible with a monastic life, too. There's no contradiction.

Because in Vietnam, for example, most monks are known to participate in politics.

You mean the Buddhist monks say this? Well, of course, in Vietnam, there is a problem. You have an emergency there and the monks feel that none of the political groups are really espousing the calls of the people, because the monks are very close to the peasants of Vietnam. They feel that the Communists are trying to use the peasants to bring them into their own cause and then throw them into revolutionary power against the land owners, and that this is really not for the peasants' interests. They're exploiting the peasants for their own political power, and they feel that the other side is simply cheating the peasants, and that somebody has to represent the peasants, and they're going to do this: that they represent the true cause of the people of Vietnam.

I would say that's perfectly good reasoning, but if there is a situation in which nobody else is doing an urgent job, then the monk has to do it. I would say that in this country, the monks should be among those who are protesting against injustice. The monks aren't the only ones, and not every monk has to—monks don't need to be marching in a parade. I don't think they absolutely can't, but I don't see any reason why they shouldn't. I think, for my part, since I have an audience, that if [monks] want to get out and say something, it's a good thing to do. I don't agree at all with those who would say, "Because you're a monk, you must not speak about the bomb," or, "You must not speak about civil rights, because it's contrary to the monastic state." I think that's a complete evasion.

Fr. Roger: But why is it that there are some Buddhist monks who say that this is not Buddhistic?

Those are the conservative Buddhists. It's exactly the same kind of situation with them as it is with us. They have the same split, and in Vietnam, you find that the progressive Buddhists and the progressive Catholics are very close together. The conservative Buddhists are not working with the conservative Catholics, but they're the same thing on different ends. The progressive Catholics in South Vietnam are very much with the progressive Buddhists, and have the same attitude towards the war.

This explains, for example, the strange fact that these [monks] will burn themselves to death, which the West doesn't understand at all, because it's a most inefficient way of doing things. "This is not efficient. It's not practical to burn yourself to death. What do you get out of it?" That's precisely what they're trying to say. They're trying to say, "I'm not getting anything out of this." They're trying to say, "I believe this so strongly that I will kill myself to make my point without getting anything out of it. I can't get anything out of it. I'm dead." But the West doesn't understand this. That's not our kind of talk and that's the tragic thing about that.

Fr. Roger: I see that now. You were talking about Hinduism and I've seen it through Buddhism.

The thing is that Buddhism does very much the same thing, but it's not as systematic as in Hinduism. Buddhism is much more monastic. In Hinduism and Buddhism, a monk has a different place. In Buddhism, the monk is definitely a privileged person. In Hinduism, the monk is just one among many social states, but in Buddhism, the monk is the one who really has the preferred position in society. The monk is automatically closer than the layman to salvation. In popular Buddhism, it would be understood that the layman is not proximately about to be saved; i.e., if he's a good layman, in the next life he'll be a monk. He'll get a better chance. This is strictly the Buddhist way of looking at it; whereas, the Hindu idea is that the layman, by karma yoga, if he lives it faithfully, can certainly achieve deliverance by it. He doesn't have to be a monk in the next life.

Fr. Roger: You are in touch with the monk, Francis Mahieu, who is now in India?[12]

We exchanged some letters. I didn't know him. Did you know him?

Yes.

Well, of course, he's with Dom Bede Griffiths.[13]

Yes. That's true. Another point, too, is that through India, many of the ideas of the Hindu, of the Buddhist, came into eastern [Christian] monasticism. You see it by the third century.

Those same ideas got into Alexandria and you find some of them in Origen, for example.[14] Origen is full of Hindu ideas, and the Alexandrian school is full of Hindu ideas. Through them, this sort of thing has come

---

12. Francis (Acharya) Mahieu, OCSO (1919–2002), Belgian-born Cistercian monk of Scourmont Abbey, who, along with Bede Griffiths, founded Kurisumala Ashram in Tiruvalla, Kerala, India. There is an unpublished letter (in French) dated December 30, 1961, with the heading "Lettres de Kurisumala," signed by Mahieu and others, archived at the Thomas Merton Center at Bellarmine University. See also Marthe Mahieu-De Praetere, *Kurisumala: Francis Mahieu Acharya, A Pioneer of Christian Monasticism in India* (Collegeville, MN: Liturgical Press, 2008). Mahieu also attended the Bangkok meeting of monastic superiors in December 1968 and was photographed standing next to Merton (see Michael Mott, *The Seven Mountains of Thomas Merton* [Boston: Houghton Mifflin, 1984]).

13. Bede Griffiths, OSB Cam. (1906–1993), founder of Shantivanam Ashram in Tamil Nadu, India. Griffiths visited the Abbey of Gethsemani during Merton's lifetime and offered conferences both in Chapter and to the novices at Gethsemani (see "Bede Griffiths' Visit to the Abbey of Gethsemani," in *Merton and Hinduism*, 347–52).

14. Origen of Alexandria, influential second- to third-century biblical exegete and theologian. His cosmology included teachings on the pre-existence of the soul, which were later condemned as heretical by the Church in the sixth century, unfortunately tarnishing his reputation as a brilliant and original thinker until a revival of scholarly interest in the twentieth century.

into the West. All the Hellenic world, after Alexander [the Great], whether Syria or Egypt, or what was later Byzantine, was in a great deal of contact with the East. At that same time, there was contact between India and China. I've been reading a very interesting travel story by a Muslim in the thirteenth century who went to China. A Muslim from Morocco.[15]

I think that we should face the question of, "Should we or should we not live under redwood trees? Why, or why not? Is this wrong or is this right?" The first thing that I would say is that there are some very poor people up the road living under redwood trees, so you don't have to be a millionaire to live under redwood trees. It's a valid choice.

Mother Myriam: To me, there is to be this type of life here, too. I intended to discuss this with you, if there was an opportunity. I think that there should also be a monastery, a center for meditation and contemplation in New York City.

Oh, absolutely. Well, there are.

And why not in the middle of the city? It's my hope, if we did allow it—

Have a place in San Francisco.

Yes, and those who should or could work outside a very simple job, a factory job, and then come back there [to the monastery]?

Sure. That's very practical.

It's good. I think that this has to stay.

Yes, exactly. The problem that comes with a monastery in the country, is that the mentality behind it is essentially medieval and feudal. This is where the whole concept of [medieval] monasticism has broken down. For example, say you put a great feudal castle surrounded with walls in the redwoods, and then fill it with people who never go out. And because

---

15. See the "East with Ibn Battuta" section of Merton's *The Geography of Lograire* (New York: New Directions, 1969), 82–88, based on a 1929 translation by H. A. R. Gibb of *Travels in Asia and Africa*, 1325–1354 (see pp. 146–47).

they're within these walls, you give them all kinds of pleasant things—in the end, it becomes a country club in which there's a certain amount of business that has to be done in order to make a lot of money. It becomes then a little city where there's a business operation going on and then recreation for the rest of the time—and some prayer. This has no reason for existing, but the modern man needs the kind of thing that we have, and nobody is giving it to him. Nobody is sharing it with him, and the reason why nobody is sharing it with him, is that nobody's got it. You can't give what you don't have. It is necessary, therefore, for us to be away somewhere where we can develop this real contemplative consciousness. We should have little places in the city where we can go and share this with other people. We should be able to share it to some extent with people who come out here.

The only problem is not at all whether it's right or wrong, it's to do it right: to do it in such a way that it is effective. The way that it has been done with the big retreat house, where everybody comes rushing in on the weekend, and you preach three conferences a day, and make the stations of the cross after dinner—this doesn't do it. Therefore, I think, that this is one of the most important places in the Church in America at the present moment. Here [at Redwoods Monastery]. Because this is one of the only places in the country where you really have a monastery. This is one of the few places where you've got a real contemplative community. This is not necessarily true of other Cistercian monasteries.

Mother Myriam: I feel that in the future, with improvements in communication, there's [the real possibility of] exchange. That's what's happening. There is a real exchange between the city and here, towards the people, but I feel that they should always come on a personal basis.

People should come because they want to come, because they know what they're coming for. And you see what you will get. You will get people who really are interested and who come for the right reasons, and who need it. But there will be an exchange. Once again, this business of filling a guest house with people that the monks never see—it's a Jesuit retreat practice that we've got at our guest house there. You're "cranking the crank."

This is so necessary to have something like this in redwood trees as a witness to the beauty of God's creation. It's always necessary to have somebody who has left the modern world and gone back to the primeval forest, which this definitely is, and simply to live there quietly, peacefully, and to develop a whole different consciousness. That really is important. The thing that we can give to the modern world that's so important is that we are different. We have a different kind of consciousness, and a different kind of awareness, because even if they don't come here to share much, the mere fact that they see that it's possible is a sign of hope for many people.

Mother Myriam: I agree on this idea of the different states of life in Hinduism, and of course it would be a special gift, that some would then develop this consciousness also in the city. I was struck by what Father Schillebeeckx[16] said, that the monks went to the desert not so much for the solitude, yes, but also because they thought that the powers of evil were concentrated there. And he asked, today, "Where is the concentration of evil if not at the center of the city?"

I wouldn't agree entirely, because where are the devils?

In ourselves.

They're in ourselves.

The difference between solitude and the city, in that point of view, is that in the city, we don't recognize and we don't come to grips with the devils in ourselves, because there are so many devils all around in the city itself [laughter], and we haven't got time. In the city, we don't have time for the devils in ourselves. There are too many other [people]. I really do think that there are certain things in ourselves that we never come to grips with unless we're solitary, because otherwise, they never surface.

Mother Myriam: On the condition that we get the solitude also in the center; because otherwise, without that, we don't get it, and we would destroy the real periods of silence and solitude, I think. We will never reach that bottom where we meet evil in ourselves.

---

16. Edward Schillebeeckx, OP (1914–2009), influential Belgian theologian who made important contributions to Vatican Council II and twentieth-century Catholic theology in general.

Yes, because if it's just a question of chat all the time.

Comment: You said that in the city, people will be too busy to come to grips with the devil in themselves. Would that be an illusion in apostolic life, too?

Oh yes. Of course, it's true that when one is dealing with the devils in other people, to some extent, God takes care of our own [devils]. That's one of the graces of the apostolic life, is the apostle forgets himself, forgets his own problems. To some extent, he leaves God to take care of his problems. We can become too involved with our own devils, too, in solitude. There's more to life than just fighting devils.

I would say that there are certain people that would have to come to grips with that, and to me, it's preferable to struggle with evil in myself rather than to get [involved] in the apostolic life. But also, with me, I feel very skeptical of the value of the apostolic life, the way it's structured.

Comment: You mean the so-called "active life."

Yes, I'm terribly skeptical. Just imagine how much time could be really wasted in terrible routines in these institutions. I've often thought of myself. I was once thinking of entering the Franciscans. If I had entered the Franciscans, I would have had to put out these magazines that they put out, and then write these articles. Whereas here, there's no magazines!

Fr. Roger: Start one!

Well, I started one, but it's a good one [laughter]. It's certainly nothing like that.[17] Well, it's about 6:00pm. Aren't you getting hungry? How are these two [conferences] for you? Are they too long? Are you falling asleep? [laughter]

Mother Myriam: Not too long. But I think I could have a bottle of beer.

Oh, fine. That's great. Should we have one after supper?

Maybe together after supper.

17. This is a reference to Merton's literary magazine, *Monks Pond.*

Let's have some beer together after supper. That would be very nice. That will stimulate [laughter]. We'll probably be inspired. We'll have some beer, and then I'll leave, and you can have chant practice with the beer [laughter].[18]

18. A discussion then ensues over whether the community should celebrate a shorter or longer chanted Mass, which would require rehearsal. Merton quips, "You don't have to be perfect," referencing the previous discussion, with much laughter, followed by the comment, "Instead of practicing singing, let's practice what we preach," to even more laughter.

Chapter Five

The Origins
of Modern Consciousness

What I was really aiming at this morning[1] when I talked about this, was that when you have a community in which everybody loves one another, the situation is set for natural development: a vital, organic development of the things that you need and look for. Renewal comes by itself in its own time, and in a very harmonious way, in a way that everybody is ready for. When it happens, you're ready for it. I certainly get the feeling here that you are all more or less [together] with what you're doing, and that you may not all agree perfectly on everything, but still, when something happens, I think you're all ready for it. Whereas with us [at Gethsemani], it's in a much bigger community, with many different types of people, so that when something happens you get the feeling that there's a wave of shock going out through the community, and this sense that there's a central power group that's doing this. Then you've got the people on the outside who are offering it up [laughter], and then you've got these repercussions going around the community. Of course, in a situation like this, a fair amount of monastery politics gets involved [laughter]. That's the disadvantage of a big community. Big communities have all these problems, and you are fortunate that you don't have to worry about things like that, and thank heaven you don't.

Well, I don't think I had anything else along those lines that I wanted to get to. I had one brilliant idea riding over here, but it's completely gone [laughter]. So, I don't know what's left of that.

---

1. This is most likely a reference to Merton's homily from the morning Mass. This conference begins mid-discussion.

I want to talk about this yoga of love today—bhakti yoga—but first, I want to say a few things about the modern mentality, and the background of the modern mentality—modern consciousness, and its development since the Renaissance—just very superficially, and with one or two examples to help us understand where we're at.

Medieval Christendom had a similar outlook as I've been describing in Hinduism. Basically, there's one reality, which is God, and all is rooted in Him and preserved in being by Him, and everything is pretty solid. It's changing; it's moving and evolving, but it's basically a very stable universe in which the Ground of everything is God—present, very real, immediately experienced. Now, if the Ground of our existence is an immediate experience of God, or an immediate contact with God, or even an immediate all-embracing faith in God, you would get a radically different kind of consciousness, because everything else tends to become secondary. The fact that things are changed, or the house falls down, or there's a tidal wave, this is all too bad, but things like that are always happening, and it's not the beginning or the end of anything, it's just something that happens.

Underneath this is the unchanging reality, which, in our Christian thinking, we have retained some of this. You can't get away from it. But at the same time, we are modern people, and I think that can cause us quite a lot of complications, because now you have a certain modern theology and modern philosophy, which is explicitly rejecting this ancient metaphysic. This is the problem of books like *The Future of Belief* by Leslie Dewart—which is a good book, and it's got a lot in it.[2]

I just received a couple of letters from him; it was in the package that came yesterday, as a matter of fact. He sent an article from the recent *Continuum*. It's an excellent article in which he gets himself off of the various hooks that he gets himself on in his book by saying, "What I'm really talking about is God, not as Being, but as Presence." He can't swallow the notion of "Being." To say that God is "Pure Being" is no longer relevant, because he says that for modern man, the very concept of "Being" is meaningless. I don't know, is the concept of "Being" meaningless to you?

---

2. *The Future of Belief: Theism in a World Come of Age* (New York: Herder & Herder, 1966). Dewart (1922–2009), a Canadian philosopher, taught at the University of Toronto. For Merton's correspondence with Dewart, see *Witness to Freedom*, 282–99.

Mother Myriam: The concept of "presence" implies a more direct related-ness to man.

Yes. The trouble with "Being" is that it has been vitiated along the line by abstract content. The thing that always sold me on it—I've always had a great difficulty in seeing the objection, because to me, my whole conversion to Christianity was the concept that God is *ens a se*.[3] It's very non-fashionable to be converted by that kind of an idea, but all of a sudden, I did. Here, you have a pure actuality, whose very essence is "to be" and to exist: "cannot not be." That struck me very forcibly. But apparently, for Leslie Dewart and people like that, this doesn't mean anything; but alright if you say "presence."

The thing that he says is that for modern man, the idea of "Being" does not equal the idea of "Reality," necessarily. "*Ens*" and "Real" are not necessarily interconvertible; he's probably got a good technical point, I don't know, but then he ends up with—what to him seems very radical, but it doesn't bother me. He says that really, you can speak of the ultimate reality as "non-Being." I've got no objection to that.

What you've got is two metaphysics: the Hindu and Asian metaphysic regards the Ultimate as "Void," whereas we regard it as "Pure Being." Well, as far as I can see, those two are perfectly convertible. It's simply two ways of saying the same thing, because after all, if Pure Being is what we say it is, then you have to immediately do the *apophatic*[4] thing on it and say, "It is, of course, not what you would think of as Being; therefore, it's also non-Being," and I don't see any problem.

One interesting point he does make, which I haven't studied, but I'll just say it: he says that this goes back to differences in language. In the Indo-European languages, we are always saying "A is B," subject is predicate. In Asian languages, it doesn't work like that. You never have an "is." You just have "A," "B." You've got quite a different concept of the verb. Very seldom, "This is," so that the concept of tagging a predicate onto a subject with "is," is alien to Asian thought. With us, you make a statement,

3. See Merton's letter to Mario Falsina dated March 27, 1968: "Reasons for my conversion, besides the grace of God. First of all the discovery of a metaphysical sense of Being, and an intuition of God as *ens a se*, pure actuality" (*The Road to Joy: Letters to New and Old Friends*, ed. Robert E. Daggy [New York: Farrar, Straus and Giroux, 1989], 348).

4. *Apophasis* (Greek), "to deny," or "unsay." A theological term for negating that which can be said in order to affirm that which cannot be said; also referred to in later Latin medieval mystical traditions as the *via negativa*.

"A is B," and the word "is" signifies a reality. You're stamping it; you're authenticating it, saying, "This is real." That's the kind of statement we make. But in Asia, they don't say, "This is real," or anything like that. They just say "real" or "not real," or "has real." I don't know. He illustrated this with some things I didn't understand too well.

But anyway, in the Middle Ages, there was this definite sense of a basic Ground of either Pure Being or Pure Void, which comes to pretty much the same thing, religiously. Basically, an experience of solidity in what is unquestionable; what one doesn't question, what one can't question, and what it never occurs to anyone to question. If you question it, it's because you've never experienced it. I think, basically, this whole Asian thinking and medieval thinking was based on experience—somebody just didn't read a book, and then say, "Oh, I think God is really Pure Being." The reason they said God was "Pure Being" was because they experienced God as the Ground of all Being. The reason they say in Asia, for example, that the ultimate self is undifferentiated *atman*, or Non-Being, or Void, is because they experienced it that way.

But along came the cadence of the Middle Ages, and with it the new mentality of the Renaissance, and right away you've got a split. On one hand, you've got a totally new sense of time. This is a very important development in the Renaissance. One of the great changeovers in the Renaissance was a new urgency about time. This gets back to the big question of yesterday—this is going to keep me on track, because this has a lot to do with depression, and sadness, and discouragement. In the Middle Ages, people were not worried about time. Time was seasonal. It came and it went. They didn't have clocks. Even in the monastery, you go to the refectory after Sext, and either dinner is either ready, or it isn't. If it isn't, you can sit down and wait, and maybe it'll come along eventually [laughter].

The clock got into the monastic life as part of the reform of the Council of Trent.[5] Until Trent, they weren't that particular about time. But Trent came along and organized everything; got it all regular. There was a time for everything: you had to be on time for the Office [the Liturgy of the Hours], and everything was measured by the clock and the ringing of the bell. This is the heritage of Trent. Now, in the secular Renaissance concept, you have an optimistic concept of time as the field of action,

5. The council was held in Northern Italy from 1545 to 1563.

in which man, by getting in there and doing something can, secularly speaking, manifest his divinity. Now, here you have not only a different concept of time, you have a different concept of man: as autonomous, as creator, as a get-out-and-doer.

Remember, this is the language of artists, of medieval humanism, and Lorenzo de Medici and people like that—medieval princes and the language of the society that later produced Machiavelli and Michelangelo—in which man is interested in personal immortality *in the world*. He does a great work and then is remembered for having done a great work. This is totally different from what we were talking about yesterday. It's the exact opposite of karma yoga. Karma yoga is you work completely free from any concern about the result. Here, you're totally concentrated on the result. Everything depends on the result. Time is given to you in which to do a great work, and to leave a statue of yourself in the public park [laughs]. That's the Renaissance idea. You end up with your statue in the public park, and all we've got to do is look at the statues in the public park to see that this is not really worthwhile [laughs].

You've got this optimistic humanist concept of time, but that's only one half of a split. With the Reformation, you also get the sense of time as fallen and as corrupt, and time as a realm in which the fallen creature is powerless; he's helpless. So, what I'm saying about the modern concept of time, is that it is deeply affected by this radical split. Not that it's optimistic or that it's pessimistic, but that it is both. What you really have in modern man is a struggle between, on the one hand, the heritage of the secular Renaissance—the idea that you can be great in time, and you can step out there and really do something big—and then along with it, the Reformation, the Calvinist and Lutheran concept that you're corrupt, and that you can't make anything out of time for yourself, because each instant is an incident of more sin and more collapse. To read [John] Calvin is a fantastic experience.[6] This is one of the most gripping—he's got this terrible, terrific sixteenth-century French prose in which he simply makes your flesh creep. A lot of it has profound religious validity. He has things about the wrath of God that are absolutely shattering.

The thing you have to remember is that it's a one-sided picture. It's very biased. There's always this terrible pessimism around time being "fallen,"

6. John Calvin (1509–1564), French-born theologian and reformer in Geneva, Switzerland, most known for his doctrine of predestination, which Merton describes below.

and "fallen man" being caught in a treadmill, trying to save himself and unable to; utterly unable to do anything for himself. Into this comes a completely arbitrary concept of grace, in which it's purely a toss-up. You may or may not get it; you may be lucky. It's a roulette thing, and you may have a winning number, or you may not. But then it works around, because behind the Reformation concept of a fallen man in time is also what's behind the American, New England, capitalist, go-getting, Yankee Clipper society.

How it got there was through these fellows that started working with things backwards. If you were successful in life, it was a sign of God's blessing. New England was the land of the "elect" and America was the new paradise. If you came to this country, it was a sign of election to be sent, to be one of the small groups that had enough sense to get away from the corrupt world of Europe and come to this country. You had a new start; this was the new paradise. To be an American was to be among the elect.[7]

Incidentally, I'm in contact with a hippie bookstore in Cleveland, which is always being raided. They carry my magazine [laughter]. That's how I'm in touch with them. I send them my magazine and they send me a lot of publications in exchange. One publication is a huge mimeograph about this thick, but a lot of very good poetry in it that was a general protest about one of their members who was thrown in jail for taking dope, and they're protesting against this injustice. On the front of it is a very funny picture of this rather shoddy hippie, who was thrown in jail, standing there with his beard, looking pretty badly in need of help. And he's standing under a huge, big sign put up by some business in Cleveland saying, "You have to work awful hard to be an American, but it's worth it" [laughter].

So, you get this double concept in American culture that you are elect, but you have to prove it. Of course, incidentally, one of the things that's behind the cutting down of redwood trees is actually the Puritan conception of the Pilgrims that landed in New England who saw the wilderness as evil—the wilderness as the domain of the devil, and the Indian as a creature of the devil, and the man who gets too interested in the wilderness, it's a bad thing. "You need to stick around Salem where it's safe." So, the idea was you went into the wilderness with an ax and you cleared the wilderness. The psychology of this type of person is a psychology that likes

---

7. A belief that persists today as the so-called "prosperity gospel," or "prosperity theology."

to cut down trees. One of you were telling me about the man who had that land. He's just cutting it down for fun, cutting down redwood trees. What for? You destroy these great big things and you prove your superiority.

What came out of this was they turned the Reformation pessimism inside out, so that a person could darn well prove that they were elect. So, you took time to work hard and amass a pile of money and prove that you were one of the elect. That was the way you showed it. What you then have is this very complicated split and conflict within the modern consciousness, and which we all have to some extent. We are all affected by this, to some extent. We no longer can have the pure Asian or medieval sense of undisturbed reality over which things just happen to flow accidentally. A basic reality that's never touched. We don't have that, because what happened with this was the transfer of the center of balance into the individual soul; whereas before, the center was God. No matter how individual a medieval man might've felt himself to be, his center was really God. Everybody felt that the one basic reality was God, and that God was really much more fundamentally real than his own individual self. But this was transferred in the Renaissance and the Reformation. This big shift took place, and since then—this has been somewhat irreversible—the only thing that can be done with it now is to move forward.[8]

We've got into the age of individualism. Rather than trying to go back to the metaphysical center, it's a communal center that we're moving towards. Centeredness in a community of persons with a new center of gravity, which is not merely in the individual—it's in the community—but it's a wholly different concept of community. It's not the medieval concept of community at all. It's not a natural concept of community. It's a completely free idea of community. This is what we're moving towards. This is the salvation which is ahead. It's the only thing that I can see that we really can do with this, and it's what God has given us to do: to find a new center in a freely formed community, a created community. Don't you think so?[9]

---

8. Merton's interpretation of medieval consciousness, both here and prior, is perhaps overly generalized, idealistic, and romanticized. On the question of the "individual" in medieval society, see the section entitled, "Did the Twelfth Century Discover the Individual?," in Caroline Walker Bynum, *Jesus as Mother: Studies in the Spirituality of the High Middle Ages* (Berkeley: University of California Press, 1984), 82–109.

9. A portion of this discussion has been omitted due to cross-talk among several members of the Redwoods community—each speaking rapidly with thick accents, and at a distance from the microphone.

Mother Myriam: Yesterday, after the conferences, I was thinking about the idea to live, or to be, the self—as in your poetry from a Hindu text—in a "non-affective commitment." And yet [isn't this] a negative of the good of creation.

It is and it isn't.

What do we do in this "non-affective commitment"? Because this is a Hindu idea, but the Christian message is to love one another—the Christian message is, after all, [about] people and persons. So, I was wondering—I don't know how yet—but if the contemplative life is, or should, move towards a life in depth in person-to-person relations in community?

It is a question of creating community. The way I see it, is that we have to create community and freedom, and not according to nature. For example, in the medieval concept of community, you were born into your community and there wasn't any problem about it. You stayed in it all your life. You were born as a peasant and you stayed a peasant; you were born a feudal lord and you stayed one; you were born into artisan families and you had to learn how to become an artisan. That's where you were, but now we cut across all these things, because we choose our community.

The other thing I would say is that we can choose a community, which would be dedicated to Zen, for example. You can choose a Christian Zen community. If you want to, you can, and neither one excludes the other; it is simply a new dimension of the whole thing. The Japanese person of the thirteenth century was born into a civilization in which Zen was natural. He would naturally gravitate towards Zen, if he was that kind of a person. But now, you can create it out of a whole cloth; instead of feeling that it's artificial, you can go ahead and do it.

With the Renaissance, you can say, quoting this man, "Human thought no longer feels itself a part of things. It distinguishes itself from them in order to reflect upon them, and thus, is no longer upheld by their own power of enduring."[10] Now, the thing about negation here—it's a negation, which is within a sense of identity. These people are so immersed in kinship with all creation that they negate the whole thing to get to a different level of understanding. It's not at all the individual standing

---

10. Georges Poulet, *Studies in Human Time* (Baltimore: Johns Hopkins Press, 1956), 13.

back from creation and negating it. It's the individual trying to affirm himself by getting loose from it. But with the advance of this different kind of thought, you get the Renaissance man described as being, "like a bird in the air with no stable support, maintaining his possibility"—not as actuality, but as possibility—"by beating his wings." This is what we're all in, and this is the source of this constant threat of depression. It is the basic conviction—which I think is an illusion, but it's us—that you have to be constantly beating your wings, or you fall. That time is given to you to keep acting, keep moving, keep swimming; otherwise, you will sink. Each individual is the one who has to make this choice.

Before that, there was no problem for the individual about subsisting. He might have problems with eating [i.e., physical survival], but for maintaining himself as a reality [i.e., existentially], there was no problem. We are people, however, who are deeply wounded with the sense of our possible nothingness, and with the sense that if we don't do something about it right away, we will disappear. But when we do that, and when we act on that kind of basis, it's extremely depressing, because it's actually unreal. We're not like that, really. This is an illusion. I think it's one of the great modern illusions.

This is the thing that we bring with us into the contemplative life, and of course, in the contemplative life, this becomes very difficult if a person tries to do this, but we do. We come into it, like it or not, as individuals; unlike the Middle Ages, where community was quite spontaneous. But for us, we are extremely insecure individuals in a community, and we have to struggle with this insecurity all the time. It takes an awful lot of effort.

We don't do it consciously, but what we do, as I was suggesting yesterday, is that we try to prove ourselves by the results of our actions. We're always trying to get results by which we can verify [our existence]. We do this "wing beating" thing to prove we're still there. Every day then becomes a challenge to prove that we're still around; that we're still real. Of course, what this means is that we doubt our own reality all the time. A Jesuit once told me that in their library there's a big flashy sign that says, "Convince yourself that you exist!" [laughter] Do we have to convince ourselves that we exist? "Oh, so I remember"? Well, that's kind of rough. In a situation like that, like it or not, community is the only thing. "Convince yourself that you exist"—this is the voice of utter despair.

What we are really struggling to convince ourselves of, is "are we loved?" Are we worthy of love? Can we be loved? And of course, if you say, "Convince yourself that you exist," it means you have despaired of the other one [i.e., love]. You chase your own tail around in a circle, indefinitely, to prove that it's still there. Well, that's plain despair, and if that's what we're doing unconsciously, we're going to be terribly unhappy and terribly depressed. What I would say is probably one of the reasons for depression in our life is that we're unconsciously doing that. We unconsciously doubt, not our own existence, but we do doubt our own worth, terribly. This is a modern sickness—constantly questioning our worth. Of course, this would be a good place to talk about things like the punishment of faults, the Sacrament of Penance, things like that. The routine, for example, of Confession; the way it normally is in religious communities: you've got to go once a week, and if you haven't got anything, find something; invent something, make yourself feel cheap about something.

There was a time about 10 years ago when they were trying to save the Chapter of Faults at all costs. You have to persecute each other in order to keep this institution moving; to keep this thing in existence. That's the extreme manifestation of it, but if we don't persecute each other, we still persecute ourselves. The official persecution is less, but in our own hearts, we're still doing it. Those of us who have been through that are, to some extent, incurable. It's like having had an arm shot off in the war; there's something irreplaceable, and there's nothing that we can do about it. In a situation like that, you're bound to be constantly questioning your worth.

Whatever way you look at it, the modern man is left in this kind of a position where he is like a bird in the air, constantly beating his wings to reaffirm his worth and his reality.

Now, with the development of the eighteenth century, for example, you've got . . . [11]

11. The recording stops here mid-sentence with a gap in the discussion before beginning again with the following chapter.

Chapter Six

Mystical Consciousness in Yoga and Life in Solitude

It is good not to have to judge things. Certain things you have to judge; but as a rule, it's good not to. A lot of judging you just don't have to do. A lot of deciding, you don't have to do; therefore, as part of our religious training, we have to have systematic training in what they call nondiscrimination. Not dividing things up to be good and bad. We have to know the difference between "good" and "bad," but at the same time, not to be constantly categorizing everything, "this is good; this is bad." Simply be open to it. Don't decide whether it's good or bad. You label it as "good" or "bad," and then you don't have to experience it.

The reason why we do that is we are afraid of being overwhelmed by experiences. That's the point of the monastery. What you've got here is a place where experiences are controlled. You are immensely rich in being surrounded by decent experiences. You've got a nice surrounding, you've got a nice choir, you've got a nice monastery, nice communities. It's not only bearable, but it's even nice [laughs]. This is most unusual! There are a very small minority of people in this country that have that kind of thing. Most people are surrounded by things which are meant to be nice and thought to be nice, but are really horrible.

Comment: The deeper our consciousness, the better we are able to accept and integrate where we are different. Because we can reconcile difference, diversity, and variety with that deep point [of consciousness] where we are at, we can then comprehend the whole.

Yes, exactly. I'm going to come to that later. The Hindus would say that we are all basically one in *atman*, but that there are different kinds of yogas for each different temperament—that one should have one kind of yoga, and another a different kind of yoga, because they have different dispositions. There's a special yoga, for example, for the man or woman who's more intellectual. He or she has a special kind of yoga. It's a very rare kind of yoga. The intellectual yoga easily gets to be academic, but it's a real, highly philosophical yoga.[1] There may be somebody in a community that would have that.

Another one would have a yoga that affects more a devotional, emotional kind of thing, which is a perfectly legitimate kind of yoga, a devotion yoga.[2] There's a place for that. Very often you get people like that, that are always being turned off, because devotion isn't fashionable now. [You would think that] to be devout is one of the worst things that could ever happen! The person who likes rosaries and things like that. "This is prideful. What are you going to do with somebody like that?" Well, maybe that's a good thing; that's good for that person, and we have to recognize that exists too.

Fr. Roger: Devotion can be often misused, too.

Devotion can be misused when it's an escape; when a person is, as you say, refusing to confront something, refusing to experience something, and taking refuge in a devotion—then it's all wrong. But a devotion may be the way a person does meet God. If a person really does find God in a simple devotion, then fine. It's good. However, in the recent past, it has been systematically promoted as a kind of evasion. It was overstressed, and obviously, it was a substitute for real depth in our life. That is why it is really discredited at the moment.

Now, the next one of these selves[3]—this is going to be problematic—because this is what we really call "the soul." It's what they call the *jiva*

---

1. Jñāna yoga.

2. Bhakti yoga.

3. The recording begins here mid-discussion on the Hindu *kosas*, or "sheaths" of the self, a multi-layered psycho-spiritual physiology, which begins with the more material aspects of the self, and proceeds to the most subtle: food, breath, mind, wisdom, and bliss (see, e.g., *Taittiriya Upanishad*, 2.2-5). Merton offers an extended conference on this topic upon his return to Gethsemani in May 1968 for the gathering of contemplative prioresses (*Merton and Hinduism*, 354–61). Merton's source for this material, as well as the "four

[in the Hindu tradition], and it's the individual soul.[4] Where we would have to dialogue with them, and where we could both learn from each other, is that the individual soul is not the person. There's a distinction between the individual soul and the true person. That's what they would say, and that's what we would say. But it is an empirical "I" consciousness. It is what we experience as "I," and that is where we tend to be a bit superficial. When we talk about "the person"—"personal expansion" and "personal development"—we are talking too often in terms of this more or less empirical ego consciousness, which is not enough. It is good for a person to develop that level of consciousness, but it's not the whole story. One of the things that I will do if I get around to people like [Michel de] Montaigne, [René] Descartes,[5] and people like that—the great thing that they did, was to develop this thinking subject, the self-aware subject in various ways. Of course, modern literature has done this in so many ways with [Marcel] Proust, and all these people have gone into this in very subtle and manifold ways. The psychoanalyst, too, to a great extent, is dealing with this ego.

It's a good thing, but we assume that this is the end of the road; that this is the whole story. This empirical ego consciousness, which we can say is "my soul"—this is the whole thing—but it isn't. There's much more. This is where it's going to be very important for us, because this is getting into our special field, because we are the ones who are professionally engaged in experiencing a deeper level of consciousness than the "I," and to know that the self is something more than just what I call "I," or what I experience as "I." You get this in St. Bernard as well. This is what you get in mystical literature in terms of these moments of "self-forgetfulness" and "self-transcendence."

But this has to be re-studied and re-experienced by us. We have to go through all this in our own modern way, and restate these things in a modern way, because they're so often stated in a way that is no longer comprehensible to modern man. This is very important.

_____

yogas" (karma, bhakti, jñana, and raja), is Swami Nikhilananda's *Hinduism: Its Meaning for the Liberation of the Spirit* (New York: Ramakrishna-Vivekananda Center, 1958/1992); especially Chapter Two, "The Soul and Its Destiny," 49–67.

4. Nikhilananda, *Hinduism*, 49–50.

5. Sixteenth- and seventeenth-century French philosophers, respectively.

[Returning to the *kosas*], what's even more important, is that there is a mystical self, which is beyond this empirical "I," and which is called the "self of bliss."[6] This is the self which is experienced in the highest contemplation; yet this is not the self [*atman*]. This is again a covering. This is the "turned on" self; the self that really lights up during any kind of a deep transcendent experience. But as long as there is any experience at all, it's not me, because the ultimate "I" is in this deep, undifferentiated realm, which has no form that I can grasp and experience. It is in a deep, undifferentiated area, which cannot be limited by any kind of experience or definition.

I'm thinking now in terms of the Hindu concept of the undifferentiated *Brahman*, because there is a differentiated *Brahman*, which is God manifesting in some intelligible form, for example, an incarnation, or a manifestation.[7] This [undifferentiated *Brahman*] is [Meister] Eckhart's "Godhead." This is the ultimate Godhead. Eckhart had all this. This is Meister Eckhart to a "tee"; he's the one in the West who got closest to this.[8]

This is a good example. I knew very well the great Zen man, [D.T.] Suzuki. We were quite good friends, although I didn't see much of him, but we'd written and exchanged things, like dialogue.[9] He was very good on Zen and very good on Eckhart, and liked Eckhart very much.[10] Suzuki died quite suddenly at the age of 96. He was writing an introduction to a book by another Zen man. He wrote it the day before he died. That

---

6. *Anandamayakosa*; Nikhilananda, *Hinduism*, 56.

7. See Nikhilananda, *Hinduism*, 49–50.

8. Merton read the thirteenth/fourteenth-century German mystical theologian Meister Eckhart extensively and favorably in the early-mid 1960s, although also critically, and includes a section on Eckhart in his 1961 lecture notes to recently ordained monks at Gethsemani (*An Introduction to Christian Mysticism*, ed. Patrick F. O'Connell [Kalamazoo, MI: Cistercian Publications, 2008], 199–217; see also O'Connell's "Introduction," xliii–xlv).

9. D.T. Suzuki (1870–1966) collaborated with Merton in Part Two of *Zen and the Birds of Appetite* (New York: New Directions, 1968), entitled "Wisdom in Emptiness: A Dialogue" (pp. 99–138). *Zen and the Birds* also includes Merton's essay, "D.T. Suzuki: The Man and His Work" (pp. 59–66). Merton met Suzuki in New York City in 1964. Their letters are collected in the now out of print, *Encounter: Thomas Merton and D.T. Suzuki*, ed. Robert E. Daggy (Monterey, KY: Larkspur Press, 1988). Merton's side of the correspondence is included in *The Hidden Ground of Love* (pp. 560–71).

10. See Suzuki's *Mysticism: Christian and Buddhist* (New York: Routledge, 1957), chaps. 1 and 3, "Meister Eckhart and Buddhism," and "'A Little Point' and Satori."

was the last thing he wrote within 24 hours of his death. He was writing this little introduction, and he said, "Zen is this, and Zen is this"; and he said, "Finally, I would like to make one last statement in this Preface, and that is, if you want to know what Zen is, you should understand what Meister Eckhart meant when he wrote, 'Christ is born in my heart at every moment.'"

The Christian version of this is Eckhart's constant birth of God in us.[11] The procession of the Son in the depths of our Being, that is what this is. This is our true identity. The Son coming forth from the Father in us. This is Reality. This is Ultimate Identity. And this is not something that can be known objectively. It is not something that you stand back and look at, because as the Hindus would say, "It is beyond the knower, and the known, and the knowing." It is just simply straight consciousness. It's not consciousness *of*, it is just pure consciousness. It's not *my* consciousness, it's *His* consciousness, because it's *in Him* that I am real—in His awareness of me and Him, which is beyond any grasp of any experience of mine. There, I am truly real. That is basically what they are saying.

This is not something that one stands back and experiences; yet it can become a kind of consciousness. That is the whole thing, to develop this consciousness. One who has developed this consciousness is, in terms of Hinduism, a liberated person [*jivanmukta*]. He's liberated, he's illuminated. He knows, he is a knower.

The purpose, then, of this whole Hindu thing, is what they call *darshan*. *Darshan* is what corresponds to our notion of "philosophy," only it isn't anything like philosophy. Philosophy is love of wisdom, and *darshan* means "direct seeing," immediate vision; not through the medium of any idea or even experience. Not vision *of*, just direct vision. There's a Zen saying—there's a whole story attached to it—but it finally ends up with this: "The true seeing is where there is no seeing." That is what this is: "The true seeing is where there is nothing to be seen, there is only seeing." Sayings like this are very strange, because they can't be translated too easily into our terms, because we always think in terms of subject and

---

11. E.g., Eckhart's "Sermon 101"; for a study, see Bernard McGinn, *The Mystical Thought of Meister Eckhart: The Man from Whom God Hid Nothing*, chap. 4, "The Preacher in Action: Eckhart on the Eternal Birth" (pp. 53–70).

object, and what a statement like this means, is not subject and object; it's beyond that. But it is very simple, too.

Therefore, the whole aim of discipline for a Hindu is to take off, one after the other, these five "garments," so that one remains in the utter nakedness of direct seeing. That is the purpose of yoga. That's the Hindu concept of consciousness, and the fruition of this is called *samadhi*, which means to say it's this pure consciousness. It's not ecstasy; that's not a good translation of it. It's sometimes translated "ecstasy," or "contemplation," but it just means *pure seeing*.[12]

Yoga, incidentally, comes from the same root as *yuj*; it means "union." Yoga is simply getting rid of all division so that there's no longer anything else between the self and God, because they are one. This is not a question of an idea, which one gets out of a book and then practices in order to become convinced of it. The Ignatian type of meditation, for example, gives you a package, and then says, "Grab on to this, until you're convinced." Then this conviction becomes a glossy experience, and this is very bad.[13] It's all right if you're going to do some simple practical things. For example, in something like the practice of a virtue, this might work, but it ultimately comes to the old business of, "Act humble, and you'll be humble," and that doesn't necessarily work. There is a certain approach; for example, you give a person an idea of what a humble man looks like, and you tell him, "Go be like that, act humble"; that is to say, put on a humble act. Even if it isn't real, keep on doing it until maybe you experience it. But this is very bad. That's what they used to do at a certain point

---

12. Comparativist Mircea Eliade perhaps further confused the issue by translating *samadhi* as "enstasy" in his influential book, *Yoga: Immortality and Freedom* (Princeton: Princeton University Press, 1958), attempting to locate the experience of *samadhi* internally ("being within") vs. "standing outside" of one's self in "ecstasy." To Merton's point, in *samadhi* one is neither "inside" (enstasy), nor "outside" (ecstasy), as there is no referential "self" to stand either in- or outside of.

13. Merton's comments regarding Ignatius of Loyola's (1491–1556) *Spiritual Exercises* are based upon a pre-Vatican II rigidity in spiritual pedagogy of which Merton is critiquing. For a more balanced approach, see Merton's *Introduction to Christian Mysticism*, 217–19. The *Exercises* have received much renewed scholarly and pastoral attention in the later part of the twentieth and twenty-first centuries. For a translation with introduction, see George Ganss, SJ, ed., *Ignatius of Loyola: Spiritual Exercises and Selected Works* (New York: Paulist Press, 1991).

in the religious life: they would train people like that. If you go around with your eyes down all the time, you'll become humble.

At the end of the road is what [yogis] call a *jivanmukta*,[14] a free soul, who has reached realization. When I prepped [for these conferences], one of the best things I could do would be to read statements from this little book that I've been using for meditation. Read some of the statements in which this *jivanmukta* is described. What it really amounts to is like Zen. It ends up as a person who lives an entirely normal life. He's a completely ordinary person. That's the real thing about it. Zen ends up with that, too—a person who is not at all extraordinary; he's not one of these fellows that's buried in the sand with his hands sticking out, which is what you sometimes see in India. Ed Rice, who used to be editor of *Jubilee*, has gone all over, taking pictures. He sent me a terrific picture he took of a pile of sand and a couple of heads sticking out, buried there, and then nearby, a receptacle in which people put coins. This is a very ancient thing in India. This is pre-yoga, in a sense. This is a very old custom of people who practice these things, are recognized in society, and they accept it.

Here's one of these descriptions, what this person [*jivanmukta*] is like, "Sometimes he's like a fool; sometimes he's like a sage. Sometimes possessed of royal splendor; sometimes wandering about. Sometimes behaving like a motionless python; sometimes wearing a benign expression. Sometimes honored; sometimes insulted. Sometimes completely ignored; thus lives a free soul, ever happy in the knowledge of *Brahman*."[15] You get all these beautiful statements.

What one has to remember with all these rather complicated and sophisticated things, is that a man who attains this realization is not at all removed from ordinary life, but he's in full possession of ordinary life. So that what happens after [attaining liberation], his bodily life is perfectly normal and real. His *prana* life—he breathes right all the time, and his mind is perfectly clear, because it's not bothered with a lot of useless judging. His "I" consciousness is in its right place. He's not denying that he has an ordinary everyday ego, but he knows what it is. In other words, he doesn't throw each one of these things away, but each one of these things is transfigured, so that he becomes a complete person.

14. Translated from the Sanskrit as "liberated while living."
15. Nikhilananda, *Hinduism,* 66.

Because he does not place himself in any single one of them, he's beyond all of them. He is his true self, because that's the only self that one can be. Then all these other things become instruments. There's an expression that some mystical people, like Elizabeth of the Trinity,[16] become an extra incarnation, so to speak. The Christian gives Christ an opportunity to be incarnated again, in this particular body. But what we become is a kind of incarnation—by grace, of course; not by hypostatic union.

It gives us some really good ideas about what the monastic life is about. This is what it's really about—to really develop this. It's a full-time job, and that's what we have to get down to. That's what renewal means for us. The best thing is to be aware of this.

One thing I would suggest is perhaps somebody like Raimon Panikkar ought to be getting around more. Do you know who he is? He's a Hindu philosopher. You've heard of him, haven't you? He is a Hindu who is also a Catholic priest and he's teaching at Harvard Divinity School now. He's bound to be on the [Pacific] Coast sometime or another; he'd probably love to come see the place [Redwoods Monastery].[17] I haven't met him, but I know he is a very interesting person, and he's in touch with all of this that's going on. Then there's a monk at Mount Saviour—the one that's at Columbia and going to the Zen Center in New York—Br. David [Steindl-Rast], who's a real sharp, good man.[18]

He gave Panikkar the idea, and Panikkar gave it to Dom Leclercq, and it got around to me that way, and then David came to see me and we talked about it. [Br. David] has the idea of forming a study center for monks of

16. Elizabeth of the Trinity (1880–1906), French Discalced Carmelite nun, author, and mystic, canonized by Pope Francis in 2016.

17. Raimon (Raimundo) Panikkar (1918–2010), Spanish Catholic priest and pioneer of interreligious dialogue. In 1966, Panikkar became a visiting professor at Harvard Divinity School, and in 1972, made his way to the Pacific Coast as a professor of religious studies at the University of California, Santa Barbara, where he taught for many years. One of his best-known works remains, *The Unknown Christ of Hinduism: Towards an Ecumenical Christophany* (London: Darton, Longman & Todd, 1964). See also Thomas Cattoi, "*Theoria Physike* and the *Brahma-Sutra*: The Rediscovery of the Cosmotheandric Dimension in the Work of Thomas Merton and Raimon Panikkar," in *Merton and Hinduism*, 180–96.

18. David Steindl-Rast, OSB (b. 1926), Benedictine monk of Mount Saviour Monastery in Elmira, New York, has taught extensively and internationally in the areas of contemplative spirituality and interreligious dialogue, and was a formative presence in both the House of Prayer movement and early Zen-Christian dialogue, as well as at the Esalen Institute in Big Sur, California. Brother David attended the October 1968 conferences held at Redwoods.

different traditions. There would be a little community with a couple of Hindus, a couple of Buddhists, a couple of Christians—all monks. That may or may not have possibilities, but definitely whatever does happen, we should really be in contact.

One of the things that I've always wanted to do, would be to get Nhat Hanh, my Buddhist friend, to come to our place and give some talks on Buddhist psychology. It's rather difficult, though; it's so complicated. When you really get into the academic presentation of this stuff, it's just like Scholastic philosophy, and sometimes worse. There's a real Indian Scholasticism—Shankaracharya,[19] for example—Vedantic Scholasticism is extremely tough. But still, there's a great deal in this.

How about any questions? We could turn [the recording] off here, and then have questions from now on, and then go on with some more tomorrow.

Fr. Roger: I have a book written by a Benedictine who went to India—Denys Rutledge.[20]

What do you think of that?

He seems to me to be prejudiced.

I think so, too. He's very English [laughter]. I don't think he gives them a fair break. He's extremely critical. There's one part that the Hindus are shocked at. He was going through India, and he was going to find out if these yogis—he wasn't interested in the essential thing; he was interested in something quite accidental. There is a side-product in yoga, the *siddhis*. These are the miraculous powers; for example, making yourself invisible. This is supposed to be one of the side effects of Patanjali's *raja yoga*.[21] There's a little section about how you make yourself invisible.

---

19. Eighth-century Indian philosopher who was enormously influential in the development of Advaita Vedanta.

20. Dom Denys Rutledge, OSB (1906–1997), Scottish monk who spent three years at a Benedictine foundation near Pune, India. Merton wrote the Preface for *In Search of a Yogi* (New York: Farrar, Straus, 1963) at the request of his publisher, Robert Giroux (see *Merton and Hinduism*, 270–76).

21. See Chapter III of Patanjali's *Yoga Sutra* on the *siddhis*, often translated as "miraculous powers." Invisibility is mentioned in III.21 as a result of intense concentration, or *samyama* (Edwin Bryant, *The Yoga Sutras of Patanjali* [New York: North Point Press, 2009], 347). For Merton's reading notes on the *Yoga Sutra*, see *Merton and Hinduism*, 321–33.

It's got nothing to do with the essence of the thing. Sometimes you have yogis who have practiced this, and done these things [*siddhis*]. Now this fellow [Rutledge] wanted to go around through India, and find out if any of these yogis actually had these miraculous powers, and I guess he didn't find any. He did admit that he found one or two real good souls. The people that were really, deeply developed. Then there's one part where he finds these two real good fellows. They're hermits up in the Himalayan mountains somewhere. He attends their prayer rite, and comes out saying it was diabolical, which is just absurd.

[*Inaudible comment*]

I think that the only real solution to the question of, "What is a person?" is going to have to be worked out in dialogue with Asian people. Buddhism is supposed to be strictly anti-personal, but it isn't. There's the Buddhist philosophy, for example, of Kitaro Nishida,[22] who's now dead, but one of the big Buddhist philosophers in Japan. He ends up talking in terms of a personal God. But by personal God, he also means the Buddhist idea of "Void." So, for him, Void is personal, and this is very important, because then the idea of "Void" gets taken out of this whole crazy context that we've got it in.

I have no way of saying it or stating it, but I believe that the root of our personality is Christ.[23] That the true personality is not just a psychological thing, but that our true personality is in God. How to prove it, I don't know, because "the person" is not nature. That's one of the things about it. If you go at it in the Thomist point of view, and you say, "The person is just an individual"—that's not it. It's got nothing to do with it. Of course, I'm not that kind of a professional; I can't handle that kind of thing. I don't get in to the learned journals making statements like that—but it is a real problem. I think a Christian, or anybody, is truly a person when he does what these people [i.e., yogis] have done. To find ourselves in God is to be true persons, and we are persons to the extent that we are free with the freedom of the Sons of God. Of course, personality is tied up with the order of grace. I don't know what you're going to do about that. It's a gift, though. It's certainly in the order of "gift."

---

22. Kitarō Nishida (1870–1945), Japanese founder of the "Kyoto School" of philosophy. See Merton's essay "Nishida: A Zen Philosopher," in *Zen and the Birds of Appetite*, 67–70.
23. Merton bangs on the table with each word to emphasize his point.

Comment: I'm not a theologian.

Neither am I [laughs].

What is grace? God communicates Himself to man?

I think that's the thing: God communicates Himself to every man in that man's personality. So, with everybody, there is a grace of personality, which is given to him—and that this is the real heart.

Fr. Roger: You would call it a grace?

Well, this is a poetic use of the word "grace."

Mother Myriam: Tom . . . [laughter from Fr. Roger, who repeats, "Tom"]

Well, that's the way. That designates the person [laughter], which "Father Louis" doesn't. "Father Louis" designates a role, and "Tom" designates the person.

Mother Myriam: To me, what helps to grasp experientially that we are more than our empirical self, is to know that this empirical "I" blinds us every second.

Yes, that's great. That's a very Buddhist notion. That is really the Buddhist idea, that we are constantly changing. The "I" is not permanent. We work to make it permanent, all down the line. We are constantly rearranging this identity and keeping it—this is not Hindu, now, this is Buddhist— this is absolutely the key to the whole Buddhist thing, and on this, I'm absolutely in agreement with them. This is what they call *avidya*. This is the basic ignorance—maintaining, by sheer willful effort—and constantly rearranging the conception of a solid identity, which is permanent, when it isn't. It's something we construct.

What makes us so vulnerable, is that we won't let go of this. Our Lord said, "He that will save his life, would lose it."[24] We have reached the point where the Gospel and Buddhism [meet].

---

24. Matthew 16:25.

This again is very important in the kind of consciousness we should develop in our life. We have to be absolutely free from the necessity of maintaining a fictitious personality. It's ingrained in us. It's original sin. That's what St. Bernard would say, "What would be the effect of duplicity?" Preferring a role, which is relatively simple, and that which we can stand back from, and which we can manage and manipulate—and to prefer that [rather than] to be vulnerable and naked—in the sense of vulnerable. Completely open to unpredictable experience. It's very easy to talk about this, but it certainly isn't easy to do.

Comment: I was just going to ask you [laughter].

Don't get around with that [laughter]. I think that probably the way to do it, would be to get out on that point out there [on the coast], and [get] in a hut, and just live there.

Mother Myriam: It would be a sin not to go.

Oh, absolutely. It would be crazy not to go. The beauty of that is that it is a situation in which everything is portrayed for you. The nakedness and aloneness of the person is just spread right out there, because there's nobody around; you've got this windswept hillside, and this empty beach. It's like looking at a picture; it just tells you: *this is what it is*. This is the human condition. In our kind of life, you have a basic need to experience the nakedness of the human condition. If we never do that, we can't be happy, and our happiness depends on occasionally doing this: really experiencing the complete emptiness and nakedness of the human being.

Comment: Is that what it means to live the life of the hermit?

Yes. Normally, in the hermit life, it is a question of being completely dependent directly on God. It's this idea of direct nakedness. It's the business of *no veils*. Solitude is a very funny thing, and we'll talk tomorrow about this. There is in Hindu tradition something beyond just a solitary life in one place. The ultimate [life] is the wandering life. The begging—

Mother Myriam: I had to hear that, I never read it. I think, when I am 65, if I really want to be in the monastic vocation, perhaps I should go and just be—when you go to San Francisco, or a big city, and you see those lonely old people, sitting in the parks, so terribly lonely, and I thought this would be really the ultimate human condition, in God, and finish your life simply. I don't know . . .

Neither do I, but it is a question. The question should arise. That is the point, that this whole question of stability with us has become a complete fetish.

Mother Myriam: Yes. I agree with that.

Comment: The thing is, if you pull all these veils away—perhaps this is not necessarily what the Hindus are getting at—but if you pull all these veils away, that means you can function.

Yes. They are no longer an obstruction.

Then you're free to go into them and look at them, and play with them.

Mother Myriam: And they become a part of you, and are reconciled with your real self, so that instead of being obstacles, they become channels of Being and communication.

And they become fully real, and then they do become you, in a sense. You're no longer identified with them; you use them freely. This is like wearing clothes; you just wear your clothes, and your clothes express you. A person who knows how to dress, wears clothes that suit her and express—

Mother Myriam: Well about that, I often wonder, because to me, just as you say, a dress expresses so much personality. This was one of my deepest renunciations in coming to the monastery, in a way.

What happens to people in the world, especially to women, is that they work it the other way around, too. They create for themselves an identity by dressing in certain ways. You have to get free from that. Your clothes have to express you, but that doesn't mean any kind of a studied thing at all. They just express you, that's all. Nothing has to be done about it. All these things are simply things that fit, that's all. They're your clothes. If they are on somebody else, they don't fit.

Comment: My whole thing with clothing is that, if the way you have to dress gets to a point that it's taking you away from [simply] being, then sure, it's like anything else.

You should never have to think about clothes.

It's in the middle of winter and you have to wear summer clothes, because that's the Rule. I mean, it's absurd.

It's usually the other way around. It's the middle of summer, and you have to wear winter clothes. It used to be some fun sleeping with all your habit on at Gethsemani, in the middle of the summer.

If a mini-skirt is going to take a Sister away from Christ, then she probably wasn't in Christ too much to begin with.

If you want to continue talking about this, and you've got further questions, we could go on after supper. I haven't anything more prepared for tonight.

There is a request by one of the Sisters for additional discussion on solitude

We could have a completely informal session on solitude after supper, then. Is that all right? One thing I could say about what I've got at Gethsemani—it's not real solitude, what I have there. I've been living in a house by myself. It's so crowded there. There are people around all the time. Good Friday evening—and this isn't bad; it's alright—I'm in bed already. And then bang, bang, bang on the door, and there's some kid: "I've come 1600 miles and I want to see you." Fine, ok. I put some clothes on, go sit down on the porch with him. He didn't have a darn thing to say; he just wanted to see me.

That's alright; it's fine. You've got to be ready for something like that; but you're always involved with something, and then people know you're there. For example, I'll be on my way home, and I'll see a car there, so I'll hide in the bushes—especially when it turns out to be one of the local clergy. There's a nice young Zen guy in Louisville. I'm glad to have someone like that come out. He plays in a jazz band; he's got a little combo. He plays in a nightclub, and he is a very nice fellow. He's got a little Zen temple going in his apartment in Louisville; a little Zen group there. He's a lot of fun. I like him. He and his Zen friends come out once in a while.[25] That's a different matter. But on the other hand, I think it's just not remote enough there. It's 50 miles from a big city, and the monastery is always full of people on retreat. So, that's a problem; that's not real solitude.

Comment: We had no idea. How come it is so easy to reach you?

It's all wide open. All they've got to do is know where [the hermitage] is. Most [visitors] don't know where it is, but sometimes people tell them.

Is it far from the monastery?

It's about a 10-minute walk. Oh, you remember, you saw it.

Mother Myriam: That's the cinder blocks?

Yes, the little house. It's just right up the hill [from the monastery]. Somebody comes along with apocalyptic messages [laughter], "I have a mission for you. The Lord says . . . " Who says? Solitude is getting to be more and more hard to find. Real solitude. Here, you've got it now, but what will it be like 10 years from now? Anything can happen. This is a very quiet road now, but I mean—

Comment: The population [near Redwoods] is growing very rapidly.

Mother Myriam: But there are no jobs.

Response: Well, you can have people with money who are moving.

That's what you're going to get.

---

25. This reference is to Merton's friend Richard Sisto.

A discussion ensues regarding the disappearance of wilderness places in the U.S. and the rapid development of urban and suburban centers.

The East is finished. I mean, maybe some parts of West Virginia, but that's the end. There's no hope for any real solitude in the East. Maybe Northern Canada is the best.

Mother Myriam: The solitude of Mendocino County—

Well, this is certainly one of the best. That beach [at Needle Rock] is one of the best things that I've seen. That's one of the best things in the country.

If we assume that there is validity to the real life of complete flight from cities, then one has to find a real solitude. I was saying yesterday that it's a good formula to live near the monastery. But at the same time, it's not very different from being in a monastery. The formula that we've got there is okay, it's fine. It is certainly an improvement over being in the community, as far as time for prayer goes, but you might as well be in the community. But the thing of solitude is really just being alone with God.

Comment: But this becomes quite a problem if you have to support yourself.

A discussion then ensues regarding both the practicalities and best practices of supporting oneself in the monastic life.

What should I say about solitude? What aspect do you want to talk about? The way it's working out with me and the hermit thing—it's not simple. When you want this thing, you say, "This is it." And I've always wanted it very much, and I still want it, and I know it's what I want. But it's not easy to do. It's quite complicated, actually. You can have a great desire for solitude and a certain aptitude for solitude, but you're always tripping up. It's very subtle. Community is much simpler. Community life is much easier. It's not always more pleasant—it's certainly more fun in solitude, you [can] do what you want—but you suddenly find out that you're not so sure that you know what you want. You might do things that you think you wanted to do, and go into it quite deeply, and suddenly find it's just wrong. It's just stupid. But of course, that's one of the good things about it.

Comment: Did you find out?

Yes, and one of things that I found out, is that I don't want to read as much as I thought. The hermitage is full of books; I've got books, and I can't read them. When I first got in there, I read piles of stuff: you wake up at, say, three o'clock in the morning, and you have your Office. I anticipate the Night Office, because I like to say that outside, walking up and down. Then I say Lauds when I get up, and then I have about an hour of meditation or 45 minutes. Then I make breakfast, which is coffee and bread, and if I've got some eggs, I'll fry an egg, and then I sit down. I used to study for four hours and really cover quite a lot of ground.

I read, first one book, and then another. I'd work hard for four hours, and get quite a lot done. And then I found that I [would] still read for about four hours, [but] I didn't get anything done. It's funny. I mean, you just don't do anything. Something happens to you—you block yourself; you can't do it. I'll read a sentence, and I don't think. I read a sentence and all of a sudden, I find I'm in the woods, walking around in the dark.

Mother Myriam: You mean that you need diversion from your books?

Well, that's very good. Normally, I used to do quite a lot of manual work at about eight o'clock. I'd finish a lot of study, then I'd do manual work; but of course, I've had a back operation. I have to go easy on the wood chopping, which is what I like to do. So now, I don't do more than necessary of that, but I enjoy it. I mean the manual work is fine. I cut brush and trim trees. Burn brush, and keep the thing clear around the house. That's a great help, but I can't do too much of it. I just clean the house out, and that's another drag, keeping a place. *Ugh* [laughter]. I wouldn't dare show the inside of that house to any woman [laughter]. It's like a stable, really. It's terrible. Papers all over the place, and the Venetian blinds—before I go back, I want to find out how you clean Venetian blinds, because I just can't do anything with them. Dust this thick.

Merton then receives instructions from various members of the community on how to best clean his blinds ("Just close them and run over it with a brush").

The big problem for me is keeping the thing clean, and then cooking. What I do for supper is usually either a can of soup or a can of beans [laughter]. A whole can of beans isn't really easy to eat [laughter]. These are the problems. You do a lot of silly things. This comes under the heading of "public confession": one night, I'm sitting up there and I'm ready to go to bed. In come three or four friends of mine, and they say, "Come on, let's go to Louisville." I went to Louisville [laughter].

Comment: That'd be nice.

I know, but it's a real mistake, because then the whole next day is ruined. You get back, and you sleep late, and then your whole schedule is out of whack. Then you don't get anything accomplished, and you find out that you didn't want to go to Louisville, that's the main thing. Certainly, one of the things I do find is that ordinary social life is terrible. Just the ordinary thing of having to talk to—nice people—but, I couldn't live if I had to go through that every day. If I had to go to parties, and go out to dinner with people, it would be just intolerable. One of our other men who left to be a hermit, he went to the Bahama Islands. Have you heard of him?

Comment: Yes.

He was within a stone's throw of one of the biggest casinos on the Bahama Islands. He became friends with all these movie stars, and he was having a time. What did you hear? [laughter] Were you there? [laughter] He sees all of that wasn't working, and he took off from there. I think he went to Europe.

It really is a difficult thing. You can do it, if you want to be very rigid. That would be easy, but I'm not that way. It wouldn't be right for me to do it that way, because it's not myself. But then, on the other hand, if you spontaneously just do things, you find you get—*phoof* [makes an exclaimed, overwhelmed noise]. So, from that point of view, you realize that community life is a great [blessing].

It's not at all simple. It's fine. It's beautiful—if something doesn't happen to upset the thing. It's nice when you have an ordinary day, and you can do your regular schedule, but then you get sick and that's a problem. It's not bad, but it's rough. You wonder, "Should I go down to the monastery, or should I stay here." On the whole, I think I've learned much more there than I've learned in community. You're the only one that's living the life. In community, everybody's going along, and you can be automatic. In solitude, you're up against it, and either you're living or you're not. That's the real problem.

What is best about it, is just simply doing nothing. The real thing in the hermit life is to do nothing. I wish I could do nothing better. I work too much. Then of course, with me, I have a terrible problem with letters. It's a big problem. I'm getting more and more, so I don't answer them at all, but still, you have to answer some. Again, public confession: I think I'd be a lot better off if I just dropped everything and just lived. If I could just be completely alone and just live, and do a minimum of writing work. I have to do some of that; that keeps me sane, really. The writing. If I didn't do that, I think I'd really be [lost], because I can see where you can go completely nuts [in solitude]. You're much more emotional. Your emotional life is dynamite. You cry a lot. Things hit you very hard. Things you read. I've had times there where something—really tragic things—I'll hear some news, and you're just simply shattered for about three hours, because things hit you very hard. I can see where people could be having visions and things like that. Suppose a person starts hallucinating up there, and doesn't realize that you could really go off. I think I've got a pretty hard head, but you have to have a certain amount of—

Fr. Roger: Consciousness.

Yes. Consciousness. The way I feel about solitude now is, I just don't think I've really begun it yet. I think it's just been sort of *half*. What I really think I should do, would be to have much more complete solitude, and then come out once in a while to something like this. But I'd then go back [to solitude] for something like two months.

Mother Myriam: Yes. That's what I was going to ask you.

Comment: Is it all right if I talk about myself for a minute?

Yes.

I came to the woods to be alone, because I have had 25 years of city life. And I find myself getting more involved with people than I had thought. I mean, not just this community; I'm not that involved in the community, but all these people from the outside.

Well, perhaps more at your age. I'm 53. Perhaps at your stage of the game, that's what you need to be [doing].

I don't know. I'll talk to people. I saw this girl today for two hours, and I said, "Okay, it's time to go back." And immediately, I just went out, to be alone. That was just enough.

Mother Myriam: There is a real difficulty [I have], with people outside, not to extend myself beyond my possibility. Because, if you have a minimum of empathy for people, it's extremely difficult to be yourself.

That's why, for a solitary life, there has to be a real separation somewhere that cuts off the problem before it starts. Because when you're caught, you're caught. It's too late. And the problem always arises when it's too late to do anything about it. That's the way it is with me. When you realize it's a problem, it has already gone too far.

That's why I've never allowed the road to be put in [to the hermitage], but they can drive [up]. There's a field, and if it's dry, they can drive up through the field. There's supposed to be a gate at the road; it's supposed to be locked all the time. But some of the monks will come through, and they won't lock it; they'll just leave it open, and then somebody's going to drive in. That's a real problem.

That's why, in the traditional solitary life, they had a place really difficult to access. Then you can figure, if somebody does get through to you, it's God's will. That's what these characters would do. There's a beautiful prayer in a Syrian liturgy for the Blessing of a Hermit.[26] There's a long blessing, and then finally at the end it says, "And at this point, the hermit pulls up his rope to his

26. Merton references this story in his final novitiate conference before entering the hermitage full-time in August 1965; published as "A Life Free from Care" (*Cistercian Studies Quarterly* 5.3: 217–26).

cave." He's in a cave halfway up a cliff, and he pulls up his rope, and there's no more access [laughter]. It has to be something like that, somewhere.

You have to really take care of yourself. The one reason why I need to stay where I am as far as getting things goes [is], because if I run out, if I find I haven't got a loaf of bread, for example, at bedtime, I just go down to the bakery and get one.

Comment: Do you have a small refrigerator?

Yes. All those things; there's no problem. And the heat is alright. The material side is okay. The only thing, if you will forgive the reference, is outdoor plumbing, complete with an outhouse that the snakes like to get into [laughter]. You go in there and you have to be very careful to go over the whole thing with a flashlight at night, because you don't know what's in there [laughter]. That's pretty bad. It's worse in winter when it gets zero weather, it's very unpleasant. But they're putting in inside [plumbing] for me now. We're getting civilized. There are a lot of snakes, but they're not bad.

Comment: Big ones?

Big ones. Yeah, six feet. They get big, but they're good because they eat the mice and the rats.

Comment: They're not poisonous?

They're not poisonous, and a king snake will kill poisonous snakes. So, I never kill them. I never fuss with them. It's good to have them because I know as long as they're there, the copperheads won't be there. So that's good [laughter].

Mother Myriam: It would seem [to me] that a certain time of your life you could do that. But for a whole life, I wonder.

Yes. I think that would be a very special kind of vocation. What I feel about myself—I don't think that what I want to do is just simply to disappear for the rest of my life. But I would like to have real solitude for certain periods, and then to be able to do other things for another time. To operate from solitude as from a good base. What I would really like to do would be to go, say, three months at a time, absolutely cut-off, and then come out to here and maybe make a circuit to two or three different places. And then go on back for another three months and do some writing.

Comment: What about the Orders mainly just for hermits?

A long discussion then ensues regarding the state of the Carthusian and Camaldolese Orders both in the U.S. and in Europe. The discussion concludes with Merton's comment:

I think that the only real hope for any kind of solitude is probably in connection with a renewed monasticism.

Mother Myriam: I think so, too. I see that even for women, here, as a part of the community that could be either temporary or [more permanent].

Sure, and I think one of the things you will find are a few genuine hermit vocations in other Orders, but I think they're very rare.

Merton then mentions some correspondence he has had with a Carmelite foundation in New Hampshire.

They had sent me their program [brochure] that they have. I saw the quotes from John of the Cross and St. Teresa and well, they've challenged me on something that I had said on a tape, that it was not a good idea to try to be continually concentrated on a conscious idea of God. They said, "Well, what do you mean? Isn't our life a life of continual prayer?" And we had some correspondence on that, because I just don't believe that it's the right interpretation of a life of continual prayer to think that you're constantly thinking about God. Because, as I said, God is not an object, and if you're constantly hung up on an idea of God, it's not an immediate, direct knowledge at all.[27]

---

27. See Merton's correspondence with Carmelite priest William McNamara (*School of Charity*, 281–82, 387).

It's self-defeating, because you're thinking about an idea. Real contact with God is not through ideas. The whole point of our kind of contemplative life is to deal with God without the medium of ideas. To learn how to be constantly, in a completely simple, direct union with God that does not involve thinking. I tried to explain [this to them], and I think they agreed with that when we were through. But you don't think about God, or don't think of an idea of God all the time. In fact, the further you go along—Eckhart made the scandalous statement which has to be properly understood, and I think people who have had some experience with the contemplative life can understand it—but Eckhart said that, "You have to be so poor that you do not have a God."[28]

This is understandable in the context of this Hindu thing where God is so close that you do not "have" a God. You cannot place Him in an object relationship. You can't stand back and look at Him. He is so close that you simply live, and He is your life, and you don't see it. I think that is a terribly important thing. In spite of John of the Cross, the Carmelites have this temptation to be too consciously hung up on their kind of meditation. They're not free at all. That's the one thing that John of the Cross did have, was this complete freedom to not be hung up on a kind of conceptual meditation. He said, "Do not deliberately meditate." Meditation is a sort of non-meditation: "To enter upon the way is to leave the way." Or, you can put it the other way around: "To leave the way is to enter the way." It's not to have "a way."

Tomorrow, we can take some of the *Ashtavakra Gita*, which is one of these Hindu texts.[29] I had never known it before. It has some real good stuff in it just about this. He says contemplation is for beginners. The thing is to be beyond contemplation and beyond meditation; beyond all of those things. I think it's a good idea to go through them to get beyond. The problem is if you try to get beyond without going through it, then there's a lack. Let me see if I can—what time is it?

---

28. See, e.g., Eckhart's "Sermon 52" (in Bernard McGinn, *Essential Writings of Christian Mysticism* [New York: Random House, 2006], 438–43).

29. The *Ashtavakra Gita* is a ninth or fourteenth-century Indian text highly influenced by Advaita Vedanta philosophy. Merton was reading it in translation throughout 1968 (Hari Prasad Shastri, trans. *Ashtavakra Gita* [London: Shanti Sadan, 1961]); see *Merton and Hinduism*, xviii, xlii, 382–84.

Fr. Roger: It's twenty to eight.

Well, let's just open this up at random; I've marked one or two [passages]: "Neither do I recognize the state of contemplation or the state of knowledge. The state of bondage and of liberation are one." This is where they eventually end up: when a person has reached liberation, he accepts bondage, because he knows it isn't there [i.e., "bondage" no longer has a sense of substance or permanence]. There is no longer a division between [liberation] and a bondage that you've gone beyond. It's a question of realizing that bondage and liberation are the same thing. This is a deep idea, because what we always do—we're fine on the beginning stages. In the beginning, there has to be a division. There has to be a seeker, as well as something that he is seeking. But there comes a time when that division is no longer there.

Perhaps one of the things about the hermit life is that you find what you're looking for very soon, but you don't dare admit it. I think that is probably one of the great problems, because the whole thing is a complete gift. A person could be there and God could give Himself completely to a person who feels himself completely unworthy, and not understand that that's the proposition. That's the way it is: the whole idea of the hermit life is not that you start on it and you think about finding ways of becoming worthy over a course of 40 or 50 years. Then, finally, with a cry of triumph, you gain your objective.

It's quite possible that you begin and you get everything immediately, but you don't realize it. I think that probably is the source of the real problems that come up; because they're not real problems.

I've never felt this way at all in community life. But I feel very often [as a hermit] that I do something that has no consequence whatsoever—it's neither good, nor bad, nor anything—but I get the feeling of tremendous infidelity. Quite possibly, what the infidelity consists in, is not recognizing that God is there. That I'm fooling around with some other thing that I think is worth doing. In another form of life, it is possible to do this, but in the solitary life, it's not allowed, and you get that feeling. I would say that this is what a "Rule" means for hermits.

It's an incomprehensible Rule, in which, when you are doing the thing that you're not supposed to do, you know it, but you don't know why. You can't tell why. I suppose quite possibly, you have to struggle with that for a long time until you suddenly find out, because there's no logical reason for it. It's usually not something bad, or even useless; it may be something quite useful.

It's not a question of irrational guilt. It's a genuine guilt. It's not psychological, obsessive guilt. It's a sense of real wrong. It's a personal thing. For example, suppose I've spent a day doing a certain job, and all of a sudden, at the end of the day, I'll say, "This was a complete waste of time. It was stupid. It's silly to do this." I feel that I should have done nothing. It's not that I should have meditated or spent time in contemplation; I should have kept the day empty. To be concrete, what I should have done would have been to go for a walk in the woods rather than doing this thing. That's the way it usually comes up. It's coming up more and more with me that if I work during the day, or if I write too many letters—which I think I have to do—I will realize very clearly that I should not have done this. I should have just left the afternoon completely open: not to have meditated, just simply left it open and gone out into the woods. I think that it could possibly be that it's a way of telling myself I would have had more fun in the woods. I don't know.

Comment: Maybe because you realize that you're totally free.

Well, I'm not being faithful to the freedom that I've got.

That's scary, when you realize that you're totally free. You can write your letters and go for the walk in the woods.

Maybe I'm writing the letters from the wrong motive?

Sometimes, things like that happen to me, so it's like coming back and looking at yourself—

Well, it just hits you.

It's kind of like a mind snap.

Yes, that's right. All of a sudden it hits you that you're being unfaithful to something, or that you don't have to do it that way [so] stop. Usually, it's that I'm not being free. It'll be something like, "You tell yourself, 'You ought to be free'—go ahead and be free." That's the thing, but you don't know.

How long have you been committed to this [solitude]?

Well, I've been sleeping out there. I date the complete [living as a hermit] from sleeping there. It will be four years this fall. Before that I was half-day there. The place was built in 1960. Even before that, I was spending at least the afternoon in the woods for a long time, back in the '50s. So, I've been out with at least a half a day of solitude for almost 12 years. Full-time about four, although I still had to go down to the novitiate for a little bit. And then completely full-time with no job, going on three years. But you don't really get into it the first year. The first year is just the introduction. A lot of the first year is just wasted with love, you know, just "flap" going on.

It's useless—thinking or explaining things to yourself. One of the first things, it was really a shock. I moved in, I've been in about three days and I was all steamed up, working like mad; really doing manual work. This was before the operation. I was out cutting brush like mad and I dug right into a hornets' nest. Oh, did I get it. They were all over me. I ran back into the house, and some of them followed me into the house. If you've ever been chased by mad hornets, well, when they're mad, they give off this smell—there's a burning smell that they've got—and these sons of guns, they were mad at me for days. They didn't come after me, but there were some patrolling that house for several days afterwards. Every time I came out, they were there. What happened was, the ones that were real mad were biting me, and they were leaving this smell on me. So, I was marked by that particular nest. They knew that I was a marked man [laughter]. What I finally did was I snuck up on their nest in the middle of the night and I had to spray it; I had to knock it out. But that was a real unpleasant experience, to feel that you're in the woods with these very hostile creatures [that] don't like you [laughter].

You do have to contend with natural forces. We had this blizzard, and four big pine trees came down all around my place with the weight of the snow. There were two right over the house. I slept with my shoes on that night. I didn't know if I'd have to get up and get out, because they were hanging right over the building. That's just something that you contend with.

But the real problem is this question of evading freedom by getting into unnecessary routines and doing unnecessary work, and getting involved in unnecessary projects because we don't dare be idle. We're afraid of idleness. There's this compulsion to produce something—especially with us.[30]

There is also the question of fidelity [to a Rule]. There's no Rule, and there's no real logic. It's a completely personal thing. You don't know yourself that well, and you just do things that you find out the hard way that they shouldn't be done.

Fr. Roger: It's not for everybody.

No, but anybody who does it is going to have the same situation, unless they do it in what I think is the wrong way. Namely, have somebody predetermine the whole thing.

Mother Myriam: A rigid structure.

Yes, and just do it that way and then no other way. I think that would be just wrong; unless a person absolutely had to do it. Oh, it's eight o'clock.

Fr. Roger: Another question, though, is the connection—quite often anchorites start in cenobitical communities.

In Palestinian monasticism, it has been built in. In the Palestinian monasteries, there have been recluses back in the caves and then hermits attached to the monasteries. It was the accepted thing in Palestinian monasticism that after a certain number of years, you lived a totally solitary

---

30. A discussion ensues here that is difficult to transcribe due to crosstalk and microphone placement. In summary, Mother Myriam questions if this experience might be different for women. Merton responds that "women so seldom get a chance to try it" (i.e., opportunities for "idleness"). Mother Myriam then describes a three-day solitary retreat in which she experienced an intense sense of fear due to the isolation, and without some activity to engage in. Merton shares that in his life at the hermitage, he is not quite out of contact with people for extended periods of time. Interestingly, he then references living in Greenwich Village in New York City (in the 1930s) as "contemplative," though he admits that he would frequent jazz clubs, which Merton also felt had a contemplative dimension. The exchange focuses on what it means for women to take time for personal solitude rather than feel ensnared in constant or compulsive activity (I am grateful to Sharon Duggan for this summary).

life, either in a hermitage or in a reclusive place in the monastery, and they didn't bother you. St. Sabas, for example, had a lot of hermitages down in the *wadis* there.[31] Whereas, in the West, communities did go to them [the anchorites], and then they became abbots right away.

Comment: It seems to me that it would sometimes be difficult to make a discernment between [all of that] freedom and laziness.

Yes, but I would say if a person in solitude were simply giving in to laziness, it would be unbearable. He'd be terribly bored. He wouldn't be bored the first day, but boredom would be a great problem. Boredom is never a problem for me in solitude. Never, never. That's the last of my problems. I get bored when I'm in town. Then, I get terribly bored, just bored to death. Especially when I'm with people who are having fun. There is nothing so boring as people having fun [laughter]. Well, I suppose we'll have to end here.

Comment: I was just wondering if, to some degree, this busyness, which could be an evasion of something, is what we sometimes experience here. When we get rid of some structure that there once was, and each person somehow has to find her own way.

I think that's happening now at Gethsemani, to some extent. There's a great deal of talk in our place—which I don't feel too confident about at all—about things like, "Let's have some baseball." We've given people all this time, and what they want to do is play softball. Of course, this is only a minority. This is not everybody, but there's a certain group that's discussing this. The last that I heard, is there are various dialogue groups that they've got, and they're hashing this out now. I think that the consensus of opinion is, "It's all right if they're not contact sports"—like football, or wrestling. "So long as you're not wrestling!" [laughter]

Well, this was a very nice session. We'll start again tomorrow. Thank you.

---

31. On the monastery of St. Sabas and Palestinian monasticism in general, see Derwas J. Chitty, *The Desert a City: An Introduction to the Study of Egyptian and Palestinian Monasticism Under the Christian Empire* (New York: St. Vladimir's Seminary Press, 1999), 101–22.

Chapter Seven

Hindu Stages of Life and Karma Yoga

Merton opens this conference with the following prayer:
Lord, help us in all that we do and think, to come closer to You, and to
love You more and more, through Christ, our Lord. Amen.

I think we're ready to have a whole session on various kinds of yoga.[1] What we've had so far, I mean, if I suddenly stopped now, after what we've had just for the first two days, it would be very insufficient, because you would get a wrong idea of Hinduism. Hinduism is very, very varied. There's an enormous amount of variety and pluralism in it. To take just one aspect of Hinduism and generalize about it is what always causes all these wrong impressions. People get all sorts of wrong ideas because it's done like that. They just simply take one side of it. For example, the kind of ultimate principles that I was talking about yesterday, about *Brahman* completely undifferentiated.

This is fine, but this is a basic principle. Many Hindu people don't live anywhere near anything like that. It's something quite different, and yet, it's in touch with that. For example, even in the most popular manifestation of religion in Hinduism—ritual, cultural, pilgrimage things; pilgrimage to the source of the Ganges, which is very earthy, and deeply religious, too. It's always conceived of as being somehow in touch with something deep and unknowable, but it's in a knowable form. So that for Hindus, one of the great things is the multiplicity of manifestations of

1. See Nikhilananda, *Hinduism*, chapters 5–8, for Merton's source on the "four yogas" (pp. 94–144); especially chapter 5 on "karma yoga" (pp. 94–104).

what is unknowable. Even though *Brahman* and *atman*—this ultimate self—is One in everybody and in everything; nevertheless, it has an infinite number of manifestations.

The world of appearances, and the world of ordinary life is nothing but a constant—you hear the expression—Dance of Shiva. But the whole of the cosmos and nature, and everything in it, is the play of God—the various manifestations of *Brahman* as Shiva, Krishna, and so forth, as personal gods. He manifests Himself in a variety of personal gods who suddenly appear as personal incarnations. These are all part of this great Dance of Shiva, which is His play. God is ultimately One.

For example, the term *maya*, which means "illusion," or it tends to be interpreted as illusion, is the term which is used for "visible reality." It doesn't mean that it's a trick or a deception. It means that it is the play of God. And play is real. So, all created things *are* real in the sense of being the play of God, and they're *unreal* in the sense that they're not the ultimate reality. They're a game of hide and seek, in which God manifests Himself and yet remains hidden.

What we can talk about now are some of the different kinds of life, different kinds of consciousness, which Hinduism promotes. You've got a wide variety of consciousnesses which all work together. Whereas with us, we have a tendency to oppose them, one to the other, in our life—action versus contemplation, for example. We'll have just one or two, and maybe we'll find it easy to reconcile them. And the one who is on one side is trying to say, "This is the only one." But with them, you've got this great variety, and all sorts of possibilities.

For example—this is always something that I found very interesting—in your life cycle as a Hindu, you go through four states of life.[2] Every Hindu should traditionally live through at least, let's say, two, maybe three states of life, and he's got a chance of a fourth. The first state of life is that of the student or the *brahmacharya*, which also means "chastity." The student life is a life of chastity and discipline, in which the young Hindu is under a master, a guru, a teacher, who teaches him yoga. He learns his

---

2. Merton is discussing here the *ashramas*, or four states of life. Merton presented similar material for the gathering of contemplative prioresses at the Abbey of Gethsemani upon his return from Redwoods Monastery in May 1968 (see *Merton and Hinduism*, 361–62).

way of life, his way of discipline. He learns to be a fully developed human being. I don't know exactly what kind of training this would be—largely a lot of ritual training, but also some yoga of the body, and knowing how to do these things that keep you healthy and balanced. This is the ordinary life of a student.

Then, when he reaches maturity, he enters into another state of life, which is that of the *grihastha*, or the householder; the married man, the married householder with children. Now for this state, there is a special kind of yoga—the yoga of the active life, which is the yoga of the married layman, and the man who is in business, or who is a warrior, or a governor, or a lawyer, or a prince. That's the yoga that I'm going to talk about today, the yoga of action, in which the ordinary, active life is a spiritual discipline. The life of the layman is a spiritual discipline, and to be understood, it has to be lived as a spiritual discipline.

How you know when you change to the next state is when your hair is beginning to get gray; you change to the next state of life, which is forest life. The man, either he and his wife, together or separately—they could either separate, or they could just go and live in the forest as hermits together—but they're no longer having any more children. This is now a life of renunciation of active life, renunciation of the cares of the world, and a life of solitude and prayer—which is not considered the highest life. It's just simply a life of retirement in the forest, and then peace and quiet.

Then there is finally the last state, which is *sannyasa*, or the life of total renunciation, which is the life of the monk. What actually happens is the same thing that happens with us, only instead of going through all these stages, with us a person becomes a *sannyasin* at age 18, and he misses some of the others. He hasn't been a householder, and he hasn't had the forest life. I suppose it's not practical to think that when a person, after he has retired from married life, and then retired from the hermit life, starts a life of wandering, but that is what they say. But the ultimate life is the life of wandering; the life of homelessness—of not having a fixed abode anywhere; living entirely on alms, free from all ritual obligations.

Comment: Would they be free from caste too?

Yes, they're free from the caste obligations; they're no longer members of a caste. When they're in *vanaprashta*, the forest life, they still retain their caste, but the *sannyasin* who has totally renounced everything, he has renounced his caste, he has renounced his social being. *Vanaprashta* still is a social category, but these other people have renounced their social being and renounced everything except the one concentration on final liberation. The final achievement of complete liberation from attachment to the ego or from any kind of illusion about the self. That gives you a pretty nice picture of this very varied society. Nobody is obliged to take on the last two at all, but it's a great variety.

It shows you what a real complex and subtle picture you have; that within Hinduism there's a vast choice, not only for each individual, but for the individual in the development of his own life. There are different times of his life, so there can be very different choices. There's always an opening for a new life, and there's always some way of doing it. There's a way provided. You don't have to suddenly invent a new way. The way is there.

Now, in line with these things, cutting across it, you also have different ways for different temperaments. This is what would be useful for us here. What we were talking about yesterday was really only one side of this thing. What I was saying yesterday about this Hindu concept of God as beyond all forms doesn't appeal to everybody, and it's not supposed to appeal to everybody. A lot of people won't "dig it," as they say. They're not going to particularly like this. It's not going to mean that much to them. It doesn't have to. There's no reason why it should.

With some of the schools, especially with this intellectual [jñāna] yoga, there is a way of saying, "Really, the intellectual yoga is the real one, and that anybody who doesn't practice this is not doing so well." But it's not real Hinduism to say that. That's one school that says that, but it's not the real thing. The yoga of the active life is perhaps less noble and exalted than the yoga of contemplation, but it still has its value. It's just as good for attaining liberation as any of the others, and if it's for a given person, it's the thing to do.

Now, this is the first one I want to talk about. This is very useful for us. The two I want to talk about today are very familiar to us. They're the sort of thing that we learn in one way or another in our own life. One of them, for example, bhakti yoga, which is the second one I want to talk about, is really the yoga of St. Bernard, the yoga of love. There is a yoga of love, and there is a yoga of work. So, the two we're talking about today is first, the yoga of work, and second, the yoga of love. These are both very familiar.

Karma yoga is the yoga of St. Benedict. Remember, St. Benedict's *Rule* is actually for the active life, which, in the original sense of the word, is the *bios praktikos*,[3] the work in which you do what you have to do. And he suggests at the end of the *Rule*, that when you have kept this *Rule* for beginners, which is the *Rule* of the active life, of ascetic purification, then you go on to these other [sources]. He says you read Cassian, and you read the *Lives* of the Fathers, and Basil [the Great], and then you go on to—he doesn't say the contemplative life, but I think that's what he means.[4] But everybody has to go through karma yoga.

It would be utterly fatal to try [to skip this]—as some people do in this country. You're liable to get somebody who has just gone to the library and discovered yoga, and he's just going to jump right into *rāja yoga*: "None but the best for me," and off he goes. Well, no. There has to be a basic, fundamental understanding of the yoga of work, and how work and action are a spiritual discipline. We find it all the time in our life that a person who does not work, or does not know how to work, or can never quite get around to working, cannot be really successful in our life. You cannot be a contemplative in our life unless you also work.

Fr. Roger: By work, do you mean particularly purification?

Well, partly ascetic purification, but also doing what you have to do. I'll skip a few points and cover that right now. The work of the Hindu is expressed by the word, *svadharma*, which means one's own—it's almost the same as saying, "One's own thing." It's not the duty of one's state of life, exactly, but it is the thing which God has destined for me to do, and in doing that work, I am doing a spiritual discipline. But that is not at all the Western idea of work. The Western idea of work tends to be a glorification of work for its own sake, which is work not as a discipline. That's not a discipline, and it's not purifying. It's the opposite of purifying. It's an obsession.

---

3. βίος πρακτικός (Gk.), literally, the "practical life."

4. Merton is referring to Chapter 72 of the *Rule of Saint Benedict*, which explicitly mentions Cassian's *Conferences* and *Institutes*, as well as the *Rule* of St. Basil the Great. Benedict advises the monk to keep his "little rule. . . . After that, you can set out for . . . loftier summits" (*Rule of Saint Benedict 1980*, 297).

Of course, one of the problems in our life, dealing with Western vocations, is that they have this obsession with work—some of them—or obsession with not working. Neither one of these goes. Either an obsession with having to keep busy all the time, or an obsession with not working. Both are wrong. For the Hindu, it's made quite clear that a person who understands karma yoga is able to work without desiring the fruit of the work, or without desiring not to work. He doesn't work for the sake of working; he works because it is his *svadharma*, it is what he should do. We'll explain that as we go along.

The ideal of this work is totally different from the ideal of Western business, for example. This is where you begin to see the real distinction between the East and the West. The real distinction isn't at all that the West is active and the East is contemplative; or rather, that the East has nothing to do with work or action. The distinction becomes clear in a real, different view of what work is, a wholly different view of what action is. For example, you get a saying like this, "He who sees non-action in action and action in non-action, he is wise among men. He is a yogi."[5] This is karma yoga. It's action in non-action, and non-action in action. That is to say, you're working and yet you're not working. You're working in such a way that you're free. It is freedom in work. Of course, we'll see in a minute what that means.

Comment: It's amazing how similar this is to the concept of Benedict.

Yes, exactly. This is purely St. Benedict. The whole idea of humility and obedience is a karma yoga. To free the person from attachment to his work so that he does it with perfect freedom; as at the end of the Degrees of Humility, for example.[6] Having ascended all these degrees, he simply works in the Spirit. What he does, he does without care; working without agitation. This is pure karma yoga, and somebody who really is formed

5. *Bhagavad Gita* 4.18.

6. Chapter 7 of the *Rule of Saint Benedict* outlines the twelve degrees or "steps" of the ladder of humility, the twelfth being, "that a monk always manifests humility in his bearing no less than in his heart" (*Rule of Saint Benedict 1980*, 201). For an extensive discussion, see Merton's monastic conferences on this topic in *The Rule of Saint Benedict: Initiation into the Monastic Tradition* 4, ed. Patrick F. O'Connell (Collegeville, MN: Cistercian Publications, 2009), 152–216.

by the *Rule of Saint Benedict* has this kind of spirit. They do a great deal of work, but it's all quiet and peaceful. There's no big fuss. You just go along and you work. This is your life.

There's nothing wrong with work. That's the sort of thing that gets people terribly disturbed. If I'm in a contemplative life, should I work? One of the reasons why it's a problem is that it has been handled with a great deal of ambiguity. For example, there's a tendency in some communities to emphasize an ideal of contemplation, and yet to demand a great deal of work out of the men—work for remunerative purposes; work for business. While at the same time, saying, "This is a highly contemplative life and we are the most contemplative [Order]." But you get in there and turn out a whole lot of work—money-making work. Work on a business basis. Of course, that creates tension in people, because there is a contradiction. It's not karma yoga; it's a different kind of thing.

Now, the word *karma* means "action" as a burden, action which brings with it a burden of consequences; action with consequences. In popular Hinduism it's tied up with the idea that you get reincarnated because you've got a certain amount of karma. We would say you have sins that you have to expiate and get rid of in purgatory. They say you have karma: a burden of the consequences of past actions you have to work out in another life. You can have good karma or bad karma. You can have consequences of good actions, which get you a better chance the next time.

Whether or not people really believe in personal reincarnation is a moot point in Asian philosophy. It is a kind of myth. Some Hindus definitely think that the individual soul is reincarnated in different bodies, but a lot of them don't. It is sort of a myth, corresponding to the idea we have of purgatory. The idea that there is a retribution, a burden that one has to take care of; that there is a debt.

But karma yoga is taking actions and their consequences in such a way that the very action itself becomes a purification. What could be a burden, becomes a purification. In other words, they're saying don't fly from it. Don't run away from action, but use action in such a way that it leads to liberation.

Behind that is a deep idea, which I haven't really gone into, and I don't really understand, but a Hindu concept to do with their cosmology. They've got three principles: energy, inertia, and a peaceful balance between the two.[7] There is a principle of energy which works in everything, and which is at work in the whole cosmos. In other words, everything is active, and then everything at the same time is inert. The action and the inertia work together to form a kind of balance, and all these three are part of this world of illusion. It's a part of the play of God. But karma yoga presupposes that since we are involved in something that is full of activity, *we* are full of activity, and we have to do something about it, and one of the things to do is to act in such a way, to work in such a way, that one is really in harmony with the whole cosmos—with the principles that are at work in nature. I think that's good common sense. That's in our Western tradition, too. It's in Stoicism, for example. I would say it's pretty strong in St. Benedict under the form of "God's will." We generally speak of God's will as being the principle behind this energy. God wills all these things to be working, and He wills us to work with them.

The key to karma yoga is the renunciation of the fruits of action. To act without demanding results, which is to say, to act without caring about the results. Not, of course, in the sense of complete indifference to the effects [of one's actions] on other people, but *not* to want to have the fruits of the action. In connection with this, they have a pretty deep psychology. It takes you back again to this idea of karma as the residue of actions. When we act, everything that we do, whether conscious or unconscious, involves a residue of impressions, effects, and seeds of further action.[8] Everything that you do is tied into a chain of causes and effects, conscious or unconscious, and it's leading to something. We act and do things during the day, and then a great number of people dream about [these] things at night. The dreams form part of this context. You have unconscious memories [that appear, for example, during dreams], and that's why a person's dreams are often quite important. Although, most of the time you don't remember them, or most people don't. Sometimes you do; sometimes you don't.

7. Merton is referencing the three *gunas* of Samkhya philosophy: *tamas* (inertia), *rajas* (action), and *sattva* (harmony).

8. Merton is referring here to the concept of *samskaras*—latent karmic impressions or "seeds" that need to be "burned up" in the heat (*tapas*) of yogic discipline. *Samskaras* can be both positive (and stored up) as well as negative, as in *Yoga Sutra* 1.50-.51 (Bryant, *The Yoga Sutras*, 162-68). The concept bears resemblance to modern notions of the unconscious, which is interesting given Merton's connection to dreams.

In Sufism, incidentally, dreams are very important. The spiritual director wants to know what the person's dreaming. I met a Sufi—we'll have to talk about him when we get further into Sufism—but a Sufi master came to Gethsemani.[9] A real Sufi master from Morocco, who knew no French. He had a French translator with him, but he spoke only Arabic. A very Biblical sort of man, a very nice person, a very cheerful person. Most radiant. He only had one eye. He lost an eye somewhere earlier, but a radiant, cheerful, really sparkling person, and very smart. No wasting time, no nonsense about him at all. He was brought to this country by a man at Temple University to talk to mostly secular students. He would go around talking to people, and if he wasn't interested in them, he just wouldn't talk to them. He'd be with them for a while, he'd sort of look them over, and then he would say to his companion, "There's no point in talking to these people," and he would leave.

I got about a dozen monks at Gethsemani to come out and talk to him. These were all monks that I knew very well. They'd all been my students. I knew all the ins and outs of their inner life. They were asking him questions about the spiritual life, and he would give them answers that went right to the center—not even what they'd asked, but he would go behind their question to what their real trouble was, even though they weren't talking about their trouble [laughter]. *Bam*, like that. One of the things that he really set me back on was—we got along very nicely and had a good time, but after we got to know each other, he says, "Did you have any dreams before I came?" I didn't remember if I had or not. He wanted to know what kind of dreams. You know what he said? Listen, this is very strange. I just remembered this. This was almost a year before Dom James retired. He said to me, "I wish you could come over to my place in Africa." I said, "I can't, I've got an abbot that won't let me travel." He says, "In about a year, you're going to have a change" [laughter].

Really, he did. And this other fellow that's with us said, "You pay attention, because he's usually right" [laughter]. This is one of the old, traditional directors, traditional Sufi masters. You get this in Hinduism,

9. Sidi Abdeslam (1900?–1980) and Merton met at Gethsemani in 1966. Bernard Phillips from Temple University arranged the visit (Nicole Abadie, "The Visit of Sidi Abdeslam to Gethsemani," in *Merton and Sufism: The Untold Story* [Louisville, KY: Fons Vitae, 1999], 182–92).

too; people who have lived in a tradition, in which a certain kind of consciousness and experience has been handed down from generation to generation. People really absorbed this, and they have this sense of the meaning of existence. They are very much aware of things that we're not aware of; that even psychoanalysts are not aware of—the rather subtle forces at work in what we do, and the way we do things that bind us instead of liberating us.

This is terribly important for us. To be in our monastic life, doing the things that we have to do in such a way that we're not tying ourselves up by what we do. It's not enough to do what we are always told to do: "Purify your intention." It's not enough to do that because that's purely a mental operation. A person can purify his intention while at the same time tying himself up by the way he does it. The thing is, then, to learn to act freely, and there I need to practice karma yoga. If I am hung up on the need for results, the need to succeed, spending the whole day thinking, "Will it work? How is it going to come out? What do I do?" And if it doesn't work, "What will I do? How will I explain this if I fail?" I've been through enough with the writing so that if a book flops, I couldn't care less. But with some other things, it's not so true, and if I act on that basis, I am tying myself up. Everything I do, even if I succeed at it, it is binding me. It is taking away my freedom. The great thing, then, is to learn to act freely.[10]

So, I think what we should get out of this idea of karma yoga is an awareness that if we are going through this kind of a cycle with everything that we do: reproaching myself for the last time I did something, whether I didn't make out too well; it was kind of a flop and I feel embarrassed about it; I feel sad and I'm kicking myself. Then it comes around again: "This time I'll really make a go out of it." So, I rush into the thing—*bam*, it succeeds—and then I feel really good. And the next time it comes around, I'm not paying any attention, and—*plop*, it fails. Each time I do this, I'm in a little spider web, and I'm getting more and more caught. What I have to do is not stop doing it, but start doing it in a completely different way.

Now, another one, especially one for us—and this is for [vowed] religious and especially for enclosed people—is the need to act perfectly.

---

10. Merton then offers various examples of attachment in regards to one's work: either the need to experience pleasure, or alternately, the "need for results, the need to succeed."

This causes trouble because no act is ever perfect. We cannot do things perfectly. Of course, we all know this. We know we can't do something perfectly, but still, there's something down in the depths that says, "I ought to do this perfectly." This is tied to the other thing. This is the kind of result that we really look for. We're not looking for material gain; we're not necessarily looking for praise. We're not looking for appreciation, but we are looking for a little approval down in there that says, "That was good. I did that very well. That was a perfect, or a nearly perfect act. It wasn't totally perfect, but it was close." When we do that, you go through the same kind of cycle, and it's the seed of sadness and discouragement. Because the cycle that we go through with all this is a cycle of ups and downs. You're high and then you're low and you're on top and then you're down below.

This ends in a great deal of sadness, because a lot of energy goes off into this. Living like this, one goes through periods of deeper depression than one should go through; then you have to spend a lot of time fighting this discouragement: "Nobody can help me. What am I going to do?" You spend much more time with everything [feeling] very heavy, and it's hard. Of course, this is part of life: no matter how you live, you've got to have some of this, but there is much more of it if we are in this cycle of expecting a perfection that's impossible, and wanting to get results that are not possible, and to do better than we can. I would say, this is central. Don't you think?

A discussion ensues regarding the reality of anxiety and depression in religious life, particularly around the issue of "addiction to perfection"[11]— and rigidity. Merton traces some of this lineage to Catholic roots in American culture as well as parenting practices in the U.S. before stating:

Competition and success are built into American society. The religion of this country is success. You've got to succeed. This country has this terrible anxiety about not succeeding. One of the places where you get it as a child growing up in this country is that you're brainwashed by advertising. In all advertising in this country, in one way or another, there

---

11. For a Jungian approach to this topic, see Marion Woodman, *Addiction to Perfection: The Still Unravished Bride* (Toronto: Inner City Books, 1982).

is an implication; every ad to some extent is implying that you are on the brink of the abyss. It doesn't actually say so, but it represents a picture of life in which you are walking on a razor edge. You are under judgment by the whole of society, and you will either be accepted or rejected by our affluent society—you will be happy or miserable—depending on what? Depending on if you buy our product.

If you buy our product, you will be happy. You'll be accepted. You will be a really nice person, and everybody will say you're wonderful. If you don't, you get the opposite. And from morning to night, people are getting this all over the radio. They're getting it all the time. How can a person have any kind of peace or security in his heart if he's constantly thinking that? And in order to buy these products, you've got to make money, and you've got to keep going; you've got to get a better job; you've got to feel you're really grooving in the business world, from the competition.

Comment: In schools, too.

Sure, I bet. It's probably more of the same in another field. When I was in school thirty years ago, it was much less intense, and when I taught 30 years ago, it was much less intense. I mean, where I was teaching, there was no spirit of competition at all. Nobody cared. I was glad to have the job because I could teach one hour in the morning, and actually spend the rest of the day in the woods [laughter]. It was perfect. They paid me a hundred dollars a month and I was delighted. I would've done that for the rest of my life, except I thought it'd be better to get into a religious order where you didn't even have to teach.

I've got an idea just beginning here. It has to do with technology. Technology as karma. Because what you've got in technology is a great network or chain of causes and effects. What happens in technology, it works strictly like karma, because there's a great determinism in technology. Once you have the ability to do something with certain mechanical means and certain technological means, it becomes necessary to do it to the fullest extent in order to recoup your investment. Once you get involved in doing this, with the way things are now, you inevitably run into improvements that have to be made. When a new improvement comes in sight, at the moment when it does, if you don't make it, then you might as well drop out. So, you make the improvement, but the effect of the improvement is that you've got to produce more, or you've got to produce in a different way. This steps the thing up. You do that, and another improvement comes in, or another merger with some other thing; you tie in with something else, then you have to produce more. No matter how you do it, you're like a squirrel on a wheel.

This is no longer a matter just of psychology. Even if everybody's psychology was perfect, it's now in the system. The system is now running autonomously on the basis of a huge karma. The Vietnam War is strictly the U.S.A.'s technological karma at work. There should be a deep philosophical, sociological, and economic study of how something like the Vietnam War was a necessary result of what had gone before in the previous 10 years in American technology. You have a society which was increasingly built on war technology. Obviously, such a society needed a war. The Vietnam War came along and the technology moved into Vietnam, but unfortunately it wasn't the right technology for that kind of war.

So, what you have in Vietnam is the awful spectacle of experimentation with technological means that have nothing to do with what's going on. A purely gratuitous use of technological means of destruction that have no reasonable connection with the aims of what they're trying to do. This is horrible. This is really demonic, and behind it are a lot of perfectly nice people. They're kind to their children, and they love their pets, and they are very nice to everybody. They would never kill a fly—except with a spray [laughter].

Comment: Could another result of technology be that you no longer feel responsible for what you've done? Or if you discovered a new way to do something, the result of that is not your responsibility?

The people who have the real moral insight into this are atomic scientists. One magazine that would be worth having is the *Bulletin of the Atomic Scientists*. This is a very worthwhile magazine because what it has in it is a moral, ethically-based study of what goes on in the world. It takes all these problems, not only atomic war and napalm, but also air pollution and ecology. It started with the atomic scientists after the bomb was developed, when they tried to prevent its being used in war. They tried to say, once they had developed it, "Now look, let's take care of this thing." They wanted it to be first used, if it all, in a purely demonstrative way—use it on some rocks or some trees, but the government wouldn't do that.

Ever since then, you've had these atomic scientists insisting on trying to maintain this [ethical stance]. But you've got these others [that are against it]. It's a strange, psychological thing. Why some people are one way and some are the other; some have this moral sensitivity and some don't. The best ones have that moral sensitivity. Incidentally, just talking about atomic scientists—I'm no physicist, and I don't know too much about science—but one of the most contemplative groups of people in the twentieth century were scientists like Niels Bohr at Copenhagen.[12] There was a fabulous group of people at that Center in Copenhagen,[13] which did the groundwork in nuclear physics, out of which the bomb came. One of the great men there was Niels Bohr. These people were very brilliant, but they also had an almost contemplative intuition—like St. John of the Cross, almost—into what happens when you get so far down into matter, that matter itself disappears. You no longer know what you're dealing with. The idea of Heisenberg, for example, that when you try to investigate what's going on in the structure of the atom, the moment you start investigating it, the whole thing changes.[14] You never really see, or you never are in direct contact with what you're looking at. It gets away from you all the time, so you've got this sense of operating almost in the dark, in the depths of matter, and with the smallest thing. You have to advance by—[15]

One of the standard problems in our life, with novices and so forth, [is] wanting to have religious experiences to justify their existence and their

12. Niels Bohr (1885–1962), Danish physicist, quantum theorist, and 1922 Nobel Prize in Physics winner.

13. Institute of Theoretical Physics, founded by Bohr in 1921; now known as the Niels Bohr Institute.

14. Werner Heisenberg (1901–1967), German theoretical physicist and pioneer of quantum mechanics; awarded the 1932 Nobel Prize in Physics.

15. The recording unfortunately cuts off mid-sentence. One almost expects Merton to finish this statement with "faith alone." There is a gap in the conference material which begins again in the following section, picking up the discussion of karma yoga and the development of "modern consciousness."

vocation, and wanting to feel drunk with grandeur once in a while. If Easter comes along, Christmas comes along, and I'm not drunk with a sense of the grandeur of the whole thing, [then] there's something the matter.

Well, anybody who can get himself feeling drunk with grandeur once a week is going to feel pretty bad for the other six days. It would take so much effort to do this, and if we are too dependent on this, we will get in a situation where we are inevitably going through a cycle. We'll get the moments of grandeur, but then we will have the moments of depression afterwards.

I think that one of the remedies for this is karma yoga, where you don't do anything with the implied condition that this has got to pay off in a good feeling or consolation. You just do it because it's the thing to do. It's what has to be done, and in doing it you're doing God's will; you're acting as an instrument of God, and it's a consolation to be an instrument of God, and this is enough. Then you somewhat get out of this cycle.

Of course, this has now gone to the point where all of a sudden, somebody discovered you could do it with a pill. Timothy Leary goes around giving speeches saying that LSD is a sacrament that really works [laughter]. This is the final perfection of the theology of *ex opere operato*[16] [laughter]. This is it.

Then you've got Voltaire saying, for example—because Voltaire was no fool, but he's kind of detached—and he says, "Let us forsake our delights in order to recapture them" [laughter]. There you have your cultivated eighteenth-century man. But this is very much built into our society, too, now. You get one of these characters [unnamed], who says, "He who has the greatest number of sensations and ideas has lived the most." This is an eighteenth-century man who says this, and it's just simply [that]—you multiply experiences.

Now, whether we like it or not, this is in us. We're stuck with this mentality. We're living in a society that thrives on this, although of course it's been developed much further. I could quote people like Montaigne, but I don't think I will. I think what I've said about this is good enough. I think I'll just skip to this Hindu idea [of bhakti yoga]. Although of course, Pascal

---

16. Latin phrase meaning "from the work performed," or more literally, "by the work worked"; used in sacramental theology to distinguish the efficacy of a sacrament independently from the minister or recipient of the sacrament.

realizes all this. Maybe I could talk about him some other time. But Pascal realizes all this and then goes under it, and sees the contradiction in it and the tragic despair that it really implies. He's so profound and really good on this kind of thing. He goes into this whole business of diversion and distraction, and then how to react against that.[17] I might take that some evening after supper if I can't think of anything else to say, because it's really so deeply moving; it shows you the kind of hell that we live in as a result of flapping our wings in order to stay there. As I said, really for us, the only practical answer is a community in which we actually create freely an atmosphere of love in which this is no longer necessary.

That's our real mission, I think, and then from that all sorts of things can follow. The capacity for solitude really has to come from that kind of an ambient to begin with. Have you any more questions about this sort of cyclical thing? The psychology of sadness has much to do with that, don't you think?

Mother Myriam: And how unconscious it is at the beginning, before we come to realize it; it takes a while.

I think people are beginning to realize it outside now, though. There is a big disillusionment [especially among younger people].

Comment: When I was in college, and that wasn't that long ago, it was different than it is now. It was only four years ago.

Yes, things have changed immensely in just the last four or five years, as far as I know. The kids now are deeply affected by this thing. But [with] the kids now, there is much more of a sense of community.

---

17. *Divertissement*, Pascal's famous treatment of "diversion" in the spiritual life; see, e.g., *Pensées* (New York: Penguin, 1966), 66–72. Blaise Pascal (1623–1662), highly influential seventeenth-century French mathematician, scientist, and philosopher, who came under the influence of the "Jansenist" Abbey of Port Royal following a tremendous spiritual conversion that deepened his Catholicism in 1654 (see Bernard McGinn, *The Persistence of Mysticism in Catholic Europe* [New York: Herder & Herder, 2020], 321–31). Merton was reading Georges Poulet's *Studies in Human Time* in May 1968, and cites Pascal via Poulet in the opening pages of his *Woods, Shore, Desert* notebook (*Other Side of the Mountain*, 92–93).

Speaker 2: They have great awareness now.

Yes, very smart. The popular music that's coming out now is totally different. Some of it is deeply philosophical. Not *deeply* philosophical, but they're reflecting on all sorts of stuff. Do you ever hear Bob Dylan by the way?

Comment: I heard it, but I feel we have not enough of that stuff.

The new record of Bob Dylan is superb. *John Wesley Harding* is a superb record.[18] Some of his other stuff is half-good, but this is really first rate; it's a beautiful job. Some of his others are alright, but of course, he's a brilliant guy. This is the one that happened after his motorcycle accident, so he's sort of chastened by suffering.

Comment: And some of those hippies—

Do you know Simon and Garfunkel? It's two of these kids. They do some very nice stuff. Beautiful reflective songs about life; it's quite nice. Something I would really like to go into is the religious dimensions of the deep jazz that's going on; its rather powerful stuff. I'm thinking in terms of [John] Coltrane, who died recently. I don't know what they call it now; they used to call it a jam session, where they simply get together and improvise and go ahead. It's two sides of a long-playing record [LP]; it's called *Ascension*.[19] It's very full of dissonances, but the second side is one of the most moving things I've ever heard. It's really a musical meditation on the [Black] experience; it's a protest in music. It's something fantastic. You have to know quite a lot about jazz before you appreciate it, though, because the first side is very shocking. You don't know what they're doing, and then all of a sudden around the second side, you begin to realize that this is meshing into something that's really tearing you up. If you ever get a chance to hear it, it would be worth trying.

18. Dylan's eighth studio album, released December 1967.

19. Released in 1966, *Ascension* marked Coltrane's bold, experimental leap into avant-garde "free jazz." He died the following year, July 17, 1967, aged 40.

Chapter Eight

Bhakti Yoga and Inter-Monastic Dialogue

Let's talk a little bit about bhakti yoga.[1] Now we're back in the old view in which God is real and He's the only reality and everything else is secondary. The reason I said it's the yoga of St. Bernard is because the basic idea is that you love God—that's practically St. Bernard's statement—that you love God without any reason simply because He's God, and without any measure.[2] Also very important in this is the idea of grace. You love God because God loves you, and God gives you the grace to love Him.

The thing that's so fantastic about Hinduism is that, with this basically impersonal concept of Void, you also have a completely serious personal God. The underlying Void is the undifferentiated *Brahman*, who in order to give Himself to people manifests Himself as a person. The personal manifestation is in bhakti yoga. He manifests Himself in order to be loved, and in order to give love.

In bhakti yoga, the whole thing is love and nothing else but love. That love simply sweeps everything else out of the way. God appears in various personal forms, in order that this overwhelming love may sweep everything else out of the way. You don't worry about anything, you simply love, and the result of this is a love which reaches out—yes?

1. See Nikhilananda, *Hinduism*, chapter 6, for Merton's source on bhakti yoga (pp. 105–18).

2. As articulated, e.g., in Bernard of Clairvaux's *On Loving God* (Kalamazoo, MI: Cistercian Publications, 1995), 3.

Mother Myriam: Would you say that this personal God, if I understand correctly, is a manifestation of this undifferentiated Void, which personifies Himself in order to be loved; that this love is a kind of an imperfection—

Well, no, it is for the people who are hung up on the undifferentiated. But they will say that for the others, it [bhakti yoga] is just as real and better.

Yes. Because it would be then an essential difference with the God of Christianity.

The thing that's so perplexing is that they take both. Even somebody like Shankaracharya, who's one of the big intellectual yoga persons, and says it's all a matter of concentration [to] get [all of the] sense objects out; but in the middle [of his philosophy], he'll go into a bhakti routine.

The same with [D.T.] Suzuki, for example, with his Zen. Suzuki had the most-strict Void Zen thing, and yet was completely sold on Pure Land Buddhism, which [includes] personal Buddhism, and salvation Buddhism, and the invocation of Buddha. The whole thing of Pure Land Buddhism is that all you have to do is say, "O, Amida Buddha, save me." You say this once, and you're saved, but you keep on saying it because you love Him. You don't do anything else. There are a lot of Japanese housewives and that's all they ever do, from morning to night, "*Namu-amida-butsu.*" All you've got to do is "*Amida butsu*" once—the whole thing's finished.[3]

Fr. Roger: Would you relate that to the Jesus Prayer?

Oh yes, it's exactly the same kind of thing. You don't have to know anything, you just love, and you just say with every breath, "*Amitabha tsu.*" Of course, in that, there is a sort of playfulness, but it's just the same as with us: some great theologian might have some very simple prayer life, or some very simple devotion.

[Bhakti yoga] is absolutely serious. It should not be regarded at all as something for the common people. This is just as serious, just as important as anything else. It's not a second-rate yoga. That's the thing that you have to remember, because normally, the Westerner tends to look

---

3. See Suzuki, *Mysticism: Christian and Buddhist*, 138–43.

at the supermarket display of yogas, and, "What's the real top yoga? I'm not going to fool around with some sort of a substitute yoga. The real top yoga is raja yoga?" Okay, but that's the most difficult one; that's the hardest one to understand. This is an easy one for people to understand.

What this does, instead of just simply negating one's sensible life and one's emotional life, it channels the whole thing into love. It just grabs the whole thing and puts it into the love of God. This is what I think is interesting. These are the elements that are considered important to make this thing work. First one, you wouldn't guess: importance of diet [laughter]. This is strictly Hindu: the importance of clean, vegetarian food, and a nice, simple diet, and also importance of the intellectual diet. The intellectual diet has to be very good. Simple ideas and good, pure ideas, and good, clean art, and good music.

Comment: May I ask you, what do you think about a vegetarian diet?

I think personally that most of us need more than that; in this country, at least. Don't you think we do?

I think so.

The Hindus seem to be able to manage it, but they've got a heritage, a background that helps them do it.

Would there be a connection between this conflict that we're suffering, that they may not have?

This is a very funny thing; whether we really could get along better without meat, I don't know. Whether we do get along better without it, I don't know. Without eggs and fish, without any living foods, even. Gandhi used to do it without meat, eggs, fish, or even milk. Just plain vegetables. But you know how Gandhi looked, he's pretty thin [laughter]. Well, evidently, they could do it.

Personally, the way it makes sense for me is, I think it's better to go for certain periods eating whatever you can get ahold of [laughter]. When enjoying the hospitality of [others] you do the best you can [laughter]. To eat well when you can, and then fast. I mean really fast. Get a good breakfast for three months, and then fast without any breakfast at all for a while, which is what I do. You can do it quite easily if sometimes you get a good breakfast and sometimes you don't eat breakfast. Or, if you eat well at certain periods, then you can simply skip breakfast and just take one meal a day in the evening once in a while. It's perfectly possible. But if you're always going on a subsistence diet with a little bit of bread and you're lucky to get a dish of apple sauce, you just have to take everything you can get, and there's no chance to really be free about it. I would say that it is probably true that one should watch one's diet with bhakti yoga or any other yoga.

But [back to] bhakti yoga: the importance of poverty, in the sense of keeping pure of desire for possessions, because this is going to interfere with one's love. The whole idea is that if you have the wrong diet, your love isn't going to work so well, and if you have too many possessions, your love is going to be interfered with—strictly a middle path in asceticism. Bhakti yoga does not go with strong asceticism. It has to go with a reasonable, balanced life. Of course, that's very intelligent. What you have here is a strong, emotional, affective loving devotion with a moderate asceticism and moderate self-denial. Great emphasis on constancy, and not letting oneself get depressed.

Of course, if you have an emotional and affective devotion, the depression is more likely. This is very much the same kind of thing that you have if you're cultivating any kind of rather intense thing. You're going to have ups and downs. This is not something that I personally do much of. I don't systematically do this. I'm emotional enough without being systematic [laughter], so I don't have to make a system out of it. I'm more or less in this Void business, and then the emotions come when they come. I think that would be the way to do it, but then this is another approach: this constancy in spite of ups and downs, and then not to be upset by dryness and the absence of the Beloved.

St. Bernard has all these things: the *vicissitudo* and the whole doctrine of St. Bernard on the ways of the spouse. *Dei vis domini*, how he comes and goes, and how you're supposed to understand all these little [movements]. This is very good. It's very much like bhakti yoga. Understanding the comings and goings of the spouse.[4]

---

4. Merton is referring here to "spousal" or "bridal" mysticism, a popular medieval trope in mystical writing, which St. Bernard developed extensively, particularly in his *Sermons*

There's a lot of bridal mysticism involved in this. The *Brautmystik*, as they say. You know the two big divisions, *Brautmystik* and *Wesensmystik*.[5] *Wesen*, the [mysticism of] "Being." Hadjewich is a little bit of both, actually. She combines the two. But Eckhart is more *Wesensmystik*, and then Lutgarde,[6] or someone like that, is more *Brautmystik*. St. Bernard, to some extent, combines the two.

[In bhakti yoga] there is great importance [placed] on unselfish service of others. That's emphasized very much. These yogas, they overlap; at this particular point, bhakti yoga and karma yoga overlap. Unselfish action is very important, and service. Avoidance of despondency comes in here twice, so they have quite a lot of emphasis on that.[7] But how [does one work with] avoidance of despondency in bhakti yoga?

What we were saying before was the need to feel one's own worth. Here, it's not our love of God that's important, it's God's love of us, and emphasis on the fact that He loves us, not that we love Him. That's St. Bernard again. St. John's statement, "He has first loved us."[8] This is fundamental in St. Bernard, and the whole first section of the *De Diligendo Deo* [*On Loving God*] is that: "Why do we love God? Because God loves us," and all the reasons and indications.

Even the familiar spiritual doctrine of the awareness that because God loves me, everything that happens is for my good, is intended for my good. [Bhakti yoga] stresses this very strongly. Everything that happens is "grace." Everything is for my benefit. Not just my individual good, but also the whole cosmic good.

---

on the Song of Songs (e.g., "Sermon 74," in *The Cistercian World: Monastic Writings of the Twelfth Century*, ed. Pauline Matarasso [New York: Penguin, 1993], 77–83).

5. A term specifically referring to the medieval affective "bridal mysticism" of the European "Low Countries" as represented in the thirteenth-century writings of figures such as Beatrice of Nazareth and the Beguine Hadewijch of Antwerp. The term *Wesensmystik* refers to the more "intellectual" or speculative mystical theology of this region, e.g., Meister Eckhart (see Oliver Davies, *God Within: The Mystical Tradition of Northern Europe* [Hyde Park, NY: New City Press, 1988/2006], 1–4); see also Merton's *Introduction to Christian Mysticism*, 181–93.

6. Lutgarde of Aywières (1182–1246), medieval mystic of the Low Countries. See Merton's early work, *What Are These Wounds? The Life of a Cistercian Mystic, Saint Lutgarde of Aywières* (Milwaukee: Bruce, 1950).

7. On both selfless service and avoiding despondency, see Nikhilananda, *Hinduism*, 111.

8. 1 John 4:19.

This, I would say, is the kind of thing that we have to cultivate. This ties in perfectly with our faith, so there's no problem at all for us. That's what we have to have, a strong faith, and recover this strong faith that everything that happens comes from the love of God. This is an old, simple, time-worn thing, but it doesn't wear out. This is solid. This is the sort of thing that you have to fall back on every once in a while.

Did you know Dom Vital,[9] Fr. Roger? You might have met him at Gethsemani. Yes, you met him? Well, he died at Gethsemani a couple of years ago. Every time he would preach in Chapter, this was all he ever preached. But it was good. Of course, he had a few somewhat comic routines, because his whole idea was, "Everything that God gives or permits must be for my good—even sin" [laughter].[10] One of our fathers denounced him to the Apostolic Delegate for preaching that sin was good for the spiritual mind [laughter]. He was so strong. He had this doctrine—he was novice master; not in my time—he had this whole business that, "Look at the manure, it's so horrible, but you throw it on the garden, you get nice potatoes, nice tomatoes" [laughter].

Dom Vital was always very good on that, but every sermon was the same thing. Everything, no matter how terrible, is bound to be for your good—but it's true. He was one of the few people that had a real doctrine that really impressed everybody. The other element in it was a strong emphasis on Christmas trees [laughter]. He believed in Christmas decorations to the "nth" degree. When he was novice master, he would have the novices put in so many Christmas trees that you could hardly get into the novitiate [laughter]. They had this little place with all these corridors going through, and you would open the door, and you were in this corridor filled with Christmas trees. You had to fight your way in to get in there.

Basically, this idea of everything being the love of God is again something quite fundamental. Another point [in bhakti yoga] that they insist on is the need for a guru or spiritual master.[11] Obviously, when there's a question of a rather emotional thing, your guru has got to be on hand to tell you which is which. This obviously could not work without some

9. Vital Klinski, OCSO (1886–1966).

10. Merton does an impression here with a thick accent.

11. *Hinduism*, 112.

kind of direction to be able to tell the difference between a real love of God and just an emotional experience.

Then there's a strong emphasis in the beginning on images: pictures of God, and pictures of various incarnations.[12] These images tie in with another very important element, what is called "*Ishta*."[13] The *Ishta* is one's chosen manifestation of God, or one's chosen ideal or incarnation. With us, it would amount to a special devotion. This is not just a question of saying prayers *to* a particular person. It is a question of becoming completely absorbed in—not imitation—but identification with the *Ishta*. Again, it's like St. Bernard. For St. Bernard, Our Lady was a kind of an *Ishta*, and Our Lord on the cross, a kind of an *Ishta*, and this whole idea of emphasizing the contemplation of Our Lord in some form or other, or Our Lady in some form or other. And then meditation and contemplation completely centered on this. Constantly returning to one's *Ishta* as the needle of a compass constantly comes back to the north. All these things work. There's no point in going around forcing them on people, but they do work, and if a person wants to do something like that, maybe it's a good thing.

Finally, one last thing about this, and then I will have more or less run out of material on bhakti yoga, and we'll just go on discussing until I start Sufism tomorrow, maybe. The question of identity comes up here in bhakti yoga. This is very curious, and I think this also gives you a real insight into what Hinduism's really like. We tend to think, "Well, this is a systematic business, and maybe you climb the ladder and you go up different kinds of yogas, but sooner or later you really should get to the point where you just lose all identity. The whole principle seems to be that you're supposed to lose your identity; just get submerged in God, and all this other stuff is second rate." Not at all. In bhakti yoga, you've got a choice. It's very curious. Either you can slant your bhakti yoga towards a total loss of identity, total submersion in God, total self-annihilation; or, you can preserve your identity, you can emphasize your identity, in honor of the Beloved, in order to have an identity with which to worship Him. Something like that is very significant. It's equally good. You don't

12. *Hinduism*, 113.
13. *Hinduism*, 114.

have an aristocratic view that this is somehow less good. It's fine. It's not necessarily for everybody, but it's fine if you want to do it.

Of course, you will get certain writings in the negative school [*via negativa*] that do give the impression that that's the only thing to do, but that's not at all the common line. Much more characteristic of Hinduism is this idea, on the one hand, to absolutely admit that "I am nothing but *Brahman* and there's no distinction," and yet to preserve an identity, a separate identity, in order to honor *Brahman* as manifest in some particular form. Then, maybe the person at the same time has at the back of his mind, "Of course, we're really all one anyway."

But it shows you the kind of religious complexity of Hinduism, and that's really the point that I'm trying to get across: the thing that we don't recognize about Asia is this enormous richness of possibilities and choices that they have. We're so narrowed down from that particular point of view. We don't have this richness, and we're always looking for just one right way, and if we haven't got just this one right way, there's something the matter with it. The spirit here is totally different. There are all sorts of right ways, and they can all coexist together, and there's no need at all to say that one's better than the other. You can take your choice.

Admittedly, this belongs to a different kind of culture from ours, and yet it seems to me something that we can do, too. We've got the choice in another form, and we've got all these things lying around. We've got the books now; we have access to these things. I think in a community, it's perfectly logical that everybody should be one on the basic essential things, and yet people should have a completely free choice in some of these personal things.

Incidentally, a book on karma yoga, which I think would be very good to have, if you could get it, is *Talks on the Gita* by Vinoba Bhave.[14] It's a fine book. You know what he did, don't you? He came after Gandhi, and his idea was, "All right, the poor should have the land, and so people who have land should give their land to the poor." So, he got this poor people's march going through India, and would go all through India from village to village and persuade the rich people to give some land to the

---

14. On Merton, Bhave, and the *Bhagavad Gita*, see Christopher Key Chapple, "Thomas Merton and *The Bhagavad Gita*," in *Merton and Hinduism*, 133–41, and Swasti Bhattacharyya and Bernadette McNary-Zak, "Merton Discerning His *Svadharma*," *The Merton Journal* 30.1 (Eastertide 2023): 26–33.

poor. Admittedly, it wasn't efficient, but quite a lot of land was given to the poor. It hasn't solved all the problems, but it's in the millions of acres. Just given away, which is the Hindu way of doing it. Just as Gandhi's Salt March is a strictly Hindu approach. Do you know the Salt March story?

In the 1920s, the English were taxing salt in India, and every purchase of salt was taxed the same. Therefore, for the poor man who had to pay for salt, the tax was an enormous proportion of what he had to pay. It was a real imposition on the poor to have to be taxed for salt. So, Gandhi said that it's unjust for the poor to be taxed for this salt. One of the implications of the government law was that you had to buy salt from the government. You couldn't get it from some other untaxed source. So, Gandhi got about 30,000 people together, and they all marched from Central India somewhere to the sea, and went down and started making salt, getting salt out of the sea, and saying, "This is our right."[15] Eventually, he was put in jail for doing it, but the Viceroy of India understood the proposition, and they came to some kind of an agreement as a result of that.[16] Gandhi also fought against the old Indian cultural things that were unjust, especially this business of caste, the untouchables. He fought that very strongly.

But Gandhi's policy didn't really succeed. It didn't actually unite India at all. India was divided and they were all fighting each other, and that was the cause of his death. He just couldn't keep the Hindus and Muslims from fighting each other. India is by no means a purely pacifist nation, but I think there is something in the genius of Asian culture and religion that would enable them to handle these things if they could get it moving— and they don't have to do it strictly by Western methods. Personally, I feel very implicated in the spiritual aspect of that. I think it's very important that it should be a two-way dialogue. Instead of just simply the West imposing on the East technology, I think we should be taking from the East the lessons of what they have to teach us in these various things.

There's a fairly good chance of some of that happening, but it's too late almost, because now in China, they're stamping out every vestige of the

---

15. Begun on March 12, 1930. Tens of thousands were arrested for acts of nonviolent civil disobedience during the Salt March which covered 241 miles in 24 days, reaching the Arabian Sea at the town of Dandi on April 5. See also Paul Dekar, "Merton on Gandhi," in *Merton and Hinduism*, 142–57.

16. The 1931 Gandhi-Irwin Pact removed the salt tax and allowed coastal Indians to produce and sell their own salt.

old Chinese culture—everything, systematically. Anything to do with Buddhism, anything to do with Confucianism. Of course, that's really frightening, because there's so much that's really good, but for me, one of the most stimulating things has been this work with Buddhism and Hinduism.

The thing that's always surprising is when you meet these people—a real Buddhist, an ordinary Buddhist person; for example, a group of *hibakusha*—these are the survivors of the atomic explosion in Hiroshima. They occasionally travel around and come to dialogue with people in the West, and try to tell them to think before it's too late. They had three groups going through this country, and one of the groups came to Gethsemani. They came up to the hermitage, and it was a beautiful thing. There were about a dozen of them, and we had them talk. They all liked the hermitage very much.

When it was all over, there was one lady, a very sweet Buddhist lady who came up. Real quiet, just a lovely person. One of the things that the *hibakusha* do, they make these little paper cranes, which is a symbol of the peace movement in Japan. I wrote a little poem about paper cranes, and I just read the poem. When it was all over, she came up. She had a little paper crane she'd made while I was reading the poem.[17]

There's an enormous gentleness about the Buddhists. They really are a very, very gentle people—if they're real Buddhists. And it's not fooling. It is a very real thing, and they've got something quite peculiar to them. The thing that strikes me—we Christians should be so gentle, but we're so—and the thing that is so heartbreaking, is that you get Christians saying, "Oh, Buddhists are life denying," and, "It's all negative, and they deny life," and there we are bombing Vietnam with napalm and burning down Buddhist villages, and saying they're life denying? I mean, if they follow their principles, they don't even kill flies without necessity. I don't call that life denying. They respect life.

But there is something, a kind of an existential quality about them. Of course, it's tied in with a culture that's disappearing, and it has to come into technological developments. Like cameras. A Japanese camera is a beautiful one, but the question depends on something like this ecologi-

---

17. "Paper Cranes," in *The Collected Poems of Thomas Merton* (New York: New Directions, 1977), 740.

cal consciousness getting in there, and not a purely technological thing in terms of pragmatic utility and profit. In other words, it's a question of values, because these are unquestionable values that you got in these Asian traditions, and they're definitely life-enhancing values.

But anyway, it's nice to keep in contact with these things, as long as they're there, to know about them. Well, I've more or less run out on the Buddhism thing. Any questions?

Fr. Roger asks if Merton might send a list of sources mentioned in his talks.

I'll write out a list when I get back [to Gethsemani] and send it, because I'll have access to things.

Comment: How much is Hinduism transformed when it's presented in this country in something like the Ramakrishna Mission?

That's hard to say. They're pretty authentic, but again, it's loaded with a particular aspect of Hinduism. The Ramakrishna movement was a pretty authentic thing. Ramakrishna was one of the big Hindu saints of the nineteenth century, and of course he's kind of eclectic. He incorporated a lot of Christianity into Hinduism, into his Hinduism.

The one problem with that kind of approach is that they get awful foggy. It gets to be, "Everything is fine. Christianity? Fine. Oh, everything is Christianity. Sure, it's all just like this, and everything corresponds to everything." If everything just corresponds to everything, it gets to be rather slippery after a while. You don't know where you are.

I'll tell you one man that would be good to know, and he'd love to come here. He'd be delighted to come here. He's a friend of Gandhi. He travels around a lot. He's at the U.N., and he's also teaching at New York State University somewhere. A fellow called [Amiya] Chakravarty.[18] I'll get in touch with him. I think I was telling you about him, he taught at Smith College a couple of years ago, and he's a friend of Gandhi and very good on Hinduism. He loves monasteries. If he came here, he'd be absolutely in ecstasy [laughter]. And a very nice person. He would be telling you

---

18. On Merton's friendship with Amiya Chakravarty, see Merton's letter to Myriam Dardenne dated October 29, 1968 (p. 413, fn. 54 below).

from morning till night, "This is the best thing I've ever seen" [laughter]. He really means it, too. He's very good. I'll suggest if he's around San Francisco, that he should come by.

Perhaps what I could do, I might run down to my room before supper, and pick up this letter from Brother David [Steindl-Rast], that I was telling you about. He sent a *prospectus* for his study center. I might run down and get that between now and after supper, and we might have that to talk about after supper.

Mother Myriam: This idea came spontaneously to mind—to have monks with different types of consciousness.

Yes, exactly.

The only [material] I have [to offer] is this project for different monks from different traditions. Shall we go through that or do you have some other questions first? This is the thing that I told you about from Brother David of Mount Saviour. He has a project for this inter-monastic thing, and this gives you the real details of what it's like. He has a first page, which I think is very interesting. It has a good lineup of an aspect of the monastic life. Then he has what the proposal is, and then how it'll work. It has [these] three sides to it. It's not just for monks of different traditions, but also for students and for professional people, scientists and people like that, who would also get into it. I think it's a little bit too complicated, but it would only be for a couple of years at a time. There'd be successive teams coming in. I think it's a bit too much like one of these professional think tanks.

I like this first page quite a lot. It's the general basis for explaining why it would be possible to do something like this and why it should be [done]: "There is in our time a growing urgency to search for the meaning of life. The monks of different times and cultures have made this search the dominant theme of their lives, radically subordinating everything else to this preoccupation. The monastic form of life is determined by an attempt to make every detail of daily activity and environment serve this existential quest for ultimately meaning." I think that's pretty good, don't you? He says that because all the monks of different traditions do this, they have a common language. I think that makes a lot of sense. I think that's good, and I think it's useful to think of our monastic life in those terms. It isn't just a question of getting merit. It's finding out the meaning of life, and if you find the meaning of life, you have to live a meaningful life. I think that's a good way of starting out.

Then he says, "The monk's quest is associated with the ideal of detachment. But detachment is merely its negative side. It liberates the monk from whatever tends to make man lose himself in distractions." This is quite Eastern. I think it's a good idea. "And sets him free for a single-minded search for man's true identity." This is a modern statement, but I think this statement is good. This is a Christian monastic statement influenced by Eastern backgrounds, because he's a Zen student. He's a Benedictine Zen student. "And this single-minded quest for meaningful human existence unites all monks, regardless of their cultural or religious background, on a deep level of human experience." It's always emphasizing these good, basic things. "This accounts for the fact that monastic life everywhere shows decisive resemblances in its forms and the inner attitudes these forms express. We can speak of a Monastic Order, which transcends the differences between different monastic traditions, and even the dividing lines between religions." That's a good statement. I think we should recover the Christian idea of the Monastic Order within Christianity!

He says: "The monastic form of life is exceptional, sets the monk apart. His special commitment to the common human search for meaning unites him deeply with all other men. His solitary stand is not a private affair but of vital concern for all of us. Our expanding horizons demand a deepening search for meaning." I think that's a good statement. And then he says, "Today, many alert laypeople consider monasticism a matter of increasing importance and possibly of great promise." I think that's a good side remark implying that a lot of the clergy don't! [laughter] And then the next page is about what it is: "A Center for Monastic Studies, where monks of different religions are brought together for a period of time to establish contact with one another, with leading members of lay society, and with students of the monastic life." In other words, I think that this means that while they're there, they're not really living monastic life.

Mother Myriam: Would they be searching for a common meaning?

Fr. Roger: Exchanging ideas?

That's what it would amount to. I think he wants it to be deeper than that.

Fr. Roger: And information?

I wonder about that. If I'm a student—say I'm from Berkeley—and I go to the Monastic Center, and there are three Hindus and three Buddhists and three Cistercians, and then three Greek Orthodox—although you might not get the Greek Orthodox, so I wonder about them—I don't think I'd want to be one of the monks. If it were two years of that or two years of Needle Rock, I don't know! [laughter]

The thing that I don't like is that a monk can't be on display. It's like something in a World's Fair. Like the "monastic building" in the New York World's Fair of 1970: "And in the monastic building there, you got three Buddhists meditating . . ." [laughter] But then, "It will help the monks grow in mutual appreciation on a personal level." "Deeper understanding of one another's traditions." That part's good. They should be doing that. "The laymen present can help them in this task by giving a wider frame of reference to the discussion of monastic life." They're going to be discussing monastic life. What's a common definition of a monk?

Then the third: "The atmosphere of the center would be conducive to various forms of exchange, by being both genuinely monastic and truly academic"—I don't like the "academic" part, it's much too "bookish"—"a place of honest work and of creative leisure." "Our time calls for forms of interaction . . . Monks all over the world speak a common language. Cooperation among the monks themselves . . . monks and laymen." Well, that's alright. "The activities are to be shared by three concentric circles of participants: monks, students, short-term residents. The monks would be small groups from different parts of the world to form the inner core of the project, each group consisting of three monks of the same monastic background: well-trained men alert to the concerns of our time. Attached to each of these core groups of monks is a group of students who enroll at the center for one academic term or more to study one particular monastic tradition." Now you've got the guys taking "Cistercian Monasticism 1A, 1B."

Mother Myriam: It's kind of an intellectual center on the study of monasticism.

"The third circle consists of men engaged in such fields as science, industry, education, or social service. They come for shorter periods of time to share their insights with the monks through lectures and discussions, and might want to stay for a few days of recollection at the center." That makes it a lecture sort of thing.

Comment: It sounds like the Chapel House at Colgate [University].

Exactly, yes. Probably he's very much influenced by that. That's the sort of thing that is growing up in these different universities. I don't know too much about it.

I've been there for a couple of weekends.

Have you? How is it?

Well, it was now about six years ago, but each person in the basement had their own room looking out across the valley, and then upstairs there was a library, both a library of music and a library of books, with all religious traditions. And then the chapel, which I think had a cross on the wall, because it had been donated by Christians, but you also, if you preferred, you could have a statue of Buddha or Shiva or Vishnu, or a crucifix, or whatever you want.

A supermarket. This is the kind of thing that ultimately you have to look out for in the business of being interested in different traditions. You have to watch out for just getting into a mishmash. The way I look at it is the things that I find in Eastern traditions, I've got to use myself [to see] if they're good for me. Not to just study them. I'm much more interested in something I can use. If I can't use it, I'm not going to bother with it. Sitting around and saying, "This is what one thing is and this is what the other thing is," that empties the whole thing. And you know what happens when you do that? After a day of, "This is interesting, and this is interesting, and isn't this interesting?"—you're empty.

Comment: That's another way to lose your identity.

Exactly. We have to really keep an identity in these things. Well, it's an interesting document. It's something that's going on in the monastic world of our time.

One thing that's always good is to see people [from outside one's own tradition] and appreciate them just as people. One very moving experience that I had was meeting at Gethsemani a Protestant from Czechoslovakia, from behind the Iron Curtain, who is involved in this business of accepting the conditions of Communism yet living the Gospel under Communism in a very radical way.[19] In the sense that Communism is a complete threat to the institution; so therefore, you can't bank on an institution. So, you have a completely non-institutionalized Christianity behind the Iron Curtain, in which you're not resisting Communism, you're simply helping people and witnessing Christ. It was the first time he had ever been in a Catholic monastery. He was in this country and he came to Gethsemani, and we sat up late talking together in a room, and the sun was going down and we were sitting there. It was a very Emmaus-like experience, this sense of: here is this man who is completely my brother and we just didn't know each other, and had complete agreement from totally different parts of the world, but somehow the presence of Christ was there. It was very moving.

I think that's what we need. We need these very real people that come in as pilgrims and pass through. You find that there is something basically the same in everybody. There is this existential quality of a religious reality, but the moment you put them around a table, then everybody is just, "This is his idea and what's your view? What do you think about it?" It just becomes all relative. Because the real thing—again, it expresses the Hindu view—is that underlying all these accidentals, there is One Reality. There is one God. And everybody, in some way or other, is trying to manifest a true experience of God. You go through the accidentals of

---

19. A reference to Jan Milic Lochman (1922–2004), Czechoslovakian-Swiss Protestant theologian and professor of systematic theology at the University of Basel. For an account of their meeting, see Merton's journal entry dated March 6, 1964 (*Dancing in the Water of Life: Seeking Peace in the Hermitage, Journals, vol. 5: 1963–1965*, ed. Robert E. Daggy [San Francisco: HarperCollins, 1997], 86–87).

what they say about their experience to this one central Unity. This One Big Reality, which is God. But if you forget that, and just talk about the accidentals, it'll keep going around and around in circles—it gets totally lost. There's nothing left.

In Hinduism, for example, when Dom Bede Griffiths went to India to start a Christian ashram, he took over the distinguishing marks of the Hindu *ordo monasticus*; that is, they all have the same habit. It's the saffron robe. He's a Christian monk in India but he has the saffron robe of the *sannyasin*.

Fr. Roger: Is he accepted by the Indian population?

Yes, he is. They understand him, and they visit, and they like the monastery. He is accepted by them. They fully understand the situation, because he has real poverty. They never accepted before the Christian monks with a purely European setup and European customs, because it can't come close to their kind of poverty. They've got real poverty there. They all sit on the floor. That's what they do in their country. He is very well accepted, and Monchanin was very accepted. Monchanin was less accepted by the Catholics than by the Hindus. The Catholics were very upset about Monchanin.[20]

Monchanin started out as a missionary and then eventually he was able to start a little community. There were two of them. There was this Benedictine Henri Le Saux. There have been some good books about Monchanin.[21] He had a really rough life, sleeping on the ground and snakes crawling in. But that's what you have to do if you really want to do it in India.

What will ever happen in China? Will monks ever get back into China? There's a Chinese professor at Indiana University that I'm working with.

20. Jules Monchanin (1895–1957), French Catholic priest who, along with Henri Le Saux, founded Saccidananda Ashram in Tamil Nadu, India, where Bede Griffiths later joined them. On Monchanin and Merton, see David M. Odorisio, "Introduction to 'Yoga and Hesychasm' by Jules Monchanin," and Francis X. Clooney, "Thomas Merton's Deep Christian Learning Across Religious Borders," in *Merton and Hinduism*, 46–49, 171–77.

21. For a collection of Monchanin's writings, see *In Quest of the Absolute: The Life and Works of Jules Monchanin*, ed. and trans. J. G. Weber (Kalamazoo, MI: Cistercian Publications, 1977).

He did this edition of one of these Zen texts and I had done an introduction on it. I want to find out more from him on this, but he was not only a Doctor of Philosophy from both Oxford and Cambridge and a very advanced student of modern logic, but he was also trained by an authentic Zen master in Northern China—who sounds very interesting, indeed—who died about 20 years ago. Apparently, he was a completely uneducated man, but who had a very deep Zen training. I would really like to find out more about him because it sounds like he had a terrific knowledge of how to form people and train people. What happens if you don't have a few people like that around? As long as you've got people like that, you have true disciples, something can go on.

This is a very interesting man, too, Dr. Chi. [22]

Fr. Roger: What does he say about China and the future of religion?

He's not very optimistic at all. Under Communism, there doesn't seem to be much hope. They are totally against all of these old traditions. They don't want any part of Buddhism or Confucianism. I'm sure that you can't stamp those things out. There are bound to be people that are keeping this alive. Of course, one thing that happens [is], we had a postulant who went to seminary in Hungary and then got out after the Revolution, and he had a brother who was a Communist in Yugoslavia and had no religion. But this brother, who was an engineer and was an international chess champion, and a Communist, was also very interested in yoga and was practicing yoga. I don't know where he got it, but he just decided that he needed to do some yoga. He was practicing yoga.

I think you can expect that in these people. They're going to be intelligent, and they're going to be looking around and they're going to say, "Okay, I'm going to do this, I'm going to do some Zen." In Russia, all they can stop is the institution; they can't stop the real thing. They can stop you putting up buildings, and they can stop you having schools, but they can't stop you following what you believe. I think these people are simply going

22. Richard Hu See-Yee Chi (1918–1986), authority on Ch'an (Chinese Zen) Buddhism. For Merton's correspondence with Chi, see *Hidden Ground of Love*, 121–25. Chi also contributed to Merton's literary magazine, *Monks Pond*. See also the reference to Chi below (p. 290, fn. 46).

to do that. Of course, in the Communist countries, at least in Europe, they're getting much more independent. In Poland, for example, there's a great deal of independence among the intellectuals. When they decide they want to do something, they go ahead and do it.

Comment: Do you know if there is a monastic movement in South America? Which Orders?

There's some Benedictines there. The best thing that I know of is in Latin America. I think I mentioned it before—this former novice at Gethsemani [Ernesto Cardenal]. He hasn't got anybody, but he's on this island. I think that they could be very good. I think there's a real need for monasticism in South America.[23]

23. A long, winding, and difficult-to-transcribe discussion ensues regarding Merton's various contacts and connections among Central and South American hermits and monastics in Patagonia, Chile, Nicaragua, Ecuador, and Bolivia, as well as a general discussion of the state of the Catholic Church in South America. The topic then shifts to the practice of group psychoanalysis in American monastic communities (with the example of Saint Meinrad's in Indiana), followed by a humor-filled critique of the Chapter of Faults at Gethsemani rife with anecdotes and much laughter.

Chapter Nine

Introduction to Sufism

Lord, send us your Holy Spirit and teach us to understand what we need to understand in order to let you work [through us]. Through Christ, our Lord. Amen.

When I originally came, I was going to talk quite a bit about Muslim mysticism, and now we're more than halfway through and I still want to talk about this. There's a lot that can be said.

First of all, one of the best people to read on this is Louis Massignon.[1] He's really very good. He's the one who was converted [to Catholicism] by Charles de Foucauld.[2] Massignon was an Islam scholar who used to work in the desert. I think he ran into Charles de Foucauld out in the desert. Massignon was a very powerful personality, and a very interesting personality. There's sort of a cult of him at the moment.

One of the things that is interesting about Massignon is that he was a married man who had some kind of Eastern Rite [Melkite] priesthood. He was ordained. He said mass in his own home most of the time. He was a priest secretly. He was very prominent in the French peace movement and

---

1. Louis Massignon (1883–1962), Catholic convert and pioneer of Islamic-Christian dialogue. On the tremendous influence of Massignon on Merton, see Sidney H. Griffith, "Merton, Massignon, and the Challenge of Islam," in *Merton and Sufism*, 51–78. Merton's letters to Massignon are included in *Witness to Freedom*, 275–81. On the remarkable conversion and trajectory of Massignon's early life, see Jeffrey J. Kripal, *Roads of Excess, Palaces of Wisdom: Eroticism and Reflexivity in the Study of Mysticism* (Chicago: University of Chicago Press, 2001), 102–13.

2. Charles de Foucauld (1858–1916), founder of the Little Brothers of Jesus, lived as a hermit in the Algerian desert among the nomadic Tuareg peoples. He was canonized May 15, 2022, by the Catholic Church.

French non-violent movement. Especially during the time of the Algerian War. He was very involved in this whole struggle for the Algerians. He's really a great man.

There are many reasons why Sufism is interesting; for example, it's in between us and India. It has a lot to do with Christianity, and a lot to do with Hinduism, but of course, be careful, don't follow the arguments of those who say that Sufism is really derivative. The Muslims don't like that. If you say that Sufism comes from Christianity, they get very upset.

There was definitely a tie-up with Christian monks. Muhammad liked monks. It's either in the Quran or one of these *Hadiths*, these Sayings of the Prophet. If you have anything to do with anybody in Islam, your conversation is almost 90% Sayings of the Prophet. This Sufi man that I told you about, that came over to our place—in order to really get into a conversation with him, you would have to keep up a running fire of Sayings of the Prophet. I'm not too strong on Sayings of the Prophet. I can maybe respond with one or maybe with none—or sayings of Muslim saints. In a sense, they are still very Biblical. They have a great fondness of sayings. They act very Biblically.

At Gethsemani, we went out for a walk and we climbed up onto this big hill outside in front of the monastery where there is a statue of St. Joseph. We climbed up on top of that, right by the highway, and there are four or five of us sitting all around in the grass. Three of them with turbans and beards. Sitting around. We had brought some oranges. The way you sat around eating the oranges was that the master would peel the orange and then divide it up, and give a little bit to each disciple. We're sitting there eating these oranges, and while we're sitting up there, their hour for prayer came. They got up and there they were bowing towards Mecca. It was beautiful, really—a very, very touching thing. Sufism is grounded in this desert-type culture, although it is also a city phenomenon. Underlying it is this basic Islamic substrate.

Now what is Islam?[3] I guess it would be a good idea to talk about that first. The term "Islam" itself means pretty much the same thing as our term "abandonment," total abandonment to God. Actually, it has

---

3. For a modern introduction to Sufism in its Islamic context, see Annemarie Schimmel, *Mystical Dimensions of Islam* (Chapel Hill: University of North Carolina Press, 1975) and Carl W. Ernst, *Sufism: An Introduction to the Mystical Tradition of Islam* (Boston: Shambhala, 1997). For Merton's monastic conferences on Sufism, see *Merton and Sufism*, 130–62.

different levels of meaning. The first meaning is just complete obedience. Complete obedience to God is "Islam." So, a Muslim is a man who obeys God totally, and obeys the one God.

The idea there is you obey not only God, but His messengers. Total surrender to the Word of God, either in the Quran or through His various messengers. Of course, one of his messengers is Jesus. He's accepted as a messenger of God. The Muslims make a great distinction between the idolaters who are the pagans and the People of the Book.[4] The People of the Book are the Christians, the Jews, and the Muslims. The People of the Book have a special preferred position. In spite of all the enmity there has been between Christians and Muslims, it was usually the Christians who were more aggressive, at least after the first big wave of invasion. For example, when the Muslims were in charge of Mount Athos, when that was under Turkish rule, the monks never had any problems. There was a Muslim garrison on the peninsula, but they never bothered the monks. The monks had to pay taxes or something like that, but that's about all. There wasn't much problem there.

There's some statement from Muhammad either in the Quran or in the *Hadith*, in which he says, if you go out into the desert, you may find some of these Christians living in caves. These Christians living in caves, they're alright. They're monks. You can get along with them. Actually, the Monastery of Saint Catherine at Mount Sinai has always had very good relations with the Muslims; although completely surrounded by Muslims at all times, they've never been particularly molested by them. They have always tended to share any kind of goods that they would have with the poor in time of hunger. The Muslims around Mount Sinai Monastery have always been very friendly. There has been basically a respect for Christian monks traditionally in Islam.

The religion of the Muslims consists of three things: *Islam*, which is complete surrender, complete abandonment to God; one who surrenders completely to God is a Muslim. The second element is *Iman*, which is faith, and the Islamic faith is absolutely centered on the unity of God, *Tawhid*.

Incidentally, talking about jazz, there is a jazz record, which I have ordered and I hope it'll be there when I get back—it's called *Tauhid*.[5]

---

4. *Ahl al-kitāb* in Arabic.

5. Saxophonist Pharoah Sanders' second album, released in 1967.

It's the great Muslim term. The central object of the Muslim faith is the unity of God. This *Tauhid* is probably quite a good record. I don't know what Muslims would think about it. I don't know if this man is a Muslim or what he is. It's probably a very good record. It's interesting to see that these jazz musicians are now basing their compositions on religious ideas.

Then the third thing is *Ihsan*, which is virtue, but virtue in the sense of adoring God and serving God as if you saw Him. Muhammad said you should serve God as if you saw Him, and if you don't see Him, remember that He sees you. A Benedictine statement in a way.

Two things about Islam: They are very meticulous about observing these religious precepts. For example, during Ramadan when you have to keep absolutely fasting from all food and drink from sunrise to sunset. You'll be riding around, I'm told, in a taxi cab, for example, and the sunset gun goes off; the taxi driver stops and gets out, and runs in and gets a cup of coffee, and then he comes out and you ride along some more. They observe exactly the precepts that they've got, and they insist very much on being faithful and regular about these things; not for any other reason except in order to obey God. There is something deeply religious about the fact that they care about the way in which they do this: "God wants this and so this is what I'm going to do."

That's the background. Sufism is something much deeper than that. The Sufi tradition is something that is concerned not just with living your life as a good Muslim, fulfilling your duties, and then dying. It is very much concerned with a complete transformation of man; the total transformation of consciousness. That is the central thing in Sufism. There's no particular point, they believe, in living according to the Muslim religion unless you use it to be transformed, because really what God wants of man is to transform him. Because when man is completely transformed by the Word of God, then he becomes on earth a perfect reflection of God.

They will never say that you can be united with God. Some of the Sufis do, but Muslims have to be extremely careful, because if they say you're united with God, this is mixing something else with God, and it's against this *Tawhid*, which is basic unity. God is completely transcendent. The only way they can get around the idea of union with God at all is that you just totally disappear, and there's nothing left but God. Then this perfect unity is not affected.

What Islam tries to do is to return man to his original, deep, inner identity, which is veiled from him because of his "dream of negligence."[6] Now, this ties in with what we've just seen in Hinduism: this idea of a deep center. Of course, for the Muslim, man is not metaphysically rooted in God as he is in Hinduism. But nevertheless, God is this center, and we are alienated from our deepest identity—which is either in God, or very close to Him, centered in Him—because of a negligence and alienation, by which we have drifted away. Our ordinary state of consciousness is, therefore, one of alienation from our true self, because of an ingrained tendency to negligence, and indifference to who we really are.

This is the typical Muslim approach. It's a version of "original sin" in a sense. The idea that man is congenitally disposed to neglect his real being and his real identity, and to live in an area which is foggy and obscure, in which things are never quite what they ought to be. Man avoids as much as possible coming to grips with who he really is. It's a little different from the Hindu approach, but not much. It's the same basic kind of idea.

We all experience this to some extent. This is another formulation of something that everybody knows. We are aware of this fact that we have moments in which we come to ourselves and we feel that we are not being true to ourselves. That's the simplest way of putting it. I would say that is the kind of situation that the monastic life is meant to handle. We are put into the monastic life in order to be completely true to ourselves, and in Muslim terms, that means being completely true to God by following Islam, by totally surrendering to God, because God has in Himself "the secret," and the secret is also a grace: the secret grace or gift of revealing to us who we're meant to be.

What is this deep identity? This is an interesting thing that we run into in Islam. For a Christian, this is Christ Himself. We are all meant to approach, as close as we can, to Christ, and the Holy Spirit forms in us a new identity as Christians; we are "new men" in proportion as the Holy Spirit forms Christ in us and identifies us with Christ.[7] In Islam, it's not quite the same. You're not conformed to Muhammad. In a certain sense, Muhammad is a model. You can imitate him.

---

6. Nasr, 22, 33 (cited below).

7. Merton develops this Pauline theme of a "new man" (e.g., Eph 2:15; 4:24), and a "New Adam," extensively in his book *The New Man* (New York: Farrar, Straus and Giroux, 1961).

There's something very interesting about this basic idea that the perfect man always turns out to be a kind of Universal Cosmic man. In other words, there's some reflection of the idea of a New Adam. It's in there somewhere. It's hard to say where it came from, but there is some idea that if we wake up to who we are, and if we're perfectly faithful to God's will, and accept the grace that he gives us, then we are transformed and deepened to a point where we become Cosmic Universal men.

What does that mean? I think it means pretty much the same thing as St. Paul is talking about when he talks about being "all things to all men."[8] In other words, you're no longer restricted. Going back to this book that I told you about, this is precisely what Reza Arasteh's book is about. The book on "final integration," on Sufism and psychoanalysis. "Final integration" is when a person transcends all possible limitations of his society and his milieu, and becomes a completely open Cosmic Man in the sense of cutting across all cultural limitations. It seems to me that a practical application of this kind of thing is openness to all forms of religious experience.[9]

Not being restricted to the external limitations by which a particular kind of religious consciousness is described; to be able to be faithful to one's own religious tradition, and at the same time, to be completely aware of the possibilities of other traditions throwing light on what we have, and even to some extent, participating in their experience. But to do this, one has to be universalized.[10] We use the word "Catholic."

It's funny what's happened to the word "Catholic." It has come to mean "parochial": a Catholic is somebody who is limited. It's lost its meaning of "universal"; at least, in this particular deep sense. Really, a Catholic man is a universal man, and in Christ, he should be a universal, wide-open man: all things to all men in Christ and in the Spirit.

For the Muslim, history is a series of cycles of prophecy in which each cycle is followed by a decline and then a new cycle of prophecy. We're in the last cycle of prophecy, which is that of Muhammad. This is now the end. There's great emphasis on the Last Judgement in Islam. I don't know

---

8. 1 Corinthians 9:22.

9. On the radical implications of Merton's interreligious thinking, see David M. Odorisio, "*Yes to Everyone*: Thomas Merton's Radical Ecumenism and Inter-Monastic Mysticism of the Ground" (*The Merton Seasonal* [46.2]: 3–11).

10. This is nearly identical to Merton's later notes for a talk to be given in Calcutta in October of 1968 (*The Asian Journal of Thomas Merton*, ed. Naomi Burton, Patrick Hart, and James Laughlin [New York: New Directions, 1973], 313, 315).

exactly what they're figuring in terms of where we stand in regard to this, but [to Muslims] we are in the last age.[11]

The cycles of prophecy are, for example, Moses, who was the Prophet of the Jews; Jesus, the Prophet of the Christians. Moses revealed the Law to the Jews; Jesus revealed the way of love, which is regarded by the Muslims as esoteric, as a mystical way. Moses and Jesus are contrasted as Moses being a way of life for earthly man and Jesus a mystical way for esoteric, spiritual people. Then Islam is regarded as a union of the two and is the final religion.

It is possible to regard Islam as a combination of a very legal religion, on one hand, with a highly mystical inner core, which is hard to situate in it. It's an extremely legal religion. It's just as legal as Judaism, if not more so. That's why they, to some extent, have trouble with Christianity, because for the Muslim, Christianity is much too free. They fear this kind of liberty of the Spirit, which is essential to the New Testament. They don't know quite where to place it, except the Sufis. The Sufis accept that perfectly. They have no particular trouble with it.

For this transformation of man to take place, there's a great deal of emphasis on spiritual commentary on the Quran. I'm not going to go into that because it's an extremely complicated procedure. There's a book by a fellow called [Henry] Corbin,[12] which incidentally that's another place where you can find a great deal of information on this.

Have you ever seen any of the *Eranos Yearbooks*? It would probably be very well worth having. Selections from that have just been done in English. There are three or four volumes.[13] These are conferences given at a place in Switzerland, mostly under the auspices of C. G. Jung and

---

11. There is a similar concept in Hinduism regarding the final age, the *Kali Yuga* ("epoch" or "age"), which is considered the current (and darkest) chapter in the history of humankind.

12. Henry Corbin (1903–1978), influential French scholar of Islamic thought, particularly Sufi mysticism. Presumably a reference to Corbin's *Imagination Creatrice dan le Soufisme d'Ibn Arabi*, published in English translation as *Creative Imagination in the Sufism of Ibn 'Arabi* (Princeton: Princeton University Press, 1969).

13. The *Eranos Jahrbücher* were compiled by Eranos organizer, Olga Froebe-Kapteyn (1881–1962), who would invite leading interdisciplinary scholars and scientists to her home in Ascona, Switzerland, beginning in 1933. For a history, see Thomas Hakl, *Eranos: An Alternative Intellectual History of the Twentieth Century* (New York: Routledge, 2014). The English volumes Merton is referencing were edited by Joseph Campbell and published in the Bollingen Series by Princeton University Press (see below).

his friends.[14] People like [Jean] Daniélou were there; Hugo Rahner was habitually there.[15] Massignon used to go there. [D.T.] Suzuki used to go there. Some very good psychoanalysts have been. Each year, they have met and continue to meet, and have a symposium on certain things that have to do with the spiritual life and our deepening of consciousness, and the Jungian approach. An Islamic scholar will give his part; a Buddhist will give his part. They're very good collections. In English, there are four big collections, one on *Man and Spirit; Man and Time; Spiritual Disciplines*, which are some of the best essays.[16] That's a very good source for material on Islam. They're very worthwhile. Anybody can really profit by them in a monastery.

There, you will find what you need to know about Quranic exegesis, because Corbin will have four or five articles there about this very elaborate spiritual commentary, like the Fathers of the Church, only much more so. I could see where it could be a very engrossing hobby to get involved in—it's extremely interesting.

One of the things that has come out of it is this idea of the "creative imagination," the part played by the creative imagination under the impulsion of this symbolic use of commentary, which is a little alien to us, but it's very rich and very profound stuff.[17] I'm not going to get involved in that because it's terribly complex, but very interesting. It's St. Bernard, but pushed far, far out—way out.

You've got a statement like this about understanding the Quran and understanding the spiritual meaning of it. It's a penetration into the inner meaning of a sacred text written by someone who has experienced the meaning of the text in his own Being. Again, it ties in with this Cosmic Man thing. Maybe it's a bit Platonic, but somehow there's the idea that the God who dictated the Quran—because Muhammad just took it down straight, the whole book. No various authors or none of that nonsense.

---

14. Influential Swiss psychiatrist and comparative psychologist of religion, C. G. Jung (1875–1961) was an instrumental and central figure in the annual Eranos gatherings.

15. Jean Daniélou, SJ (1905–1974), French Cardinal and Jesuit theologian; Hugo Rahner, SJ (1900–1968), German Jesuit and brother of influential theologian, Karl Rahner, SJ (1904–1984).

16. These are actual titles of volumes in this series.

17. See, e.g., Corbin, *Creative Imagination*.

Took it straight down on paper. Textual criticism—they don't fuss with that sort of thing.

The God who dictated this is also the God who created man. So, the Bible, the inner constitution of man, and the constitution of the cosmos, are all really aspects of the same thing. In proportion, as a man enters deeper into the revealed text, he also understands himself better, and then in him, opens out the secret laws of the cosmos. When he becomes a Cosmic Man, he is one who completely corresponds to the revelation that's in the Quran, and the inner laws of the universe. Nature and revelation come to a double focus in him. That's what a "Complete Man" is.

Then, in such a one, all that God has willed to place in His creation and in His revelation is brought together and manifested [in the Cosmic Man]. Now, when you get someone like Ibn al-Arabi—who was a Spaniard from Andalusia, and ended up in Damascus as a [spiritual] master—he has developed this to a fine art, and he's really a most exciting person to read.[18] It's a great aesthetic philosophy, in which you've got this sense of different levels of consciousness and being and meaning, all jammed together with an enormous amount of brilliance. It's very interesting to read.

I was doing some work on him last year,[19] and some of his stuff about creation—I was sitting up at the hermitage at dawn about this time of year. Each day at dawn, I would be working on Ibn al-Arabi and the sun would be coming up and the birds would be singing. You really would "turn on" [laughter].[20] It's immensely complex, immensely imaginative, and yet at the center, you get this feeling that everything is all coming to a focus. There's a feeling that it all points to one thing, which is to this creative design of God. You get this tremendous sense of wonder, which is a very important religious dimension of life, this admiration, which is very important in Islam.

18. Ibn 'Arabi (1165–1240); *The Bezels of Wisdom* (New York: Paulist Press, 1980) remains one of his classic and most enduring works.

19. There are five audio recordings that Merton made with a tape recorder between April and May 1967 based on his reading and notes on Ibn Arabi, archived at the Thomas Merton Center at Bellarmine University. See also Merton's 1961 poem, "Song for the Death of Averroës (from Ibn Al Arabi . . .)" (*Collected Poems of Thomas Merton*, 325–29).

20. Merton uses the phrase "turn on" here within the context of late 1960s counterculture.

One of the things we most need to recover today in our worship and in our spiritual life is this admiration for the wisdom of God. A sense of the great wisdom of God's design, in which all things so marvelously come together. Of course, you've got this in the Middle Ages; the medieval people were full of this. You get the same kind of thing in some scholars that go into medieval art. For example, you have people who have studied medieval architecture in relation to medieval music, and in relation to a background of Platonic philosophy and medieval Scholastic philosophy, coming up with clear demonstrations of how, in certain buildings, for instance, Chartres, or places like that, you can work out mathematically how the intervals between certain parts of the building correspond to intervals in music.[21]

There are parts of Chartres which are fourth tone, and parts of Chartres which are third tone. You get the same kind of impact visually as you do from these modes in music, but to do that, there must have been something very rich going on, even though they may not have been fully conscious of it. This is one of the things that always gets me excited about this: you suddenly realize the enormous richness of these religious cultures, and it's the same out in the East. It's the same with Buddhist religious culture. We still have too much of a tourist mentality: you just go there; there's this huge temple, and, "I saw that temple, check off another one." But really, what you're in is a great whole world of all kinds of rich correspondences, and to enter into this is to really open out to a much higher kind of consciousness. I think that's certainly one of the things that monks have to keep alive on earth: this possibility for expansion of consciousness, appreciation, and awareness.

So, "This authority, then, who himself has been completely penetrated by the wisdom of God in scripture, then sees in the sacred scripture what he is himself and the type of knowledge he can derive from the text depends precisely on who he is."[22] That's very revealing. Whether or not we are interested in the spiritual interpretation of scripture, this is the principle behind it. There's a tendency to dismiss the spiritual interpretation of scripture as purely an allegorical gimmick. What it's really about is an interpretation in which one lives the deeper and inner dimension of scrip-

---

21. See, e.g., Otto von Simson, *The Gothic Cathedral: Origins of Gothic Architecture and the Medieval Concept of Order* (New York: Pantheon Books, 1956), 3–60.

22. Nasr, 57 (cited below).

ture. St. Bernard had this perfectly, and that book about St. Bernard and the Bible by Dumontier brings this out pretty well.[23] I'm not crazy about that book all the way through, but it does bring this to the fore a little bit.

The idea is that what Bernard was doing was in point of fact, completely illegitimate from the point of view of scientific criticism and scientific exegesis. But what he was doing, was deepening as far as he could, the correspondence between his own experience of life, and what the Bible said. Now, if you want to experience the Bible, you have to do something like that in some way or other. If you're going to live the Bible, somehow or other, you have to enter into this experience. We are, for example, all familiar with Abraham and Isaac and Jacob; our God is the God of Abraham, Isaac, and Jacob. And Abraham, Isaac, and Jacob are much more to us than just simply figures that happen to be in Mesopotamia at a certain time, or in Palestine at a certain time, in so many centuries BCE. Abraham is to us as familiar as our own father. He is our father. How is this possible? I don't know, but it certainly is true. The Sufis are very strong on this.

Incidentally, I'm following this Persian scholar [Seyyed Hossein] Nasr.[24] He gets around this country every once in a while. I haven't yet met him, but I hope to. He's got some very good books, and he is completely a Muslim. He's very trustworthy as a scholar. He's writing about Islam from within. He quotes Rumi[25] here about understanding the Quran, and about Quranic exegesis, "If you draw aside the veil, you are repulsed. The act itself tricks you, and you see the Quran as ugly." That is to say, if you approach the book in a purely subject-object relationship, and you say, "I'm going to get out of this what I can"—you don't get anything out of it at all. If I go to the book the way you go to a store, for example, "I'm going to walk in and take something from this"—you don't—and it repels you. You lose your taste for it. "But if you do not draw aside the veil," he says, "and seek only it's good pleasure"; [i.e.] give the book time

23. *Saint Bernard et la Bible* (Desclée De Brouwer, 1953).

24. Seyyed Hossein Nasr (b. 1933), Iranian-born professor and Islamic scholar. Merton's notes are based on Nasr's *Ideals and Realities of Islam* (London: George Allen & Unwin, 1966).

25. Jalāl ad-Dīn Mohammad Rūmī (1207–1273), highly influential and celebrated Persian Sufi, poet, and founder of the Mevlevi Order of Sufis. See Nasr, 58 (paraphrased).

to reveal itself when it feels like it. The book is now treated as a person [laughter], "Watering its own field and attending on it from afar, toiling upon that which pleases it best, it will show its face to you without your drawing aside the veil."[26]

This is a typical Sufi statement. First of all, it's cryptic and poetic. Secondly, it is highly paradoxical; it turns around on you. It says that if you want to understand the book, live with it without trying to force it to reveal anything to you; that if you dwell with the book, and water its sown field, and toil upon that which pleases it best. I don't know what he precisely means by that. What do you think he means by that? How do you please a book? How do you toil?

Comment: I was just reflecting; he's treating the book like you would treat people.

Yes, yes, yes. I think what he means is that in a relationship with a book, you start it, and yet, there is a kind of "book providence." There's a funny kind of psychology that goes with books, and I'm astounded how things work out with books. A book all of a sudden seems to come along just at the right time; something falls open right at that page that hits you. But you may have to struggle with it, too. You'll get books that you may have three or four days of sleeping over them and having an awful time. Very probably, there's a psychological resistance. Something's telling you, "You're going to get something [out of this]; this is going to hit you—stay away from it," and then all of a sudden, you get really involved in the book. There is a kind of interrelationship that takes place in reading. You go through a whole development over a period of a week or ten days when you're reading this book. It changes your whole outlook on everything and the whole tempo of your life changes and leads you in all sorts of new directions. With me, it gets into work, and starts a new line of work. Some of the most important things that happen in your life happen in relationship to some book—for a monk.

Of course, that's another problem: we are not really in the age of the book anymore. I still am, but I think for a lot of people now, books aren't going to work that way anymore. If that's the case, then they're much more

26. Nasr, 58.

at the mercy of other people, because if you're going to be depending on TV, you're going to have a different kind of "providence." Not that there's anything wrong with TV, but it is predetermined by a whole lot of other people. The production of a TV show and the production of a book are entirely different.

I was talking to somebody who has had a lot to do with TV and they were saying that when you're involved in a TV production, what's actually being shown is the least important thing. In other words, they're shooting, say, two people having a discussion about something, and there's an enormous amount of activity going on—the filming, the lighting, the sound; all the engineering that's involved in it. What happens in a TV production is that you've got all these different influences at work to produce the thing, and they all go into it in some way or other, and that's part of your "TV providence." I haven't really thought this out very deeply, but I think there must be some kind of implications there. There's a great difference between a man just simply reading a book on his own with his own reactions to deal with—think of all the reactions of all these people. Because what you do is to such a great extent determined by the situation in which you're in, how you feel, and how other people feel, and what they're thinking.

Fr. Roger asks a question about the role of salvation in Islam and the Quran.

It's salvation by corresponding to the will of God. This is where the spiritual commentary comes in. The spiritual commentary by the Sufis either injects this, finds it, or imagines it, but they conceive this to be the most important thing about the Quran. They read what is said in the Quran not just as a revelation of what's going to happen in history—

Fr. Roger: The way this is presented appears to be a communication of the sacredness or wholeness of God.

Yes, but as manifested in His creation. The holy will of God and His power as creator is manifested in creation and as corresponded with my own life when I open up to these deeper levels of consciousness. In other words, God has created the world and put man in it, and man has to discover himself in discovering the world and in discovering God; and discovering this through the Word of God.[27] For the Sufis, this means deepening consciousness to a profound, mystical dimension, and that's the way they approach it.

Fr. Roger: How do they conceive that in the personal relationship between man and God?

Entirely in terms of love, obedience, and surrender; entirely in terms of will, and of course, contemplation and intelligence. But it's a relation of surrender. "Islam" means surrender—obedience to God's word. This deepening of consciousness is, in the end, obedience to God's deepest purpose in creating me. He created me with these secret dimensions of my being, and the purpose of my life is to work at opening these up by studying the Quran, and by these other methods that we'll see in a minute. They have these various ways of breaking through to deeper [levels of consciousness].

They're full of the love of God. It's very much like bhakti yoga. When we get further into it, [you'll see] this deepening of consciousness, and this discovery of one's deepest inner self, corresponds to the kind of thing in bhakti yoga, where a person dedicates himself totally to the love of God, seeking to even be absorbed completely in God by love. It's all in the same kind of a deeply, self-dedicating kind of love. But in Sufism, the thing that is quite characteristic of them, is this gnostic sense of God's wisdom having placed in me these various secret dimensions, which correspond to his plan in the cosmos.

Fr. Roger: You speak about "secret dimensions" quite often; but it cannot be related to Gnosticism.

It can, and that's one of the things you have to look out for. Sufism and Gnosticism are close, but you have to take each man on his own merits. For example, one of the elements that you aim at in Sufism is *marifa*, which is "gnosis." But I think it is not so much a purely esoteric thing. The esoteric element of Sufism is more a matter of keeping things hidden

---

27. Compare to Merton's celebrated passage in *New Seeds of Contemplation* (New York: New Directions, 1961): "[T]here is only one problem on which all my existence, my peace and my happiness depend: to discover myself in discovering God" (p. 36).

from the official establishment of Islam. It's not a question of a higher elect group.[28]

Comment: Is that why it was so suspect?

Oh, yes. What was so suspect about Sufism was this whole element of union with God by love. But they would have to be very careful about saying that, because the official people would keep coming in with, "You people are heretics. You are saying that the relation between man and God is not just a relation of 'man way down here and God way up there giving him commands'"—which is the standard Islamic view of things—"You're saying that you get so close to God that you're united with Him by love," which the official position tries to avoid.

Some of these Sufis became so carried away by their love for God that they would say extraordinary and even provocative things.[29] The man that Massignon was interested in most was Hallaj.[30] It's evident that Hallaj perhaps provoked his death. He was put to death by crucifixion, and the reason why he was put to death by crucifixion was that he was so convinced that he was one with God that he said, "I am God." It's a very strange case. Massignon makes a tremendous thing out of it. Massignon says all the time that Hallaj is really a crypto-Christian mystic;[31] that there was something in there that was more than just Islam. That may be

---

28. Sufism and the Gnostic communities of early Christianity who sought an "elect" or "elevated" form of spiritual knowledge ("gnosis") are utterly distinct traditions. The similarity—and issue in question—is in regard to the use of the term "gnosis" among many scholars (e.g., Corbin) to translate the type of spiritual knowledge Sufis are seeking (*marifa*); however, historical Gnosticism and Sufi "gnosis" are not to be conflated.

29. "Ecstatic utterances" or "theopathic locutions" (*shathiyat*), such as those of al-Bistami ("Glory to me!") or Hallaj (cited above); see Michael Sells, trans. and ed., *Early Islamic Mysticism: Sufi, Qur'an, Mi'raj, Poetic, and Theological Writings* (New York: Paulist Press, 1996), 212–13; Schimmel, *Mystical Dimensions of Islam*, 41; and Kripal, *Roads of Excess*, 114–17.

30. Mansur al-Hallaj (d. 922), early Sufi mystic and martyr, gruesomely executed for proclaiming "*An al Haq*"—"I am the Real." Massignon wrote his dissertation and later a four-volume scholarly work on al-Hallaj, entitled *The Passion of al-Hallaj*. For an abbreviated English translation of this later work, see Massignon, *Hallāj: Mystic and Martyr*, trans. and ed. Herbert Mason (Princeton: Princeton University Press, 1994).

31. It is important to keep in mind Massignon's own conversion to Catholicism and the ways in which he perhaps identified with Hallaj (see Kripal, *Roads of Excess*, 112–13).

so, but Hallaj was deliberately provoking this. I think he got to the point where he saw that the best thing that he could do was just simply push it so far that it couldn't be evaded anymore.

What I think he was saying was that he had experienced mystical union with God at such a point where he felt that there was no longer any distinction between himself and God. He experienced it that way, and instead of making fine distinctions, he would just throw it at them and see what they'd do. So, they crucified him.[32] He's a legendary man. Apparently, his disciples carried on this tradition [of ecstatic utterances]. There's a great deal [written] about him, but he's not the one that I'm most interested in. There are problems about him. It's a little bit bizarre, when they come out and say, "I am God." It troubles me, too, in a way. I much prefer people like Rumi, who simply say ordinary outrageous things [laughter].

The esoteric aspect of Sufism has these two slants: one where they're getting away from persecution and saying things so cryptically that nothing can be found wrong with them; and another way where they provoke persecution by making outrageous statements—which could be explained. I think Hallaj was simply trying to say that he had had a genuine mystical experience, but he just didn't want to bother to explain it. He would just put it in the most outrageous terms and then let them kill him [for it]. I think that was perhaps his grace; it was the way he approached the problem.

Fr. Roger asks a follow up question regarding the influence of "gnostic" tendencies on Buddhism and other Eastern traditions.

Much less in Buddhism. Near Eastern mysticism is deeply affected by Gnosticism, Platonism, Neoplatonism—some good, some bad. With the Sufis, you have to take each man on his own terms. There are some in Sufism that are obviously influenced by Hinduism. You have to take each one on his own terms. Then, of course, there's also the Zoroastrian background.[33] All of this is there [too]. So, you have to take each man on

---

32. According to tradition, Hallaj approached his execution laughing and singing. One of his most celebrated poems begins, "Kill me, O my faithful friends / for to kill me is to make me live; / My life is in my death, and my death is in my life" (Massignon, *Hallāj*, 285; Schimmel, *Mystical Dimensions of Islam*, 68–69).

33. Zoroastrianism is an ancient Persian religion that predates both Christianity and Islam and is based on the teachings of the prophet Zoroaster.

his own merits, and you have to also get something of his background. But as you get further into the Middle Ages, they have very much their own character; for example, Ibn Arabi, in whom there is obviously some "gnosticism." It can be handled in such a way that you don't get sunk in it, and it doesn't affect the reality of the mystical experience, but it's obviously there. Of course, that's for the scholars, and they handle it objectively. Corbin is clear on what's gnostic and what isn't, and they can do that now, because they've got enough material on it.

Moving on here. We're dealing with these symbols and the sacred texts that transform a man. One of the things that is involved in this contact with symbols in the sacred or revealed text is the transformation of man's sense life from exterior to interior. This again is like bhakti yoga: the idea of taking your emotional life and your imaginative life, and taking it from the ordinary, external level of contact with sense objects, and developing interior senses. This ties in with Origen, and this is very important in Sufism: a systematic effort to deepen man's consciousness by taking his exterior senses, and through various disciplines, interiorizing them so that they become interior spiritual senses.

Mother Myriam: I imagine it as a kind of monasticism?

Yes, it is. It is the kind of monasticism of Islam, although they're not celibate; they're married, mostly. They're not ascetics. They continue to live in the world. I'll talk later on the question of Sufi schools, but normally in Sufism, what you've got is a master and disciples—just a group—and there are different Orders of Sufis, quite a number of them. These different groups are related to these various orders.[34] What you do is go to a regular meeting, a religious meeting, with dancing, and with prayer—*dhikr* is what they call it.[35] It's a discipline like hesychasm.[36] The

---

34. On the variety of Sufi Orders, see Schimmel, *Mystical Dimensions of Islam*, 228–58; and Ernst, *Sufism*, 120–47.

35. On the practice of *dhikr*, see Ernst, *Sufism*, 92–98; and Bonnie Thurston, "Thomas Merton's Interest in Islam: The Example of *Dhikr*," in *Merton and Sufism*, 40–50.

36. Hesychasm is a prayer-practice originating in Eastern Orthodox Christianity, which, in its traditional expression, connects the recitation of the "Jesus Prayer" ("Lord Jesus Christ, Son of God, have mercy on me") with the breath, while focusing on the heart. These writings are compiled in the classic text, *The Philokalia*, trans. and ed. G. E. H. Palmer, P. Sherrard, and K. Ware (4 vols. [London: Faber and Faber, 1979–1995]). See

ideal way to learn *dhikr*, which is this breathing discipline, breathing and prayer—incidentally, when these Muslims were here, they were doing this all the time. Every breath is "Allah," and we'd be walking along and conversing, and then there'd be a lull in the conversation, and I'd hear this great big Moroccan "*Allah*" [makes an exhalation sound]. They have a whole system—I'll see if I can find it in these other notes and give it to you in detail—because it's very interesting.

The idea is you breathe in and then you breathe out, and there's a mental image that goes with this. But the way you learn *dhikr*, the rhythm of it, you don't just hear about it and then try to apply it yourself. When you're a novice, you've been under a master for a certain period of time. When he thinks you're ready, he will set aside for you a long session in which he sits opposite you and you sit opposite him on the floor with crossed legs, and he breathes and you breathe in time with him. Then he says the invocations and you listen carefully to how he says them, and you try to reproduce the thing as he does, until finally, you can completely reproduce the breathing prayer of the master. Then you go on yourself. You simply do everything that he does: you pray just as he does, and the interior follows.

This breathing prayer is centered on bringing the external senses to a focus in the heart.[37] And that's, of course, another thing about the Sufis: they're called "the people of the heart." The idea of concentrating one's senses and one's experience in the heart is standard for Sufism, and hesychasm, and for yoga, especially bhakti yoga. It's a practical way of enlisting one's body in living a life totally focused on a spiritual center. The heart is really not the center. But a good way of feeling as if one were centered, is to experience whatever one's prayer is—the invocation of Allah, or the invocation of Jesus—as coming from the center of your physiological being, or what we imagine to be the center of our physio-

---

also *Merton and Hesychasm: The Prayer of the Heart*, ed. Bernadette Dieker and Jonathan Montaldo (Louisville, KY: Fons Vitae, 2003).

37. On Merton's connections between Christian hesychasm and Sufi *dhikr*, see Bonnie Thurston, "Thomas Merton's Interest in Islam," in *Merton and Sufism*, 46–47; see also Seyyed Hossein Nasr, "The Prayer of the Heart in Hesychasm and Sufism," *Greek Orthodox Theological Review* 31.1–2 (1986): 195–203. The volume, *Paths to the Heart: Sufism and the Christian East*, ed. James Cutsinger (Bloomington, IN: World Wisdom, 2002) also takes up this theme.

logical being. Consequently, in all these disciplines, you have a tendency to be conscious of your breath going down to your heart.

In hesychasm, what you're supposed to do is get your Jesus Prayer from your head into your heart. In other words, you have to experience it. I'm not saying this is a very good thing to do. This may be a very bad thing to do. For a lot of us, it might be exactly the wrong thing to do. I personally don't advocate it or do it, but I'm just saying what they say. The Russians made a great point of trying to follow their breath down to their heart until they'd found the place of the heart. That is to say, they experienced their spiritual activity as taking place down around here somewhere. It's a kind of self-hypnosis in a way; an innocent form of self-hypnosis, but no form of self-hypnosis is necessarily a very good thing.

You have to be very, very careful with techniques like this. It's all very well to explain them. If I explain them, it's because I think it's interesting. It's useful to refer to this kind of thing, but not to go doing it too much without help. Especially some of the hesychast ones, because it's very easy to hypnotize yourself. You can hypnotize yourself if you don't look out. That doesn't mean to say that you get yourself into a trance and can't get out, but auto-suggestion is a very frequent thing. That's one of the troubles about the life of prayer—our own life of prayer—is that you have to be careful of an auto-suggestive, "Prayer of Quiet" type thing,[38] in which a person becomes very body conscious, or people become either conscious of their whole body, or conscious of part of their body.

Comment: Because most people, when they practice those things, they have not the philosophy behind it.

Yes. This is the precise opposite of what they're supposed to do. If a person, without any training or background, simply decides to empty her mind and just stay there praying, what will happen is, since there's nothing particularly going on, she may become very conscious of just being there; very conscious of her body. That's the wrong kind of consciousness. The interiorization of the senses hasn't worked. The word that usually applies is "narcissism," a narcissistic kind of prayer, in which a person is simply aware of being there.

---

38. Merton's concerns here are in reference to the so-called European "Quietist" controversy of the sixteenth–seventeenth centuries (see p. 32, fn. 3 above).

Comment: Could this happen easily with Dom Déchanet's book on Christian yoga?[39]

Oh yes. Anywhere you're fooling with the body; anytime you are paying attention to your body, if you're not doing it right—this is same way in athletics. It's a fundamental thing in athletics that you have to, for example, in some of the more complicated sports, like rowing, where there's a great deal of emphasis on technique. It's very easy to get completely hung up on your style: how's your wrist going, and how's the seat going. You can find yourself just simply doing the worst possible kind of rowing because you're conscious of every muscle. The whole thing in any sport is that you cease to be conscious of what you're doing. You just do it completely. Playing a musical instrument is the same thing. A person can be so hung up on where the hands are, what's the next note, and if a person's conscious of that, they never play.

So, the whole thing in prayer, and in everything else: the purpose is freedom from any kind of a hang up. But if you go about it in the wrong way, you get exactly the opposite. That's what these people mean by "the interiorization of the senses," so that they become objective. Father Roger was talking to me about that last night at supper, whether bhakti yoga is not completely subjective. If it's properly practiced, it's objective. It is directed; it channels all one's emotional drives to God, conceived as object.

They fix it in such a way that it's a workable subject-object relationship, or an I-Thou relationship, which is more than subject-object. All the emotion is channeled out. It's not just dammed up inside ourselves, because if we simply steam up an emotion and then stay with it, it just simmers. It's like a pot that has some water in it, boiling. It's useless. How do these people get away from this? In a thing like that you have to have somebody to tell you exactly what to do, and exactly what not to do.

---

39. J. M. Déchanet, *Christian Yoga* (New York: Harper & Row, 1960). For Merton's reading notes on this text, see his "Exercises to Help Bring the Body Under Control of the Spirit," in *Merton and Hinduism*, 337–39. Merton practiced a series of postural sequences based on Déchanet's book and even taught some yoga postures to several novices at Gethsemani (*Merton and Hinduism*, xxxviii–xl; Paul Quenon, "Yoga in Merton's Novitiate," in *Merton and Hinduism*, 334–36).

Therefore, never try any of these breathing prayers. With *pranayama*,[40] you don't need that much. That's more innocent. It's just deep breathing. You don't need any guidance on that. But anything like the Jesus Prayer with breathing, or Muslim *dhikr*, or something like that with breathing, you would absolutely have to have somebody tell you precisely what to do. Otherwise, you get all messed up. But it's very interesting to know that this kind of thing exists, and to understand a little bit of the principle behind it, in order to see that we may be able to do the same thing, much simpler and perhaps not as deeply, but this sort of freedom from oneself can be arrived at, perhaps in a lot simpler ways. This whole thing is a question of getting down to a spiritual center.

How's the time by the way? Has anybody got any more questions?

There is a question regarding the interiorization of the senses.

For example, take the sense of sight. I see light and colors and form and objects and people. If my life is lived entirely on a more or less exterior level, that's all I seek; for my sense of sight is to see visible things and to use my sight for that. If I am completely hung up on that, my interior sense of sight remains undeveloped. If I realize the potentiality of an interior sense of sight, and become detached from the need for [external verification], I then make a choice of not letting my senses wander all over the place, seeing only what's necessary for me. Instead, I develop an interior sight, which is like exterior sight, in which you see the intelligence and the imagination. You experience spiritual realities in a way analogous to your experience of sensible realities. This is perfectly ordinary Christian doctrine. The spiritual sense of sight is tied in with faith, and to develop a sense of spiritual sight or spiritual vision, it's simply a matter of praying and developing one's faith to the point where one sees—not visions—but sees in a way in which things become quite clear. You experience things directly and immediately in a clear, direct, personal way; not just conceptually—you *see*.[41]

---

40. Sanskrit technical term for yogic breathing; literally, the retention (or expansion; *yama*) of life force (*prana*). Merton references practicing *pranayama* on several occasions in his journals (*Merton and Hinduism*, xl).

41. Recording ends here; there is a slight gap before beginning again in next paragraph.

When you say, "Taste and see that the Lord is sweet," it really is a kind of taste. It's hard to explain, but there really is. And the word "sweetness" is adequate. It's sweet. But the trouble is, if you get too self-conscious about it, then the whole thing gets fouled up, which gets back to the thing that Rumi was saying about the veil. If all these things are to keep the interior senses pure and healthy, one must not be too conscious of them. One must simply direct his consciousness toward God, or toward some deep, important, central, truth, faith—towards the center. Again, this is imagery. I don't know how you would describe this scientifically; perhaps one would say that when a person is truly centered in that which his whole life is oriented, there is a feedback loop of wellbeing that affects your nervous system. I don't know. It probably all cooperates in that. In these Eranos studies people take up things like that, for example, modern psychologists. If you get those *Eranos Yearbooks* and look through them, you will find an essay on this kind of thing. Someone will have given a conference on this; either a Jungian psychologist or some other kind of scholar will have something to say about this. They're open to this. A lot of psychologists absolutely wouldn't touch it with a 20-foot pole, but these people dare to go into this. And there is a phenomenology of this kind of experience. Again, I would say, this is for us; there's no harm in reflecting on these things and seeing what they mean.

Comment: But you do have both the internal and external senses.

We always do.

Isn't it possible that the two should always continue to work in harmony? What about the factor of renunciation and detachment?

Renunciation and detachment are only necessary insofar as your exterior senses impede the action of the interior. If they don't impede it, then there's no need.

Right, and if they don't impede it, isn't it possible to have a community that's fully involved in external things?

Sure, this is quite possible. It's just a matter of the cultural situation and the situation of the individuals. But the only thing is that you've got to choose something. The state of being completely balanced with external, internal, and all that, is the paradise state. It's the way man was supposed to be. Now, it's quite possible. I would say that as people get less fouled up, they can get back to this. If a person is completely simple.

We never [seem to] psychologically get to this state, where we don't need the rules and can rely on more of a democracy.

Exactly. From a certain point of view—again, this is suspect saying it—but there's a perfectly justified Christian tradition which says that the monastery is the *paradisus claustralis*, that the monastery is the restoration of man's paradise state in Christ.[42] The sacramental life of the Church should do this, and the liturgy should do this. Everything should conspire towards doing this. Now, when I say that one should deny one's external senses, what I mean by that is not to be carried away with things that interfere with [this work of restoration]. If a person is going to drink a bottle of bourbon a day, then his interior senses may work, but what they do is not going to be reliable; in other words, we have to consider the health of the senses. The normal thing is for man's interior and exterior senses to work together.

The man who had this to a super eminent degree in the last 200 years was William Blake.[43] Blake, at the age of six or so, saw a tree full of angels, or saw Elijah walking down the street. Blake would be a very good man to start with. Incidentally, one of the "God-is-dead" theologians has written quite a good book on Blake—[Thomas] Altizer—it has finally come out. I think it's Altizer's best book.[44] I just had to do a review of it for the *Sewanee Review*.[45] I disagreed with one or two points, but I like it, and in

---

42. Merton takes up this theme in the final chapter of his early work, *The Waters of Siloe* (New York: Harcourt Brace, 1949), 332–52.

43. Merton wrote his Master's thesis on William Blake, entitled, "Nature and Art in William Blake: An Essay in Interpretation" (Columbia University, 1939; included in *The Literary Essays of Thomas Merton*, 387–456). For a recent study, see Jason Whittaker, *Divine Images: The Life and Work of William Blake* (London: Reaktion Books, 2021).

44. Thomas J. J. Altizer, *The New Apocalypse: The Radical Christian Vision of William Blake* (Lansing, MI: Michigan State University Press, 1967).

45. Published as "Blake and the New Theology," in *The Literary Essays of Thomas Merton*, 3–11.

general I think it's very good. Blake is a tremendous man. Blake is very much of a Sufi.

The consciousness of Blake is as close as you can get to this very elaborate fellow that I was talking about from a while ago, Ibn al-Arabi, although it's a different kind of thing. But it's that same kind of fantastic consciousness that works on five or six levels and has this enormous scope. What Blake did, he created this whole cosmos of spiritual beings, a whole spiritual cosmology, which Altizer takes very seriously, and really works it out. He says that Blake was the first prophet of the radical Christian God-is-dead movement. He gets the whole theology and cosmology of his God-is-dead theology from Blake, which of course means, when he says "God-is-dead," you know what he means? He means that a complete epiphany of God in the world—that God is no longer remote from us at all, because he's completely here. It's not at all a "dead" theology, and not at all even irreligious—well, it is irreligious in a certain sense—but it's by no means preaching "spiritual death" or anything like that. It's trying to say that God is so close that now, everything is filled with Him; that if you look for Him in heaven, you won't find Him, because He's here. It's an eschatological theology that he's developed there.

Blake has this whole idea of fourfold vision. What's the thing that he says? "Now I a fourfold vision see."[46] And what he sees is a thistle, and then he says on one level, it's a thistle, but on the fourth level, it's a divine being or an angel. It's some flaming thing. Then he ends up by saying, "may God preserve us from just having single vision." So, what's wrong is not just seeing the thistle as a thistle, but seeing *only* the thistle as a thistle. So, the development of the interior senses with Blake is that you see clearly: you know it's a thistle, but you see it as an angel.

Comment: If both sides of the senses bring one to God, I think you have a deep responsibility for yourself and to God [to develop both].

---

46. "Now I a fourfold vision see / And a fourfold vision is given to me; / Tis fourfold in my supreme delight / And threefold in soft Beulah's night / And twofold Always. May God us keep / From Single vision and Newton's sleep!" (William Blake, Letter to Thomas Butts, January 10, 1802; in Philip Pullman, "William Blake and Me," *The Guardian*, November 28, 2014). "Beulah" is Blake's mythopoetic location for inspiration and dreams.

You do. Absolutely. What's meant by "renunciation" is purely the one-dimensional view. But the problem is, as you were saying the other day, there's a certain type of person that looks at a redwood tree and all he sees is cubic feet of lumber. That's the vision that makes the interior senses impossible to develop. He sees a redwood and sees only board feet and dollars. I think that's a very good example. It's a good thing we've brought this up. You do have to clarify this, because [there are] people [who] think that you're not supposed to see the sunlight, or you're not supposed to enjoy it.

But the whole point is the hang-up that sees this purely with eyes of greed, which therefore doesn't see it. This is a transference into another realm, so that you have to maintain both [interior and exterior vision]. And Blake did. Blake was a terrific draftsman; he really saw things. But the point is the purification of exterior vision, which makes it possible for the two to go together; for all four to go together.

Well, I've been skipping through here. Here's another point about Sufism being a *way*: "It exists in many different forms, corresponding to different spiritual temperaments." This is, again, getting back to what we've been talking about with Hinduism, that all these religions and all these mystical systems have a great respect for diversity. They make sure that there are all kinds of ways that fit everybody. In the last analysis, everybody has his own way. One way, one person, ultimately, but you can group them in such a way that there are certain types that fall together as we did with yoga. You've got your karma yoga types, your active yoga types; and love [bhakti] yoga people, and intellectual [jñāna] yoga people.

The distinction that he makes here—I skipped over it in my notes—where Sufism talks about Islam being a wheel in which most people are content to be on the outside circle, on the periphery, just keeping the law. But the outside circle is always related to a center. The rim of a wheel wouldn't be a wheel, if there wasn't a hub and spokes going to it. But most people are content with the outside circle of the wheel. But there are certain people who are not happy unless they are going to the center—these are the Sufis, and these are the monks. That's what a monk is: a person who is not content to just go around the outside circle; [he] wants to get to the center. That is what Sufism exists for, to bring that about.

Now, in Sufism, it's not just important to have a discipline, but the discipline is supplemented by a grace. The discipline is supposed to open you up to a grace, a special grace. And each *way* is a grace, a special way is a special grace. Therefore, there is an immense importance of finding one's proper grace. Seeking your own identity means also seeking your own way, and means seeking your own grace. In Sufism, it means that you have a director or a guide who is telling you or helping you find what your grace is. That's the function of a director. That's what he has to tell you: "What's your grace?" If you don't know, he should tell you, or he should be able to help you find it. Most of the time, it seems to me, that's so simple; most of the time we don't need that much direction to be told that. I think we tend to know what we need. I don't think we need to be told that much. I think we need to be reassured sometimes. What do you think?

Mother Myriam: I think people should find themselves in their own way, and that a good helper would try to bring them to find their own way.

Yes. I think so. But in Sufism, the director, the master, is very important, because of these breathing techniques and things like that. And also, to push them. It's probably because it's more intensive. But when it comes to finding one's real way, I think that we have to realize that nobody can tell us. Nobody can tell us what our way is, but people can reassure us; although there comes a time when we have to get along even without reassurance. There may be moments when we can't be reassured. If we can be, fine. But if we can't be, well. . . . And I think that in all these traditions, too, there's a great deal of talk about people getting rid of their doubts. But it's the doubts about our own way that are the doubts that count. There comes a point when we have to realize that there can't be any more doubts; we just have to [live]. Of course, when they get into a different situation, and new questions may arise [there might be need of direction], but there comes a point in one's spiritual life when one has to drop all doubts about the fundamentals of one's way. One's way is now set.

At that point, then you know at least what your way is. There may be questions about this or that turn on the thing. But that is very important for Sufism; that's one of *the* graces. But how to begin about that? How does one start on that? Of course, it usually starts from the outside and works in. One sees somebody else that seems to represent this and you follow that person or imitate that person, but sooner or later, you're on your own.

I suppose one of the reasons why there's so much emphasis on the spiritual master in Sufism is that it presupposes an oral culture, in which there weren't that many books, and you had to have somebody tell you all these Sayings of the Prophet because you couldn't read them. You couldn't go down to the library and get them. Somebody had to tell you all these things. So, Sufis are people of the *way*. Another name for them is, "people who learn through allusion"—not illusion, but allusion—because their statements are always very hidden and perplexing and paradoxical.

"They aim to bring a person to the totality of the nature of Universal Man." We're coming back to something that I said before, "who thereby becomes the perfect mirror in which God contemplates himself. And the Universal Man is the mirror in which the Divine Names and qualities are fully reflected and through which the purpose of creation itself is fulfilled."[47] That's getting back to that central question that you brought up about what is it that's revealed, and bringing together in our lives God's Word and God's creative design in us. The purpose of the creation is that there should be men who work to realize in themselves God's plan, cooperating with God. That's the purpose of Islam. That's what obedience means: obeying God in such a way that we become the kind of man that he wants all men to be; that is to say, universal, open to everything.

Then we're back again to some notes on *dhikr* and breathing, which I've pretty much already said; except there's one other angle, an Islamic saying that in all creatures and in all the cosmos is the breath of the compassionate. This is one of the beautiful things. Sufis have these Names of God: the 72 beautiful Names of God. And the two main ones are the Merciful and the Compassionate. One of these standard sayings [the *Basmala*]—every chapter of the Quran begins with it—"In the name of Allah, *Al-Rahman Al-Rahim*," "the Compassionate, the Merciful."

Fr. Roger: [Is God merciful and compassionate] even to people with bad faith?

For the Sufis, the whole universe is pervaded with the breath of the compassionate and the merciful. If God is not compassionate or merciful to anybody, it's not God's will, it's the person's resistance. And everybody has a chance; they may have a predestinationist theology, but that's in the

47. Nasr, *Ideals and Realities of Islam*, 138.

legalistic schools. You don't need to worry about that in connection with Sufism. Sufism is a complete reaction against that.

And so, "breathing is not just a question of finding one's own heart, but also breathing in union with the breath of the Compassionate One, which is the whole universe"—another poetic expression of this—and this prayer, this breathing, and this *dhikr* and this invocation is a way of "awakening from the dream of forgetfulness." This is this whole problem, again, of the habitual state of torpor that we tend to be in—torpor, forgetfulness, and mindlessness, and automatic behavior. We've gone into most of that. "Prayer in this sense then makes and transforms man until he himself becomes prayer; he becomes identified with it. And his real nature is the prayer in which he discovers who he really is."[48] That's what Nasr says.

That's a good expression of what the prayer life means: in prayer, man finds his true identity. Don't you think that's kind of incontrovertible? I think that's a pretty good description of what prayer is. Instead of being hung up on an image and a narcissistic self-awareness, in prayer, a person really finds himself, and then with that, finds certainty, dispels these inner doubts, and dispels these other things.

It is not a purely subjective thing because it does involve correspondence with external reality willed by God. The basic condition for it is acceptance of the reality which God has imposed externally, and then complete internal obedience to this and abandonment to this, [along with] acceptance and understanding. Once this act [of surrender] has been made, then our own identity comes clear at last. The compassion of God is manifested in this. The mercy of God is manifested in this; so that the thing that has to be renounced is the will to resist this. One of the sources of this will to resist—that the Sufis understand so well—is what we're all up against now: an iron-bound institution.

It's a real problem for Sufis, and for everybody else, to find oneself in a bind where a completely intransigent institution is bent on keeping people in a condition where they can't realize themselves, in which they are forced to accept a definition of themselves imposed by the institution for the institution's own sake; for the institution's benefit—or what they think to be their benefit. The Sufis are very strong on this. But what we could all learn from the Sufis is that there should be a little bit of esotericism

48. Nasr, 142.

of our own. I think the Sufis would say, "Go ahead and do what you're supposed to do and make sure that it doesn't necessarily have to be in the *NCR* [*National Catholic Reporter*] next week" [laughter]. I think that is an important point, because in this country, we've got this feeling that unless you're getting good press mileage, it doesn't mean anything [laughter].

I think we should be an esoteric Cistercian movement, because it certainly has to come to that. I think it would be very effective. I think it would work very well, because nowadays people think so much in terms of press and media—that if it's not in the press, they're not going to bother with it. They'll leave you alone if you're not getting headlines. Maybe that's the solution; I don't know.

Well, that's about it on that [topic]. Let's see. I've got this article by Fritz Meier here. This is one of these Eranos papers now, from the book called *Man and Transformation*. This is an essay on the transformation of man in mystical Islam, by Fritz Meier. I think he's a psychologist.[49] He starts out with the idea—again, we're looking for our true identity. What is the model of perfectibility? He comes at it from another angle. It's quite interesting. He alludes to the fact that when people have a limb amputated, they think that they've got a limb there; there's a phantom limb. From this, he goes on to say, that this is an illustration of what happens in our own heart when we start seeking spiritual perfection. That is to say, we are people who have a sense of lack because there is something lacking—of course, the amputee can't get his own limb back—but we can, according to this.

He asks the question, "What is the model of human perfectibility that arises in the mind of a Sufi?" Where does [a Sufi] get this idea? Where do we get this notion that we want to be men of prayer, or men of God? Where does this come from? He says, this is not "arrived at inductively, but it stems from a higher spirit, and it is only through vision or faith that man can understand or feel the soundness and necessity of the plan to which he submits."[50] In other words, this is something that God makes known to us. He makes known to us that there is secretly—but this secret is not gnostic. This is "secret" in the sense that it's not immediately

---

49. Fritz Meier, "The Transformation of Man in Mystical Islam," in *Man and Transformation: Papers from the Eranos Yearbooks, vol. 5*, ed. Joseph Campbell (Princeton: Princeton University Press, 1964).

50. Meier, "The Transformation of Man," 38.

obvious—you have to dig to get to it; that there is a secret plan for us to which we have to find. We have to discover a way—that God has a way for us. This is the way we begin. This is what gets us coming to monasteries; wanting to enter monasteries because we feel that there is a way, and that God has a way for us, and what is it? And we start looking for it—and that there's a plan, and that this plan is sound; it's ultimately sound. It ultimately has meaning, and if we yield to this, we will find our way.

[Meier] illustrates it in that way. He says this leads to a sense of division from God, a sense of basic being in contradiction to the will of God. At the same time, we get the sense that there is a way—and the sense of resisting it. The sense that there is something opening up, and yet we refuse. We want to submit; yet we can't—and of course, we all go through this business of wanting and not wanting.[51] So, there are two wills: there's God's will and our will, and we tend to be in conflict; therefore, the whole idea of Islamic unity is to overcome the conflict, and how do they do it? Well, they emphasize the fact that the "I"—the isolated individual ego—is a "false God" that we have to renounce, and that we have to submit totally to God. This is another way of saying what we said before, that Islam is total surrender to God. This ties in with the basic Islamic idea of the unity of God. That God alone has to be the One who is adored, and that our own being has to be surrendered in a sense of dying away and being completely surrendered to Him. But we can't do this by our own efforts.

Well, I've just got a couple of quotes here. I'll read these few quotes and then I think we can discuss things for a little bit—or it's almost supper time. Here's one Islamic mystic who says, "He who believes that he can reach God by his exertions hurls himself into an endless torment. And he who believes he can reach [God] without exertions hurls himself into an endless, wishful dream."[52] So, there's this balance. But how true that is, though, "He who believes that he can reach God by his exertions hurls himself into an endless torment." This is again that unhappiness thing that we've been talking about so much. One of the roots of this

---

51. The classic instance of this ambivalent desire in the Christian tradition is found in Paul's "I do not do the good I want to do, but the evil I do not want to do" (Rom 7:19); mirrored in Augustine's *Confessions*, and perhaps even in Merton's own autobiography, *The Seven Storey Mountain* (New York: Harcourt, 1948).

52. Meier, "The Transformation of Man," 45.

unhappiness—from the depression that we get into—is constantly doing something that can't be done, or constantly beating our heads against the wall. It makes us very discouraged; it's bound to.

Comment: I didn't ask what you meant by the bird comment ["flapping your wings"].

Trying to do something which you cannot do, or in that particular case, something you don't even have to do.

Mother Myriam: It can be given to you.

Yes. The purpose of that illustration—this was yesterday—the idea was that in medieval times, there was no anxiety about reality, because God was *the* reality, and everything was completely sustained by Him. So, you didn't have to be like a bird in the air, flapping your wings to keep going, because God sustained you. You just went on and did what you did. There was no anxiety about existence.

Of course, there was anxiety in the late Middle Ages. Presaging what was to come later, this deep sense of death in the fourteenth to fifteenth centuries, for example; the dance of death and the Black Death—the plague. But fundamentally, in the Middle Ages, there's no real anxiety about existence. They're not Existentialists in that sense at all. But with the development of the Renaissance, we get this idea that man was given time, in which—as an individual—to manifest his powers and his genius, and create himself as immortal in history. And, at the same time, the Protestant sense that he was doomed and liable to collapse at any moment—which left men isolated like a bird in mid-air—and to keep going, he has to constantly reaffirm his existence by doing something and reassuring himself that he's there, which is our modern condition. Even though we believe in God, we can't have the security that medieval man had, because we don't have the same sense of the reality of God.

Personally, I think that it's not impossible for us to have that sense. I don't see why it should be impossible for modern men to have that sense of God sustaining everything. Maybe we'll get back to that, I don't know. What do you think about that? That would be one of the central questions, because you have people who insist that it's just not possible to have that kind of sense; that a modern man doesn't have that sense of God. I don't think that's true. What do you think? We're bound to have some anxiety.

Mother Myriam: I would say that our sense of God being present in the world is real, but that it's not a type of security. We have lost [that], in a way.

Yes. It's not really a metaphysical security. Personally, I think it's possible to alternate. It seems to me that we could have moments of a deep metaphysical sense of being sustained by God; but at the same time, we do have our sense of being lost in the void, like Pascal says, "the infinite spaces."[53]

Today, people would say that this was a form of self-deception, which the Middle Ages were able to practice because they were simple people; that they didn't know any better, and that for them it was alright. But for a modern man to do it is dishonest. Sartre would say that this is an example of "bad faith." Sartre says that man invents for himself a necessary being in order to justify his own existence. This is the whole question of Sartre. Maybe we could talk about that after supper, if I've got some notes on him. This whole idea of Sartre as the extreme modern consciousness of the pessimistic kind. The whole idea of "bad faith," which is a big point with him, and the idea of justification, which is very strong in both Sartre and Camus.[54] I don't think people have studied this enough, because these people are both preoccupied with justification. Why would they be preoccupied with justification? They are. The idea of justification, for example, in Camus—the whole problem of *The Fall*, for example. Have you read that book, *The Fall*, by Camus?[55] That's something that every monk should read.

---

53. "When I consider the brief span of my life absorbed into the eternity before and after . . . the small space I occupy and which I see swallowed up in the infinite immensity of spaces of which I know nothing and which know nothing of me, I take fright . . ."; "The eternal silence of these infinite spaces fills me with dread" (Pascal, *Pensées*, 48, 95).

54. French Existentialist philosopher and playwright, Jean-Paul Sartre (1905–1980) and French novelist Albert Camus (1913–1960) were major influences on Merton's thinking in the 1960s. Merton wrote seven essays on Camus (included in *The Literary Essays of Thomas Merton*, 181–304), and references him in at least six monastic conferences in 1967. See David Belcastro, "Merton and Camus on Christian Dialogue in a Postmodern World," *The Merton Annual* 10 (1997): 223–33.

55. New York: Random House, 1957. First published in French in 1956 as *La Chute*.

Mother Myriam: I read that years ago.

It's an amazing book. You could call it a study of pride, but it's also the study of the total isolation of modern man. This is modern man as judge and penitent. It takes place in Amsterdam. A man enters a bar in Amsterdam and this old geezer is sitting down in the back of the bar and engages him in a conversation. The whole book is a monologue of this odious character, who was a terrible person, and who is full of pessimism and misery and guilt, and tells more or less the story of his life. But actually, it is this totally useless self-examination of a completely individualistic being. Here's a man who is a totally isolated individual. He's got no community or anyone. The only kind of community he has is somebody who's ear he can bend, and to whom he tells this story with all this analysis of guilt, which is completely fruitless; it's totally pointless. It's a complete confession that is totally pointless. It's a gloomy book, but it's very funny in a lot of ways.

Sartre goes into this idea of "bad faith": the person who thinks that he can be justified in any way, or believes that he has a right to some kind of justification.[56] The man in bad faith is the one who can give you a reason for his existence. But there is something to this. It is true that some people have made a practice of hiding behind a lot of rationalizations for existence, and then not really taking responsibility for their own existence. That's Sartre's point. He pushes it too far and he twists it around too much, but there is something to it.

Fr. Roger asks an inaudible question that shifts the conversation back to Sufism.

They're looking for a center. They believe that there is a way; that a way is open to them, and that if they seek, they will find [the way]. And that there is a possibility of a breakthrough in which your life can take on a totally new dimension. This is common to all religions. One thing we might talk about after supper would be the [Native American] Indian, the practice of the Indians around this part of the world [i.e., California]. The idea of spiritual formation of the Indians. And this was for everybody;

---

56. Sartre articulates his concept of *mauvaise foi* ("bad faith") in chapter 2 of *Being and Nothingness* (New York: Routledge, 1943/2018).

this wasn't just for monks. This was for every Indian. But we'll talk about that after supper.

Comment: Thinking of that point of transcendence and perfect unity, wouldn't modern man bridge the gap of the void?

There's no reason why not; there's nothing against why modern man couldn't, or anybody else couldn't. He's got what he needs. The problem isn't in man. The problem is in his culture. I think that a lot of people can't handle the culture in that particular way. They're so passive in it. If you've got a culture that simply manipulates and alienates people—it's built on alienation.

But if you know you're being manipulated, then—

Alright, but yes and no. Maybe so. Maybe not. You mean if you let yourself willingly be manipulated?

If you enjoy these forces; you're aware of them.

Yes. You're hip.

You're bemused by the interaction and you swing with it, you flow in it.

It depends what you mean by that. This can be a big problem. My feeling would be that you have to resist it; you have to fight it. If you're not fighting it, I'd wonder. I'd have to fight it.

You're aware of it and you're not blocking it; you're accepting it.

Yes, but then the first thing you know, you're swinging with it, and then *bam*, there's an atomic bomb dropped on a bunch of people and you're with it. It becomes very difficult. If you buy it and get on the train, you're going with the whole thing.

You don't want to reject the reality of it becoming a bomb being dropped by [implicating] yourself in the system.

What you have to do, I think, is to fight the system from within. But you do have to fight it.

If you fight it, you've got to be really aware of it.

Sure, there's no question about that. You really have to know what's going on. Of course, in that way, you're part of it. But the real problem today is to be able to fight in such a way that your fighting means something. I know what you're saying, though, and I agree with this completely. Take Sister Corita, for example.[57] A person can say, "Okay, these ads are all real crummy and it's disgusting and it makes me vomit." Or, you could be like Corita and make something out of it that's beautiful. I absolutely go along with that; I'm doing that to a great extent now with poetry.

Comment: Well, your last [poetry] book—[58]

I'm glad somebody [read it]! It's very easy to do; this is a very rich thing. Talk about Blake being rich; talk about Ibn Arabi being rich; our culture is immensely rich in this particular way. There's this fantastic generation of forms and colors. This is great. I'm absolutely with that, and electronic music, and things like that, too. Everything. You could do all this. But that's not what I'm talking about. There is this enormous, sinister power that does result in the death of millions of people, and it makes you stop. But there's so many people within the thing that are fighting it.

Mother Myriam: And also, is there not the cultivation of sensation? We are that, too, to a great extent.

Yes. Well, again, I think she's bringing up that same point, but from another [perspective]. Now I'll agree perfectly; that almost the only thing

57. Corita Kent (1918–1986), artist, educator, and advocate for social justice, entered the Servants of the Immaculate Heart of Mary (IHM) in 1936. She served as faculty in the Art Department at Immaculate Heart College in Los Angeles for twenty years, eventually leaving the Order in 1968 and relocating to Boston, Massachusetts, where she continued to work as an artist and sought-after graphic designer.

58. A reference to Merton's *Cables to the Ace or Familiar Liturgies of Misunderstanding* (New York: New Directions, 1968).

you can do with this bombardment that you're getting is to really accept it. Because there's actually no point whatever in simply shutting your eyes to the whole thing, because you still get bombarded anyway. It's irresistible.

Comment: Reality is truth and truth is God!

Yes, well . . .

Mother Myriam: With the exception that you shouldn't be the slave of your TV.

Yes, exactly.

It is a great possibility of choices anyway.

I think what's happening is that the new generation is so able to handle all this, which we weren't, and I think we can learn [from them]. Some of you have probably been exposed to TV since as long as you can remember. That puts you in a totally new position. Your whole generation—of which there are lots of them—is therefore able to handle all these things, and you can see it. I think the rest of us should go along with you. I think your bunch should lead us in this particular direction. I'm willing to follow [laughter], because there's no point in just fighting all these sensations, as you say. Because I don't think they're slaves of TV. I think the intermediate bunch are. I think your parents are, probably, but not necessarily the younger generation.

Comment: It's in this sense that I wonder about when you asked us what we thought about being secure with the presence of God [and] the way we're brought up. When I hear you speak, I see in my own upbringing, my child-hood school, everything, is totally against that. How can we, as a generation that's in this now, try to embrace something like this?

Maybe you shouldn't even try to embrace it. All I'm saying is "what's what."

Mother Myriam: The little I know of you individually, as Americans—each act so differently. Even though you are all in the same culture, what you make of it is very different for each of you.

The one thing that I've been saying all along is there's this immense possibility of choice now. Even though, as you say, the situation has been very hostile to this kind of thing, I think you can buy any of it. All these consciousnesses are now open to everybody.

I feel in the young people who come [to Redwoods], that they have such an individualistic richness, because they have that broad possibility of choices.

Yes, and I think as monks, that's what we have to keep wide open. Even in a community as small as this, there should be all kinds of variety, every possible kind of—Sufis—you take your choice! [laughter]

Comment: [American] Indians?

Indians, absolutely. We'll discuss the Indians [later], because that's very beautiful.

Comment: Do they have monks?

No, in tribal society, your society is so small—the whole tribe is a monastic setup. Your little village is a monastic setup, but you have a "novitiate." You go through a novitiate for society, and you've got a common "liturgy" and everything like that. It's very interesting.

It's about supper time now, isn't it? [laughter][59]

59. At this point in the recording Dardenne plays a hauntingly beautiful recording of guitar music for Merton, which lasts approximately fifteen minutes (for a later reference, see her letter to Merton dated August 28, 1968; p. 407, below).

Chapter Ten

Native American Ritual and Practice

What happens tomorrow? What's the program?

Mother Myriam: Tomorrow is our last day.

I've got to make a routine. I've got to save my soul [laughter].

About the [Native American] Indians.[1] One thing I can say about the Indians is that this was the normal "novitiate" for Indian society. To become a full-fledged member of the tribe, he had to go through a regular formation period, and as a final test made a solitary retreat. They used to renew these retreats frequently during their life. It's a standard procedure when they're about 14 or 15 [years old]. It's very interesting to see how deep this really goes. It's the same thing in another way of finding a deep inner identity; a center and a focus on which one's whole life is centered.

It's the idea of "fasting for vision." That's what they call this retreat. Suppose a 14- or 15-year-old boy is ready for his initiation as a mature warrior in the tribe—a warrior or a hunter. He has to go off to some very isolated spot, some fairly dangerous kind of place; the top of a cliff, or a mountain, or some holy place. I suppose he picks his own place. But in some tribes, it was more complicated than others; in the Dakotas, there was a whole ritual of tracing out a special area, a circle, a holy circle with

---

1. Merton became particularly interested in Native American spirituality in the final years of his life. See his collection of writings, *Ishi Means Man: Essays on Native Americans* (New York: Paulist Press, 1968/2015), as well as the volume, *Merton and Indigenous Wisdom*, ed. Peter Savastano (Louisville, KY: Fons Vitae, 2020).

a cross in it. It's marked out in some special way. They may even put up some posts. And then he doesn't leave that area. He stays in there and has no food, no drink—maybe a little water—and stays there for three or four days. The idea is not that he has just any vision; but the purpose of this retreat is to bring him into contact with what's called his "vision person." This vision person is in the context of a totem society. They have various ways of going about this. In the Crow Indians, you were definitely supposed to have some kind of a vision. And then some of the other tribes, you could settle if some bird flew in at the right moment, or some significant sign like that. Yes?

Fr. Roger: Would you hold on at any point to the superego?

I don't think so. I think it's something much deeper than that, because [Freud's concept of] the superego is simply the interjected values of the society. This is more than that. This is what's so interesting about it. It's not just simply the formation of a person so that he gets complete grasp on the values of society. It's more than that. This is outside his society. It's interesting because you've got a whole society in which there are certain members who are in contact with spirits and are outside the framework of the social structure. But the structure is also raised in such a way that there's an intercommunication between these levels; because you've got down in the village, four or five chiefs who are well-versed in this kind of thing. They are in constant contact with vision persons—not only their own, but other peoples'—and consequently they can judge; when this person comes back from his retreat, he has to present his vision for approval to one of the old chiefs.

The fruit of this retreat is that the Indian, ideally speaking, has a real vision; but of course, once again, it does get to be somewhat institutionalized. There are only certain beings that you would normally have a vision of—it should be one of the approved totem animals or a spirit that could be identified as some totem animal—so I suppose it does get socialized. But they would feel themselves in contact with a spirit who was definitely given to guide them and to tell them what to do. Thereafter, they've got to obey that spirit, and they've got to be very careful what they do. If, for example, they make up their mind that they're going out to fight, they don't just go out to fight. They have to make a real retreat, and get in contact with their vision person, and see what he thinks about it. And then he may, either in a dream or in some other way, tell him what he thinks. He may say, "Don't go out to fight," or "Do go out and fight," or "Go here," or "Go there." And then eventually it gets institutionalized. It is very interesting to see how it gets built into the social structure.

You have a medicine bundle that goes with this. For example, if your vision person turns out to be an eagle, he will instruct you how to get together your medicine bundle. You have to have an eagle's feather or maybe a little bit of bear skin. You get this little package together and then every once in a while, you have some further experience; then you add a little bit to your medicine bundle, and you carry this with you when you go to war; you wear it around your neck. Of course, it gets to be superstitious in a way, but behind this are probably quite widespread and authentic experiences.

The people who really made contact with a spirit, and really lived in contact with a spirit, usually made out pretty well. They were good hunters and good fighters, and they followed the guidance of the spirit. I did a review of one book by a Crow Indian,[2] in which he narrated all his experiences with this in a very honest way—because he cheated a bit with this. It was very striking that when he cheated, he got into terrible trouble. He never had a really good vision. It was always sort of "not quite," and he would come back and say, "Well, now, this and this," and the teacher would say, "I don't think so, be a little careful with that." And then he'd say, "Oh, the heck with this."

He was repeatedly doing this. He was very ambitious. He wanted to be a Chief, and he never did; he never made it to Chief. He just got to be the next degree under Chief, but never made it to Chief. And then one time he got a bunch of people together—it's a very free kind of society, because if somebody gets an idea—"let's go hunting"—he can. If he's got sufficient prestige, he can get a bunch of people together. They can just go off and start hunting, even though the rest of the tribe may not feel like it, or may even disapprove, but they do it. So, one time he took off with a bunch of other fellows, and one of them was a pretty good vision man, too. And he tricked this other fellow into thinking that he had a really

2. Peter Nabokov, *Two Leggings: The Making of a Crow Warrior* (New York: Crowell, 1967). For Merton's review, see "War and Vision," in *Ishi Means Man*, 17–24.

good experience and a real good vision bundle, and that he was going to get a lot of bison. So, they went out and they got trapped by a whole herd of bison. And he somehow fell off his horse. In the end, he was thrown into a river by a bison and almost killed [laughter].

He told this story with great simplicity: how this was the result of cheating. He fixed up a phony medicine bundle, and this is what happened to him [laughter]. He went through his whole life and narrated all these experiences, and then finally, at the end of his life—it's a very sad story. He's still going on with his visions and vision quests, and he doesn't seem to notice that things are changing considerably, and there's a railroad coming through, and more and more white men around, and he cooperated. The Crows were cooperating with the white people against the—[3]

Anyway, they're still fighting these other people and they don't seem to realize that all the whites are taking over more and more. Then all of a sudden, one day, he has another dream: he's after somebody, and he gets this fellow's scalp right by the railway in the middle of the night, and then he's called in on the carpet to the white captain, who says, "What'd you do that for?" "Well, he stole my horse." The white man says, "Alright, but don't do it again. Here, I'm going to give you this; go get yourself something." The white man gives him a $5 gold piece and the Indian looks at it, "I wonder what that is." The captain says, "You take that to the store and find out what that is." The last sentence in the book is, "I went to the store and I found out I could get a lot of things for this little $5 gold piece. But after that, there was no more hunting, and there were no more warriors, and there was no more medicine bundle. There were no more visions."[4] It was just the end. [These practices had] become so socialized, it became a system. But they didn't tell him anything he needed to know. Originally, it probably was a really deep breakthrough to some source of psychic energy that they needed to have.

What happened was this became discredited pretty widely when the white men came in. The old Indian religion was completely revised in

---

3. The recording cuts off mid-sentence and continues with the paragraph below.

4. See the concluding lines of Merton's poem "Ghost Dance": "After a while the dreaming stopped and the Dream Dance turned into a Feather Dance. It was just a fun dance. It was mostly a white man's show" (*The Geography of Lograire* [New York: New Directions, 1968], 137).

many places about 1850. There's a long book by Paul Radin[5] who got in with some Indians up in Wisconsin who revealed to him the secret esoteric rituals of certain groups. They had an Indian renewal in which everything was simplified. The rituals were extremely long and complicated, and the whole thing was simplified. And then that broke down about 1870. Then you've got the Ghost Dance, and then peyote came in, simultaneously.[6] Peyote was definitely a kind of eschatological cult; so was the Ghost Dance.[7] I don't know about peyote, but the Ghost Dance was entirely centered on the messianic hope that the ancestors were coming back and were going to drive all the white people out, and that all the animals were coming back; all the animals that had been killed were going to return. And then the Indians would live happily ever after and the white people would be swallowed up by a flood, or something to that effect. That started just north of Reno [Nevada]. And then it worked right up into the north of the state here [California], and then up into Oregon, and then back down again through Wyoming, and all the way down to Oklahoma, finally.

It was very strong in the north of the state here. There were even a couple of wars fought about the Ghost Dance.[8] There was one war in the 1870s up in Oregon. Sitting Bull was largely concerned with Ghost Dance.[9] It was the Sioux. Then there was a terrible massacre at Wounded Knee where the army had rounded up these Ghost Dance people and had

5. Paul Radin (1883–1959), American anthropologist, who studied with and published extensively on Native American mythology and cultures. Merton's reference is perhaps to Radin's 1923 *The Winnebago Tribe* (Lincoln, NE: University of Nebraska, 1973), which includes one of the earliest anthropological accounts of the peyote ceremony.

6. For a complete history of peyote usage, particularly during this time period, see Mike Jay, *Mescaline: A Global History of the First Psychedelic* (New Haven: Yale University Press, 2019), 51–76. Mescaline is the psychoactive compound found in the peyote cactus and was the "first" psychedelic to emerge among the 1950s American counterculture due to the popularity of Aldous Huxley's 1954 *The Doors of Perception* (New York: Harper & Row).

7. On the intersections between the Ghost Dance and peyote usage, see Jay, *Mescaline*, 58–59.

8. "The Ghost Dance War" refers to U.S. Government attempts to violently suppress the Ghost Dance movement among the Lakota Sioux 1890–91.

9. Sitting Bull (1831–1890), celebrated Lakota leader and resistance fighter who fought and defeated Custer's army at the Battle of Little Bighorn in 1876. Sitting Bull was involved in the Ghost Dance movement and also performed in Buffalo Bill's "Wild West Show."

them all surrounded; there was absolutely nothing they could do.[10] One of the things about the Ghost Dance was that they thought they were invulnerable. Finally, when they were surrounded by these soldiers with guns, the medicine man got up and started blowing his whistle, and they all got up and said, "Let's go and attack."[11] And they were all shot down. But there was a big development, an evolution—and there still is. Now, the Indians are legally allowed to have peyote in their church, the Native American Church.[12] The peyote perhaps fulfills the same purpose in another way as a vision, but it's no longer a question of a vision person. I don't know.

It has been tied up with Christianity in some places, though. I don't know too much about that; maybe it has gone through a further evolution. That's what these Cargo Cults do. In the Cargo Cults you've got a definite period when it's all very Christian, and then after that there's an anti-Christian reaction. It could quite possibly be that way with peyote. I'd like to try some peyote; apparently, it's extremely unpleasant to eat.

Mother Myriam: We don't know what you're talking about. Is it food?

Oh, it's a psychedelic. It's a cactus.

Oh, now I understand.

You eat this; and they really do have visions and see lights.

There is an inaudible comment here about Navajo sand paintings.

Yes. Can you tell us something about that? I read a little bit about it, but I don't know too much. How does this work? What happens with sand paintings?

10. As many as 300 Lakota were massacred at Wounded Knee, Pine Ridge Reservation, South Dakota, on December 29, 1890, by the U.S. Cavalry.

11. It is unclear who instigated what became the Massacre at Wounded Knee; Merton's version is contested.

12. On the founding of the Native American Church (NAC), see Jay, *Mescaline*, 122–28, and Robert Fuller, *Stairways to Heaven: Drugs in American Religious History* (Oxford: Westview Press, 2000), 38–48.

Comment: The shaman comes into the hole [of the structure or dwelling]; the person is sick and on the floor with colored sands. He paints it with a symbolic design. Then when the whole thing's over, he destroys it.

Yes. Some of them are very beautiful. I've seen reproductions.

They're fantastic designs.

Yes. It is so interesting. The Jungians get into this, too, to some extent: the relation between these symbolic designs and what they conceive to be an inner, psychic pattern of the person, and how these shamans know the correspondence.[13] There are several good books about sand painting that are around. There's one huge, great big thing I got in the library once and spent an afternoon looking at it. It's a beautiful thing. There's a biography of some Navajo sand painter that I saw in the library, too.

Comment: It seems to survive even though—

Oh yes, they're still doing it.

I received a paper from an anthropology professor at Berkeley with regard to Indian beliefs in healers. He did a study of a man in Mexico and Southern Texas, and the things that he did—they really weren't legend; they were fact.

Of course. They had a terrific knowledge of natural medicine and herbs. I've never had enough contact with Indians. This would be something to really go into.

Fr. Roger: You don't have Indians in Kentucky?

No, Kentucky never was a place where they actually settled.[14]

---

13. See, for example, Maud Oakes and Joseph Campbell, *Where the Two Came to Their Father: A Navaho War Ceremonial Given by Jeff King* (Princeton: Princeton University Press, 1943/1991).

14. The state of Kentucky, specifically the land around the Abbey of Gethsemani, is historically Shawnee, Eastern Band Cherokee, and Osage territory (https://archive.kftc .org/indigenous-lands-acknowledgment).

Mother Myriam: There is a reservation near Eureka.

The Indians are in some sense much more in despair than anybody else.

Mother Myriam: It is a tragedy.

The Indians have had a terrible time. Not only have they been oppressed, but then they've been shifted around so much. Some of them just have no hope.

Fr. Roger makes an inaudible comment regarding plans for the next day which prompts Merton's following comment.

I think what I'll have to do is just put my cards on the table and stay permanently [laughter]. I don't want go back! [laughter]

Mother Myriam: We have two hollow trees.

Sure! A bag of cement to make a floor in a hollow tree! Well, this will be news to Father Flavian! [laughter] I'll take a tree and he'll take my hermitage back there [at Gethsemani] [laughter].

A discussion ensues regarding housing development in proximity to the Abbey of Gethsemani, followed by an extended conversation regarding the realities of alcohol and substance abuse on Native American reservations ("This was their land, and they were just completely beaten"). Much of the discussion is hearsay, based on Merton's and various Sisters' impressions of what is happening today on reservations and the interplay of traditional Native American culture and local Catholic communities (e.g., Christ in the Desert Monastery). It is an informal conversation, with much of the dialogue inaudible, rendering it difficult to transcribe.

The Indians in this country go back a long way; something like a million years ago[15] [in the American Southwest]. It must have been a really

15. Merton is perhaps using hyperbole here. The earliest human inhabitants of what became known as "the Americas" dates to approximately 16,500–13,500 BCE.

impressive thing. It was a rich culture around here [California]. Linguistically, they were very sophisticated. Some of the tribes in this area had such a sophisticated language that you had a different syntax for women and for men. The women used a whole different syntax than men did.

The earliest languages were the most complicated, not in grammar, but they have these fantastic vocabularies. There's one very interesting man writing in anthropology, Claude Lévi-Strauss;[16] there's some very interesting stuff in him. He's bringing up how these early people had this fantastic vocabulary—the kind of vocabulary they would have, not only for trees and plants, but for parts of trees and parts of plants, and for slightly differing varieties of animals. And then for animals of different sizes and different ages. Thousands of words. We don't have anything like it.

Lévi-Strauss takes all these legends and myths, and he takes them in all the different forms that you find them in this tribe, and this tribe, and this tribe. He works mostly with Central South America, below the Amazon. He lines all these [myths] up and then puts them all together and tries to come out with a systematic interpretation. For example, he has all the myths he can find about cooking, and all the myths he can find about tobacco, and myths about the origin of cooking, and myths about the origin of tobacco, and the rules that came out from these myths, and he systematizes it and comes up with the conclusion that the thinking of these people was extremely sophisticated.[17] That they had a very coherent worldview that fit together pretty well, and worked pretty well, except that it wasn't scientific at all [in a modern sense]. It worked fine, just as a different kind of thing. It was a worldview that just classified everything in terms of myths. And you can remember everything, fit it all in, and just live accordingly. But he's quite an interesting person.

Do you want to go to Compline? Is it about time?

16. Claude Lévi-Strauss (1908–2009), influential French anthropologist and originator of the theory of "structuralism," which Merton outlines below in his interpretation of myth.

17. See Lévi-Strauss, *The Raw and the Cooked* (Chicago: University of Chicago, 1964/1969).

Chapter Eleven

Sufi Spirituality

Surrender and Mercy

Benedicite. Let us pray: O Lord, send us your Holy Spirit, and may He do this in the fullness of all truth. In Christ our Lord. Amen.

There's a lot to say. That dance was very impressive; really, very good.[1] That's a Sufi practice. Dancing is essential to the Sufis, and for many different reasons. One of the reasons is because the dance has something of the note of *excelsus*[2]—it goes beyond the normal limit, and you've got to be pretty mature to do it. It takes something to do it. You have to be strong. And the person and the community have to have the courage to let go, and do something—because you have to let go. In the spiritual life, to be able to let go requires a great deal of—you've got to have something [laughter]. So, the whole thing [dancing], it's a very good point. In Sufism, they always ran into trouble with this dancing. It was regarded as a rather questionable practice. The Sufis were constantly reproved or criticized for their dancing, precisely because of the element of *excelsus*. It scares people [laughter]. The average person can't handle it.

Comment: The dervishes—are they Sufis?

Exactly. That's one of the branches of Sufism. The whirling dervishes. What they do is go around in a circle, and then one gets in the middle

---

1. This is a reference to the liturgical dance that Merton had just witnessed during the Redwoods community Mass just prior to this conference. The audio of this Mass was recorded, but a transcription is omitted here. See also Merton's journal entry of May 14, 1968 (*Other Side of the Mountain*, 98).
2. Latin for "sublime," "surpassing," or "highest."

and really goes fast, and the other ones go slow; then they take turns going out in the middle. This going around is to let everything go. What I want to talk about today—it's the last conference—but we might as well get into the root of this thing: what's behind this idea in Islam of Sufism and letting everything go. That's what I want to talk about, because it's the basic thing with them, and it is what corresponds in them to our idea of death and resurrection. The structure of the Islamic consciousness is definitely a death and resurrection one; it's built on that. You can contrast it with the official death and resurrection thing that we've had for so long, the legalistic kind of thing, which perhaps you could say corresponds to the more or less legalistic external structure of ordinary Islamic piety.

With us, death and resurrection has been reduced to obedience, to authority, and that's it. The only death that is required of you is to do what you're told: follow out the rules and keep the laws, and that's it—that's sufficient. And then morning, noon, and night there are exhortations to obedience in this sense only, and no other aspects of it at all; just simply this business. You just put your head on the block and let them chop it off. Well, this is alright. There is something to it, but it isn't the only thing.

In Sufism, there's definitely been a much deeper development of that kind of idea. For example, in Sufism, they push the idea very far of not even being aware at all of having any virtue. It's not that they disregard the practice of virtue, but the idea is to be a person who has lost all status. Of course, this is an extreme view. Remember, in Sufism they use paradoxical expressions all the time; they're using extreme expressions. It's like the desert fathers.

Desert father literature is a special kind of literary form, in which you have to be very aware of precisely what is being done, because each desert father's story takes one particular point and pushes it way out here. Then you get the next desert father's story, [where] it takes exactly the opposite [point] and pushes it way out here. Each time, they seem to be saying, "This is the only thing." Somebody will say, "What is the main virtue that should be done?" and someone will say, "Hide in a cave and don't see anybody." Then the next man will come along and say, "What is the only virtue that should be practiced?" "For heaven's sake, stay away from a cave, go into the city!" One of the things that explains that, is that really these *Apophthegmata* [Sayings] were usually directed to individuals. Each desert father was telling the individual, "This is what you should do," but then it got to be canonized as having general validity.[3] But in Sufism, there is a tendency to pick up one thing and then push it way out to the extreme.

One of the things that Sufism does stress is the theme of welcoming a scandalous reputation; that it is good to be, to some extent, a stone of stumbling, because then this will keep you from being an official figure. Nobody's going to light any vigil lights in front of you. For example, there's a Syrian story of two Christian saints, which is part of a tradition. There's a whole series of stories like this. That's one of the things I had to do at Columbia. I had a course in Medieval French. One of my first contacts with monasticism was a comparison between some story in the *Apophthegmata* or the *Vitae Patrum* [Lives of the Desert Fathers], and the same story in the French Medieval version.[4] This was the story of St. Paphnutius,[5] who is praying in his cell, and very humbly says, "Oh Lord, if there is anybody else around as holy as I, show me who it is" [laughter]. So, the Lord immediately shows him this dancer down in the town, this juggler. And Paphnutius goes down to the village and says, "How come you're so holy?" And he says, "Who me?" This story has all sorts of versions. For example, one of the variations is that the saint goes downtown and finds a married couple. In another one it's the three married women who do works of mercy. But it's always the idea of a corrective to the man who is living fully the monastic ideal. He is always shown that there's something superior. And that superior state is the state of the person who's completely hidden.

So, this story of these two Christians—which is believed to have had an influence on the Sufis. Two young Christians—hippies in a way— Theophilus and Mary. It's a Syrian legend. They lived together chastely, but he pretended he was a juggler and she pretended she was a very wild

3. For Merton's translation of the Sayings of the Desert Fathers, see *The Wisdom of the Desert* (New York: New Direction, 1960).

4. See Merton's *Seven Storey Mountain* for his initial mention of this essay, which refers specifically to the medieval legend of the juggler of Notre Dame (p. 171).

5. *The Lives of the Desert Fathers*, trans. Norman Russell (Kalamazoo, MI: Cistercian Publications, 1981), 95–98. In this version it is a flute player. For an additional summary, see Merton's novitiate conference notes in *Pre-Benedictine Monasticism: Initiation into the Monastic Tradition* 2, ed. Patrick F. O'Connell (Collegeville, MN: Cistercian Publications, 2007), 37–38.

girl. So, they were reviled by the populace. Everybody thought they were just a bunch of hippies, but *really* [laughter] it always comes out like that: if somebody peeks under the door there's this light and they're both three feet off the floor [laughter]. But it's a typical kind of story. Of course, they're forerunners of the idea of the Russian "Fool for Christ."[6] This has always been strong [in the tradition]. Now, Theophilus was converted by a "tramp" whom he saw secretly praying on a manure pile in a stable [laughter]. This is always the same kind of literary form.

So, the Sufis emphasize very strongly, like the Rhenish mystics, the idea of being "secret friends of God." Ruysbroeck has this terrific lineup of "hidden children" and "secret friends."[7] The real top of the ladder for Ruysbroeck is being a "secret friend," in which this union with God is completely hidden, even from oneself. Really, what it means is [living] outside of all social [inaudible], including religious ones; [living] without any indication that there's any kind of holiness involved.

Now, this is probably one of the explanations of that man Hallaj that I was talking about yesterday. The man who deliberately presented the idea of the mystical life in a completely provocative way, so that he would not only be blamed, but would even be put to death. The reason for this is tied into the basic concept of Islam, which is *Tawhid*, that God alone is. Of all the religions on earth, Islam is the one that pushes that the furthest. God alone is real. There's a verse ascribed to Hallaj, who says, "The disappearance of myself is the greatest favor. My persistence as I now am is the worst sin." Of course, it's utterly exaggerated and pushed to the limit. But the idea behind it is that since God is the only reality, the only thing left of him is to lay down his life and disappear into God.

Of course, it's an extremely exaggerated expression, but behind it is a pretty deep idea. And this is the one I want to talk about today. If we go

---

6. An antinomian practice in the Eastern Orthodox Church, particularly in Russian Orthodoxy. "Fools for Christ" or "Holy Fools" would often forsake wearing clothing or enact other radical renunciate behavior in order to openly critique—or mock—the material or even ecclesial attachments of society. There are comparisons with the "Crazy Wisdom" tradition in Tibetan Buddhism and the Pashupat lineage in Indian Shaivite yoga.

7. Jan van Ruysbroeck (1293–1381), influential Flemish mystic and author. For an English translation, see *John Ruusbroec: The Spiritual Espousals and Other Works*, trans. James Wiseman (Mahwah, NJ: Paulist Press, 1986). Merton references Ruysbroeck throughout his *Introduction to Christian Mysticism* (see p. 411).

around in circles, all right, but it is this whole question: How do the Muslims and the Sufis handle this idea of our individuality, our freedom, and the unity of God? And God's initiative and our initiative. How do they deal with this? And the question of God's mercy. How do they fit that in? That's really what I want to get around to, but in connection with this, the Sufis are faced with a choice of being scholars who study the law and study theology, or being friends of God who *live* the union of the prophet with God.

Islam is a prophetic religion, and the idea is that the scholar interprets to the Islamic community the heritage of the prophets, and the prophets are, of course, Abraham, Moses, Jesus, and Muhammad, especially, but also all prophecy included in the Bible and the Quran. The Sufis are to reproduce in their lives the union of the prophets with God. To experience in their lives the secret union of the prophets with God, without revealing anything about it to men; therefore, anything they say about it is cryptic. That is to say, they are the people of allusion, who refer to these things in funny, strange stories, and then people have to make the best of it.

Incidentally, talking about stories, there's one Sufi called Nasrudin who's famous in the Persian tradition.[8] The thing that's peculiar about him is that even today there are jokes going around, real worn-out jokes of a vaudeville circuit, and if you trace them all the way back, they end up at this Nasrudin, who was a Sufi, and they have a Sufi meaning. There are quite a few jokes like that, something like six or seven that I know I've heard; I can't think of them right now. These are well-known jokes that are all over Europe and America. One of them, which is standard—you've probably heard some version of it yourself—is the one where Nasrudin is found by somebody in the street at night, looking for something under the streetlight. And they say, "What are you looking for?" And he says, "I'm looking for the key to my house." And they say, "Where did you lose it?" He says [laughing], "Three blocks down." And they say, "Why are you looking for it here?" He says, "Because the light is better" [laughter].

This is a typical Sufi story. They will just tell you that story and you [have to] make the best of it you can. Of course, there are two ways in

<hr>

8. Mullah Nasrudin (1208–1285), Sufi and storyteller; see Idries Shah, *The Exploits of the Incomparable Mulla Nasrudin* (London: Jonathan Cape, 1966). See also Merton's February 24, 1966, letter to Mark Van Doren for a further recounting of Nasrudin stories (*Road to Joy*, 50–51).

which you can handle that: one is positive and the other is negative. The one I assume is right is: that's what we do. We go where we think the light's better. When we're looking for God, we go where we think the light's better. For example, it could be an implicit criticism of [scholarly] study. If the man is looking in books—instead of going into the dark where the thing is really lost.

Of course, this idea of the "lost pearl" and the "lost treasure" is a big Sufi thing. There's a whole slew of stories. I haven't heard this one in any modern version, but it's quite a good one. Nasrudin is going down the street and he meets a bunch of friends, and he says, "Why don't you all come home to dinner with me?" So, 15 of them all go to his house. He says, "Wait a minute. I've got to go in and tell my wife that you're coming" [laughter]. So, he goes inside and says, "I'm bringing 15 friends for dinner." She says, "What?!" She refused to cook for 15 friends, so then he just goes upstairs and hides [laughter]. The other friends are waiting outside. They probably get tired of waiting; they knock on the door. The wife comes to the door, and they say, "Where's Nasruddin?" She says, "He isn't here." And they say, "But we just saw him walk in," and then Nasruddin sticks his head out the window and says, "But I could've gone out the back way, couldn't I?" [laughter]

All these stories have a Sufi meaning. I don't know what the Sufi meaning of that one is, but there is this whole series of stories around being a secret friend of God, and expressing it in these strange ways. Some of the Sufis express it in exorbitant terms, and others in these rather funny comical terms; but the basic thing behind it is to preserve, under a humorous, paradoxical, or hidden form, the real life, which cannot be expressed anyway. Simply to live this hidden life of secret friendship with God and to express it in ways that don't really communicate it—but which keep people curious. Then the person who is really serious about it is initiated into this by a Sufi master and comes to understand it.

I'll try and get to the roots of this. This is all very amusing, but what is the real root of all this? I suppose you could call this a basic [theological] anthropology that underlines Sufism and Islam, [and it can be found in the Quran]. The opening chapter of the Quran is very important. It's a prayer that they use all the time, and it sums up the whole essence of Islam. I haven't got the whole text here; it's hardly longer than the Our Father. It's that kind of a text; one of those basic texts that really contains everything. It starts out with the praise of Allah, the Lord of all Being, the all-Merciful, and the all-Compassionate. This is Allah the Merciful and Compassionate, which is a central thing [in Islam]. There's a theological dialectic between mercy and compassion, which gets very technical, and I'm not going to go into that—because I don't really know how to do it anyway—but that's how it starts out.[9]

There are two levels of being, one of which is covered by mercy and the other by compassion. But the underlying idea is that everything is mercy and everything is compassion. And the question that you brought up yesterday about reprobation; how do they handle that? We'll see today exactly how that works. But for the Muslim who really knows what Islam is about, mercy and compassion are the whole thing. They all cover justice. Justice is absorbed in mercy and compassion. If justice does stand out, it's only because there is some particular reason for it in some particular case. But God is essentially merciful and compassionate, and man's whole being is penetrated by mercy and compassion. If, by chance, he comes under wrath, it's a particular case, and it never excludes the presence of mercy and compassion to which he can always turn, if he wakes up. But, of course, not on his own initiative. The thing about Islam is that it's always a gift of God, but you can always do it. It's the same old thing that you get into when you start talking about grace and free will. So, Allah is merciful and compassionate. He is the master of the Day of Doom [i.e., Last Judgment]. The end is in His hand as well as in the beginning. And we are all hastening toward that end. In the end is God Himself.

Judgment is seen in this life, not just as punishment and reward, but everybody is going back into God—whether they want to or not—because there is only God. The basic thing in Islam is "God alone is": *Tawhid*. There is only one reality, and this is absolute. You have to do all your thinking and all your statements in terms that do not interfere with this basic truth. No Muslim will ever say, "Tomorrow we'll take the train"; [instead] it's, "If Allah wills it." You never even make any statement about yourself as an independent agent. The only way you can conceive of yourself at all, as an Orthodox Muslim, is to see yourself completely as an instrument of God. Yes?

---

9. Merton is paraphrasing here the *sūrah al-Fātihah,* the opening verse of the Quran (1:1-7), which he cites directly below.

Fr. Roger: How do they consider the individual personality?

That's what we're coming to. It's a very interesting concept. To me, it's a really exciting concept, but we'll get to that; we're building up to that. To me, it seems shocking, and offered in these terms it seems absurd, but the way they handle it is really quite exciting. They get themselves in this bind and then how they respond is: you are not an independent agent, God alone is; we're unreal. Well then, how do we get in there? What happens? Well, we'll carry on with this and we'll get to it.

"Thee Alone we serve, thee Alone we adore. To thee Alone we pray. To thee we take refuge. Lead us by thy straight path"—which is the path of Islam, the path of mercy—"and not by the path of those against whom thou art wrathful; to the unbeliever, who is closed to mercy."

How do the Sufis handle this? Your hardcore, ordinary Muslim is liable to interpret this and say, "Get out the sword and clean up the unbelievers." But Ibn Arabi goes at it a different way. This is the man from Andalusia, who ended up in Damascus. "Verily, God's way is the straight way. The way it is exposed to sight everywhere, is to be perceived in great things and small. In those who are ignorant of the truth, as well as those who know it well. This is why it is said that his mercy covers everything. Everybody walking on earth is on the straightway of the Lord."[10] This is, in a certain sense, completely in contradiction with what the legal scholars would say, but the Sufis, taking this completely different dimension where everything is compassion, will accept the same statements the other people take, but say the whole thing is still compassion: "Everybody is under the mercy of God." But how does this work? How can it be? "Both wrath and going astray come into being only secondarily. The great thing is mercy."[11]

---

10. Quoted in Toshihiko Izutsu, *Sufism and Taoism: A Comparative Study of Key Philosophical Concepts* (Berkeley: University of California Press, 1983), 123. Merton was reading the original edition of Izutsu's work, entitled, *A Comparative Study of Key Philosophical Concepts in Sufism and Taoism: 'Ibn 'Arabi and Lao-tzu-Chuang Tzu* (Tokyo: Institute of Cultural and Linguistic Studies, 1966–67). See Merton's letter of May 12, 1967, to Masao Abe: "I am at present reading a most revealing book by a Japanese scholar, Toshihiko Izutsu, comparing the Sufi mystic Ibn Arabi with Taoists. The first volume only, on Ibn Arabi, is available, I believe. Others will follow which will show the resemblances. This is very important. If you do not know it already I recommend it to you, and it is easily accessible to you, being published by Keio University" (*Witness to Freedom*, 332).

11. *Sufism and Taoism*, 123.

Primarily, for them, Being Itself is mercy. Existence is mercy. The mere fact that one has been called into existence is a gift of God's mercy. It is all to be seen in the light of mercy. To stop seeing it in the light of mercy is the beginning of justice. But each time, the person *chooses* not to see it in terms of mercy. If you don't want to see it in terms of mercy, okay, see it in terms of justice. But what it really is, is mercy. What they're saying is, the way you want to look at it doesn't change what it is. If you want to regard this as justice, well, that's your business—but it's mercy. And if you let it go long enough, it will turn out to be mercy—if you let it. "To love the true good," he says, "in everything, without personal"—the danger of the personal preference in terms of choosing between things which are merciful and choosing to put another label on them. For example, I get sick and I choose not to see this as mercy. If I choose to put the label "justice" on it, that's my prerogative, but it's a silly choice. I should see it as mercy, because mercy is what it is. What I have to do is to train myself not to make these personal interpretations of what mercy is, because then I falsify the mercy. What is essentially mercy I turn into something else.

"To love the true good in everything without personal preference is to be on the right way of Allah, to be like Muhammad, to be under mercy, and to manifest mercy." Muslim thinking is like Muslim art, where you get a design that weaves in and out around a central point. That's what you're getting [here]. It's an Arabesque, which has one center, and you're constantly weaving around that center. The same idea comes up here and there, but it's always pointing to this center. So, there is one thing in everything that one must see, which is mercy. To choose otherwise is not just a question of personal [preference]. It can be, of course, a question of going to sleep on the job; a slackness or torpor. Or, it can be dictated by custom. Society can train a person to make these choices, to not see in terms of mercy. Everybody thinks it's something else, and you get to thinking that way; or, an idiosyncrasy of some sort. But in the Quran it says, "My mercy covers everything," and then, "God's mercy forestalls His wrath."[12] So, everything is praised as mercy. Everything is praised by mercy before it is judged by wrath. There's the absolute primacy of mercy.

Again, this is Ibn Arabi: "Everything which is remembered by the Mercy is happy and blessed. And there is nothing that has not been re-membered by the Mercy and the Mercy's remembering things is exactly

---

12. *Sufism and Taoism*, 128.

the same as bringing them into existence."[13] So, everything that happens, then, is something that comes under God's mercy, because it is God remembering it. This is a Biblical turn: "God remembers this." This is tied in with a very important example in Islam, the story of the first son of Abraham, Ishmael,[14] because he is their ancestor. Massignon has a beautiful exposition on this: how Hagar was driven out into the desert, and she takes Ishmael and puts him under a tree, and says, "Well, let him die." Then God, "Remembers the child," and there's this beautiful Biblical concept of the mercy of God, remembering this child, with this long plan that nobody knew anything about; that He has in mind: "You're going to be a Muslim." Because Ishmael is the ancestor who ties the Muslims in with Abraham. The way, then, to be under mercy—we always have this choice, to return, to awaken to God's intention in things, and to return to that. And where is this? It's in us. It's built into us. There is this divine design built right into our being. The only problem we have is that we forget it, and we're not aware of it; yet this is our true identity, which is placed in us by Him. And that is the center where mercy is found.

This is what we really want to investigate. Ibn Arabi says, "There are two ways in which people ask for mercy. Those who know, and those who don't know"—and they both ask for mercy.[15] "Those who are veiled from the truth"—that is to say, they're not Muslims—although he might admit Christians here. "Those who are veiled from the truth, ask the Lord to show mercy on them" in particular events. They ask for particular signs of mercy, or particular evidence of gifts of mercy. They ask for mercy piecemeal. They're always saying, "Well, give me this in mercy, and give me mercy in that. Help me to recover from sickness." He says, that's fine, but it is a veiled way of understanding mercy because it implies that everything is not mercy. It is nevertheless a recognition of mercy, but it doesn't see that everything is mercy. It's all mercy. If everything is mercy, then you don't [need to] ask. On the contrary, the people of the unveiling—that is, Sufis—and, I guess everybody who is a person of unveiling in any religion; Ibn Arabi would certainly mean that, because we'll see that he's a very ecumenical Muslim. "The people of the unveil-

13. *Sufism and Taoism*, 128.
14. Genesis 21:10-12.
15. See *Sufism and Taoism*, 129.

ing ask the mercy of God to subsist in them. And they ask in the name of Allah and he shows mercy upon them by making his mercy subsist in them."[16] This is the idea that we're getting towards, the way they're going to solve this. Your personality itself is the core of mercy—in you. Your own liberty is mercy, but your liberty works on a periphery of something even deeper, which is what we have to try to explain.

Incidentally, I spoke a little too soon about that Ravier book, *La Mystique*, because he has some very good stuff on this.[17] It comes way at the end of a long, long chapter on Islam in which he talks about ordinary, everyday conduct. But what he has on this is quite good. I'm following him here now: all the point of the mystical life is concerned with finding this particular personal center, which is the center of mercy, and to see how it subsists in freedom, in the context of this almighty and all-pervading will of God, which is mercy and compassion. How does this work? The first point is that even before man comes into existence, even before there was any humanity, even before anything was, there was a covenant between God and man, in God Himself.

This covenant is called the *Mithaaq*. It's the starting point of a metaphysical concept of man. In other words, even before man is created, in God's very design for man, there is built a covenant in which man has already said, "Yes." So, the very first step in God's "plan" to bring man into existence, is he plans man as one who not only can say, "Yes," but has said, "Yes." "Man is the one who says 'yes' to God. This is what man will be. He will be the one who says, 'Yes.'" Later, I've got a whole page of a text from Junayd,[18] in which he quotes God as saying to Adam before Adam was even created, "Am I not your Lord?" And Adam says, "Yes." I think that's absolutely beautiful. This is a wonderful conception of what the nature of man is. Man is he who says "yes" to God. That's his whole being. And it's because of this, that man is essentially rooted and grounded in mercy, because his whole life and his whole being is to say "yes" to the mercy of God, and to say "yes" to God is mercy. It's the whole thing of mercy.

There is, then, built into human nature itself, the model of a primordial "yes"; this primordial consent to God and primordial submission to

16. *Sufism and Taoism*, 129.

17. A. Ravier, SJ, ed., *La Mystique et les Mystiques* (Paris: Desclée de Brower, 1965).

18. Junayd of Baghdad (830–910), influential Persian Sufi mystic and saint.

God. Since Islam means saying "yes" to God completely, it follows that every man is a Muslim. Man is by nature a Muslim. Man is by nature one who obeys God. To be a Muslim is just simply to be a human being. The only distinction between Muslims and others is that a lot of people simply don't realize it. They don't think about it; [whereas] a Muslim is somebody who is aware of who he is. Of course, they would have great respect for a Christian—a Christian who follows his Christianity faithfully is a Muslim, or as we would say, a Muslim who follows Islam faithfully is a Christian—because he obeys God; as long as he is true to who he really is: to this basic, inner "yes," which is built into him.

This is not at all a Platonic idea. It's dynamic; it's not a static essence. It's a dynamic, existential readiness to respond to God, rather than as an irrational animal. With Plato, man has this static essence, like a mirror, which he polishes—incidentally, this static contemplation is something that is very alien to the modern consciousness. And incidentally, I won't have a chance to talk about Zen much, but there is one very good Zen story that relates to this. One of the central things in a real understanding of Zen is that this "Quietistic" purification of the heart is not Zen—it's anything but—and this story illustrates that: a master comes and sees his disciple sitting in meditation, and he says, "Why are you sitting in meditation?" The disciple says, "Because I wish to become a Buddha." The master picks up a brick and starts polishing it. The disciple says, "Why are you polishing the brick?" And the master says, "I'm trying to make it into a mirror" [laughter].[19]

This shows that Zen, especially Rinzai Zen, has absolutely no place for [this]—although they do sit for hours in meditation, but that's not it. It is important to sit in meditation, but it's not Zen—although they make people do it and they go through all that. But it is not [meditation] which makes Zen. It's a totally different approach altogether. But Zen does have a similar idea that we have here in Islam, not that man is saying "yes" to God, but that man is essentially in Nirvana, but he doesn't know it—and he won't find it out by sitting in meditation. He has to push, he has to try to break through into it in some way, but he finds it out when it finds him out. All of a sudden, one day it hits him and he sees it, but it can't be taught and it can't be reached by practice. It has to be reached by a kind

19. Merton recounts this story in his *Mystics and Zen Masters* (p. 20).

of sudden illumination. But that's a very complicated topic; it's not what I'm talking about now. We've got to stick to Islam.

"As in humanity, there is this covenant, so, in each human being, there is his personal 'yes,' which is built into his being and the ground of his being." That is his person. I don't think they'd put it that way. But this is unconscious. It is in the deepest ground; what they call, "the inner secret of the heart"—the *sirr* ["secret"]. There, in this deepest ground of unconsciousness, [i.e.] beyond consciousness, in the depths of my personality, is my "yes" to God, which is inalienable and unchangeable. It's there and it's not something that I choose. It's in me, and there's absolutely nothing I can do to get rid of it. Whether I like it or not, there is, in the depth of my being, this "yes" to God. Not only because I am a human being and a member of the human race,[20] but because of His personal creative act, which has called me into being. The fact that I am in being is already a "yes" in response to God's call. He's called me into being and I've said "yes." As long as I'm there, I'm saying "yes," and I can't do anything about it. What I have to do, then, is appropriate this inner "yes"; I have to make it mine, consciously. That's the one thing that I can do.

Incidentally, I think this inner "yes," this personal "yes," corresponds almost exactly to Eckhart's idea of "the spark"—the *scintilla*—the little spark in the depths of your being, which is always there, and which has to be activated by the love of God.[21] It is, I think, practically the same concept. I think this is very close to the same thing. This I buy. Everything that I've been telling you, I didn't buy; but this, I buy. This, I think, is absolutely straight, and I think this is very important for us. Doesn't it strike you as being quite modern in a way? It's dynamic; it's not static.

20. This, and the following paragraph, is remarkably similar in tone and language to Merton's "Fourth and Walnut" experience: "It is a glorious destiny to be a member of the human race. . . . At the center of our being is a point of nothingness which is untouched by sin and by illusion . . . a point or spark which belongs entirely to God" (*Conjectures of a Guilty Bystander* [Garden City, NY: Doubleday, 1966], 157–58). The influence of Louis Massignon on Merton is apparent in Merton's use of the term *le point vierge* (*Conjectures*, 158; see Griffith, "Merton, Massignon, and the Challenge of Islam," in *Merton and Sufism*, 63–68).

21. See Merton, *Introduction to Christian Mysticism*, 200–201; as well as Erlinda Paguio, "Blazing in the Spark of God: Thomas Merton's References to Meister Eckhart," *The Merton Annual* 5 (1992): 247–62.

What would you say? It's existential. It's a question of personal freedom, but of course, you don't create your own.

Mother Myriam: How can we know? Of course, I speak from my own background; [but for] somebody who would not have been raised in a Christian milieu—how would you know then? For us, is it the reserve of Western culture, or is it really in man?

I think it is. I think that you could say that there are enough people around, who, even if they've been brought up in something completely alien to this, might experience it, or might respond [to this]. Because the real point in all this, is not how men tell each other they experience things. It's how God has made them that really counts. And, it seems to me, He really has made us this way. It seems to me, this is the best account of how we're made, in a religious sense.

Comment: I was just wondering if this would be comparable to what is called "religious consciousness"?

Yes. I think this is the religious consciousness.

Speaker 3: You speak of universal or inalienable—

Yes. This is perhaps the best description of the religious consciousness, and of course, it's tied up with man's capacity to love, too. A person could conceivably experience it, not as a "yes" to God, but as a "yes" to life.

Mother Myriam: We touch here the whole area of the sacred and the secular today.

Even in the secular, a person who, with a certain innocence, says "yes" completely to life in whatever form, provided it's really life.[22] Put into

---

22. Merton is collapsing any distinction between "sacred" and "secular" here for those who fully say "yes" to life.

other terms, take either Freud or take Erich Fromm, for example.[23] Take Fromm's whole ethic of "life affirmation." That's what this is. It is an acceptance of life, a consent to life, an affirmation of life, a dedication to life. It seems to imply that. And I think if you translate it into those terms, it's exactly the same thing. This is it. It doesn't have to be ["yes"] to "Allah."[24] This is Life. But of course, there is the question of God's will.

Fromm is really a very religious man. I've been in correspondence with him for a long time, since his book on psychology and religion,[25] in which he said, "I'm an atheist."[26] But ever since then, he's really coming out more and more. He likes the Sufis very much, and reads Rumi a lot. In fact, I have a copy of Rumi, which he gave me. He said, "Here, read this. This is very good. You'll like this." His whole problem with religion is purely and simply with popular religion, which to him has a concept of God, which he finds blasphemous. That's the whole thing. He simply can't accept the popular concept of God. And the radio idea of God. He won't touch it. He says, "Such a God as that can't exist and I won't have anything to do with that." Actually, he was brought up as a devout Jew, and I think he's still very strong in the Jewish tradition and the Hasidic tradition. He's always using Hasidic stories.[27]

The next thing is, [from] where does this act of personal response [come]? There is built into me, whether I like it or not, an unconscious "yes," and the only thing left to me is to accept this, and to make it mine, consciously. That's my job. I can reject it. I can say "no" to it. I can make

23. Erich Fromm (1900–1980), influential and prolific psychoanalyst and humanist, who fled Nazi Germany for the U.S. in 1934.

24. Again, Merton seems to be stating that even a "secular" or "non-religious" person can operate from within a "religious consciousness" through saying "yes" to life. This, and the previous section, represents Merton's "mystical humanism" at its best (to borrow a phrase from Jeffrey J. Kripal, *The Serpent's Gift: Gnostic Reflections on the Study of Religion* [Chicago: University of Chicago Press, 2006], 88).

25. *Psychoanalysis and Religion* (New Haven: Yale University Press, 1950).

26. For Merton's correspondence with Fromm, see *The Hidden Ground of Love*, 308–24. Merton first wrote Fromm in a letter dated October 2, 1954. See also Merton's Working Notebook #31 for his reading notes on Fromm (Thomas Merton Center at Bellarmine University).

27. The recording for this section ends here before beginning again in the next paragraph.

some other choice, but this must be a personal response. Now, this personal response is an act of God, because God alone acts. But we don't have to get hung up on that particular point, because whatever it is, it is an act by which I appropriate this "yes." I make it really mine.

But before we go any further on this, we're on a moving stairway. This isn't the end of anything. This is on the way to something else. This happens to be a moment in what's really a dialectical procedure. We're going somewhere, but at this particular point, we have reached a place where I say "yes," and it's an act. It's my act—although, it's God's act—but this act is a total abandonment to the power of God. It is, for Islam, a recognition that God alone acts. Here you get your Arabesque. We're weaving out from this center again. So, the "yes" by which I appropriate this deep unconscious "yes" is saying, "Yes, God alone is real. God alone acts." This is the total submission to God, which is Islam. This is the act of complete obedience. Therefore, the act by which I say "yes" to God is the renunciation of the act. I am saying, "Yes, it's true, I can't," and then, in that, I act. When I say "I can't," then I can. When I admit that I can't act, then God acts in me and then I do it. This is typical Islam. This is exactly the way they think. It is this very sophisticated metaphysical view of things. He who says "yes" in this sense is therefore admitting that he's not an agent, and yet he, in a certain sense, is an agent, but with God; therefore, he's united with God. He's obeying God and that's Islam.

But he could say "no." If he says "no," what would happen? He would be the bird. This is where the bird [metaphor] comes in. When he says "no" to this inner "yes," then he's got to do it himself; then he rejects God as the only agent. Then he really has to begin. God says, "Alright, you want to do it all yourself, go ahead." This is the crucial point: the person does not have the religious consciousness, which accepts this "yes" to God within himself, and [instead] prefers [the opposite]. People in our culture often take for granted that the answer is "no" on this, but it's not because they've thought it through. It's just taken for granted. It would be quite easy for anyone under the appropriate impulse of grace, or in a particular situation, to suddenly wake up to the fact, and say "yes"—but ordinarily, it's "no." Consequently, we're stuck. We're in the void, where we've said "no." Of course, we're still in God's mercy—but God's mercy, because of our choice, has now become a void; an emptiness in which we have to maintain ourselves. We're under "justice": the bird who has to flap to keep himself up in the void. That's the condition of being under wrath, and everything that follows from that is wrath. The guy who has to maintain his own existence and his own powers as if there were no God, is still maintained by the mercy of God, but he has doomed himself to a condition of "metaphysical wrath," which leads to pointless activity; to utterly useless activity. He has to be an agent when: 1.) he can't be an agent, and 2.) God's doing it anyway. But he has to convince himself that he's an agent and that's where the flapping [starts]. Therefore, if the bird wants to stop flapping, all he has to do is realize that he's sustained by God, and go on from there, with this different conception of life.

Comment: Would the Sufis believe that most persons are in this state?

I don't know, that would depend on the situation. Perhaps a Sufi in the thirteenth century would say that quite a few are. The one who isn't is the one who accepts God's reality. But I suppose a Sufi looking at the effects of this in our society would say that they were. Suppose you look at something like the Vietnam War, which is such a tremendous fabric of screw ball decisions and funny things that are happening for no purpose at all—and then ending in the death of lots of people. Behind that, there must be something very screwy. The kind of thinking that has gone into that implies a real alienation from reality. The war is "unreal" in that sense. It has no connection with what the people themselves think they're doing. I may be wrong on that, but it certainly seems to be going that way.

Comment: We just read today an article by Bishop McGrath regarding Latin America.[28] *A part of it says that one of the things that's happening in Vietnam is a loss of confidence in each other, for people. Isn't this almost the key to Communist aggression? But how do the people who see this react?*

One of the ways we can't react is by doing something that destroys confidence even more. One of the real tragedies of Vietnam is that we've destroyed all confidence *in us*. It's obvious in the last 5-6 years, that what

---

28. Marcos G. McGrath, CSC (1924–2000), bishop in Chile from 1961 to 1969 and archbishop of Panama from 1969 through 1994, was a leading figure in the Latin American Church in the conciliar and post-conciliar period.

has happened to America in the eyes of the rest of the world has been a tremendous nose dive. They don't trust us now. And what's happening with the Communists is that their stock is going up. Not only because their guerrilla-tactics are effective in certain situations, but because people are beginning to think, "Well, maybe the Communists are right. Maybe they are the only ones that can help us." That's the tragic thing. This is another subject, but it seems to me that where the real problem has arisen all down the line is probably that the people in the middle who could have given another alternative have systematically been eliminated, not only in Vietnam, but in South America, too. Most of the time, what we end up doing is backing some two-bit dictator who has meanwhile thrown into jail everybody who would be neither Communist, nor neither extreme left nor right, but a kind of a liberal or a socialist. I think that's the tragic thing, that anybody who's got any other alternative seems to get eliminated. I don't claim to be an authority on this, but that's the way I look at it.

To return to the Sufi thing: I would say we certainly do live in an atmosphere in which this basic "yes" is pretty much ignored. "The human response to God is a punctual and an ungraspable emergence of the human being." When you say "yes," you come into being fully, the full emergence of your being is the conscious "yes," which appropriates this unconscious "yes" which is in us. I think that's great. That's just the way man is; that's the way we're supposed to be, and that's what the monastic life is. That's St. Benedict on obedience—it's all centered on this fundamental appropriation of a "yes," which wants to obey. There is in our hearts, something that above all wants to surrender to God, and the acceptance of that, and the appropriation of that is life and happiness.

At the point between absolute reality and absolute unreality emerges [from] our being a "yes" to absolute reality. You're hanging on the edge of a cliff. There's another Zen story like that; one of these Zen koans. You're hanging by your teeth on a branch over a cliff, and somebody comes up to you and says, "What is the meaning of Zen?" And you have to answer. If you open your mouth, you fall into the abyss, and if you don't open your mouth, you just remain hanging there anyway. This is perhaps really the answer to that. The only answer is not something that can be formulated. The only answer is a total commitment to the Real, and a total non-commitment to the unreal. And you can't do that in words. I don't know what the answer to that particular koan is, but I think this reflects that situation.

Then you've got this "pre-eternal covenant," which is beyond the existence of man, and which founds that existence. Then you've got the inner unconscious "yes," "pronounced in the secret of the heart, in the course of a dialogue with God, which is situated beyond our own consciousness, but which is at the origin of the consciousness of ourself."[29] I think that's great. A dialogue with God, in which we are responding to God and saying "yes," which is situated beyond our own consciousness, but which is at the root and the origin of our consciousness of ourself. That's our identity, that's our personality; that's who we are.

In those terms, then, it's altogether different from the kind of despairing predestination that you get in Calvin, for example. Because in Calvin, you've got a totally different thing. You've got this isolated, monadic individual, all locked up in himself, and nothing ever penetrates in there. He is completely self-enclosed; a completely self-enclosed unit who was brought into being like a stone. And nothing has ever penetrated this little stone. And the stone starts wondering whether it's accepted or rejected. It can never know. This is the result of the switch that took place in the Renaissance, and in the Reformation, in which everybody became an Adam. Each one is his own private little Adam; his own private little locked up being. And God has to reach him from the outside, so that here we all are, some stones lying around in a creek, and I suppose God comes through as would a child, who's picking up interesting stones, and maybe he'll pick up you. Maybe he'll pick up another one; maybe not. It's pure luck.

But the Islamic thing is totally different, because the choice is already made. You've already been chosen; all you have to do is ratify it, because it's already in you to say "yes" to God. This is our true self, to which we may or may not be faithful. The appropriation of this central "yes" is fully becoming a person, and this inner "yes" is the ground of personality. I think this is something really worth investigating. Because personality cannot be reduced to nature. It has to be free. Personality is not just part of a man's "essence." The Boethius definition of personality as an individual of "rational essence" is totally hopeless.[30] It doesn't get anywhere near the real meaning of personality. Personality has to be seen as freedom;

---

29. Merton is following the Ravier text, translating on the spot from the French, hence the sometimes awkward sentence structure here and in the following sections.

30. Boëthius, sixth-century Roman senator and philosopher.

yet it is something created in man by God. And in these terms, I think it comes out that way.

So, "Man only becomes himself by this 'yes.' The divine act which gives faith and the human answer which accepts faith, coincide in an indivisible instant—an intemporal instant—which belongs to the intimate secrecy of the heart." I think that's great. What we were saying yesterday about time is that there is a time when this intemporal instant has to [break through]—and of course this doesn't just happen once in life. For the Sufis, life is a constant development, in which, starting from the basic act of faith, there are moments where this same kind of "yes" reproduces itself on different levels. They have a whole list of states and [stations], and you pass from one to the other by another "yes."[31] Sometimes situations of trial, sometimes situations of joy. What we have to be, then, is constantly alert; to be obeying God at all times; to be saying "yes" to Him. Then, if we are always disposed to say "yes," when the right moment comes, we'll say a "yes" that really gets things going, and we break through [even] further.

But what happens, though? As I said, this thing goes somewhere. There does come a time when the "yes" that one makes is so profound that it also involves the renunciation of the ground of one's own self. The ground where this unconscious "yes" originally was has urged us to appropriate it by repeated "yeses." Then, all of a sudden, one day, the thing that we're supposed to say "yes" is: "Yes, the ground of the self must go." The real point of Sufism is to reach the place where the whole ground of one's liberty is completely renounced. And then what happens, as the Zen people say, "You fall through the hole in the bottom of the bucket." At that particular point, there is nothing left but God. And when you realize that there is nothing left but God, you realize *that's you*. You fall through the bottom of everything and you come out in God with, as they would say, no separate existence apart from God. This is the Sufi's final affirmation of *Tawhid*, the unity of God, which is where we began and it's where we end. So that the annihilation of our being in God is not at all just simply being absorbed in God, but being lost and found—it's a death and resurrection.[32]

31. On the various "stations and stages" denoting varying degrees on the Sufi mystical path, see Schimmel, *Mystical Dimensions of Islam*, 109–29.

32. Merton is describing the Sufi states of *fanā'* and *baqā'*; see his essay, "Final Integration," in *Contemplation in a World of Action*, 227–28.

This ground of being, in which we have a personal "yes" of our own, is a provisional thing, on which, first of all, you build a structure of "yeses," and then all of a sudden, the whole thing collapses. It's like a scaffolding for a building. You have a ground on which you start putting up a scaffold, which is this unconscious "yes," and you build a scaffolding of "yeses," and then all of a sudden, the whole scaffolding is taken away. And what is left is God. But, I-in-Him. They speak of the dissolution of our being and its reconstitution in God. Dissolution [only] is not it. It's dissolution and reconstitution. What this is, in Christian terms, is dying and rising in Christ, so that "I live now, not I, but Christ lives in me."[33] The value of going into something like this, is that it gives us a slant on that Christian truth, which people don't ordinarily go into. We tend to rattle off terms like that, "I live in Christ; Christ lives in me." We say it so often. But something like this gives us a deep insight into what this could possibly mean; what kind of implications this could have.

I think the best thing I can do after that is just to read this one last text, and then we can either discuss it, or I can just leaf through notes and quotes here and there. The one thing I wanted to develop systematically was this [on dying and rising], because I think this is very important.

33. Galatians 2:20.

Chapter Twelve

The Interpretation of Dreams, Sufi Spirituality, and Religious Inclusivity

This is simply saying again what I've said before, but in typical Sufi language. This is from one of the Sufi mystics called al-Junayd. This is about the creation of Adam and Eve and the response of man coming forth into being at the call of God—even before they existed. Incidentally, I would like to see this in a liturgical text. This would be beautiful to say in our own Office. "God called them and they replied at once. He replied for them in conferring existence upon them, and they were a call coming from Him. He made himself known to them, when they were as yet only a design conceived within Himself. He made them bear witness for themselves, saying, 'Am I not your Lord?' And they replied, 'Yes.' God made known the fact that He addressed Himself to them when they existed only insofar as He created them. But then they perceived God without perceiving themselves—God being present in a way, unknown to any but Himself, a way no other could discover. Finding them, embracing them, seeing them, He created them in a state of *fana*"—dissolution. "Thus, they perdured in extinction in their pre-eternal state"—this is just like Eckhart; this is pure Eckhart—"in which He revealed to them the hidden abysses of His knowledge and united them with Himself."

"Then He separated them from Himself and made them absent in their union and present in their separation. Their absence became the cause of their presence, and their presence the cause of their absence. He ravished them with signs, which He caused to appear to them in making them present. He deprived them of signs in making them absent. He perfected their extinction in the state of persistence, and their persistence in the state of extinction. This existence He has given them is the most complete, the most fundamental, the most sublime, the most apt to receive the violence, the triumph, and the true domination, which pour out upon them from Him, so that all traces of them disappear; all sight of them vanishes and their existence goes away. Then there is no longer any human attribute or existence that can be known or any perceptible trace, for all such things constitute vices, which hide from spirits, but belong to them from pre-eternity." Terrific text.

He's bringing in all these different aspects. First of all, the fact that man actually is created in a state of dissolution in God, which is his proper state. But there's no idea of a fall. There's no "fall." It's just that God also lets them be outside, in order that they may see Him from that angle, too. That they may be outside Him and return to Him with a response and a "yes," which calls [man] back into himself, into extinction. And when they are outside Him, then they have to be awakened to Him by symbols, by signs. This is the real way of awakening for the Sufi. And this is one of the problems, again, of our particular culture. The Sufi would say that it is essential to understand symbolism, because of what I was talking about yesterday regarding the spiritual interpretation of the Quran. You have to understand these symbols by which Allah is drawing you; not just observance of the Islamic law, but inner transformation.

But the symbol is only the first step towards inner transformation. The symbol simply awakens you to the need for inner transformation, but the symbol [itself] doesn't do it. It simply awakens the need for this response. "He ravished them with signs," with these symbols. To go back with what you were saying yesterday, I think a Sufi interpretation of this today—you could say that everything is sign. We could turn everything inside out in modern society. Instead of simply rejecting it and trying to start something else. To see it all as a sign. If Sister Corita says Mary is the "juiciest tomato of them all," well, fine.[1] I think the world is full of these signs. I'm not nearly as reverent as Sister Corita with this.

Was it *Cables to the Ace* you were talking about? That somebody's reading it? *Cables to the Ace* is strictly about signs. Have you got it? Oh, you don't have it. I'll have to send you one. I've asked them to send you

1. This is a reference to artist Corita Kent's famous, "the juiciest tomato of all" (1964).

some others; I'll send you one of these, too. I didn't think of sending it to you before; I didn't know if you'd like it or not [laughter]. It's a little bit problematical. I don't know what kind of reviews it's going to get. One whole section was written when I went to Louisville to see the doctor, and I went down to have some lunch in a hotel, and I was late; I was drinking a glass of Chablis and sitting there quietly in the middle of the afternoon, just getting fragments of conversation coming through—some from the waiters and some from the people—and you weave the whole thing together and you get this weird mosaic, which doesn't make sense, and yet in a certain sense it does.

All this is coming out of everybody's unconscious and there's a great deal going on in everybody's unconscious, especially in our culture. You've got all this churning going on, so why not tune in on it? It's all right there. And it's much more interesting than to, say, go to the library and take down a lot of books and then study some darn thing about Shakespeare's maidenhead, or something like that, and then come up with an essay about it and send it to the PMLA,[2] so you can get published and get a better job. This is much more fun. So, I'll send you that.

Well, I haven't got anything more. Do you want to discuss any of this now? Yes?

Comment: Where does it come in that the Sufis are interested in dreams?

It doesn't fit precisely here, but dreams have a great deal to tell us about where we are going with these "yeses."

Mother Myriam: You should write a book on that!

Our unconscious has to tell us a great deal about what God's asking of us, and if we don't take the unconscious into account, we can't really know. We Catholics and Western rationalist people have really stunted our lives by judging everything purely in terms of rational consciousness. It's just not nearly enough. It's got to go much deeper than that. It's just not the way to think. I think that's what they [Sufis] are simply accepting. The fact that our unconscious life is a necessary dimension in our life. There [in

---

2. Publication of the Modern Language Association.

the unconscious], you have the residue of our past actions and you get a way of understanding your actions that you don't get consciously [with] the regular [rational] mechanism, [where] we're always choosing. We're selecting data that we feel to be relevant and excluding other things. Then our unconscious salvages some of what we've excluded and comes back with it and says, "Hey, you know, this driftwood looks good too." We're like people that are always doing some elaborate, fancy, Baroque, self-conscious work of art, and forgetting that the driftwood is very beautiful. And that there's a lot of driftwood which may be even more beautiful than the things that we're creating for ourselves. And the subconscious keeps telling us that, and to pay attention.

But dreams are fascinating. Although I don't remember most of mine. Of course, this has been a dream come true in a way, because one of my dreams—the Sufi told me this, too [laughter]. He said, "What do you usually dream?" And I said, "I usually dream that I've got a lot of money and I'm going on a trip" [laughter]. He said, "Well, you probably will" [laughter]. That's my standard dream: plenty of money and a ticket in my pocket, and I'm just getting ready to go [laughter]. I guess a lot of Cistercians dream that. A huge hermitage at Needle Rock [laughter]. One of the dreams I used to have—it was a much more unconscious form of this same one—it's the dream that anybody in an enclosed life is liable to have some time or other. It's the one where you're home and you're trying to get back to the monastery, and you don't know whether you're going to miss the train or not. Isn't that something? [laughter] This dream is the standard one, in which you allow yourself in your dream to be outside, and it's permissible because you're trying to get back; but you're missing the train [laughter]. You want in the worst way to get back, but you just can't catch that train [laugher].[3]

Comment: How can you know how to interpret dreams?

---

3. The recording for this section ends just as Merton begins to share the following dream: "I remember at one time, a really beautiful dream—I've had several really beautiful dreams—about a superb [Carthusian] Charterhouse; a great Dream Charterhouse, that every once in a while, I dream about." Merton had an early fascination with and idealization of the more solitary religious Orders, such as the Carthusians and Camaldolese (see Donald Grayston, *Thomas Merton and the Noonday Demon: The Camaldoli Correspondence* [Eugene, OR: Cascade Books, 2016]; see also Merton's *The Silent Life* [New York: Farrar, Straus and Giroux, 1957], 127–76).

Mother Myriam: It's your own growing out of your own unconscious into consciousness. At times I have a very key dream, and for weeks and weeks I wouldn't have the answer. And then all of a sudden it was there. It was really building up to something.

Yes. What the psychoanalysts tell you to do is "free association." I've never found that I get anything with free association. Do you know what free association is? I don't think it's terribly helpful to interpret a dream. You start with your dream and freely associate from some element in it. I've never gotten anywhere with that, though. You can go all over the [dream] and get all kinds of material, but it doesn't seem to [work for me]. I would say that a dream, as you say, if you let it cook, and go and live with it for a while, all of a sudden you see things. I've seen dreams like that work out. It's a funny thing that happens to me now—this is quite strange. In the hermitage—I'll sleep at night and dream—and then I go to make my bed and I remember all the dreams. They all suddenly come out. It's strange. I don't remember them completely, but they all come back. I wake up and forget them. Then when I go to make my bed—I really do make my bed [laughter]—the dreams all come back. It's as if they were hovering over the pillow. It's very strange.

I really do think that the Islamic concept of man as a being created to respond to God is very beautiful. I think that's very Biblical, too, don't you? I get a lot out of that. Perhaps I could just leaf through my notes at random and pick out some of these statements on Sufism. This one is nice. This is Ibn al-Arabi on different religions. He talks about two kinds of minds. Again, this would tie in with the interior senses. The distinction he makes is not just choosing between sense impressions and interior senses, but a totally different attitude towards everything. As you were saying yesterday, the idea is to see both the outward and the inward, but to see them in an entirely different way. There's a certain way of looking at the outward—a certain mental structure or structure of consciousness—which refers everything back to reason, and which always mediates everything through a reasonable analysis or interpretation in view of something else. This is the business of looking at a redwood tree and estimating right away how many cubic feet of lumber you've got. You don't really see the tree. In that sense, there are neither external nor internal senses.

So, one of the things that's very important for us if we want to develop our interior sense is that we should develop our exterior senses. That's a much more practical way of putting it for modern man. Walking in a redwood grove, and seeing the redwood [trees]. Seeing the light [shining through]—seeing all these things also develops your interior senses. The apprehension of external space can open up an internal space. Appreciation of external space and light are very important. Guardini,[4] for example, is always talking in terms of a sacred space, which is not only external in a building and in a community, but also within ourselves. The interior sense by which one would apprehend sacred space would be developed by an exterior awareness of something like a redwood grove. These things go together. Therefore, I think it would be very important to educate people along those lines: to develop internal senses by the development of external senses that favor internal senses.

Were you the one that asked the question about that or who was it? We were talking about it, but somebody asked the first question. Was it you?

Comment: Coming to your senses? That was me.

Music develops one's interior senses. Dancing has to do with interior senses in a way. It's an expression. A person can't dance unless they can outwardly manifest something that they sense interiorly—to express with your whole being. One doesn't [have to] reflect [on it], it's there. It's something one knows.

Comment: It's certainly true with music and intervals and notes. They all have meaning.

Speaker 2: I'm wondering: a person who doesn't have some form of art, or some way of creating or making art is really—

Mother Myriam: Impoverished, very impoverished. But I believe there is art in everyone.

Here's one of the things from Ibn al-Arabi: "In reality, every true knower of God, who knows God through the experience of direct, personal mani-

---

4. Romano Guardini (1885–1968), influential twentieth-century German Catholic priest and theologian. For Merton's citations of Romano Guardini's *Sacred Signs*, see *Monastic Observances: Initiation into the Monastic Tradition* 5, ed. Patrick F. O'Connell (Collegeville, MN: Cistercian Publications, 2010), 10, 49–51.

festation in himself, is actually living in a mode of being peculiar to the Hereafter."[5] It's already living in heaven. That's one of the ideas of the monastic life. I suppose it really boils down to this constant submission and "yes" to God. "Such a man has, already in the present world, been resurrected from the dead and brought to life from the tomb. So, he sees what others cannot see." Here's your interior senses. "And witnesses what others cannot witness. This is a result of the special favor [that] God grants to some of His servants."[6]

Here is Ibn al-Arabi's idea of the man who is religiously ignorant. This is great: "The religiously ignorant man is the one who judges the things of God by the light of his own reason, and accepts God only in the form proposed to him by his own particular religion."[7] Here's the [one who is] religiously ignorant: "only in the form." He's not saying that he shouldn't believe: "The religiously ignorant man is one who judges the things of God by the light of his own reason"—fundamentally refuses to say "yes" to God. Pre-judging everything that comes from God, figuring it out, and then accepting or rejecting it, "accepts God only in the form proposed to him by his own particular religion."

That's a revolutionary statement, but it's very good. "Rejecting all others as impious." It's not that that one shouldn't give primacy to the form in which God is presented, because he would say that, definitely; you have to take the form of your own religion. It's through this that God has manifested Himself to us and that's what we should follow. But, "rejecting all others as impious, he fails to see the truth of God when it appears to him in an unfamiliar form." This is what we were saying yesterday about the necessity of becoming a Cosmic Man. The ability, while being perfectly faithful to one's own religion, to also grasp the truth of God when it presents itself in an unfamiliar form; for example, as in Islam or in Hinduism—to the extent that it's acceptable. This absolutely does not mean that one must accept everything that presents itself without even examining it. You would have an awful mishmash.

But there are, in all these different religions, manifestations of God which are new to us, even today in the twentieth century, which to some extent we should be able to accept as manifestations of God [that are]

---

5. Quoted in Izutsu, *Sufism and Taoism*, 253.

6. *Sufism and Taoism*, 253.

7. *Sufism and Taoism*, 254.

relevant to us. And I think the way to do it is the way we're doing it now. In other words, these things should be discussed in a contemplative monastery of Christians; the way of each religion should be known. At least some of these fundamental ideas should, because they help us. So, Arabi says, "Beware of being bound up by a particular religion and rejecting all others as unbelief. If you do that, you will fail to obtain a great benefit. You will fail to obtain knowledge of the true reality. Try to make yourself a kind of prime matter for all forms of religious belief"[8]—or, I would say, for all forms of religious experience; different forms of religious consciousness.

"God, the blessed and exalted is wider and greater than to be confined to one religion to the exclusion of all others."[9] In other words, there is no such thing as any one religion which has all the answers, or the only relevant answers, and "everyone else is wrong." That's a good point that he's making. Therefore, for him, a true religious consciousness is one which recognizes God in all His manifestations; whereas, religious ignorance is a hang-up, which finds God only in a few manifestations, only in one or two particular ones, and then excludes all others. What he's saying, in other words, is that religious ignorance is a kind of bigotry. But it doesn't mean that one has to believe all the other religions, but one should be open to the experience implied in the other religions. "Instead of dividing one manifestation against the other that seems contradictory to it, the true knower perceives in his own heart that there is an underlying unity, and the Absolute is One in apparent contradictions. The knower knows this, because he knows through his own heart, which is grounded in the One." He can identify [with the other religions, because] it's the same One.

Well, I have about run out of things. I could read lots of quotes, but I think if we haven't got any [questions]—

Comment: Isn't exclusion a characteristic of Catholicism?

It's a perversion of Catholicism. What we have tended to do, especially since the Council of Trent, has been a defensive attitude towards Protestantism and towards error; to say, "This is absolutely wrong." Whereas, what we should have done, and are doing now to a great extent, is more a question of understanding other religions, including where they are

8. *Sufism and Taoism*, 254.
9. *Sufism and Taoism*, 254.

absolutely incompatible with us. We can say it's interesting, or we can say it might have a useful angle, but instead of saying, "This is Catholic or this is Muslim, therefore this must be wrong and I don't even look at it," what we do now is ask, "This is Muslim. What does it mean?" What does it really mean to us, and can it be useful for us? Does it correspond to something that we already believe? Is it simply another way of saying the same thing that we believe? Because I think what we went through today is really identical with our own kind of experience. It's another way of saying what is perfectly Christian. This obedience to God of the Muslims—we can practice it and it will help us. And it's not just peculiar to the Muslims. It's universal. In other words, it's "Catholic."

The Fathers of the Church used to interpret this. They used to have this famous spiritual interpretation of the Jews leaving Egypt, and they took away the spoils of the Egyptians.[10] They borrowed all kinds of golden pots and pans and walked on. Just stolen. But Origen and the Fathers of Church interpret this to mean that the Christian philosopher takes what is true in all the "pagan" religions, or any other religion, and applies it to Christianity. Just as St. Thomas [Aquinas borrowed from] Aristotle, so can we, today, go further. Aristotle was condemned when St. Thomas was using him. It was forbidden. It was forbidden to use Aristotle in teaching when Thomas was using him. And he got Aristotle from an Irish teacher in Naples who was using Aristotle against the law.[11] So, Thomas followed his example.

Mother Myriam [re-enters with a beverage]: The color is kind of funny, but it's not poisonous. And I don't think we can find the napkins.

Oh, that's fine. Thank you, Mother. I don't know what it is, but it's very nice. Grape juice?

Mother Myriam: No, I don't know. There was something in the dining room— it's grape and orange.

Oh, a cocktail! [laughter] What are we going to do after supper? Do you want to play the guitar and I'll play the drums?

---

10. Exodus 12:35-36.
11. Peter of Ireland (thirteenth century), lecturer at the University of Naples.

Comment: Why don't you read us some of your poetry, Father.

I don't have any around. Have you got *Cables to the Ace*? We might read a little bit of that afterwards. How about that? Alright. That'll be fun. We'll take a little bit on the music and then a little bit on the poetry.[12]

Mother Myriam: You say that the Sufis found themselves faced with the choice between either being a scholar and studying the law, or [being] a friend of God. But we are more or less faced with that alternative today. I feel you cannot really, with modern consciousness, exclude completely the other.

No, they were scholars, too. But what they had to refuse was the position and the status of the scholar, and everything that went with that—making their scholarship the important thing. But of course, they were scholars. Just as Eckhart was a great mind. But the important thing was something more than the scholarship. And of course, in Islam, the study of law is more highly legalistic than it is even with us, and it's much more complicated, apparently. I don't know too much about it. But there were situations where a Sufi, in order to really be a Sufi, practically had to give up this very complicated, hair-splitting legal study, which they had. I don't have a translation from the Arabic, because I don't know Arabic, but I got this from the French and translated it into English. It's a Sufi master writing a letter to one of his disciples who was studying law. It's a very good letter. I've got it in a book called *Raids on the Unspeakable*. That book is coming [to you]. There's some text from Ibn Abbad.[13] There's this letter to the one who is studying law, telling him, "Well, if you want to study law, it's too bad."[14]

---

12. A long digression ensues here with Merton detailing the difficult relationship between Fr. Frederick William Faber (1814–1863), Oratorian priest, and John Henry Newman (1801–1890). The discussion begins with Merton relaying a story about Faber's 1866 work, *The Precious Blood or The Price of our Salvation* (London: Thomas Richardson and Son), in which Merton jokingly refers to Faber as the "Cecil B. DeMille of pious literature."

13. "Readings from Ibn Abbad," in *Raids on the Unspeakable* (New York: New Directions, 1966), 141–51.

14. "Letter to a Sufi Who Has Abandoned Sufism to Study Law," *Raids*, 147–48: "[G]o ahead with your books of Law, / It will make little difference whether you do this / Or something else equally trivial" (p. 148).

In case we don't have any time to say anything more formally on this, it's been a great grace for me to share with you these few ideas about Sufism and Hinduism. I think that things like this really do have something to say to us. At all costs, our real work is to deepen our lives. And I don't think that we can do it today by simply remaining within the framework that's always been approved and prescribed for us. It's good to read the monastic fathers, we have to keep that up, but things like this [e.g., Sufism] throw a light on that. This is a very monastic kind of thinking. These people have much more in common with our monastic tradition than a lot of other things do. I think we should range widely over everything in a wise way.

I think the only problem that comes up is when you get a bunch of immature people, as you do in some monasteries, who mindlessly pick up everything without any kind of discrimination. In one breath, they're talking about something very good, and in the same breath, they're talking about something completely trivial. I think obviously you have to avoid that, but apart from that, to be really wide ranging, and to cover everything that has any kind of significance at all. But each one can't do all that, so it has to be a communal thing. You have to have somebody come in once in a while and stimulate interest in these things. I will try to dig up some books; I have some that may be duplicate in the library, so if I find some, I'll put them in a box and send them out. I think I have at least one volume of the *Eranos Yearbook* selections. You'll find some useful things in that. But this has been a great joy. Thank you very much for your patience and putting up with me [audible collective sigh of appreciation from the community].

Mother Myriam: Thank you for coming.

Well, I certainly have enjoyed it. It's been a great thing all around. I hope my abbot will feel that I behaved myself properly and that he will let me come back [laughter].[15]

---

15. The recording picks up again after supper with Merton offering an extended reading of selections from his *Cables to the Ace* with much laughter throughout.

Needle Rock, Beach, Sinkyone Wilderness

Needle Rock, Sheep Ranch, Sinkyone Wilderness

Needle Rock, View to the North, Sinkyone Wilderness

Cliffside, Sinkyone Wilderness

*Photographs by Thomas Merton used with permission of the Merton Legacy Trust
and Thomas Merton Center at Bellarmine University*

Redwoods Monastery Church Interior
(Used with Permission, Redwoods Monastery Archives)

Chapter Thirteen

Life in Prayer

Day One[1]

Anybody who wants to hold forth at length, can do so during the discussion, and we'll see what happens. Mother Myriam and I were thinking, for today, and in this session particularly, we could spend most of the time talking about what has transpired in regard to Houses of Prayer,[2] and what your mind is about that. Part of this would be devoted to educating me. Let's say that this first session could be devoted to talking about what has been going on, especially *what you want* and what you are after. I can tell you very well what I want and what I am going after, with the grace of God, I hope. And I think, what we should do is talk about it. What do we want to do? What are we after? How we are going to do it will follow from what we want.

Right at the beginning, I would say the most important thing is that we are here. We're here at this place. We're in a House of Prayer, and [Redwoods Monastery] represents a very definite expression of a very definite contemplative tradition, which is the Cistercian tradition. This is probably the best Cistercian monastery in the United States [laughter].

Mother Myriam: Not everybody agrees with you [laughter].

---

1. Merton opens with a prayer to the Holy Spirit, which is not on the recording, but is included in Dardenne's conference notes (Redwoods Monastery Archives).

2. The general theme and context for this series of conferences is the House of Prayer movement that was current among American religious orders in the late 1960s. See the Merton-Dardenne correspondence included in Part II of this volume, particularly from August 1968.

This [place] is an authentic realization of the Cistercian spirit; the true Cistercian spirit. And there are many reasons for this. This is an authentic Cistercian house from the Flemish tradition, which is closely aligned with the great mystical traditions of the Lowlands and the Rhineland. You get a very different sense of things here. So, you're at a real House of Prayer, where you've got a nice environment, and what I would say is to, first of all, enjoy this. Drink in what is here and take advantage of it: get out under the trees, and take advantage of being under the redwoods—maybe wait until the rain stops!

Mother Myriam: I suggest that you wait until the sun comes out, then we'll go [laughter].

And if the sun comes out, I suggest, too, we get over by the ocean. I was out there yesterday afternoon, and although it's threatened with development—as everything in California is—it still is most beautiful. To be simply out there with this vast expanse of land, with nothing there except for pasture and the sea. Even the sheep are gone now, because the man moved out of his sheep ranch. And these waves coming in, and sea lions playing in the sea, and hundreds of birds flying back and forth—and nothing else. Just sea, sky, waves, birds, sea lions. This is where you get your answers. This is where you find out about House of Prayer. Everything connects.

The talking, although important, isn't the principal thing. Nothing that anybody says is going to be that important. The great thing is prayer. Prayer itself. If you want a House of Prayer, the way to get to it is by praying. And if you want a life of prayer, the way to get to it is by praying. We were indoctrinated to think so much in terms of means and ends—technologically achieving ends—we don't realize that there's a different dimension in the life of prayer. In the life of prayer, you start where you are. You deepen what you already have. And you realize that you're already there.

In technology, you've got this horizontal progress where you have to start from one point and move onto another. That's not the way it is in the life of prayer. [In prayer] you discover what you already have. We already have everything, but we don't know it; we don't experience it and we don't see it. Everything has [already] been given to us in Christ. The importance of a House of Prayer is that it is an atmosphere that is removed from this linear dimension of means to ends. [Prayer] is in the dimension of ends which have already been achieved, but need to be enjoyed. There are so many problems that come from that, but that's what we could discuss as we go along.

As you know, I've been living as a hermit—sort of. I've been out of that atmosphere for about three or four weeks and talking a lot. And I get the feeling that there's so much talking that goes on that's utterly useless. You say the same thing over and over, and over and over again. Something is said perfectly well in five minutes, and then you spend five hours saying the same thing over [again], going around. This may be necessary or good, but we don't have to feel that much needs to be said. We already know a great deal of what we need to know, and it needs to be *grasped*, it needs to be deepened.

That's the dimension in which I hope we will be thinking. But now— really, since Vatican II—we are in a very unusual time; we all realize this. It's very disconcerting, because we've been pushing and pushing on the door, and all of a sudden, the door has burst open, and we're all falling over each other; and find there's a stairway on the other side, and we're all rolling down it. And after all this tremendous pushing, to suddenly break through this door and find ourselves falling, is quite an experience. Because anything is possible now. If you keep within reason, you can do anything you want, provided that it's humanly reasonable. Still, people are pushing like mad. They'll take the most impossible and most unlikely thing and push on that, because they still think they have to push. We don't have to push for anything like this. It's *there*.

And suddenly, when everything is possible, we realize that we don't really know what we wanted to do. We've just been pushing for the opportunity to do something. We spend so much time pushing that we haven't figured out what it was we wanted. And now that we have the chance to do it, here we are. So, you get the rather disconcerting phenomenon of all these little contemplative experiments being started and then evaporating, like in the Cistercians. Started by kids who have gone through a traumatic experience of wanting a real contemplative life, and somebody says, "All right, here it is. You know what you want, go ahead and do it." And they don't know what they want. And it evaporates. They buy a farm, or they rent a farm, and get themselves together in the farmhouse, and they sit around and suddenly realize that they've either got to do it the old way—which of course, they absolutely refuse to do—or, you've got to have a better way of your own, which they don't have.

So then comes the meetings and the dialogues, and then it becomes an interminable "yak session." "What are we going to create now?" You have to realize that perhaps you already do know what you want, and maybe the new structures aren't that necessary. What we were doing when we were pushing on the door, we were, each one, writing out a Rule. And this was the favorite sport of Trappist monks for some time [laughter]—go off some place in secret and write a new Rule. You have your new *horarium*, and you have it all figured out [laughter].

We should have such a fullness of what we are after that all that's necessary now, since obstacles are removed, is to *do it*. And what we want to do, presumably, is pray. Okay, now pray. This is the whole doctrine of prayer that's in the *Rule of Saint Benedict*. It's all summed up in one phrase. He's got several chapters on the liturgy: how it has to be lined up; of course, we want to change this whole thing. But the whole practical theology of prayer in St. Benedict is, if a monk wants to pray, let him simply go into the Oratory and pray [laughter]. That's all he feels is necessary to be said about the subject. He doesn't say, "Let him go in and start with vocal prayer, and then go on up the ladder." He says, "If you want to pray, pray."[3]

But then a very important other thing that he adds to this is, "But don't let anybody mess with the guy. Let him pray. If he's praying in the Oratory, don't you go into the Oratory and turn it into a place for weaving your baskets. And don't keep your baskets in the Oratory. Get them out of there, because the people who are in there want to pray." Because before that, the basket making and prayer went together.[4] You pray while you were making baskets. And in this way, prayer was continuous. So, St. Benedict divided it up to some extent.

The real problem now is, can we do this? Now that all the barriers are taken away, the obstacles are removed, and we are presented with the opportunity to do something, we find that we can't fully do it. The obstacle now is in ourselves. What is holding us up? What is keeping us

---

3. This is a reference to chapter 52 of the *Rule of Saint Benedict*. See Merton's comments in *The Climate of Monastic Prayer* (Collegeville, MN: Cistercian Publications, 1969/2018), 23–24, 47–48, 65–66.

4. This is a reference to pre-Benedictine forms of desert monasticism, particularly in its Egyptian variety.

back from living lives of prayer? This is the thing that I think we really have to discuss. First of all, we don't know how. Secondly, perhaps we don't really want to pray that much. This is one of the things that I think we have to face about the life of prayer: there is a certain ambiguity about it in ourselves. We are divided on this thing. We do and we don't want to pray. Before, what's been happening is that we took it for granted that we were entirely dedicated to the desire to pray. And that somebody else was stopping us. The ones who were stopping us with all their structure, keeping us from living a life of prayer. "That awful structure—destroy it."

Now, you suddenly find that maybe a structure helps. If a structure helps, keep as much of the old structure as helps. If some of it helps, keep it. We don't have to have this mania for throwing out structures, just because they're structures. What we have to do is dismiss structures that don't help, and keep structures that do help. And if it turns out to be some medieval thing, if it helps and we keep it, is somebody going to say it's "medieval"? That's none of their business. It helps us. Whether it's medieval or not doesn't matter. The great thing is: Does it help?

Now, to get to grips with this business of wanting to pray. This is what the Zen people do: they give it a certain amount of time. In Zen, you do have to spend a great deal of time either sitting or doing whatever it is that you came to do. We have to give it time. So, this idea of time is something that we can investigate as we go along here. One of the things we can discuss is that, in a House of Prayer, in a contemplative life, time has to be experienced in a new way. We have to approach the whole question of time in a new way. Time and place are both important, but time is most important. We have to become non-obsessed with time. We have to get rid of this mania of time; this manic view of time—which is a problem for our society—and have a whole different view of time.

It is really a question of slowing down. If we reduce our speed to some-where like 90 miles an hour, where it's feasible, instead of 300 miles an hour, we will begin to have time to listen to what is going on. Things will begin to take shape by themselves. The reason why we don't stop to pray, is because we've got this feeling that we have to keep moving. This is a real sickness. I know that Dom Leclercq has come up with—one of his latest ideas is the theology of speed [laughter]. I guess this is a theology you develop when you're flying on airplanes all over the place. But, as far as I'm concerned, an airplane doesn't move once it's off the ground. The theology of flight is the theology of stillness. You're suspended. Things do move, but what goes by is like a dream; a very interesting dream of abstract shapes. It's the most marvelous experience to see things from very high up. It's all completely abstract and psychedelic, in a way [laughter].

So, we don't have to worry too much about speed. If we simply slow down enough to a human tempo, we will hear the answer. What we need to know will be told to us; will develop by itself. And then, once we have recovered the taste for what we really want, we'll do it. But you can't do it if you don't have the taste for it. And you have to recover that taste for it by experiencing it. You experience it by giving yourself a chance to do so. The whole thing, I think, boils down to giving ourselves a chance to rediscover what we've always wanted. And then to go deeper and deeper into the implications of the fact that we have what we seek. It's there all the time; yet we won't let it make itself known to us. I think that's really the whole story.

I've got a quote here from Aldous Huxley, from his book, *The Doors of Perception*. I'm not reading *The Doors of Perception*, I'm reading Zaehner's response to Huxley, and neither book is perfectly satisfactory.[5] Huxley's book is interesting, and Zaehner's book is interesting. I think they're wrong on a lot of points. But it's interesting to go through this material. This is a wrong approach; yet it has something good in it. Do you know Huxley's book, *The Doors of Perception*? That's the one about mescaline. It's all about [psychedelics] and mysticism. This is in defense of mescaline. [Keep in mind] that people take mescaline for the same reason that we want a House of Prayer. But what are those reasons? One of things about the [psychedelic] experience is that it lets you find out something that's already inside you. But is that what we're looking for? It's not the same thing, but nevertheless, it releases potentialities that are there. Is it worth taking [psychedelics]? And do [psychedelic] drugs get us to the thing that we want? I don't know. We'll talk about that some other time, but Huxley starts with this: "That humanity at large will ever be able to dispense with Artificial Paradises seems very unlikely. Most men and women lead lives, at the worst so painful, and at the best so monotonous, poor, and limited, that the urge to escape, the longing to transcend themselves, if only for

---

5. R.C. Zaehner, *Mysticism: Sacred and Profane* (Oxford; Oxford University Press, 1957/1961), 1–29. For a summary, see Christopher Partridge, *High Culture: Drugs, Mysticism, and the Pursuit of Transcendence in the Modern World* (Oxford: Oxford University Press, 2018), 213–24. On Zaehner's own experimentation with mescaline, see *Mysticism: Sacred and Profane*, 212–26, and Kripal, *Roads of Excess*, 163–68.

a few moments, is and has always been one of the principal appetites of the soul."[6]

This is the wrong way to approach the whole thing. But it does bring to mind that there is an element of boredom in our life. There is an element of dissatisfaction in our life, and this movement between boredom and escape is the wrong movement. You can't build a House of Prayer, or anything like that, on boredom with your present religious structure—or looking for another one that is going to be an "artificial paradise." That is the problem that the kids get into. They're bored with the old thing. They're bored with the Trappist life, and this is understandable. The old Office that we used to have was boring. It was a tedious, long thing. Especially the old one, with the Little Office and the Office of the Dead every ferial day. It was extremely boring. It could happen without being bored, but basically, people were bored to death with this.

But it's not a question of escaping boredom. On the contrary, it's a question of realizing that your boredom contains everything that you're looking for. In the boredom itself, underneath, if you listen, you know how to turn the boredom inside out. It's all there. Why are we bored with ourselves? It's because we're alienated from ourselves. It's because the self that we're bored with is something we're not at home with. The present routine is to do something to change the boredom: switch on another [TV] program. You can go from program to program, all over the whole spectrum of programs; yet they're all equally boring. Perhaps some might seem less, but the thing is to not even turn it on at all; to be at home with yourself. Once you're at home with yourself, you can never be bored with anything, because you are at a center which is open to everything. Then everything is interesting and everything is simple.

There's no need for an "artificial paradise." If we're constantly escaping boredom, we simply run and run and run. There's a very interesting book by Max Picard on that, called *The Flight from God*,[7] which goes back some years, but it's still a valid expression of this whole thing. It's a really good book. It's about this idea of constantly running off on a horizontal line into an indefinite distance [where] everything becomes a constant flight. Everything is a flight, moving indefinitely from nowhere to nowhere.

---

6. *Doors of Perception*, 62.

7. Max Picard, *The Flight from God* (South Bend, IN: St. Augustine's Press, 1934/2015).

What we really need is to be at home with ourselves in order that all of the resources within us are able to be *given*. It's not to find another area where we can get something that we need, but to find ourselves where we are in order to give what we've got. But [first] we have to collect it all together, so that it's ours, and not alienated.

Still, the idea of a paradise has some validity. In Cistercian theology, in medieval theology, you've got a theology of the "cloistered paradise." And of "sabbath," rest; of quiet, and contemplation, and hesychasm.[8] Once we have set aside this view that Huxley takes—with the intended outcome that you take a pill and then all of this appears—there is a perfectly valid quest for a perfect contemplative life. We're not going to attain that by building a structure, but still, it is a valid quest. And this idea of the sabbath of contemplation, the rest of contemplation, *quies*. Dom Leclercq has a fine book about this idea of quiet and rest.[9] It's an excellent book. I don't think it's been translated, though? Or has it been translated now?

Mother Myriam: No, it's here in the library, in French.

It's a beautiful book. If anybody knows French and would like to read it, it's very worthwhile. As Dom Leclercq does, he takes these fine texts from interesting and medieval sources on this whole question of rest and quiet.

This theology, which evolved from the Middle Ages, the theology of the paradise of the cloister, the sabbath of contemplation, and quiet and hesychasm, is valid—although it has its limitations; it can be static—because it's realistic. And it's realistic, because it's based on sacrifice. The desert becomes a paradise when it's accepted as a desert. The desert can never be anything but a desert, if we're trying to escape from it. But once we accept the desert, it becomes a paradise, if it's fully accepted, [along] with the Passion of Christ.

Just to mention it now, if it doesn't come up again—it certainly should—any attempt to renew the contemplative life is going to have to include this element of sacrifice. Uncompromising sacrifice. Because this breakthrough

8. *Heyschia* is the Greek term for "silence," from which the Eastern Orthodox prayer practice of "hesychasm" takes its root (see the essays in *Merton and Hesychasm*). On *quies* in the desert tradition, see Merton's *Contemplation in a World of Action*, 285–91.

9. Jean Leclercq, *Otia Monastica: Études sur le Vocabulaire de la Contemplation as Moyen Âge, Studia Anselmiana* 51 (Rome: Pontificium Institutum S. Anselmi, 1963). See Merton's journal entry dated November 22, 1964 (*Dancing in the Water of Life*, 168–69).

into what you already have, is only achieved by a complete acceptance of the Cross in some form or other. There's no way around this. This is the only way. There is no possibility of a renewal of the contemplative life that bypasses this.

At the moment, there is a temptation to do this, because of wrong ideas of personal fulfillment as opposed to right ideas of personal fulfillment. The wrong idea of personal fulfillment is the fulfillment of an illusory self. This wrong kind of personal fulfillment is a deep engagement in a common illusion about what fulfillment consists in. And this common illusion is rooted in commercialism and selling people things that they don't need; forcing upon them products which they couldn't possibly want if they were in their right mind. You then have to keep them in their wrong mind so that they'll want all these things and think that this is giving them fulfillment.

At the center of this, the paradise idea and the sabbath idea become realistic on one condition only: that it implies acceptance of the Cross. Again, this is the liberation that opens us to everybody else, and makes the thing real, and makes it *not* a narcissistic thing.

I was thinking of going into a little bit of a history about all this. But before that, I think perhaps just one big statement: the real thing about this whole quest is the desire to live to the fullest, the consequences of our belief. This is the heart of it. All the consequences of our belief, which means to say, the Cross, the Resurrection. The whole thing. And to live it in a particular constellation of experience, which can be called "contemplative"—because there are other ways of pursuing the full consequences of our belief. Martyrdom, for example, in early Christian times. The martyr was the one who lived to the full all the consequences of what he believed. And the monk took over that same kind of absolutism; the same complete unconditional self-dedication, from the idea of the martyr, so that the desert was the place where you pushed to the limit the consequences of your belief. Remember, Antony went into the desert as a result of hearing the Gospel saying, "Leave all things and follow me."[10]

---

10. Matthew 19:21. Antony of Egypt, also known as Antony the Great (251–356), is widely considered the "father" of early Christian monasticism, particularly in its eremitical expression. See Athanasius of Alexandria's celebrated *The Life of Antony*, trans. Tim Vivian and A. Athanassakis (Kalamazoo, MI: Cistercian Publications, 2003). For Merton on Antony, see *Cassian and the Fathers: Initiation into the Monastic Tradition*, ed. Patrick F. O'Connell (Collegeville, MN: Cistercian Publications, 2005), 31–39, and *Pre-Benedictine Monasticism*, 17–24.

Now, this isn't the only way to interpret this, but this is the way some people interpret it. I presume this is the way we interpret it, to some extent, that there must be some way in which this unconditional gift of ourselves, surrender of ourselves to God, has to be done in a contemplative manner. Let's not be ashamed of the word "contemplative" anymore. I was for a while debating about it. I remember when we were having meetings at Gethsemani, we were all wondering, should we say "contemplative" anymore? Let us say "contemplative" with full confidence. Dom Leclercq is behind the word "contemplative" [laughter]. Let's say it. And no matter what anybody else says about it—it's Greek, Platonic—I don't care. We're contemplatives. What's the matter with Plato, anyway? Plato was a good soul [laughter].

I would say this is the background. Now, what is the history of all this? What lies behind all this? We don't see far enough back. At present, we're sort of hung up with the post-Trent[11] view of the House of Prayer. But it has a much longer history than that. The post-Trent idea is especially connected with the Ignatian idea of the "Long Retreat," to which you go for 30 days, at the most, to make a decision; to arrive at a crucial decision about your life.[12] This grew out of the needs of the time. Remember the background of this: what was the decision that you were likely to make in your 30 days in the Ignatian Retreat? It was the decision to go, say, to England, and face martyrdom. All this was certainly a very practical way of approaching this. But it definitely belonged to that time: a sense of means to an end. "Something has to be done." I have to go through something in order to get grace to do something else.

This is fine, and it fits this whole concept. But now let's go back to the earliest manifestation of this. One of the earliest places where this spontaneously arose—remember these early things are all very spontaneous. They did them first and then said "why" afterwards, or didn't even say "why"; they just went on doing it. One of the earliest places, of course, is tied up with pilgrimage. I suddenly discovered a great connection between hermit life and pilgrimage [laughter]. But there really is. Pilgrimage and the hermit life are very closely connected. It's not just a question of going

---

11. The Council of Trent (1545–1563).

12. For a history of early Ignatian spirituality, see Bernard McGinn, *Mysticism in the Golden Age of Spain* (New York: Crossroad, 2017), 71–99.

to find a special place, it's a question of a pilgrimage to a holy place. Where this really starts is with the Irish—it doesn't necessarily start with them, but they are the ones who really developed it in the beginning.[13] Remember, for example, the early Irish monks were able—and it was a normal thing—if summer came around, they could go to the abbot and say, "Father, can I borrow a boat for the summer? I'll be back around November" [laughter]. They would push off without oars, which some of them did. Some of them, as a result of doing that, ended up in Canada [laughter].

But they did arrive in Iceland, and then they arrived in Greenland. There are remains [of monasteries]. But you could go off for the summer. You could go off to one of the islands off Scotland and spend the summer there and come back. Find yourself a little island. Alaska has great possibilities.[14] Flying over the Alaskan coast, there's simply hundreds and thousands of these islands, with nothing on them, except a few lakes. You'd have to take a supply of something, but that would be a possibility. They're within rowing distance, some of them. On a calm day, you row off to an island, pitch up a tent, and spend the summer out there. Of course, there's always the problem of bears; you've got to compete with the bears for the huckleberry crop.

One thing that the Irish [monks] also did was go to a holy place and then become a recluse there. Some shrine in Austria, for example; the Irish were very strong in Austria. The recluses of central Europe were basically of Irish origin. The idea was that you would look for the "place of your resurrection." And once you had found the place of your resurrection you became "entombed" there. This is a bizarre Irish concept, but it's what they did. You find the place. You get an interior illumination: "This is it. This is the place of my resurrection. Now I'm dead." They would go to bizarre lengths over this. There are certain rituals for people about to become recluses, in which a Mass of the Dead is sung over them, and

13. *Contemplation in a World of Action*, 311. Merton offered several novitiate conferences on Celtic monasticism in 1964 and 1968 (http://merton.org/Research/AV/novitiate .aspx). See Merton's essay "From Pilgrimage to Crusade" (*Mystics and Zen Masters*, 91–112); as well as Monica Weis, *Thomas Merton and the Celts: A New World Opening Up* (Eugene, OR: Pickwick Publications, 2016).

14. Merton arrived in California from Alaska after spending several weeks giving conferences and touring remote wilderness areas (see *Thomas Merton in Alaska*, ed. Robert E. Daggy [New York: New Directions, 1989]).

they're even stretched out there. They're even walled into this place. This is the place of their resurrection. This is a peculiar cultural development around the ninth and tenth centuries, mostly due to the Irish.

Then you get a split between recluses and hermits. Recluses become highly official and institutionalized, and prized possessions of some monastic institutions. The great thing is to get yourself a big monastery and have two or three recluses there. St. Gall was strong with this.[15] They would have several recluses inured in the monastic church; or, they would have recluses inured in the gate of a city. Trier, for example, was quite strong on always having a recluse in the main gate, as protection for the city. There would be a holy man or a holy woman in a cell in the city gate, busy praying for the city.

This became highly institutionalized. The history is extremely interesting. It goes on down through the Middle Ages in England where they were very strong. There was a very important recluse movement at Westminster Abbey. There was a recluse at Westminster in the thirteenth or fourteenth century who was giving spiritual direction to people that were running a revolution. They would go to Westminster to ask, "What are we going to do about this king?" And they'd say, "Pretty bad man, better get rid of him." That sort of thing [laugher].

When these recluses became official and institutionalized, then you've got an independent hermit movement. What happened was, the Benedictine practice of going to a hermitage tended to be interpreted in many monasteries as "reclusion." You became a highly contemplative monk until finally you were walled in. Then the hermit movement started, because people no longer went through the monastery into solitude. They went straight into solitude. Lay people, poor people. This was a big movement in the eleventh century, in which you've got these independent hermits all over the place. They began to get in trouble when they started preaching. But it was very important that they should be, because they were preaching the Cross to poor people, whereas the monks weren't preaching to anybody. This was the seed of the Franciscan movement.

Then the big Benedictine monasteries began to permit hermits to the monastery, to take off into the woods somewhere. For example, Cluny

---

15. On the ninth-century Benedictine monastery of St. Gall, see Peter King, *Western Monasticism: A History of the Monastic Movement in the Latin Church* (Kalamazoo, MI: Cistercian Publications, 1999), 112–15.

had hermits as far south as the Pyrenees. Even Peter the Venerable's secretary was a hermit in the Pyrenees.[16] At one point, after he'd been there for some time, he got a letter from Peter the Venerable that said, "Come back, I need you." So, he'd hike off back to Cluny.[17]

In the Cistercian Order, many of these independent hermits were the ones who became Cistercian lay brothers. They were the ones that were recruited to the lay brotherhood and liked the life on the grange, when they were 15 or 20 miles from the monastery and only had to come in once a week. The grange life of the Cistercian was really a kind of hermit life. But the thing about the Cistercians is that they never dignified anything with any special term. They revered these holy brothers, but the grange life of the brother was never called a House of Prayer, or anything like that. But they were true men of prayer. They led a kind of solitary life. This started as an economic thing. The economic reasons for the granges was that since the choir monks were not supposed to be out of the monastery too much, brothers could handle it. But then a few choir monks would be with them. And then it developed.

This gives us our possibility of doing things. In point of fact, we have two hermits in Texas, who are, strictly speaking, members of the Gethsemani community. We're still wondering how this might pan out, and if it is going to be fully accepted. But right now, we are in position where a person can be a hermit, not only on the monastic property, but also anywhere. This could be done on the grange pattern. One or two or three, but the grange thing gives it a juridical foundation.[18]

And then, of course, remember the Franciscan hermits.[19] The early Franciscans were, to a great extent, a combination of hermitage and pilgrimage life—hermit-pilgrim people. Of course, this was lost in that big

---

16. Peter the Venerable (1092–1156), Abbot of Cluny (see King, *Western Monasticism*, 188–90).

17. *Contemplation in a World of Action*, 324–25.

18. Merton's general *apologia* for the hermit life, which includes much of this material in a more polished historical outline, can be found in his "The Case for a Renewal of Eremitism in the Monastic State," in *Contemplation in a World of Action*, 306–39.

19. See Merton's essay "Franciscan Eremitism," in *Contemplation in a World of Action*, 273–81.

upheaval of the Franciscans.[20] And the fact that it was lost was something quite tragic, because the whole history of Europe was indifferent to this poverty hermit-pilgrim thing. It persisted because of St. Francis; [otherwise], it would've been a totally different course of events.

But now, after Trent, you get a whole new view of things. It's much more institutionalized. Before, none of these things are really institutionalized, except the recluses. It all just happens. After Trent, for example, you get the Carmelite Desert,[21] and the Discalced Carmelite reform,[22] which, after about the second or third generation, started "desert houses" where two or three people may live permanently, and others may go for a year or for two years. This worked very well. It was a workable pattern that went on down through the years.

Then you get another interesting development in the Franciscans with the idea of the *Ritiro* in the seventeenth and eighteenth centuries.[23] Two separate kinds of houses [emerge]: one, the *Ritiro*, which was simply a house that keeps the Rule, because most of them didn't keep any—they were all over the lot by that time. So, certain small houses were set apart and they would just keep the Rule. These are houses of exemplary regularity. You would go to a house of exemplary regularity and get refurbished [laughter].

This wasn't totally satisfactory at this time with the Franciscans. It always remained a provisional thing, so that, at the same time, they started something else, which was called a *Solitudine*—a hermit house.[24] The *Ritiro* went back to the official Rule of those who had thrown out St. Francis, and the *Solitudine* went back beyond the original [vision] of St. Francis; it became an extreme hairshirt-type of outfit. It had little cells that you could barely stand in. [It was] a real ascetic [movement]. This is the post-Trent mentality, where everything has to be legally set up. This absolutely won't work now. Today, the whole thing is changing and it's bursting open in all

20. This is a reference to the early controversy and split between the "Conventual" and the "Spiritual" Franciscans in the thirteenth century (see Merton's *Introduction to Christian Mysticism*, 175–76, and Bernard McGinn, *The Flowering of Mysticism: Men and Women in the New Mysticism—1200–1350* [New York: Herder & Herder, 1998], 74–75).

21. See Merton's essay, "The Primitive Carmelite Ideal," in *Disputed Questions* (New York: Farrar, Straus and Cudahy, 1960), 258–63.

22. Merton, *Disputed Questions*, 252–58.

23. Merton, *Contemplation in a World of Action*, 277–78.

24. Merton, *Contemplation in a World of Action*, 278–79.

directions. And now, all the different Orders are asking themselves, "How are we going to do this? Should we do it on this *Ritiro* plan?"

That's about all I have to say, as far as a formal talk. I think now we could go ahead and just discuss what *we* can do, and do we have to follow this post-Trent pattern? Obviously, that's the thing that we've got to get out from under. The idea of a Carmelite Desert or a *Ritiro* isn't going to work for us.[25]

As far as the hermit thing goes, I think a great deal depends on not putting too explicit a label on anything. The only problem with the hermit business at Gethsemani, has been the name "hermit." Because when you say "hermit," right away you set the thing up in the certain way, and everybody's going to throw things at it. They will get a dictionary and say, " 'Hermit.' Well, now look what he's doing. He's not a 'hermit.' He's going to India" [laughter].

If any type of a House of Prayer is started, call it anything but a House of Prayer. Call it a "rest house" or something. Because if you say House of Prayer, right away you're going to get this whole contemplative mystique thrown at you. This, I think, is something we should consider as we go along: this whole idea of the danger of a contemplative mystique as opposed to a really contemplative life. A "contemplative mystique" is one where people set the thing up beforehand for you, and then demand that you meet this abstract standard. As an example of contemplative mystique at Gethsemani—we were running off of contemplative mystique officially for about 10 years: you never write a letter, you never look over the wall; you're always dressed in a cowl and your hood is always up [laughter].

Perhaps you might get certain people who wouldn't mind that; who would want to go on for a life of prayer, and they're just kidding themselves, because they've taken up with this wrong notion. The real thing of the life of prayer isn't that you want to meet some abstract norm, it's that you want to do the thing that God is really asking of you, which is to be yourself. And if you start being yourself, you're not going to fit into anyone's "mystique."[26]

---

25. A small discussion ensues regarding which models are—and are not—currently working in the U.S. and in Europe.

26. Another discussion ensues regarding the current state of the House of Prayer movement in the U.S. and Europe, particularly within Passionist communities, with

We have found, for example, at Gethsemani, that most people aren't hermits and they're never going to be hermits, and they don't want to be hermits. But for many of them, most of them, simply what they call a "*lectio* day" in the Benedictine tradition, is quite enough. One day a month, or something like that, where they're completely free from Tierce to Vespers; that means after the High Mass, which is very early. You get off at, say, 7:00 am, and you come back around 5:00 in the evening. You've got the whole day to yourself. You can go out to the woods, take your lunch. We will soon have little buildings that they can go to if it rains. You have a whole day like that. We've been doing this for a long time. This is very good. This helps people to get to grips with what they want during that day, and very often, that's all they need.

Mother Myriam: It's very true. If we don't have time to reflect in private, we might never get to the deep root.

Sr. Mary Aquin[27]: This whole movement seems to be [towards] a deeper contemplative way for the whole community, and not just [for individual hermits]. That was what we were envisioning; that's what the Spirit was saying: a prayer life for the whole community.

At Gethsemani, they're shortening the Office. Fine; but for what? What are you going to do? You've got the perfectly legitimate question of, "Now we have this extra time. What are we going to do with it?" Well, the response is, "We're going to play handball." And they do. You could see a real roaring game of handball up against the horse barn, back where the farm workers are. This is fine for them. I don't see why they shouldn't play handball. But then if somebody else wants to pray, let them pray—and the handball outfit shouldn't be saying that handball is the only Christian response to [the additional time] [laughter].

Fr. Ed Hennessey: Perhaps now they can play against the wall of the Chapel [laughter].

---

some summary and follow up from the Michigan Monroe Conference (see the Merton-Dardenne correspondence). The conversation eventually comes back around to the lived practicalities of life in prayer.

27. Sr. Mary Aquin, IHM, also attended the initial House of Prayer gathering at Monroe, MI.

Sr. Mary: Father, we've been hearing for some time that you have been living the life of a hermit. Would you mind telling us what that is exactly?

It's very relative.

Combined with pilgrimage, is that it?

Combined with pilgrimage, and combined with writing books. I don't set myself up as a hermit at all. It's a life of privacy. A certain amount of privacy is necessary for me. I don't care about the term—call it "privacy"—but I'd rather not be called a "hermit." I'm an anti-hermit.

What we've done at Gethsemani has been very good up until recently—it's getting too noisy around here—but we've got several little houses on the property. We have two good ones, real houses, and two trailers. Then Dom James's place, which has the latest in everything. And he deserves it. He should have this. This is fine for him.

About three years ago, [my place] was built in order to have somewhere to talk to Protestant ministers who came through, because when we talked to them in the guesthouse, everybody else wanted in on the discussion, and it wasn't right. This was a place where they could come and they'd be undisturbed. Then I put a bedroom on the back, and a chapel on the back, and then the abbot said, "What did you do that for? You don't need a bedroom up there." But it was too late [laughter]. Then it became a place to work. I've been writing up there for about 6 to 8 years. [At first] I'd spend about half the day, most of the day, or the whole day [up there]. Then about three years ago, a great event happened. The Holy Spirit struck, and I think Dom James, at that time, began to look forward to the day when he would want to be a hermit himself. And then everything started to spark.

It was then that I got permission to sleep up there. And after that, things moved pretty fast. I got permission to retire from the novice master job to live up there fulltime. This worked out very nicely. I'd sleep there, eat breakfast, then come down for one cooked meal, dinner, and the rest of the time I'm up there. I'd come down and have various contacts with people when necessary, and just live on the property. It works very well; there's no real problem at all. It's within walking distance. You're not depending on anybody. The only thing I've had to depend on anybody else for is drinking water. The man in the dairy volunteered to bring a five-gallon milk can of drinking water a couple of times a week, and as he volunteered to do it, and as long as he was glad to do it, it was no problem.

Then this was voted on by the Community Council, and the general impression was that they were all glad that this had happened, and there was no real criticism or opposition, and everybody understood it. So, this has been working fine. Where the trouble is getting to be a little acute, is now that there are many of them—three houses, two trailers, and then many temporary ones; people sleeping in little shacks that they've built for themselves. Now, the community is getting worried about it. There is a general feeling of, "What's [with] this hermit thing? Why so many hermits? Do we need all these hermits?" But every single one of them maintains a job in which he contributes something to the community. Some of them work in the guest house, some do this, that, or the other thing, but they all have to do some work. It isn't getting out of work or getting out of anything.

Sr. Marie Goldstein: Is there much communication with these hermits— together?

Four or five times a year, we've been getting together and having a party, talking over things.

You don't follow the same pattern, then?

No, each one does what he feels is right for himself. For example, I like to get up early in the morning and then say some Office and meditate for a couple of hours. Or read and pray. The great thing is the time. Just to have time. This is the whole thing. If, once a person can get time, that's most of it. That's 99% of it.

That arrangement, Father, for a contemplative Order, is good, right on the property. But for an active Order, there might be some disadvantages.

Well, the reason we have them on the same property is that we're supposed to be enclosed. But, there's no reason why you should have to have it on the property at all.

I think there's a general idea that it would be better not to.

Yes. But the great thing is the time. For a person to have time where they're free. They're not caught up by anything and don't have to do anything; [to] stop yourself from doing something. It's great just to do nothing. Even if it's just a house where you do nothing. You can't very well go around advertising that [laughter]. But it's important.

That's the unwritten law.

Exactly.

Comment: One of our big problems is that we feel guilty about being "useless." We have to have a function all the time, even for prayer. But to live without a purpose is, of course, ludicrous.

Of course. There you get to the question of, "What do we think is our purpose?" And then it gets down to the question, "Who do we think we are?" Of course, this is a big thing, and I think we can really talk about this, as time goes on, in the next couple of days. But we have to overcome all these illusions, which are forced on us by a society that profits by this kind of illusion. The illusions of the world we live in are enormous. Of course, they always have been, but now it's just fabulous illusions that people have. We've never been such a deluded people. The trouble with that is that we're deluded, and we have at the same time, this immense power for destruction or construction, and the delusion gets expressed in this power.

The atomic bomb is an expression of this; that's our delusion in action. The idea that you can force other people to submit unconditionally to your ideas—and if they don't submit, you can destroy them. People always had that. It's always been in the back of people's minds. But now, it's being put into effect. We live in a society where this is going on. What are we going to do? Of course, the opposite thing is, "Well, we've got to stop this."

Fr. Ed: Particularly in active communities, people have just been fed into the machine . . . [28]

---

28. The entirety of this, and the following comment, is inaudible.

Mother Myriam: It is something that we also have to face in contemplative communities, because the community is everything . . .

Fr. Ed: Out of this comes a very real and growing concern for how there can be developed a theology and study and process, so that there will be, not a series of rules or set patterns, but the formation of persons to enter into this type of experience and come to the new creation of a community.

Yes, so a question of not just having a variety of roles: "Here's the role of being a man of prayer." This whole question of personhood, it all revolves around the idea of alienation. This idea of people alienated in favor of the institutions. Of course, this goes so deep, because this was the whole idea of sacrifice. You just forget your own will. The will of God is expressed through the institution. You are needed to teach biology, so that's it. You're not a qualified biology professor. It doesn't matter. Teach it, "offer it up," get busy.

Sr. Marie: And the whole community will really need this basic education if they see the House of Prayer in the right light.

It would certainly have to come from a change of mind of everybody else.

Sr. Mary: Some of the reports that came from our conference—not many, but some—and in some of the discussion, too, was that this was a movement against renewal, or [against] secularity, or a movement toward "quiet"— and not in the right sense. That's one thing, and the second was that some communities who have already attempted these kinds of things have drawn up such a strict horarium that you couldn't manage—

That is the great danger. I think it's terribly important that some people should not set this up in that particular kind of way, and that should not become the idea of what a House of Prayer is, because it will completely confirm all the reasonable criticisms of it: as a reactionary thing, as a regressive thing. But even if that does happen—let's just imagine that now we all come out of this peaceful meeting here, and we open the *NCR*, and there it is: this has been decided. This is what the House of Prayer is: every 10 minutes a rosary.

Supposing that happens: does it have to bother us? Not in the least. As far as I'm concerned, it doesn't matter what any of these people do. Let them do what they do. I'm going to do my thing whether they like it or not, or whether they're interested in it or not. It doesn't matter what anybody says about it, as long as I have this in conscience—I feel this is what God is asking. It doesn't matter what kind of press it gets.

We are much too dominated; I mean, as Catholics, we are servile people, and we have got to stop being servile about these things. We've shaken off domination by the Curia, but we haven't shaken off domination by a vaguer deal—public opinion—which is always reforming itself every minute. We can't possibly depend on that. It may occasionally give us feedback on things that we absolutely need to know, but you can't depend on that. If everything that we do includes an afterthought of, "What is somebody else going to think about it"—whose business it is *not*. If it's somebody who really should have something to say about it, that's alright. But all these people, it's none of their business what we're going to do.

Br. David: It would seem to me that we should keep ourselves free from publicity and from performing with anybody else's notions. We might first try here to clarify our ideas in order to help others, and possibly even make some concrete suggestions.

I was making an extreme example, but you are perfectly right. We should also communicate with people who are doing the same kind of thing. Of course, once again, we're going to have to face the whole idea that [today] contemplation is completely discredited. The worst possible thing to be is a "contemplative," because that makes you a whole litany of other things: you're a Platonist, you're a Manichean, you're a Jansenist. Of course, that has got in there. The stream has been poisoned by this kind of thing. This is one of the reasons that we have to rediscover the reality of it.

To my mind, I think that we have strong support outside the Church. I think we need to realize that our real allies in this are very strong people: psychoanalysts and people like that who are interested in religion. For example, take somebody like [Erich] Fromm. Fromm would absolutely support the kind of thing that we want to do—if it's properly done. He's a very smart person. He's a good man. Lots of academic psychoanalytic people are very interested in the whole question of religious experience, all over the area of different religions, and they would be right behind it.

Not to mention, of course, the hippies. I think it's very important for us to realize where we are in the social context of what people are doing and thinking. We are much more with these other people than we realize, and we should be in contact with them, too. These are the people who are really interested in the contemplative life, and that will give us a little more humanly desirable security, in the sense that we do have friends.

Br. David: And not only people who are interested in it, but people who are actually living it, at least in this country.

I didn't get to Tassajara Springs, but I think that's something that everybody should get to. Anybody who's interested in this should go to the Zen Center.[29]

Br. David: It is not very easy to get in there. And this may be one of the concrete problems that we could tackle here: how we could expose people who are seriously interested, who would like to be exposed to this, and how we can actually set up channels—you can't just send somebody to Tassajara. They will either be guests there, or they won't get in at all—but to really go through a training period.

That's a special thing, but just to be a guest there would be important for anybody who's interested in the idea. This is what the Zen people are doing for a House of Prayer, to use our term. This is in connection with the San Francisco [Zen] Center, which they have downtown, and then they've got this place back in the mountains. This is their solution to our particular problem. This is how they've done it. I think just even to see it physically would be a worthwhile thing. Of course, for the training, that's another matter. That's a really specialized sort of thing; within this specialized thing that we're doing anyway, regarding a contemplative vocation, a Buddhist-type thing would be for very few people, but still—

29. Tassajara Zen Center, founded in 1967 by Shunryu Suzuki Roshi. Tassajara Hot Springs are located nearby in the Ventana Wilderness area of Los Padres National Forest along California's Coast Range. For a history, see Rick Fields, *How the Swans Came to the Lake: A Narrative History of Buddhism in America* (Boston: Shambhala, 1992), 258–65.

Sr. Mary: That seems, to the point that you made, that you really have to taste it before you can want it.

In the monastic setup, we've always approached this from a very practical way. The ideal thing is to be in a community where there are people who do experience this, and who do want this. And if you're with them, you catch it.

You have to be open in order to catch it.

Yes. You do. But on the whole, I think people really are interested. This is the old question at Gethsemani, where we did have so many of these old brothers that really were men of prayer; then people did catch something from that. It wasn't unambiguous, because they felt that they could never do that themselves, but still, there is such a thing as catching this monastic, this contemplative thing—it's infectious.

Sr. Mary: Many of our Sisters are really searching for something. They really are searching. Sometimes they realize they are searching; sometimes they don't.

Yours is really an experimental contemplative house, which is different from, say, the one in Portland. It would be entirely different for somebody to come to you, that would need to go to Portland, or to go, say, to the Louisville Carmel, or to the Poor Clares of Chicago.

Mother Myriam: At this point, I think "active" or "contemplative" is beside the point.

Sure. Meaning that it's just a juridical distinction.

I mean that we all have to go through a process of conversion and deepening.

Sure, that is the thing; as long as you have these rigid hard-and-fast post-Trent identities that we're dealing with, this messes it all up. You can't do anything until people have acquired a new consciousness, a new sense of identity.

Br. David: I have the experience in our community, for instance, that at one point we stood for following the Rule of Saint Benedict as plainly as possible—

not as strictly as possible, but as plainly as possible. Then, there came the point gradually; one time we decided—somehow it came clear—that the majority of the people simply want to dispense with the Rule altogether. And ever since, we have spent all our time and all our energy in trying to substitute something else for the Rule, and we haven't been doing anything at all. I personally, which might be terribly reactionary and old-fashioned, would say, let's keep the Rule as plain and simple [as possible]. Because at least we have something in which everybody agrees, and let's keep it and not waste any energy in substituting anything else, and work with that. Just use it as a structure within which you can really [do something positive].

I absolutely agree with that. The *Rule of Saint Benedict* is entirely different from the kind of Rule that more modern congregations have. Because it's not a "Rule." There is nothing in it that really binds you to anything terribly definite that you have to do. It's a kind of "spiritual directory," and the *Rule of Saint Benedict* presupposes a whole different view of what this is about; namely, that what is being handed on is an experience and a tradition, which has been lived by generation after generation of people, and which can only be absorbed by living in the kind of milieu that the *Rule* presupposes. I'd say it's actually essential for us to preserve the kind of Benedictine climate that the *Rule* demands. What happens is that when they throw the *Rule* out, everything becomes totally trivial. You've got this complete lack of seriousness in the religious life that comes from a lot of people who have no depth at all, trying to substitute for the depth that was acquired by generations of really deep people.

Mother Myriam: Armand Veilleux[30] once said to me at a European meeting on the liturgy, "Fidelity to the Rule is, first of all, not a liturgical problem; it's a problem of monastic spirituality. It's a spiritual document, which incarnates a certain spiritual attitude in the frame of the sixth century. And we have changed a lot, but we should incarnate this attitude in our own terms today." That's it. But of course, he's a very intelligent man.

Fr. Ed: Tom, did you have the chance to read over the reports of the workshops from the [Monroe] conference? The reason I ask is, whether the titles

---

30. Armand Veilleux, OCSO (b. 1937), influential monastic scholar and historian.

of the workshops, the areas of concern, the things they studied, seem to cover the majority of the things that you felt should be covered. It was an effort to explore the relationship of the House of Prayer to the community.

I did, but they were so schematic that I really didn't get too clear an idea of what was going on. I'll look them over again in that light and see. But, yes, the real problem is making sure that everybody understands precisely what it is all about. People are going to misinterpret this from the word "go." When we talk about educating our communities, it's not so much about giving them a new idea, [it's about] making them realize that this is something that they wanted and is a part of their vocation. What did any of us ever become religious for if we didn't want to pray? I remember when I was thinking about becoming a religious. I was at Columbia [College] and I was out to supper with Bill Tindall,[31] who is an expert on James Joyce, and his wife. They were shocked by this idea that I wanted to go—what I wanted to be then was a Franciscan. They were shocked at the thought of this awful, austere life that I wanted. They said, "Well, if you want to pray a lot, it'll be right. Is that what you really want to do?" And I said, "I guess that's what I want to do." The general idea that anybody has is that if you go into this, it's because you want to pray. Isn't that it? What do we want, if not to pray?

There is some brief discussion at this point, followed by a coffee break.

To my mind, a House of Prayer, or a prayer life, a contemplative life, fits into a somewhat traditional experience in the sense that you're going to profit by the experience of people who went before; whether mediated through a traditional Rule, or just directly mediated through spiritual formation by a spiritual master, as in Zen. That's what Zen does; it's a transmission of an experience which cannot be formulated. What are some of the other patterns that we could get into? One that I worked very hard on, and tried to do something with for a long time, was the traditional Western pattern of the Cistercians in the twelfth century, which has a great deal in it, but takes too much work. Apparently American people coming in don't come onto it at all. They won't read St. Bernard, and if

---

31. William York Tindall (1903–1981), Joyce scholar who taught at Columbia for forty years.

they do, it's out of a sense of duty, and they can't get anything out of it. It drives them crazy. This whole question of appreciating twelfth-century Cistercian stuff—which is highly sophisticated and beautiful—it just takes too much background. Somebody who's done postgraduate work in Medieval Studies could really make a big thing out of it. But the average kid that comes in and has had two years of college, and [barely] knows where France is [laughter]. What's the point of talking about Cluny? It doesn't mean a thing to them.

Then there is the Pentecostal formula—

Fr. Ed: That's very opposite.

Exactly. This, I would say, is the most likely to work in this country at the moment. It's something that people seem to have a spontaneous taste for.

Mother Myriam: It's pretty much alive in our monasteries in many places—even here!

Fr. Ed: I thought it had much to do with this question of the hang ups within religious communities about the old patterns of prayer and what you do with the new pattern as well. It's a good thing to go into a place where there's no existing pattern, and the prayer [life] very much alive, and the people very much alive in their experience of it; and then see what that has to tell you. It's a phenomenon that we would be quite stupid to ignore.

We have to understand what it is, and to what extent it is a choice for [community members] or for the average novice coming in. For me, it's no longer a choice, but for the kids, fine. Maybe it's just what they need. Let's get into that perhaps in the second part of this afternoon.

Sr. Mary: It's really a sign of the interest in prayer today.

The other two formulas that I can think of offhand are the Greek and Russian ones, which I think have a great deal of value to explore. Once again, you can say, "Okay, you have to be a post-graduate specialist." You don't. For some reason or other, there is something about the Greek and Russian thing that is immediate for us, even though it's alien and remote.

For example, the story of the Pilgrim[32] is something—I mean, it got into [J. D.] Salinger's *Franny and Zooey*,[33] and people read this book like mad ten years ago. There must be something to this.

Fr. Roger: I tend to make a distinction between the Greek and Russian [traditions].

There is. When I lump Greek and Russian together, I think in terms of the *Philokalia*; this tradition that started at Sinai, grew in Athos,[34] was transmitted to Russia through Romania with Paisius Velichkovsky in the eighteenth century,[35] and which ended up with this story of the Pilgrim and the Jesus Prayer and [eventually] *Franny and Zooey*. Evidently, this does get through, and I would say there's a great deal that could be explored there, too—a real rich field. Remember, one of the richest aspects of this in the last century, this terrific movement of the *startsy*[36] in Russia, the idealized *starets*, Fr. Zosima from *The Brothers Karamazov*[37]—something like that hits people.

I know that people at Gethsemani, when this book was on the "forbidden list," were reading it surreptitiously and getting terrifically turned on by Zosima, and this whole concept of prayer. Of course, this is really a romanticization of the Russian *startsy*, but there's great value in this. I think this could be part of this education; to get people to be aware of this particular field would open them up. There's a tremendous ignorance of all these things in the average religious community; whoever would imagine that there were all these Russian saints?

---

32. *The Way of a Pilgrim*, beloved nineteenth-century Russian spiritual classic on the Jesus Prayer (see *The Pilgrim's Tale*, ed. Aleksei Pentkovsky [Mahwah, NJ: Paulist Press], 1999).

33. American author J. D. Salinger's (1919–2010) 1961 novel; originally appeared in *The New Yorker* in 1955 and 1957. The Jesus Prayer features prominently in the second half of the book (e.g., pp. 147–49, 164–72, 195–98).

34. See Merton's essays, "Mount Athos" and "The Spirituality of Sinai," in *Disputed Questions*, 68–96.

35. Paisius Velichkovsky (1722–1794).

36. Russian translation of the Greek *geron*, or "elder."

37. *The Brothers Karamazov*, Fyodor Dostoevsky's (1821–1881) literary classic, originally published in serial format 1879–1880.

Br. David: Do you know some good people in this tradition, in this country? As you said before, I think they should be transmitted.

[John] Meyendorff[38] and [Alexander] Schmemann.[39]

Fr. Roger: Fr. [George] Maloney is in this country.[40] He is a specialist in Nil Sorsky.[41]

Mother Myriam: He was here, and he would like very much to help a contemplative group in these matters. He's at Fordham.

Simply to have somebody come in and talk once in a while to the community about Russian spirituality; to get them to feel and realize that there is this tradition of prayer that exists, that it was real—that people lived this and still do live it.[42] The Russian monasteries are still going on; in spite of everything, they're still going. One man who would be delighted to come to this country and talk all over the place about Russia would be Sergius Bolshakoff. He wanders around from monastery to monastery in Europe. He really knows his stuff. He wrote a very good book on Russian mystics.[43] He tried to get it published in this country. I passed it on to the

---

38. John Meyendorff (1926–1992), French-born prominent theologian of the Orthodox Church of America (OCA) and former Dean of St. Vladimir's Orthodox Seminary in New York.

39. Alexander Schmemann (1921–1983), highly influential Orthodox priest and theologian who grew up primarily in France among the Russian émigrés before emigrating to the U.S. to serve on the faculty (and later as Dean) of St. Vladimir's Orthodox Seminary.

40. George Maloney, SJ (1924–2005), Jesuit priest and founder of the John XXIII Institute for Eastern Christian Studies at Fordham University.

41. Nilus of Sora (Nil Sorsky), fifteenth-century leader of the medieval Russian "non-possessor" movement, which emerged in opposition to ecclesial landholdings; see Sergei Hackel, "Late Medieval Russia: The Possessors and the Non-possessors," in *Christian Spirituality: High Middle Ages and Reformation*, ed. Jill Raitt (New York: Crossroads, 1987).

42. Merton offered several monastic conferences at Gethsemani on the topic of Russian monasticism throughout 1962–63 (http://merton.org/Research/AV/novitiate.aspx).

43. *Russian Mystics* (Kalamazoo, MI: Cistercian Publications, 1976). Merton authored the Preface, which also appears in his *Mystics and Zen Masters* (pp. 178–87). Bolshakoff includes chapters on Nilus of Sora, Paisius Velichkovsky, and Russian *staretz*.

American Benedictine Foundation, and then the whole thing collapsed. I don't know whatever happened to the book, but he'd be delighted.

I think it would be a very good thing if people like this got circulating more among our groups, and got across some of the ideas of prayer that were current in Russia. And if some of this literature could be translated, because there's an enormous amount of Russian literature on this, especially nineteenth century. There's a very interesting man called Theophan the Recluse,[44] who was a Russian Bishop who retired and became a recluse. He carried on this immense spiritual direction operation from his cell.

Sr. Mary: This is just a little comment, both in regard to the Pentecostals and to the Russian [tradition]. We just had a few books that came out, The Jesus Prayer and Jesus: A Dialogue with the Savior,[45] and it's interesting that the younger person coming in can just grab that, and take the simplicity and the directness in their prayer without the hang up of the breathing [technique]. They don't have to worry that they're going to get too gone on it. They seem to be very attracted to the simplicity of it.

At Gethsemani, this is the going thing at the moment for the more contemplative monks. Fr. Flavian likes it very much. He's pushing the Jesus Prayer quite a bit, and most of the young ones like that. On the whole, I would say that probably it's the most going thing at Gethsemani; even though Pentecostal's there, too, a little bit.

Br. David: Are there other scenarios like this for the House of Prayer?

The other one that I would mention is the Asian one, the Zen one, which I think is more a minority than the other [approaches], in a way. Perhaps you could talk about Zen sometime when we have a little more time. To me, this is a matter of great interest, personally. I see no contradiction whatsoever between Buddhism and Christianity. I think you can at the

---

44. Theophan the Recluse (1815–1894); Bolshakoff includes a chapter on Theophan in *Russian Mystics*. See also the compilation, *The Art of Prayer: An Orthodox Anthology* (trans. E. Kadloubovsky and E. M. Palmer [London: Faber & Faber, 1966]).

45. Each originally published by "A Monk of the Eastern Church," later revealed as Orthodox convert and priest, Fr. Lev Gillet (1893–1980).

same time be a Christian and a Buddhist. There's no problem, because Buddhism is not, strictly speaking, a religion. [Just as] you can be a Christian and be psychoanalyzed. I intend to become as good a Buddhist as I can. In Asia, I intend to learn as much of it as I can; perhaps that will be useful.

The thing about Asian [traditions] is that there's an enormous amount of [material]; there's no end to it, really. The best that anybody can do would be to make materials available to those who are interested. People who want to read about these things. There's just no end to Buddhist texts. They have discovered piles of [texts] in caves in China, mounds of material that has [not yet] been edited.

This year, Indiana University Press is bringing out one of the most important Chinese Zen men, who has been previously very much neglected; a man called Shen Hui.[46] I had the opportunity to write the Introduction for it.[47] It was very interesting to read the text while doing this. There is a great deal there and it is very modern in many respects. It has a lot to say to people who know something about phenomenology. It also has a lot to say to people who know a bit about modern physics—which I don't. But I think that these insights are going to be very important for people who are up on atomic physics and who have a worldview affected by modern physics. I think Buddhism has a particular view of reality, which coincides completely with [physics] more completely than any other religious cosmology. It coincides with the view of modern physics of things in constant flux.

Comment: What was the name of that book?

This will be called *The Last of the Zen Patriarchs.*[48] [Zen] is basically extremely simple. Zen is the simplest thing in the world. There is nothing simpler than it. But it can be made to appear very complicated. To what extent the Asian formula can be of use to us, I don't know. The best introduction to it would be something like John Wu. John Wu has done this in a very nice, simple way; not only in his own autobiography, but he will

---

46. Richard Y. S. Chi. For Merton's correspondence with Chi, see *The Hidden Ground of Love*, 121–25. For additional background and context, see Patrick Hart's "Editor's Note," in *The Merton Annual* 1 (1988): 3–4. See the reference to Chi in chap. 8, above (p. 174, fn. 22).

47. Published as "The Zen Insight of Shen Hui," in *The Merton Annual* 1 (1988): 5–15.

48. It is unclear if the book ever made it to print.

write a very good, careful essay on how St. Teresa is saying similar things to the early Daoists. He has a very good book called *The Golden Age of Zen*,[49] which unfortunately was published only in Taiwan, but I guess it could be obtained. It's printed at the Chinese University in Taiwan, where he teaches. I'm sure he'd be willing to arrange to have some sent. I'm going to see him at this meeting I'm going to.[50]

Mother Myriam: He's going to be there?

This is a meeting of religions that I'm going to; there are Buddhists and Hindus and Jains and Muslims. Christians. And you know who John Wu is representing? Confucians [laughter]. He's a Catholic convert, but he's representing Confucians at this meeting. He's a wonderful person. His book on Zen is really quite good.

Sr. Marie: What do you think of Aelred Graham's book?[51]

It's very good. I'll be using some of his new book [later on]; it has just come out. I just got a copy. The new one is *Conversations: Christian and Buddhist*,[52] about his trip through Asia last year. I'll be bringing that in and quoting from it. It just came in the mail the other day. *Zen Catholicism* is useful, I think. What do you think, David? Do you think it's any good?

Br. David: I think it's very good. It's good for Catholics, because it opens [us] up a little and it's good for Buddhists because many Buddhists for the first

49. John C. H. Wu, *The Golden Age of Zen* (Garden City, NY: Doubleday Image 1967/1996). Merton wrote the Introduction, included in his *Zen and the Birds of Appetite* as "A Christian Looks at Zen" (pp. 33–58). Merton's complete correspondence with Wu is included in *Merton and the Tao: Dialogues with John Wu and the Ancient Sages*, ed. Cristobal Serran-Pagan y Fuentes (Louisville, KY: Fons Vitae, 2013), 171–363.

50. There is no record of John Wu attending the Temple of Understanding Conference in Calcutta; in his November 9, 1968, circular letter, Merton says he hopes to see Wu in Taiwan (*Road to Joy*, 118).

51. Aelred Graham, OSB (1907–1984), British Benedictine monk, best known for his 1963 book *Zen Catholicism*. Merton corresponded with Graham from 1953–1968 (see *The School of Charity*, 48–49, 167, 181–82, 187–88). Graham visited Merton at Gethsemani in March of 1964 and spoke to the novices on the topic of Zen (http://merton.org/Research/AV/novitiate.aspx).

52. Aelred Graham, *Conversations: Christian and Buddhist* (New York: Harcourt, Brace, Jovanovich, 1968).

time get Catholic spirituality by reading Zen Catholicism. The only thing I didn't like about Zen Catholicism is that it's a little on the patronizing side, [saying], "[Catholics] have it all, and we have also discovered it." I think we should be perfectly open and say that we have not had it [all]. We have had something else that goes in the same direction, but here is something new for us to discover, and that by having the fullness of Revelation, it doesn't mean that we know everything. Revelation is ongoing in the sense that we only discover what Christ actually brought us by discovering what we have; by learning this. This is how we see the fullness of what is there in Christ. That is not [Graham's] attitude at all; but otherwise, it's very useful.

That is very useful for educating people [regarding] more openness about [Zen]. People who read that will certainly have a better understanding of what we're saying when we talk about contemplative life. Because Zen really torpedoes the whole Manichean thing. That is [what] Zen does. People who don't know anything about Zen think that Zen is a Platonist thing, and it absolutely is not. The root thing about Zen is *no dualism*. You don't divide. You don't split man up into body and soul. It's absolutely against all that.

Comment: Father, another tradition in light of that is the Shaker tradition.

You could include that with Pentecostal. It's a similar thing. What would you call them? Not "fundamentalist," but the left-wing Protestant cult. People should be exposed to Shaker buildings and Shaker furniture,[53] and to see the spirituality that's in there. [The way they] expressed contemplation in work in a way that nobody [else did]. This torpedoes all that dualism: that you can't [be contemplative] and work, but their work was contemplation, and the results were evident: all you've got to do is look at a Shaker chair as a contemplative experience. You have this perfection of form. How do you explain something like that? It's completely beyond explanation.

They're sharing in the Spirit, though—one another's.

---

53. For Merton's photography and essays on the Shakers, see *Seeking Paradise: The Spirit of the Shakers*, ed. Paul M. Pearson (Maryknoll, NY: Orbis, 2003).

The whole philosophy of Mother Ann[54] in regard to work was beautiful. We've got a Shaker place right down in Kentucky. There's one at Pleasant Hill and one at Bowling Green. There's a lot of material in libraries there, too. The Bowling Green library has piles of Shaker stuff that has never been touched or edited. I was going to run some of it in *Monks Pond*. There was an original text about how the first Shakers came down to Southern Ohio, around Cincinnati, and then moved into Kentucky. It's very amusing about their encounters with the Presbyterians there, and how they got the Presbyterians "away from the flesh"; that is to say, they broke up their marriages [laughter]. It's a very amusing piece of writing. There's a lot of stuff like that. They wrote everything down; all about their work: "You know what I did today? I finished the chair."[55]

Sr. Mary: Father, have you had any contact with the "Movement for Prayer" in the United States, people who don't belong to any church at all and yet are trying to be contemplatives?

I don't know whether I have had any actual contact with that movement, but there are lots of people that I get letters from that are interested in deepening their own interior life without belonging to any church. Of course, this is so common now. The world is full of people that won't have anything to do with any church and yet want to pray, and many of them feel that people in the churches don't really pray. This is a real tragic thing, especially when you think of monasticism and religious life. These people look to us.

Br. David: I wonder if we all agree here what we really mean by prayer? I can't think we don't, and maybe it would be worthwhile to have a session [on this]. Some of the old concepts of prayer just aren't working anymore.

Let's have a session on that. Let's see what comes up this afternoon. I think the thing on prayer is probably one of the most important ones

---

54. Ann Lee or "Mother Ann" (1736–1784), founder and charismatic leader of the Shaker movement.

55. Following a question on the topic of mysticism after the twelfth-century Cistercians, a brief discussion opens up regarding Teresa of Avila and John of the Cross; most notably, how they have fallen out of favor in certain contemplative circles, and some of the issues around their misrepresentation and misinterpretation.

at the moment. Let's see if we can start on that and then move into this whole area of Pentecostalism. We'll cover it all this afternoon in some way or other. Let's see what happens. Do you want have a little break before Mass? What time is it?

Mother Myriam: I think we should. Fifteen minutes?

Comment: I have a question. When we're [referring to] Houses of Prayer as signs of religious life, what fundamentally does "religious life" mean? I don't know if we can settle it, but could we just say a few things about it. I'd be especially interested in your idea about commitment.

I'm not going to attempt to respond now, but let's all keep this in mind, as everybody may have something to say on this. I would go back to the one thing that I did raise this morning: the idea that behind all this is the desire to unconditionally give ourselves to following out the consequences of our belief. The first monks didn't have any vows; there were no such thing as vows until quite late. St. Benedict is probably the first one to formally profess vows. But it seems to me that the essential thing is this commitment—not at all juridical. It's something in your own heart. You seek to give your whole life to finding the ultimate root of what it's all about in your belief. Why do I believe? To go right to the root of it: our life is dedicated to this single quest. Vows finally arose as a convenient institutional way of signifying this. Then they became the only way you did it; so that if you didn't make vows, you weren't really "doing it." Then the whole thing got turned inside out. I think you're better off without vows, because vows obscure the issue. If you're constantly talking "vows, vows, vows," you don't do it because you really mean to, you do it because there's something on paper—and it's somebody else who says that this is what the consequence of signing that paper is. What we have to do is live in such a way that we're doing things because we believe they ought to be done; because we deeply believe that they are what God asks of us, and not through the mediation of a concept of a vow, or of a juridical obligation. It is always this business of putting in between ourselves and reality other things: media—

Fr. Ed: Distractions, which create a distance between ourselves and every-thing else.

Yes, which is a kind of protection. This is what I meant the other day about sin: that if we know too clearly what sin is, then it cuts us off from faith in God. This knowledge of "good and evil" in moral and juridical terms, gives us leeway where we can escape God. We put this knowledge between [us and God]. "Original sin" is that. You fall into this condition where you can get away from God; you've got a concept of sin between you and Him. You know just where it is—"You can't get me. I didn't do it"—so I'm safe. I've got this "no man's land" where I can operate and God can't touch me. This is the worst, and to have that under the guise of "virtue" is even worse. This is a terrible thing. This is what religious life tends to do.

What we have to get back to—and this is Luther's whole thing—is that this is taken away: you don't know where the boundary line is, and you are naked before God, so that any moment, you are completely under His mercy; and you don't mind, because you have experienced the fact that it really is mercy. And then, if you don't know whether you are wrong or right, but you say, "I trust in You. You figure that out. You're my Father"; this is the whole way. Get the vows out of the way and live in more direct contact with God. Of course, this is an extreme statement. There's nothing wrong with vows, and vows are perfectly okay; however, a person could conceivably live a more valid life of prayer outside the whole area of vows and formal religious commitments—but he has to have something better [in place].

Comment: That's why many are giving up their vows; they feel that they can't live as real Christians.

But then they have to know where something better lays, and that's where the problem comes in, because we are so helpless in being dominated by somebody else. If we're not dominated by a religious institution, then we're dominated by General Motors.

Comment: Earlier, when you mentioned Cistercians and [Zen] Buddhism, I was going to ask about two other methods. They seem to be a different way of approaching these [other] two: one being a method of really Judaizing Christianity, and the other—I wouldn't know where or how it would be done, except maybe as you said through Buddhism—but the idea of "space prayer" or "academic prayer." That kind of a person who is put before God— even in the right kind of "Platonistic" sense—because of studying something

that is so extremely abstract that it leaves him naked before Nothing. And
this being done through study rather than—

It seems to me that one of the great contemplative monastic communities
of the twentieth century was Niels Bohr's group at Copenhagen, where
they were working on the atomic bomb. Niels Bohr used to come up with
things that sounded like St. John of the Cross; realizing that they were in
this tremendous thing over this abyss of what they didn't understand. It
was all opening out and they didn't know what it was. There was no way
of really saying what it was even when it worked according to prediction.
This sense of being face to face with the complete unknown.

Br. David: Some of our allies in those very dedicated sciences talked to me
on two occasions at the University, speaking to a small group, and they said,
"What you tell us about the monastery—we have it right here."

Exactly.

Mother Myriam: Mr. ["Ping"] Ferry, yesterday, was very interesting. They
have so much in common with monks.

Yes, from the Center for Democratic Institutions. And it's a beautiful monastic building, with a cloister and everything. I got to [Santa Barbara]
just when I came back from Alaska, and they were having a meeting in
the morning with all these kids that had been running these university
revolutions all over the world.[56] One from Columbia, two or three from
Italy, Mexico, Germany. And they were the top men, the ones that were in
the press—some of them were in jail—but these were the kids that were
running this revolution. And I got talking to some of them afterwards
and mentioned the fact that I was a monk, and they said, "Oh yes, we feel
that we're like monks, too." Immediately.

56. See Capps, ed., *Thomas Merton: Preview of the Asian Journey.*

Chapter Fourteen

Opening Discussion

Day One: Afternoon Session

Merton opens the afternoon session with the following prayer: "Come, O Lord, open our hearts to Your light and grace, and open our wills to obey Your holy will. Fill our hearts with love and strength that we may ever come closer to You through Christ Jesus, Our Lord." The session then begins with a detailed report from the Monroe Conference read by Sr. Mary Aquin.[1] The following discussion then ensues.

One thought that occurred to me while you were reading was that the practical thing for active congregations is to expand this concept and to think of it not just as a House of Prayer, but as a "house of renewal." If you give it that title, then you can also incorporate into it something in the realm of dialogue with scientists, for example, and have people come in, giving insights from other fields, and also have a place where people are doing "spiritual research" for your own community. This brings in the idea of writing. Mr. ["Ping"] Ferry, who was here the other day from Santa Barbara, was very concerned. He asked me, and I think he asked several others, "What are these contemplative nuns *producing*?" Not in the sense of cheese or anything like that, but what comes out of their contemplative life? Do they write anything, or do they have anything to say? And I said, "No, mostly you don't have time." What's going to come out of the average Carmelite house? Of course, you have to face the fact that a lot of them aren't going to want to produce anything. "Productivity"

---

1. Much of the following discussion has been abbreviated due to its focus on specific points regarding the Monroe Conference report.

doesn't matter. But, at the same time, a really grooving contemplative life should produce, once in a while, a book or an article; something like that.

Sr. Mary: There seemed to be a tendency among the group to want to distinguish between a House of Prayer and a house of renewal. The house of renewal would be [a model where] you come in for a briefer period of time to attend classes, etc.

Since we all came to a consensus yesterday that what's important is the personal breakthrough to a deeper maturity—that isn't only in prayer. There are other ways of breaking through. The danger would be, of course, that if you mixed up a House of Prayer with a house of renewal, where there would be conferences and academic things, it might easily get swamped in classes. Maybe what you could do would be to have the general idea as a house of renewal and then have places where people could do just the prayer thing.

Fr. Ed: This came up repeatedly in the preliminary sessions when we were meeting prior to the conference, that the House of Prayer would serve as a center both for prayer and for research; of renewal of study. When we got into the larger conference, we had 160 people—60 more than were intended. As you can see, dealing with the problems of prayer itself, the relationship to the community houses, the relationship to apostolic involvement; to what degree—all of these are the first areas of discussion. I don't think it finally got through to these other areas.

But there was a great deal of work, as you can imagine, this being only the first conference ever of its kind. We thought that in other conferences, this would really be developed in a more specific fashion. But we certainly did, in our early discussions, suggest that the House [of Prayer] would have a far greater range of service to be a faithful member of the community; to render this service to the community and beyond. This was very much in our mind.

Mother Myriam: What came through to me was, at the beginning of the conference, it seemed that the general concern was the House of Prayer, but gradually the interest and the thinking about the House of Prayer gave way to a deeper concern about prayer itself, and the need for prayer if man is to keep his sanity.

Of course, there is always the danger of things mushrooming awful fast. As soon as you say something like "renewal," then almost anything gets in. A lot of talking gets in.

Mother Myriam: And if it is a center of research, it needs to take some proportions.

This prayer thing has become so sclerotic. We've fallen into this completely ossified, rigid—not that people pray in an ossified, rigid way—but all the doctrine about prayer is completely fossilized now, at least with us. It's all tied up with special rule-keeping; special exercises. We've got to break out of that. Renewal in prayer is necessary before you can have a House of Prayer.

The whole thing about this Rule business is that the Rule gets stricter and more rigid in proportion as you don't have a human leader, a "Father" who is really developing a life of prayer. When you don't get a spiritual father, then you get a Rule that replaces him. You've got to have one or the other. Either you have to have a Rule, or you have to have a spiritual leader who is really teaching prayer and telling you what to do. Because the person who enters into a thing like that cannot lead his or her own life of prayer yet. There has to be a time during which one is told what to do, asks what to do, and confronts the person who has the experience. I think a House of Prayer without that is bound to fail.

Maybe what you need in your house of renewal is, first of all, to purify and renew the idea of prayer, and then to form leaders who will replace the Rules, and who will help people to make their own Rule. The purpose of a spiritual father is to help the individual make his or her own Rule. Because the individual can't do it by herself; doesn't know how until she's fully mature. Then the House of Prayer is where you learn how to live your own life—and then live it. The gap that exists is that we don't really know how, and when we have a chance to do it we don't know how, because we've never learned. All we've had was the Rule. We can go back to the Rule, but that's the vicious circle.

Fr. Ed: But then the community itself has to be constantly reforming the Rule.

Yes.

Sr. J.²: It seems to me that the key question is, "How do you form this leader?" The spiritual leader?

The Holy Spirit has to do that. This is what you pray for. And you don't know who it's going to be. There's a very interesting Zen conversation where he says, "Oh, the Roshis. They're not all enlightened. They haven't all attained this experience." I don't know exactly how he meant this, if this is good or bad, but I think the great thing is to have enlightened people, who can really transmit the inner direction that enables you to write your own Rule and make your own Rule.

Mother Myriam: Wouldn't you say that a group of people with a certain degree of maturity, a real desire for prayer, and a life of prayer could also come together, and gradually, if they are faithful to one another and to the Spirit, one of them will emerge as expressing the consensus of the group?

Sure. Why not?

Mother Myriam: Because to be a leader is to be, if it is in a community setting—a coenobitical setting, to use the old traditional term—it's to discover the charism of each other in the community, to remake the cohesion and unity in the group.

Sure. But you can't do that unless you've got somebody that has special stuff, maybe more than one. But when it's a community, if you have more than one, you always have trouble. And then they start fighting. It's just the biological background of the human race.

Mother Myriam: Yes. This is true, too.

Br. David: I'm just wondering about the belief in the principle that a group can work something out together. I see our goal as something very highly specialized and something on which generations can work. It is true that the basic principles that lead to the building of a jet engine are the most

---

2. "Sr. J." is listed as one of the speakers in Mother Myriam's conference notes, although no additional information is given. It is perhaps Sr. Jane Marie Richardson of the Sisters of Loretto (see chap. 16).

basic mathematical principles, which everybody can understand. But you may put a group of people together for any length of time, and let them come up with a jet engine, build upon all the generations and generations that have worked on it. And so, I think we, the members of this group, will have to bring together a background of traditions. And the weightier that background will be, the more promising the results will be. We have to introduce it into this group, the wealth of the spiritual traditions of all mankind. That is the great problem.

Another thing, too, is that any group—from within a Christian context—is always, from a human viewpoint, bound to be quite unsatisfactory. This seems to be a law in Christian life. St. Paul in Corinthians, "I have chosen you. You are not all wise. You are not all rich."[3] The real Christian setting is ideally made up of people who are all mixed up—not necessarily "all mixed up" in a terrible way—but people who are weak or deficient in some way or another.

The people that are extraordinarily gifted in some other way go to General Motors, or go to put together jet engines, and the people who come to us are, in a certain sense—we are all, in a certain way—misfits. Not entirely, but to some extent, you have to be a bit of a misfit to want the religious life. They're not entirely at home in the world. And that has to be taken into account, too. Of course, then you run into this stupid mystique that we've always had, that somehow or other, the people that entered religious life were superior in the first place. "We are the absolute cream of the crop. We're the best Catholics," that sort of thing. That's a sociological thing that's deeply ingrained in our background in this country. If you were of an immigrant background, the best, quickest way to get ahead was to be a priest or a religious, and then you really had an identity.

CS[4]: We experience absurdity now. I think we all agree. This is what we work with now. We're absurd.

We are actually. That's why existentialism fits in pretty well with religious life.

---

3. 1 Corinthians 1:26.
4. "CS" is another unidentified speaker in Mother Myriam's notes.

Chapter Fifteen

Prayer, Freedom, and Doubt

Day One: Afternoon Session

Should we get into prayer? Are we ready to talk about that today? The Bible is here and anybody who wants to [can] grab the Bible and give a text and a commentary on prayer. I think we will be able to arrive at something.

The first thing I would like to say, when we talk about prayer, is that it's a dangerous topic. There is no topic in the world which is more easily inclined to become self-contradictory immediately. That's why I think it's very difficult; for the first thing about prayer is that prayer is not the object of prayer. And faith is not the object of faith. In other words, I don't believe that I believe, and I don't pray in order to see myself praying, or in order to reassure myself that I can pray, or in order to make myself feel that I have faith. I don't go to prayer in order to reassure myself that I am faithful.

In other words, I don't pray in order to pray. This is very important. You set up a House of Prayer, and you are immediately in this bind, because you throw people into a situation where they feel they're obligated to see themselves pray. "You have been rewarded by being admitted to the House of Prayer, now go ahead and pray." And then you have this obligation. Today, am I praying? Let me get myself together [in order to] see that I am praying. I verify that I am praying. Then at night, I sigh with relief, "Today, I prayed. I've earned my daily bread by praying." This is just not it. This is the dangerous thing about a House of Prayer—a rigid House of Prayer.

I might right away read to you a text from the Quran on monasticism, which is very interesting. These Muslims are very sharp people. Now the Quran has a statement on the monastic life. It's the official "condemnation," so to speak, of the monastic life in Islam. But it's not an unequivocal condemnation, and it's quite mysterious. Many Islamic people have commented on it, and they all come up with different answers, so that there is no final answer to what this is saying about the monastic life. But out of the commentary you get something quite interesting. The statement is this: "Then Jesus came . . . the son of Mary." This is a definition of Christianity as it looked to the early Muslims, to Muhammad. "And we gave him the gospel, and we planted in the hearts of those who follow him, the seeds of meekness, of compassion, and of monastic life."[1] Now these are the characteristics of Christians for the Muslims: meekness, compassion, and monastic life. By "monastic life" [they] especially mean "celibacy." That is the reason why, for the Muslim, there is no monastic life in Islam, because there's no celibacy in Islam. That's the meaning of that statement: no monastic life in Islam, because celibacy is out for the Muslim, except temporarily. October meant you're celibate. You go on your pilgrimage to Mecca, you remain celibate. You remain chaste.

"The Christians, they are the ones who instituted the monastic life, says Allah. We only prescribed it to them to make them desire to conform to God's good pleasure. But now it turns out they have not followed the method required for their rule of life. To those who have remained faithful to it, we have given their reward, but many among them have been sinners." Now, this is a very interesting statement. I think Christian monastic theology should take account of this. What it's saying is that monasticism is a human institution, which God tolerates. It's not at all God's final answer to all the problems of life. It's something he lets you get away with. It's like making a vow to fast. If you decide you want to fast or make a vow to fast, go ahead and fast. If you vow to do it, then do it. If you want to have a monastic life, go ahead and have a monastic life, but then do it. The interesting thing is, first of all, it's in this context of meekness and compassion; and secondly, it's in this context of divine good pleasure. The only warrant of monastic life at all is that it enables you to abandon yourself to God's good pleasure. If it doesn't do this, it's useless. That's what is meant as a Muslim commentator: to make them desire to conform to God's good pleasure, and the method required for their rule of life is the method required for a monk: his total abandonment to God's good pleasure, which is fundamental to Islam.

1. Quran 57:27.

This is what Islam is: total abandonment to the good pleasure of God, so that there is nothing but God's good pleasure. Nothing but God. This is the application of the idea of *Tawhid*, the absolute unity of Allah. There is nothing but God's good pleasure; get everything else out of the way, and simply go with Him. That's what monasticism is for, and if the monk is doing that, then everything else follows. But if they're not doing that, then the whole thing becomes ridiculous. Because what has happened is that, instead of the one thing necessary—which is God's good pleasure—a human institution has been put in between man and God's good pleasure. Human, institutional monasticism becomes primary, then, and is supposed to mediate exclusively God's good pleasure; so that God's good pleasure can't get to you except down the chain of command and through the Rule.

Then you get this situation that I spoke of yesterday, where you are insulated from God by a "sacred institution," which is just about the worst thing that can happen. This is the plight that we are in. We are in this situation now of having to break through this. The danger, then, becomes, anything that you take on for a life of prayer, is it going to be a life of total abandonment to God's good pleasure? That is to say, total openness to God in the world? Or is it going to be a life of insulation in doctrine and techniques of prayer? If one simply becomes insulated in a Rule and a sacred form of ritual existence, and a doctrine and technique of prayer, one is committing another variety of the original sin, which is to separate oneself off from God as an isolated, untouchable unit. The whole idea of "original sin" is to constitute for oneself an identity independent of God, which can stand back and deal with God: make deals with God through the mediation of an institution, through the mediation of a Rule, through the mediation of a life of prayer.

Therefore, the whole thing that is demanded in embracing a life of prayer is to get rid of everything that mediates between God and us, except the essential mediation of Christ's life in us, which is what our life of prayer is, and which is already the deepest root of our own life of prayer. The great thing in prayer, then, is not to pray—that is to say, not to enter into prayer in order to get to God—but to go directly to God.

Br. David: How would one define prayer if it isn't going directly to [God]? What else is prayer?

Prayer is praying. If it's not going direct to God, it's going to [a concept of] "prayer."

Br. David: That is recycling words or something.

Becoming conscious of one's self praying. This is where we meet Zen. This is the thing that Zen destroys. Who is it that seeks enlightenment? *Bang*—get him out of the way. Because there's no enlightenment possible if there's somebody seeking it. Who is it that prays? If "I" am praying, I'm finished. That's the end. The only valid life of prayer is where Christ is praying. So maybe an off the cuff method of prayer would be, let Christ pray. Be glad that Jesus is praying. Thank God Jesus is praying, or just rejoice, Jesus is praying. This is the New Testament. There is no need of anything except a prayer of Jesus. Of course, in hesychasm I can simply incorporate that into my life. I say "Jesus," and He prays in me, and I no longer watch myself praying. I forget myself praying.

In those books that ["Ping"] Ferry is going to have sent to you, there's a very good one on the Orthodox way of prayer. I forget the title of it. It's by an Englishman. The last chapter is on the Jesus Prayer, and the whole point that the man makes is that this is the quickest way to forget that you're praying. The Jesus Prayer leads you very rapidly to what [we're saying here]—forget all about prayer. Of course, this is the real thing.

What St. Antony [the Great] says is that you're not really praying unless you are totally unaware that you're praying.[2] You forget all about the fact that you're praying. But in order to do this, you do have to start. We do have to face the fact of human weakness, confusion, and helplessness. And the thing that all these people are doing now, the "God-is-dead" bunch, and the secular city people, is that they are actually taking away from weak and simple people the things they have to do to start, and they're leaving them helpless, so that something else can immediately grab them. If I don't pray, what do I do? I go get drunk or something. And then where am I?

Mother Myriam: I would say, in [Br.] David's terms, that they take away no-thing. That their life is nothing.

---

2. As cited in Cassian (see *Cassian and the Fathers*, 251–52; and *Pre-Benedictine Monasticism*, 68).

Yes, exactly. And that is the fantasy. So, we do have to "go about" prayer. Even though praying is not-praying, and praying is forgetting prayers; nevertheless, we have to want to pray, because otherwise you get into a real kooky agnostic thing. You have to start with your illusory self. Having admitted that it's illusory, then you start with it. You don't take it seriously, [that] which you begin with. In that sense, maybe you do take it seriously; so, I do have to want to pray. Where this whole thing comes in with us, is that prayer is not simply a human action—it is a response to a divine call. And in the depths of our self, illusory or otherwise, we do hear, first of all, this call, the call of life, speaking from its very source. In the terms of St. Ignatius the Martyr, in this beautiful language that he has in his *Epistles*, where he says, "In the depths of our heart, there is a living water, which says, 'Come to the Father.'"[3] There is a whole Trinitarian theology built into that [regarding] the Holy Spirit, the Father, and the Son. In the depths of our heart is the voice of this living water, which says, "Come to the Father." This is the living water of prayer. And if we let this living water say in us, "Come to the Father," [then] that's it. If it doesn't say this, it doesn't matter. But if we let it, it's saying this anyway all the time.

Now, let me break in here with a statement of one of these Zen people that Dom Aelred Graham was talking to. This is a highly conservative Zen master that I hope to meet, too. I think he's a Rinzai,[4] and he's a very conservative one; apparently a great Japanese, aristocratic, seventeenth-century Zen type that's really got the whole thing down. He's a very fine person and doesn't want to have much to do with Christians, but still, he's interested in monks. The thing that he starts saying to Aelred Graham is that monks should simply be people of prayer and shouldn't get involved in politics—nothing to do with political issues. And Aelred Graham says, "Yeah, but they should, really," and they're not fighting, but they're arguing a little bit about this. And then [the Zen master] says, "Well, this is a very difficult, fundamental problem, which both Buddhist and Christian

---

3. Ignatius of Antioch, second-century bishop, theologian, and martyr. Merton is citing from Ignatius's *Letter to the Romans*. See Merton's essay "Church and Bishop in St. Ignatius of Antioch," in his *Seasons of Celebration* (New York: Farrar, Straus and Giroux, 1965), 28–44.

4. Rinzai school of Zen Buddhism, transmitted from China to Japan in the twelfth century.

monastic life may confront. I think the monastic life should withdraw completely from social activities and not be mixed."[5]

What's important is not this statement, but the reason that he gives, because the reason is good: "And that when a person needs to come out, he should come out positively, and engage in social activities." He's saying, if you're going to get into politics, get out and get into politics, and not be coming in and out of the monastery. [For example] Dan Berrigan always wants me to come up to his trial, and stand up and say, "War is no good." Well, I've already said, "War is no good." There's no point in standing up at his trial and saying it [again], and then coming back to the monastery. This makes everything highly ambiguous.

"According to your Benedictine *Rule*"—first off, he's read the *Rule*. He likes St. Benedict. He thinks he's right on the ball. "A person who lives in a monastery should throughout his life, be in a monastery, and not come out"—except to visit Zen masters [laughter]. "A person should be in the monastery all the time, so as to not split his mind in two. Some other person may engage in so-called 'worldly activities.' There are not so many people in monasteries, even in your country, I think. This is an example of the purely religious life. This is the fountainhead. The fountainhead should not be muddied by many people's steps. It must be kept pure. Then the streams that come from the fountainhead may be drunk by other people." So, this narrow, small fountainhead is a place nobody can approach. This is very conservative. He's a conservative Zen man. They're not all like this.

But prayer is at this fountainhead. And the thing about prayer and the life of prayer is, whether temporarily or permanently, it is a realization that there is a fountainhead that is far beyond any of these other concerns, and that it is so fundamental and so deep, that these other things don't reach it directly. There may come from this contact with the fountainhead some light—how to deal with these other things. But unless the fountainhead absolutely preserves its nature as source, all intervention and other things will be useless; will be fruitless. That is an important element there. When it's done on this deep level, you don't know you're praying.

---

5. The Zen Master is Kobori Sohaku (Graham, *Conversations*, 29–41; see pp. 31–32 for the passages quoted).

You can't engage in these other things and not know what you're doing. As soon as you get involved in any of these things, you have to think about them. You have to figure things out. You have to plan action and do things, but in prayer—no. The best way to pray is just simply to stop, and let prayer pray itself in you, whether you know it or not. This is the best way to pray—and this works. Then you don't have to know it. You don't have to even look to see if you're praying, and to look and see if you're praying is a great mistake.

What this is, is a deep underground awareness of finality that is built right into our being, and is renewed in us by God. This finality is a kind of identity. Our deepest identity is not just that we are constituted as human individuals, but that we are constituted in a special kind of Christlike being, by God's call to come to Him. So that what our prayer life does, is that it gets right down to this root identity of the self that is called into being by God's direct word: "Come. Come follow Me. Come to Me. Come to the Father." Prayer, and everything else in our life, has to be built around that central thing, which is inaudible. You don't hear it, but it is the very depths of your being, and the very depths of your identity. The trouble with all that is said about the life of prayer, [is that it] tends to obscure this, and tends to make us forget that this is the fundamental thing.

Another thing that's forgotten about the life of prayer is we say, "Alright, it's a life of faith." Sure, it's a life of faith. But it's also a life of doubt. If you never doubt, you can't pray. You have to doubt. It's necessary in the life of prayer to struggle with doubt. And once again, that is the trouble with all this hard and fast, safe Rule thing: "If I get to the end of the day, and I've kept every little rule from morning to night, then I have no reason to doubt. I'm justified. So why should I doubt whether I'm justified or not?" This gets back to this central thing in faith. It's not by the work of prayer that I'm justified—I don't justify myself by praying. And if I've prayed all day, it does not make me any better than if I hadn't prayed all day. See what I mean? All of these things have to be absolutely fundamental, because otherwise, I have another kind of identity. I have an identity of somebody who has become somebody by praying. "I have prayed. Now I'm me. I'm the man who prayed all day." And you come away from prayer with a placard on your chest, "God, you know who I am. I'm the man who prayed all day."

There's a guy I quoted in *Conjectures of a Guilty Bystander*, a Bishop, who, on his death bed, got off a remark like this: "I have served God for

55 years and I hope he's not going to forget it."[6] There's a good Zen story about that. It was one of the famous Zen stories of the first Zen master who came to China. He had an audience with the Emperor, and the only thing that the Emperor found to say to him was, "Well, I have built 9,221 temples, and I put up stupas in every place. What will be my reward?" And [the Zen master] says, "There is no reward" [laughter]. So, he threw him out. Then the Zen master went off someplace and prayed 20 years facing the wall.[7]

But this idea of doubt is very important, and the thing that really comes out in our life of prayer, is that we must absolutely give up this business of trying to suppress doubt and put faith in its place, because it is in doubt that we are faithful.

Doubt and faith are really two aspects of the same thing. If you doubt honestly, you will end up believing. Because out of the doubt, faith itself will come in. Faith isn't going to come from someplace else. Then, of course, there's always this question of, "What do you doubt?" People who have temptations against faith usually don't doubt God at all. They doubt whether they have faith. And people who are tempted about the life of prayer; they're not doubting the value of the life of prayer. They're doubting whether they pray. This whole thing is so much of an illusion. It's a completely illusory form of life. This is the thing that's wrong with the contemplative life. The contemplative life, as it is officially lived, can become a life of total illusion. Complete self-kidding from morning to night, and from one end of life to the other. This, of course, is why it's a disaster. So, perhaps one of the things that we should propose today, is the total abolition of the contemplative life, and start over again *with prayer*.

Sr. Mary: [I am thinking of] the particular type of doubts that you have in each person's unique struggle with prayer. I remember last week, one of the novices said to me—you could see she was bad about faith. She said, "It isn't that I doubt things about God. I find it so hard to believe that God really loves me"—as an individual. You could see that her life, her struggle

---

6. Not a bishop but "a certain Monsignor Hulst" (*Conjectures*, 137).

7. For this story about the legendary first Ch'an (Zen) Patriarch in China, see chapter 2 of Wu, *Golden Age of Zen* ("Bodhidharma, the 'Wall-Gazing Brahman,' and His Immediate Successors," pp. 34–42).

with her vocation was based on that. "The vocation would be very logical
if I could believe that God really loves me and wants my love in return."

The crucial issue centers around: "What is she doubting?" When she
doubts that God can love her, the doubt is not centered on God. It's very
often centered on herself. She is doubting whether she's worthy of love.
This is something that has to be lived through to the point that you realize
that there's no answer, because the answer is not in determining whether
or not I'm worthy of love, because that is irrelevant. It's got nothing to
do with it, but a person has to experience that. When that doubt turns
into faith is at the point when the person completely forgets the problem,
because it's nonexistent. Whether I'm worthy of love or not makes no difference, because what happens is that God loves me whether I'm worthy
of it or not. We all know this at the top of our heads, but we don't experience it until we go through this struggle of doubt. And we've got to doubt
and doubt, and fight the doubt, until we come out realizing that what we
doubt is nothing. And the doubt itself is nothing. The doubt is rooted in
our crazy view of who we think we ought to be: somebody worthy to be
loved by God. If the life of prayer is merely a life in which we try to make
ourselves worthy of being loved by God, we're crazy.

That is the thing we have to get clear on. And then, once a person has
worked through this whole doubt thing—which is essential to the life
of prayer—what one would do in a House of Prayer is to come finally
to the realization that our identity consists, not in the fact that we have
made ourselves worthy of God by our good works, but that God simply
loves us because He loves us. Then what happens is that our whole life of
prayer, and our whole identity, becomes praise and thanksgiving. But it's
not "I" praising; it is just praise praising. Praise praises. And thanksgiving
thanks. And Jesus thanks. It is not at all that I am thanking Him in order
to get His attention, or to be recognized by Him. This is what we have to
get out of. This all has to be thrown away. Then, at this point, in the life
prayer, in the consummation of the life of prayer, the divinization of the
Christian is the realization that he is Christ, and that he doesn't have to
be in a kind of relationship where he is always banging on the door of
Christ, saying, "For God's sake, let me in." You're in. What do you want
to get in for? That's where you are. But you can't know it until you have
experienced this; that is to say, until you go through the doubt.

The real crux of the matter is that we come very fast to the doubt—this probably is what we were getting to yesterday. This, perhaps, is the point where you have to go through the doubt to get this real development. And we don't. The insecurity involved is too unpleasant. So what are the ways we evade this stuff? One of them is regularities. I become extremely regular with everything "1, 2, 3"; or the other thing is perhaps I throw myself into some brand new, wild, social action of some sort. It's another kind of justification. Here again, involvement in the world is put in the wrong place. When the Catholic should be involved in the world is after he's gone through the doubt; then he's got something to give to the world. If he is involved in the world in order to have the world justify him, he is betraying his faith. He is betraying it in exactly the same way as the contemplative is betraying it by keeping a lot of rules. He is creating for himself an identity, where he can constantly prove himself by referring back to the people who accept him.

Sr. Marie: This reminds me of something said at the [Monroe] meeting. The way it has come through to me is that the House of Prayer is a means to this end that you're speaking of. When a person has gone through this doubt stage, and truly comes to the realization that Jesus is the Lord, the natural thing—[as well as] in Ignatian spirituality—is that he or she will be drawn to serve. Many people are saying that just to pray is [of] God; rather than the House of Prayer being a means to an end. Whereas, if it's an end in itself, why not just be there to praise God?

The end is not so much whether you serve people or not. The end is to go through this [doubt], so that you become fully developed. When you are fully developed, then you're ready for anything. You are a totally new creature. Then God will pick you up by your head and send you in like Daniel in the lion's den. Anything can happen. But it would be perfectly logical for a person who has gone through this to simply live a life of praise. But that's his business. If that's what he's going to do, let him do it. It nobody else's business.

What happens is that we not only try to justify ourselves as individuals, we want to justify our institutions. Some people try to justify it by saying, "Look, we've got all these contemplatives. They're all locked up behind the wall"—this is the awful bind that you're in, in the contemplative life. You've always got these people who want to be able to point to you and say, "Look, she's been behind a wall for 82 years. She never went out. This proves everything. This means that somehow or other, things are going to be better for me; some things are going to be better for the President, and we're going to win in Vietnam, because this old [inaudible] is behind these walls." This is a strictly pagan type of thinking. It's the "vestal virgin" bit. They're locked up in that hutch and they're keeping that fire going, and Rome is going to win all their wars.

CS: Would you talk more about the relationship thing? I think we want to justify ourselves to God. All the "in" books now in religious life say that the big thing with us is that we've got this special thing going with God. It seems that the object of the relationship [becomes no longer] God, but the relationship [itself]. This bothers me very much, because I don't think that's true.

Ultimately this involves a renewal in theology, and a renewal in Christology. I don't know what the renewal in Christology is doing, whether it's going in this direction or not, but ultimately, the question is, "Has Christ truly been a mediator, or is He a block in between us and God?" He is [a block] if He remains purely an object, and this constant pushing Christ off to the level of an object complicates things indefinitely. Because we are Christ—although we are, and we aren't. Supernaturally, we are; by grace, we are; by the Holy Spirit, we are. Therefore, we shouldn't be looking for Him "out there." And yet we're not [Christ, too]: we experience ourselves as separate from Him. That's true, too. So, what we have to do is learn that our relationship with God is really Christ's relationship with God. It's the relationship of Sonship.

Now let me dictate my Bible text, because I think it fits in pretty well here. It's a good bit from Romans [Ch.] 8, which might be what other people are thinking of, too, because it's so clear. Romans 8:1: "The reason, therefore, why those who are in Christ Jesus are not condemned, is that the law of the Spirit of life in Christ Jesus has set you free from the law of sin and death."[8] Point one. This is the central thing in the life of prayer. And it is a central thing in Christian identity. The basic identity of the Christian is the identity of one who has been called and chosen in Christ, and is not condemned. "If he is no longer under judgment, he does not

8. Romans 8:1-2.

have to justify himself." This is the central thing. This is what we fail to believe. We won't believe this; yet, we say we believe it. St. Paul is read all the time. These words about law and grace wash over us day and night; yet [we say], "Paul really had a hang up about this law thing."

But the first thing is, as Christians, we are no longer under judgment. If we're not under judgment, why do we have to justify ourselves? Therefore, the first thing out of that is get rid of all self-justification. Of course, it has to be understood immediately in the context of what went before, and that messes it up, because what a lot of people try to do, the Brethren of the Free Spirit,[9] for example: "We're no longer under condemnation; therefore, we do what we want." But that doesn't work, because the conflict remains. It's very unpleasant to have to constantly remind ourselves that we're not under condemnation, when constantly we feel in ourselves things that go against God.

The real struggle, and where the doubt comes in, is in the awareness that I am not condemned, and yet I am worthy of condemnation. Then you get this horrid moral theology where you fuss around with responsibility, and you draw the fine line: "Did I really will it?" And, "Didn't I will it?" It's a form of self-justification. And the thing is, "Maybe I did, maybe I didn't, but God is merciful. Forget it. Keep on moving." This is what we don't do. This is what we absolutely refuse to do. And all renewal, of whatever kind you like, has to be centered in this kind of consciousness. The consciousness of somebody who is an acceptable son of God, who is nevertheless liable to rebel against God at any moment, but remains a son, and is accepted in Christ.

"Your interests, however, are not in the unspiritual, but in the spiritual, since the Spirit of God has made its home in you. In fact, unless you possess the Spirit of Christ, you could not belong to Him. Your body is dead because of sin, but if Christ is in you, your Spirit is life itself. Because you have been justified and the Spirit of Him who raised Jesus from the dead is living in you. Then He who raised Jesus from the dead will give life to your own mortal bodies through His Spirit."[10] In other words, the resurrection is the center of all this. I am not under judgment, because

---

9. A "mystical heresy" of thirteenth-to-fifteenth-century Europe, particularly in the Low Countries; often (mistakenly) associated with the Beguines, and a major cause of their condemnation and attempted suppression by church authorities (see Bernard McGinn, *The Essential Writings of Christian Mysticism*, 489–94).

10. Romans 8:9-11.

the risen Christ lives in me by His Spirit, and the flesh is dead because of sin. And this I have to experience, too. You have to experience both.

Br. David: How can you account for the fact that this is what you say, and what some of us may have said on occasion, but it really isn't the official teaching of the Church today. I've tested it. I have asked in Catholic colleges; I have said, "Here are two statements: Christ came to tell us what we ought to do in order to be saved." Another statement, "Christ has come to tell us we are saved, now act accordingly." Which one is correct? I had them raise hands. You have just about a few hands for the right statement in a Catholic college. And from every point you hear the wrong teaching. What has the Church got wrong? What is it?

What do you mean by "the Church"? We're the Church, too, aren't we? That doesn't mean to say that we are the only ones in the Church, but this is absolutely true. This is the evident sense of the Gospel. If the Church has missed this, then maybe there was a point to the Reformation after all. This is partly what Luther was trying to say, and maybe the Church should have paid more attention to Luther. It's a pity that instead of accepting what was true in Luther, the Church simply condemned what was false in Luther. [The Church was] so caught up on the mistakes that he made.

This gets back to the whole business of compassion and forgiveness, which is so basic in Christianity. If you don't forgive your brother and accept all that is good about him, then you're going to be in a bind, because you're going to be constantly rejecting him. If you're rejecting the "he who is not you," you are affirming yourself as separate, and you are getting back into this little hutch, where you are—all by yourself—in a position to deal with God, and to deal with other people, and to deal with God about other people. "God, see him? He is a sinner." That is self-liquidating. Perhaps this is something that we all need to understand in order to go on to renewal.

Sr. Mary: E.I. Watkin[11] said that any heresy was a partial truth that the Holy Spirit wasn't ready yet to bring above the horizon. And that Luther's

---

11. Edward Ingram Watkin (1888–1981), British Catholic convert and prolific author; for Merton's letters to Watkin, see *Hidden Ground of Love*, 577–85.

teaching was essentially that kind; that the Church wasn't ready. That's essentially the teaching of the spirituality of the Little Flower,[12] isn't it? That complete abandonment to God is the important thing.

It's trying to come through. But this isn't exclusively ours, either. This has been trying to come through in so many of the ancient religions. Although in a partial form. It's not too clear, but everywhere, it seems to me that the whole of man's religious history is the history of this truth. To what extent has it finally come through? To what extent does it come through? And when it comes through, then you get people who accept themselves in a totally different way—as people who are forgiven, and who therefore forgive others, which is the basic Christian thing,

Br. David: How can you say it hasn't come through in Asian religions but partially? I may be biased, but it seems to me that it has come through a lot better than we thought?

I mean "partially" in the sense that the theological content isn't there. In Buddhism it's come through in a perfectly straight, human, existential way, without theological explanation. And even then, maybe in Buddhism, I think if you go way down deep, perhaps there is a grain of authentic, mystical and theological experience, which got even into the explanation of it. We don't know what some of the things they have said really mean. [D.T.] Suzuki certainly has passages which say in Buddhist terms something that could be a perfect theology of grace.

Br. David: He has a beautiful passage on prayer, which is not very well known.

Fr. Ed: This means that the Pauline concept of "all things being created in Christ"[13]—the universe itself, and all things—it's really affirmed, not only by ourselves, of course, but has been affirmed and experienced in the other manifestations of God's Spirit throughout the world. But when Paul is say-

---

12. Thérèse of Lisieux (1873–1897), also known as "The Little Flower," French Catholic Carmelite saint and Doctor of the Church.

13. Colossians 1:16.

ing that the whole universe is created in Christ Jesus, and the whole thing is redeemed in Him; the whole thing is summed up in Him, that in reality, the experience of this is present in the other communities. But we have somehow interjected between this affirmation, or this stillness before the fact, or this willingness to say "yes" to the fact, without handing it all off. That others have found better ways, or more naked and sincere approaches to it, and it really tells us a great deal more about the total unity of the salvation experience. It says a great deal to us about if we do come to the point of Houses of Prayer, as to what kind of a "non-spirit" there has to be.

"What kind of a 'non-spirit.'" Yes. The great thing is to keep people from getting hung up on these self-justifying procedures. Again, that's an argument why "maybe just a little prayer" for some people, and then get them out again with other people, where they're not going to be hung up on a self-justified way of prayer. Of course, there is the historic thing that needs to be studied, too: this whole question of Western Christendom—how did this historically get violated and messed up.

Mother Myriam: How do we believe this message of "newness"?

I think the historical argument is important, because one of the things that happened after Charlemagne, especially, was the corruption of Christianity into a "Christendom"—as a sacred and secular "final package," in which everything was joined into this "secular-sacred" institutional thing: Church and State all together. It turned into, "You obey the authorities, whether secular or sacred, and you're okay."

One other point: this idea of debt. Doubt and debt go together. I have to be conscious of myself as a person who is no longer in debt. I have only one debt, St. Paul says, that is to love one another.[14] I have no other indebtedness, so that the relationship with God is purely and simply not a matter of a self-justifying thing, in which I pile up a whole lot of interior good acts. It is purely and simply a matter of forgiving my brother and releasing him from his debt, with the intention of creating in him the freedom from debt, which is my own identity. What I should go around

14. Romans 13:8, "Let no debt remain outstanding, except the continuing debt to love one another, for whoever loves others has fulfilled the law."

the world doing, ideally speaking, is going around forgiving everybody their debts.

I take away your debt; now you're free. This is what Christianity gives us the power to do. You just go through the world, taking away their debts. It's as if you were a person with millions and millions of dollars, and went through the world and everybody you found, "Do you have a debt?" Okay. I pay it. "Now you're a free man." This is what we're supposed to do as Christians: to go through the world taking away from people the imprisonment that makes them feel that they are unworthy.

CS: There's a wonderful movie called A Thousand Clowns [1965]. In one of the scenes in the movie, the main character goes into New York—

I've heard about that.

—He goes up to everybody on the street that he meets and says, "I'm sorry." And the reactions of people—[laughter]

Sr. J.: Is this just in St. Paul?

Go through the entire New Testament; you will find not theology for the sake of theology, but theology for the sake of freedom. A theology of liberation: we are all liberated. We're now released from debt. That's what the Cross is about: that there are no more debts; now we can start over. Finally, this [forgiveness] having been done, the Spirit of freedom is again everywhere, and I have at least done everything I can to open up everybody. Then I am free inside. And the freedom that comes from this is the real freedom. It's not the freedom at all of closing everybody off, and nobody now bothers me, because I've got rid of all of them, so nobody can get to me to bother me. No. I have now no debt to anybody, because I have forgiven them all their debts, and if they want to come back, I'll forgive them more debts. I will unlimitedly forgive debts. Then I am free. Then I can pray anytime, anywhere, so that the whole problem [of work] for example—if work becomes a debt that I have to pay, then it's going to disturb my prayer. If it is something that I have to get rid of, that I have to get off my conscience before the end of the day, then it's a distraction. But if it's not a debt, then it's purely a freedom. If it's something that I give, then it's not a distraction.

And all things like that. Everything. Admittedly, it's hard to do. Again, it involves doubt, because there are moments when you see it, and there are moments when you fall back into doubt. Of course, the most obvious doubt comes in, "Do I really love my brothers?" Well, I don't—not perfectly—because there is an interior resistance to others. This remains, but it doesn't matter. The whole thing is not that we get rid of all these compulsions and signs of selfhood in order to be justified, but that we are justified in the midst of all these things, if we simply are resolved on living Christ's life, which is proclaiming the Gospel of freedom from death, and that we're all redeemed in the Cross.

I think that prayer is the quest for this central sense of identity in Christ. It is the response: to come and be this kind of a Christ; come and be Christ. That is to say, come with all the weakness of your humanity in order to be a channel for the forgiveness and love of Christ to everybody. Then the life of prayer is in that: the sense, the ultimate feeling of this; that we're now sons of God, and we are not our own. We no longer belong to ourselves. We belong entirely to Christ; so, there is no self to justify, because He, to whom we belong, will justify us. That's Romans 8: "Nothing, therefore, can come between us and the love of Christ." Not even a Rule, nothing. "For I am certain of this: neither death nor life, no angel, no prince, nothing that exists, nothing still to come, not any power, or height or depth, or any created thing, can ever come between us and the love of God made visible to us in Christ Jesus, our Lord."[15] It's all there.

15. Romans 8:38-39.

Chapter Sixteen

Discussion

Zen and Non-Violence[1]

Day Two: Morning Session

Merton: This is from an old Japanese Zen Master: "In Zen, we'll start with faith." Faith in what?

The [Master] says, "Doubt, the great doubt": about the problems of man, the human situation, and human destiny. [Doubt] is the beginning of "insight" training. Faith and doubt: one emphasizes faith; one emphasizes doubt. Faith and doubt sound utterly contradictory, but after all, they are one and the same. If one starts doubting, in the ordinary sense of doubting, which gets solved in the ordinary sense of "a solution," and [simply] goes from one position to another, then it will take you nowhere. [However] if one really doubts—if one doubts true doubt—he will doubt even the doubt itself. This will mean that doubt has no objective. The doubt that has no objective cannot be doubt, and therefore is the same as faith. Typical of Zen, don't you think?

We are going to talk now about Zen. I talked to David about it and he suggests that I give you something of the essence of it, and then that he elaborates on it. The essence of Zen is a dangerous thing to talk about, because it cannot be talked about. But the essence of Zen training—and the whole thing is in the training—is something to reproduce an experience of the Buddha as he saw the morning star while sitting under the tree [where he achieved enlightenment]. He completely saw the morning

---

1. There is no extant recording of this section. The transcription follows Dardenne's conference notes (Redwoods Monastery Archives).

star. He didn't see the morning star as something else; he just saw the morning star.

When enlightenment comes through, it's a sense perception. You don't see something built on top—you just see. Zen is purely and simply a return to this immediate vision. It is not a vision *of*; it's just *vision*. There is not a "something" behind anything; it's all right there. It's just a "seeing," and it is not important that you are there having achieved "seeing." There is just "seeing." Seeing *is*. Seeing *sees*. Something like that. This is an immediate intuition of "being." It excludes all abstract statement about it.

Imagine you have been shot by an arrow and you go to the doctor, and you want the arrow out.[2] You do not go and say to the doctor, "I will not let you take this arrow out unless you [first] tell me who shot it, where it was made, where did it come from." You just want the arrow out. It is the same with Zen. It doesn't make sense. It's irrelevant. What is "being"? What is "not-being"? What is "Void"? What is "Absolute"? The important thing is to get the arrow out and to *see* what's there. And what's there is the morning star. It's seeing—not as subject and object—not seeing "an object," but pure seeing. And where there is "no seeing," that is the purest seeing. The thing that has to be avoided is getting between or placing something between us and the basic "seeing."

The whole thing is getting rid of all explanations and all intermediaries. What we had to say a while ago about justification is where Zen and Christianity come very close together. The Christian message that St. Paul is saying is very much like Zen. You don't need to be justified. While this is a theological statement, Zen is purely an existential statement. Zen is saying exactly the same thing in existential terms. Existence, your existence, does not require justification. It does not require explanation. But the way we ordinarily live, we put all sorts of things between ourselves and it; as I said before, we actually withdraw ourselves into a little, isolated, autonomous world that can defend itself against life, and justify and maintain itself, and say, "I think, therefore, I am." With Zen, to say, "I think, therefore I am," is original sin—the fundamental illusion. For in Zen, there is no "therefore." "I think, therefore I am" is my thinking

---

2. The parable of the poisoned arrow is not exclusively a Zen story, but is found in the Culamalukya Sutta of the Buddhist Pali Canon, part of the Majjhima Nikaya (Middle Discourses) #63, of the Sutta Pitaka, the second of the "three baskets" of this most comprehensive collection of (Theravada) Buddhist scriptures.

about it. This is a complete illusion. It's the beginning of illusion. This is not the kind of a statement that requires an explanation. So, Zen is a training that people go through in order to get rid of all sorts of things that get between subject and object; to get rid of this illusory identity that we construct. Justifying existence by thinking about it is an illusion. The only thing that counts in Zen is concrete experience. Br. David has had training in this and he will fill in some of the details.

Br. David: The central activity is "no activity" in Zen training. It is just sitting. Zen means sitting. You just sit. Newcomers into Zen training are given a cushion and are invited to sit. You do a little walking in silence. You go around for ten minutes, and again, you sit. The idea is to put your mind at rest. It is just a matter of breathing and controlling your breath. Put everything out of your mind, and of course you cannot do that, so you are just to let the thoughts pass; flow through them. Don't stop them, pay no attention to them. Let them pass right through. Just sit. This word "just" is important. The Japanese leader [at Tassajara Zen Center] says this is the best word in the American language. *Just*. When you walk, just walk. When you sit, just sit. When you eat, just eat. And yet this is not a *laissez-faire* attitude. It is very strict. There is ritual. The kind of ritual that is liberating. It is not doing whatever you please, but you know exactly what to do and that liberates you.

Mother Myriam: The ritualistic attitude, if taken like that, can free people as well as anything else in the monastic life.

Br. David: And, it is logical; yet, it is illogical, too, as any other ritual. And then, in the monastery proper, they would have little prayers, chants, that will keep you alert to what you are doing. Before you open your eyes in the morning, you have something to recite; something like this, "Before I open my eyes, I unite with all living beings and vow to awaken to everything"—not going off the road.

Mother Myriam: That is very Christian.

Br. David: Or, before a bath, every action [is ritualized]. This is very impressive, especially since everyone bathes in one huge bathtub, and you see them before they enter—they bow—it is just like a baptism. They recite, "As I take this bath, I unite with all living creatures and wash from my body and mind all dust and confusion, and to stay healthy and clean within and without."

The last thing is the gratitude. In my mind, this is the most striking feature; besides the warmth and kindness that you experience very strongly at Tassajara. This is also something you could experience very much in a Christian community, but I think that gratitude is something that is more pronounced and noticeable [at Tassajara]. This tremendous gratitude. Before they recite anything at all, they always fold their hands and bow. When picking up or putting down a book, especially those who have been there a longer time, you see this gesture, which they call *gravitas*. You see them pick up a book as if it were heavy; they pick up heavy objects as if they were light, and light objects as if they were heavy. It is part of the training. You are taught this way so that you become aware of what you are doing. This goes together with this awareness that everything is a gift. They receive everything with a little bow—spontaneously, to one another—to show you that this is not merely an empty ritual, but deeply spiritual.

The other day, I was walking down Riverside Park in New York City, and the wind was blowing and suddenly I felt air in my face, and it occurred to me: the air is always there, but we do not feel it unless the wind blows. Then I noticed how the sun was shining through the bare trees, and the wind, and the sun, and it occurred to me how beautiful all this was. Suddenly, spontaneously, without being aware of it, my hands came together and I bowed in gratitude. It suddenly then occurred to me that this is all that matters: to make the bow, the gesture.[3]

Fr. Roger: Sometimes, a hundred times a day, the monks in Asia do the same thing.

Br. David: And this is why it is so important for us to retain the bow.

Merton: Some are trying to get rid of the bowing [in monastic liturgy].

Sr. Mary: This whole sense of integrity is also in the Shaker ritual. When they go to a meal, they don't say grace; they sit for a while in silence, in gratitude.

---

3. Br. David is particularly well known for his promotion of the practice of Grateful Living (see https://grateful.org).

Sr. J.: Even with St. Benedict, the dishes should be handled as sacred vessels.[4]

Br. David: What happened once at Tassajara, was a few Zen masters got together and started out by speaking about not wasting the soap in the soap dishes by letting them get wet. One expected the height of insights!

Merton: This reminds me of a story about a man who had three sons and he wanted to see who would be the best swordsman. So, he put up a cushion in such a way that it would fall as the sons walked into the room. I don't remember what the first one did, but he got angry; the second one came into the room and as the cushion falls, he hacks it with his sword, and the third son reverently picks it up and puts it back where it belongs. This, said the father, is the best, the true swordsman. After all, a cushion is not meant to be hacked in half. This makes me think of non-violence: you just do what has to do with what is there. The cushion was there, just there, and didn't belong elsewhere, so he puts it back.

And then there's that other beautiful story.[5] I think I told you when I was here before. It's the one about the famous hermit who was supposed to be so spiritual, and this rich lady, to see if he really was a spiritual man—she had him living at the bottom of her garden for 50 years or something—and finally, to see if he was a truly spiritual man, she got this lady of "easy virtue" to go down and tempt him. So, [the rich lady] asks him [about it], and she says, "Now this lady was down there to see you. What did you feel?" And he said, "Oh, I felt nothing at all." And she said, "Well, you're a fake." And he said, "Why?" And she said, "You should have felt compassion."

Mother Myriam: The other day, Winifred and I were together at the foot-bridge. And there was a tree, the top of which the leaves were all eaten, and caterpillars were at the trunk. She said, "Could I do something?" So, I said, "Could you please cut the top off that tree?" Because I was afraid the cater-pillars would eat the whole tree. She said, "So what?" I said, "I feel sorry for the tree. If I have to choose between the tree and the caterpillars, I would

---

4. A reference to chapter 32 of the *Rule of Saint Benedict*, "The Tools and Goods of the Monastery."

5. The recording begins again here.

like to keep the tree." And she looked at me very seriously, and she said, "I don't know. I need the caterpillars." The caterpillars had the right to exist, too.

Br. David: This was the most striking experience I had at Tassajara; one of the most dramatic. I think I told this [to some of you] at Monroe. We were working on tearing down a little wall, and there were many scorpions there. The scorpions came out of the wall and bit one of the monks on his foot. He stepped on it, evidently. Of course, this is very painful, and also extremely dangerous. He screamed and [had] all the natural reactions. Except, also a natural reaction would have been to kill the scorpion, but [instead] he looked at it, and he bowed and went on.

Underlying this is really the idea that everything has a right to exist, because it all is part of a complex whole. We [tend to] feel that we have an absolute right to do anything we want with anything—[that] we're the complete bosses of all of nature, and anything we do is okay, as long as it suits our advantage; therefore, we can disrupt the whole of this balance. Up until now, we haven't been able to do this effectively, until the last two centuries. We didn't have the power to do this, but now, for example, we came into America and decided we didn't like Indians, and didn't like bison, and Indians ate the bison. So, we exterminate the bison in order to starve out the Indians. Or, you cut all the redwoods in order to make money. You can do anything you like, but then what you do is you destroy a balance, and when that's destroyed, it's irreparable. So, an important element in our whole moral attitude towards creatures, is a respect for the balance of living things.

Mother Myriam: Isn't there a whole other attitude behind this, that we want to suppress evil? Which is wrong, because evil is part of the ambiguity of life, and we have to learn to cope with it, first of all, within ourselves.

We think we're capable of saying what's bad. Of course, underlying this Buddhist attitude is really a refusal to judge. You don't judge that the scorpion is bad, just because he bit you; it's just his nature as a scorpion to bite people, and I shouldn't have had my foot there.

Br. David: This balance is not just on a physical level. Immediately afterwards, we got a bucket and he put his foot in the ice, and sat there for a whole hour, just in the same spot without moving away. And while he was sitting there, he said, "Oh, I had this coming. I've been pretty bossy lately" [laughter].

That's the idea of karma.

Sr. Mary: Would this whole thing, too, be that tendency in Western man to organize means to ends?

Br. David: This is one of the points the [Japanese] Zen Master [at Tassajara] makes: that the future of Zen is in the West. No bones about that. Just as Buddhism came from India to China, and then Zen came from China to Japan. [It has] always, more or less, lost ground in the country from which it [has] come. They very clearly see now that it's going to the West and losing ground in the East, which again puts a tremendous responsibility on us as Christians, because we are the ones that, I guess, are to receive it.

Mother Myriam: I would think, maybe, that the future of monasticism is in the West, too. And when I speak of monasteries, I don't speak at all of the old view, [but] a real type of life consecrated to God.

Not only here, but I think everywhere. But a whole different kind of monasticism. A "secret monasticism," very hidden and small, and nothing official; nothing terribly institutional, but structured in this other way. [For example], there's no institutionalism in Zen, but there is discipline. And I think the thing that's killed this whole reverence and discipline with us, is that it has been in the service of an institution. More and more at Gethsemani, for example, the mentality got in that the Choir had to be properly performed, and the chant had to be very good. Because there are people up in the tribune, and they come to Gethsemani because this is where the contemplative life is really being lived—and this ruined it. When the idea of the integration of the brothers came out, a lot of them resisted this, because they felt they were just being moved into the choir in order to fill the choir stalls, so that they would look even, and there'd be more people in the choir stalls in the view from the tribune. I don't know whether that was true or not, but they felt that, and the fact that they felt that was indicative of something. They could feel that they were being used. Now, I think a lot of the rebellion against bowing at Gethsemani is due to that.

Fr. Ed: If all the Zen and Buddhist traditions are under fire or deteriorating in the lands from which they came, and we are endeavoring to explore the special gifts that characterize them, wouldn't it be important for us to understand why, in those countries, this is beginning to diminish? Is it a parallel movement to what's happening in Christianity in the West? Is it important to try to seek common causes? Otherwise, we could just become enamored of an Eastern concept, which is extraordinarily rich and beautiful, but if already the seeds of decay are there . . . ?

That's one of the things that I'm going to find out when I get over there: to try and find if they are beginning to sense the same kind of problems; if they have an explanation for this. Tibetans, I'm sure, are very shaken up by the fact that they've been pushed out by the Communists. And they're probably going through quite a crisis of wondering who they are, and what it's all about, but I think they're holding up very well. The only indication I have is in this book of one of the Lamas called *Born in Tibet*,[6] where he describes his escape, and his education before, and how he grew up. I hope to meet him, too.[7] He wasn't in his monastery when the [Chinese] came; he was making visitations [to monasteries] in another place. He had several of his monks with him. The cellarer kept saying, "We've got to go back to our monastery," with a great deal of argument. The cellarer insisted on having a train of 25 yaks with all kinds of supplies. [Trungpa Rinpoche] saw that he couldn't possibly escape if he had 25 yaks with all these supplies. When he found out that they were going to have to go, he

---

6. Chögyam Trungpa Rinpoche (1939–1987), eleventh Trungpa *tulku* and founder of the Shambhala lineage and Naropa University in Boulder, Colorado. His autobiography, *Born in Tibet*, was published in 1966 (New York: Harcourt, Brace & World).

7. Merton did meet Trungpa in India on two occasions: first, in Calcutta, where they spent an entire afternoon together (October 20, 1968), and again in Delhi a few weeks later (*Other Side of the Mountain*, 219, 268). Merton's initial impression is energetic and lasting: "we are people who have been waiting to meet for a long time" (p. 219). Trungpa later remarked of their meeting that, "Merton himself was an open, unguarded, and deep person. During these few days, we spent much time together and grew to like one another immensely. . . . I had the feeling that I was meeting an old friend. . . . [Merton] was the first genuine person I met from the West" (in Judith Simmer-Brown, "The Liberty That Nobody Can Touch: Thomas Merton Meets Tibetan Buddhism," in *Merton and Buddhism* [Louisville, KY: Fons Vitae, 2007], 57).

sent a message to this other abbot and said, "What are we supposed to do? What is the plan? And how are we going to save our monastic life?" And the [abbot] says, "Now, you have to stand on your own feet. There is no plan, and everybody is going to have to stand on his own feet and work it out himself."[8] That's a realistic thing.

I think they've got this feeling that what they're doing [is that] they're coming West. This particular man [Trungpa Rinpoche] has got a foundation in Scotland,[9] and it's already very successful. It's a House of Prayer. It's a meditation center in Scotland and people are coming to learn how to meditate. They have various long retreats. Their biggest retreat is three years, three months, and three days. Others are thinking of moving West, but they're obviously going through a crisis about what they're going to do next. Probably, the reason why they seem to be so happy to receive a Western monk coming there is they probably want to know what we're thinking [too].

Br. David: This whole idea of standing on your own feet is so important for us, too. We may not realize that, but Fr. Damasus Winzen,[10] from the very start of our foundation, [has] always said, "We are not necessarily training monks here for spending their lives in the monastery, because we do not know how long this is going to last. We train people to stand on their own feet as monks, come what may," and that is very important.

Sr. Mary: That's the whole diaspora idea, isn't it?

Br. David: In answer to your question, "Why is Zen losing out in Japan?" I have at least one answer that was given by a man who does know a great

---

8. This is the advice given to Trungpa Rinpoche by his teacher, Jamgön Kongtrül ("everyone must now be prepared to stand on his own feet," *Born in Tibet*, 116). The actual letter Trungpa received was from Dingo Chentze Rinpoche, stating, "You must not depend too much on others. If all acts are performed according to the Dharma they cannot fail" (p. 144). Merton recounts this story in his final talk, delivered in Bangkok just hours before his death (*Asian Journal*, 338).

9. Samye Ling, founded in 1967. It is the first Tibetan Buddhist Center established in the West.

10. Dom Damasus Winzen (1901–1971), founder of Mount Saviour Monastery, Elmira, New York, in 1951. Portions of Merton's correspondence to Winzen are published in *School of Charity*, 18–19, 90–91.

deal about it: Bernard Phillips, who wrote the anthology of Suzuki's works, and has studied other religions very extensively, and has a good grasp of them. I think he's a fine man.

He's the one who brought my Sufi man to Gethsemani.[11]

Br. David: Is that so? He's a very good man. He teaches at Temple University now; I think he's the head of the Religion Department there. He said Zen is the one spiritual movement in history that had a built-in mechanism to counteract institutionalism. It has worked for hundreds of years, but now it is becoming institutionalized.

It had already become institutionalized to some extent when it became the religion of the Samurai, and became part of feudal society. A lot of the good, and some of the bad, results from this alliance with a military society. The great weakness of Zen that people point out is that, though a person may be completely disciplined in Zen, he may be utterly at the mercy of, say, some fascist government. Many of the kamikaze were Zen people. They would perfectly accept the idea of the kamikaze busting up battleships, and accepted the war. It's not because of Zen, but because of the hookup with militaristic society—even though what they say about swordsmanship is very beautiful.

The Zen doctrine of swordsmanship is very interesting. It's the idea that you become so much the sword that it just works by itself. You have no hatred of the enemy at all, no desire to kill the enemy. He just throws himself on your sword. The explanation of that is that you have become so completely disinterested, and so completely free from all self, and so completely trained in swordsmanship, that things just happen. You don't plan anything. You're not reflecting on what you're doing. This is the whole thing with [*Zen in the*] *Art of Archery*, too.[12] This may be to some extent mythical, but still, there is this danger of a sense of power creeping in. Power and religion have always had a very bad alliance.

11. Merton was introduced to Bernard Phillips through Linda Sabbath in October 1965. For Merton's unpublished letters to Phillips regarding the visit of Sidi Abdeslam to Gethsemani, see: http://merton.org/Research/Correspondence/y1.aspx?id=1604.
    12. Eugen Herrigel, *Zen in the Art of Archery* (New York: Pantheon, 1953).

Br. David: With every training in the martial arts in Japan, there is a [component] that is built in regarding non-violence and mercy. But they do admit that the training of Zen gives you power, and does not necessarily determine the use of this power; therefore, it's an extremely dangerous thing.

The question of power is terribly important. I haven't seen much of a real eschatological theology of power, sin, and law. It's terribly important for us in the Church now. The real problem is this corruption of ecclesiastical authority by the love of power. This is, in a certain sense, an eschatological thing, which is involved with the "powers of the air" that St. Paul talks about.[13] It isn't just an innocuous sociological fact. There is something deeply disturbing about it.

Sr. Mary: I'd like to add to Mother Myriam's comments about this false attitude of wanting to completely destroy evil. I think part of that is our American tradition of the Pollyanna idea that once you get this one thing, then everything should go alright. I'd like to have some discussion on what is the evil that is standing in the way right now of renewal; for example, the type of people who are holding onto these absolute values of security. You say you can't wipe them out, but how do you deal with it? They're the real evil in the situation right now, in the human condition.

The whole thing with all evil is that you have to identify yourself with it, because the same evil is in ourselves. Therefore, we have to be careful of standing back and saying, "I'm right, you're wrong." That famous Jewish saying, "Who is it that's stopping the Messiah from coming?" "It's so-and-so—he's eating pork," or something like that. And "so-and-so," too, with us. I mean, who is it that's stopping the Messiah from coming? We don't know. I think the important thing is not at all a victory over these aggressive people. Again, it's the story of the hermit and the woman. What we've got to offer these people is compassion. All of these people who are misusing this power.

Sr. Mary: But at the same time that you feel compassion, you have to also keep them from increasing their power.

13. Ephesians 2:2.

I think what we can do is just forget them. Get out from under their power in some way or other. Of course, this is easy to say; I'm not running an Order or a monastery, but I think the real problem is not so much to fight them. There's a kind of "ecclesiastical judo" that's necessary. What you do with power, is let it destroy itself. The only thing that you can do with power is that. You have to find a fulcrum, which will be the place that you direct them to when they attack you, so that when they hit you, they go right over your shoulder, and land on their neck [laughter].

CS: A question might be, does non-violence work in our situation?

Non-violence hasn't been tried.

Br. David: Isn't this question being asked wrong? Because non-violence isn't something that ought to work. It's a goal in itself. It isn't a means to an end.

This is the trouble with the peace movement now. I'm great friends with all these people, but all their activities now are extremely aggressive, and they are not at all using anything like judo. They're trying to fight a bulldozer with a toy wagon, and you don't run a child's scooter up against a bulldozer. You can gain the reputation of martyrdom, but it doesn't work at all. The thing to do, is to not get into confrontations at all with anybody, unless you absolutely have to. Let them do the confronting, and you with the grace of God, in whatever way you can, dispose yourself as close as you can, with total harmony, to the truth, and to God's will as you see it. Don't try to trip them up. But if they break their necks falling over you, that's their fault. Because they will. They always do, if you let them. If you don't mess with them, they will. It certainly is a good enough formula for us, with unfair use of authority. It really does work that way. Of course, there are obviously situations that are absolutely tragic. But most situations aren't like that.

There may be times when somebody has to put up a direct confrontation; [for example] if somebody burns draft records.[14] [The problem]

---

14. A reference to the May 17, 1968, Catonsville Nine draft board raid in which Daniel and Philip Berrigan and seven other Catholic activists burned 378 draft files seized from a suburban Baltimore Selective Service office and burned them with homemade napalm in

then, is if I start thinking that if I don't go out and burn somebody's draft records, then there's something the matter with me. I would say that if I were doing this, if I went and burned the draft records, it would be chiefly in order to bring into focus the issue of the draft law. Once you burn one set of draft records, [then] that's it. But what should happen, is that the draft law should be abolished, and then there would be no draft records to burn. The function of the prophetic witness is to highlight the issue so that the people who have the political obligation to do something about it, should do something about it. I think they burned enough draft records. I think they have to do something else now.

JM[15]: I feel a little differently about this, because I think we are in the realm of conscientious feeling and experience. I think if you take up the question of Vietnam, or the question of the draft, or the question of race, that these are really things which the individual person must have a conscience about.

The choice is how you express your opinion. It seems to me that you've got to come out against the war, and it's an absolute matter of conscience to be against the draft, but that's not the point. You have to do that. You have to express yourself. The only thing that I'm saying, is a question of the tactics. What is the desirable way to do this? There are more ways than burning draft records.

It seems to me that what should be happening, is that the bishops should be discussing this publicly, and saying, "Here's a draft card, and all these Catholic kids have to go to a war they believe to be immoral. What's about this?" And they should exert their influence and pressure on the governing people to change the law. They could still do this. This law shouldn't be on the books, but it never seems to get discussed in those

---

the office parking lot before being arrested. They were tried and found guilty of destruction of government property in their October 5-9, 1968, trial (see Jim Forest, *At Play in the Lions' Den: A Biography and Memoir of Daniel Berrigan* [Maryknoll, NY: Orbis, 2017], 1-6, 124-25). For Merton's ambivalent public response to Catonsville, see *Passion for Peace: The Social Essays*, ed. William H. Shannon (New York: Crossroad, 1995), 322-25.

15. Most likely Sr. Jane Marie Richardson of the Sisters of Loretto. Their Motherhouse is located in Nerinx, Kentucky, approximately twelve miles from the Abbey of Gethsemani. Merton was in regular contact with several members of their community, including a long-standing friendship with Sr. Mary Luke Tobin.

terms. Basically, it's a political issue. It's like prohibition. Enough people wanted booze so that prohibition was abolished. If enough people simply got up and said, "This war is unjust—to send kids to fight in a war that they don't believe in and that has no real justification." If this were clear to everybody, I think most Catholics would see it.

JM: Don't you think there's a difficulty here that it's political, but it's also moral.

Of course, the trouble is that what we're really up against, is the fact that the political action doesn't work now. The system has stopped working. So now what you've got is a Presidential election, which—although the country is bravely trying to make it look as if there's a choice—there's no choice. So then, of course, you do come around in a circle. If the thing has collapsed, then maybe all you can do is [take action]. I think Dan believes that. The reason what's behind Dan Berrigan's[16] actions is the feeling that no political action is of any avail, so you have to do these desperate things. You have to get yourself put in jail to prove that the only place for an honest man is jail.

Br. David: We are much too identified with a "United States Messianism" in the world, [where] Communism is "the devil," and the United States, with its Democracy, is "Christ," and is the "Messiah." This is so much the framework in which most of us are thinking, that we never penetrate to the real issue at all. We're just floating in this vague fog.

We're way overdue on that. We should have seen that after the end of World War I. We got our karma building up in a real bad way.

Sr. Marie: Believe it or not, I think that this has something to do with the House of Prayer [laughter]. I was talking with someone who was saying that going to war [is] the only way to mature young men. It was a professor.

---

16. Daniel Berrigan, SJ (1921–2016), Jesuit priest, author, and prominent anti-war activist. Merton hosted Berrigan at Gethsemani on several occasions. Selections of their correspondence are published in *Hidden Ground of Love*, 70–101. See also Gordon Oyer, *Signs of Hope*, 91–119. For a biography, see Jim Forest, *At Play in the Lion's Den*.

And then we got on the topic of prayer, and it seemed that this is really the message of prayer: that it's only living a deep life of prayer that we'll become aware, and have this great desire for peace. So, this should be more of an impulse to us and for us, to have these pockets of peace among us, and that that's the kind of apostolate of peace some of us may really feel called to.

The problem is that what a lot of people think prayer means, [is that] you pray to win the Vietnam War. You show that you've got more faith, and that your God is stronger than the Communist "non-god." You prove to them that there's a God by bombing them off the face of the earth. This is perfectly logical to a lot of people—and a lot of priests, and even bishops.

Br. David: I think that what our Houses of Prayer should do, is to make people feel fearless, because that is what the Zen training does. They are a good many old ladies, typically New York City old ladies that come to the Zendo there. And one of them went home after the sitting and a man came up with a knife and attacked her, and she was completely fearless. To the point where he put the knife away and let her go—[due to] her mere strength and presence.

Mother Myriam: This is the best way to escape a knife!

Br. David: In fact, she was very compassionate to him. He asked for her purse, and she said, "You must need money very badly, but I happen to have only $2 with me." She was meeting him as a human person that needed money. That's why she talked to him like that. She wasn't afraid at all and he just let her go.

Sr. Mary: I recently heard a speaker who brought up the fact that—I think there are two national organizations of women in the United States—if those women really exerted their power, they could change anything they wanted in Washington.[17]

17. Bells ring for Mass, ending the morning session.

Chapter Seventeen

Discussion

Pentecostalism, Poetry, and Prayer

Day Two: Afternoon Session

A significant portion of the afternoon session includes a history of the Pentecostal movement delivered by Fr. Ed Hennessey. Merton welcomes Fr. Ed to "start it all out," stating, "He'll begin, and then we'll just go on. [Fr. Ed] will talk about Pentecostalism, in a general sort of way, and then we'll go on and talk about prayer," inviting "anybody who has any ideas or any texts" to share them. The below transcription begins with the discussion following Fr. Ed's presentation.[1]

One of the basic ideas behind liturgy is developing constant prayer.[2] The life of the monk should be a life of prayer. The whole life of the monk is prayer. It's spent in the presence of God, responding to the Spirit in all it's different aspects—*lectio*, etc.—in other words, integrating all the elements of [monastic] life. A man who is a monk is a man of prayer. What I mean by prayer is the experience of the relationship with Christ, which you should have in work, in prayer, and in your relationships with your

---

1. Fr. Hennessey offers an overview of the Pentecostal movement, beginning with its origins (Acts 10:34-48), and Paul's "gifts of the Spirit" (1 Cor 12). He then summarizes the Catholic Pentecostal revival current in the late 1960s, e.g., at Notre Dame and Duquesne Universities. Sr. Aquin then offers more specifics from Notre Dame and Ann Arbor (University of Michigan), summarizing the campus experience among Catholic Pentecostal-influenced college students. The recording for this section ends following this discussion.

2. The tape for the afternoon session is defective, with the sound ebbing in and out. The following is a compilation of select audible sections along with a highly condensed summary of the discussion.

brothers and sisters [in community]. Community prayer has to be closely related to the whole life of prayer of the monk, including [personal] or "mental prayer." This is what I mean by integration.

Mother Myriam: How do we relate the reality of our life to the Office?[3]

Br. David: It is the question of the rhythm of life of the monk.

Which is different now than it was in St. Benedict's time; the rhythm of modern life as we are faced now to support ourselves in a technological society—you can't take a rhythm that was written into the *Rule* and belongs to St. Benedict's time and culture, [which was] agrarian, and [transpose it to today]. Technological man is the person of the future.

Fr. Ed: I don't see how modern American monastic communities can exist without this technological development.[4]

> *The following section's recording is damaged and opens with Fr. Ed Hennessey offering additional reflection and a summary of Pentecostal spirituality, particularly regarding the gift of "speaking in tongues." The below transcription follows Mother Myriam's conference notes.*

Merton: One thing that you said really gave me a whole new perspective on something that is happening in the literary field; not in the religious field. Whatever [speaking in tongues] may be, it reminds me of something similar being done in poetry. There is a whole movement in poetry—an unconscious process to a great extent—of putting things together in this particular kind of coincidence where the logical connection is not evident. There is a connection that you don't see. There are all sorts of things happening on the surface, under which there is almost anything possible, and you don't know what it is. You become aware of this strange

3. A long discussion follows regarding the economic context and social realities of monastic life in its concrete expression in the world today, including an extended consideration of the *horarium* and Liturgy of the Hours in light of monastic and liturgical reform.
4. Another discussion ensues regarding the monastic *horarium* and "best practices" for balance in communities also needing to work to support themselves financially.

thing that is going on. It's not intended to be religious. There are a lot of poets—hippie types—writing like this. This is in the literary field, not religious, but it seems to fulfill a similar need for our own type of people [monastics]. You get much more peace out of writing this way; it seems much more worthwhile, more real, and you get much more satisfaction out of writing this way.

Mother Myriam: Is it alright if Winifred, Bob, and Gale come in?

Merton: Sure, come on in! Hello Winifred!

[*Mother Myriam introduces their visitors*]

Merton: Maybe Winifred can help us out with this. Do you know of anybody who is writing this kind of thing? We were talking about the Pentecostals and speaking in tongues. My contribution to this was through writing and poetry; although it's not speaking in tongues, and it's not religious. I think in poetry, a lot of us are doing this. What you do is establish these strange correspondences. What is important is not the correspondence, nor any logic; but when these [disparate] things are put together there is often a great depth underneath it, and you don't [always] know what it is. What you have to do is set up one thing after another—you can do it with art and also with music. You can do it with found stuff. I've started doing it with the "funnies." There's one I discovered in Alaska, "Buz Sawyer."[5] When you only read it every other day or two, you start to get [combined] phrases like: "Why are they flooding the exploratory cross cut at the 37th hundred-foot level," and then you start lining these up, one after another. Then you throw in something from an ad, and you get this weird effect of something that could make sense on a logical level, but doesn't. And then underneath it, anything might be happening.

There's no message—that's what speaking in tongues is doing—but there is utterance. And the utterance may be largely borrowed from someone or somewhere else—with a million possible implications, none of which are stated. Then you just line these things up. For example, I've got

---

5. "Mosaic: Alaska Papers and Funnies" (*Other Side of the Mountain*, 183–85).

this big long poem now. The last of it is all stuff from the Ghost Dance,[6] from a sociological study made at Berkeley all about Indians in this area, and in Southern Oregon.[7] Just statements made by these Indians. When you line them all up together, you get a much more poignant picture of what the Ghost Dance was all about. This is like [Pentecostalism] too; it's another kind of apocalyptic movement, in a way.

When the Indians realized that they were [faced with an attempt to annihilate them], suddenly this Ghost Dance movement spread. It started in Nevada, and it moved up to Oregon, and out to the Dakotas. That's where the massacre ended the whole thing. They massacred the last Sioux who were doing the Ghost Dance. The idea of the Ghost Dance was that, if you danced, for three days or so, and then bathed, the white people would all fall into the ocean, all the animals that had been killed would come back, and all the Indians would come back. Everything would start over. They kept doing this, and of course, none of these things happened. But still, they would keep on doing it; keep on dancing and going around, until finally, the white people got into such a state of paranoia. There was nothing threatening about it. It was just people dancing. But these [white] people got into such a state of paranoia about it that finally they massacred them—for dancing.

This is not in connection with Pentecostalism, but similar things have been going on, for example, the Cargo Cults.[8] I've used this in the same poem.[9] What a Cargo Cult is, is this: the natives see these white people coming in—this is before the First World War. These white people come in; they sit down and they do no work. They sit at a desk. The native does a whole lot of work [while] the white man writes out all these little things on pieces of paper and hands the papers to somebody, and pretty soon, in comes a boatload of goods, because he wrote on this paper. The white man gives the native a little bit of what comes off the boat, but not very much. The native says, "What's going on here is that these people have a special system for making this boat come from the land of the ancestors."

---

6. *Geography of Lograire*, 131–37.

7. Cora DuBois, "The 1870 Ghost Dance," University of California Publications in Anthropological Records III.1 (1939–46). See Merton's extended discussion of the Ghost Dance in chapter 10 above (pp. 218–20).

8. See Merton's extended discussion of the Cargo Cults in chapter 3 (pp. 71–73).

9. *Geography of Lograire*, 91–116.

The boat comes from where the ancestors are—across the sea where the ancestors live. The white man doesn't trouble to explain about factories. So, they say, "We will do what the white man does, and we will get a cargo boat that will come for us."

First, they adopt Christianity, because they think Christianity has the secret. And they are very faithful Christians, until they realize that this Cargo secret is not being transmitted: "The white people must have torn out of the Bible the part about how you get the Cargo, and they are not being fair with us. They are not telling us the whole story." Then they start a Cargo Cult. For example, they set up an airstrip. They build a little airplane out of bamboo, and put it on the airstrip as a decoy, and wait for the airplane to come. Nothing ever happens, but they keep doing it, and it gets more and more complicated. That's the basic set up.

The anthropologists that have worked on this have spelled this out in a very good way. What these [Indigenous] people have always done, is that they have understood human relationship in terms of sharing goods. If you are somebody's friend, you give him certain things, and he gives you certain things. Everybody has a certain amount that they can share. This is what constitutes society. It is what constitutes human relationships. The first problem that these people ran into was that there was no capability of any kind of sharing with a white man. Why? What happened? What was wrong? The purpose of the Cargo Cult was to get on a level of parity with the white man, so as to be recognized as a human being, and to be able to share things.

The way this is spelled out, is that these people who are thought of by the white men as a bunch of "mad men," are really telling everybody what we ought to know as Christians; only they are saying it in an imaginative way, and we don't get it. We don't understand it. They are just saying: "Look, we are people." These people, in their way, are speaking prophetically, but nobody knows it. This is where prophecy is [in the world today]. Prophecy isn't just a person standing up and giving a particular prophetic message. Prophecy is going on in people all over, but you have to be able to read it, and you have to be able to respond to it.[10]

[Therefore] when we talk about Pentecostalism, the important thing is not to see it as this isolated thing, but to see it as part of this whole big picture—of everybody, everywhere, trying to say something in a new

---

10. Merton summarizes here the work of Lévi-Strauss, "totemism," and current anthropological research on the topic.

way. Because all the old, cerebral ways have stopped. The "brain way" of saying it has gone dead. It has to come from somewhere else. It seems to me what the "speaking in tongues" people are saying, is that it's got to come out of some place that you are not in full control of—and to let it.

CS: Don't you think the art form that comes closest to this now is film?

Merton: I guess so; I don't see enough movies! Bob Lax[11] and I want to make a movie some time. I haven't seen any movies in so long. I've seen only about 3 movies in 25 years, and they weren't very good! [laughter]

Sr. Mary: I am thinking of Sr. Corita's art.

Merton: She's following what's been done, for example, by Paul Klee.[12] The things that he did were absolutely beautiful—slapped together in a real strange way that's terribly significant. This is where it's all being said. Pentecostalism consists in listening to all of it and being open, as much as possible, to the whole thing.[13]

Short break

Merton[14]: The best experience I have had of "community" this year has been through a poetry magazine [*Monks Pond*]. It was really fabulous, the way this thing built up. The 4th issue is on its way. This magazine was a real thing, and some terrific people showed up in it from all sides. [Initially] I wrote to

---

11. Robert Lax (1915–2000), American poet and longtime friend of Merton's from Columbia College. Their correspondence is collected in, *When Prophecy Still Had a Voice: The Letters of Thomas Merton and Robert Lax*, ed. Arthur Biddle (Lexington, KY: University Press of Kentucky, 2001).

12. Paul Klee (1879–1940), influential Swiss-German modern artist and art theorist.

13. Merton digresses here to a discussion of religious diversity in Indonesia in light of his upcoming trip, including Muslim mystical sects, the prominence of Pentecostalism, and shadow puppet performances, e.g., of the *Mahabharata*, which Merton describes, following Aristotle, as a kind of "catharsis" for the audience. This leads to a discussion of "madness" and irrationality in the Middle Ages, following Michel Foucault's *Madness and Civilization* (New York: Vintage, 1965), with Merton postulating that Pentecostalism serves as an outlet for the "irrational" in our modern, hyperrational world.

14. There is no extant recording for this section; the transcription is an edited summary of Mother Myriam's notes.

two or three people and asked them to write poems, and they immediately wrote five or ten each. Poems were coming in from all over the place. Terrific poems by a 16-year-old kid,[15] and beautiful stuff from out of nowhere. This wonderful woman from Arkansas wrote a fantastic book of poems—all Mexican stuff—she's been around all this time and nobody's published her poems, and it's a terrific book; I've got most of it in my magazine.[16] And this guy, Alfred Star Hamilton, a radical from the 1930s, living in a rooming house in Montclair, New Jersey, who rode the freights in the 1930s. He writes fabulous poems, real simple kinds, some of them sound like the *Book of Job*. He says the same thing over and over again, but in slightly different ways. It's very Biblical; very solemn and prophetic—and very funny. He was one of our favorites when we started on the "concrete poetry."[17]

Everybody was just so happy to do this. Nobody was charged anything; the [magazine] was free, and if anybody wanted to write anything, they could—and everybody wanted to. And it really shook up the monastery, too.

When the first issue came out, they thought, "Gee, this thing seems sort of crazy, but maybe he knows what he's doing; after all, he's an author." And then, after a while, they began reading about the poets, and they'd come in and say that all this is very interesting, and then, after that, they started to read the poems, and they thought, "Maybe it's not so bad, and maybe he's really saying something; maybe he's really got something [here]."

This was another kind of Pentecostal thing. Once you get the idea of just letting things happen, they can. That's the Pentecostal thing, and that's really the thing to do. You don't have to plan anything.

Br. David: Maybe you just have to set things up so that you are no longer controlling things, but you are letting things take hold of you. Abandon yourself—then, it happens.

Merton: Yes, but with a House of Prayer, you do have to work at it. You can't just let a House of Prayer happen if it's going to be a part of an institutional structure. You do have to make it fit. But, still, you are right on that.

15. A reference to Christopher Meatyard (*Monks Pond*, 117, 268); actually 13 years old according to the contributors' notes (pp. 207, 346).

16. This is a reference to American poet Besmilr Brigham (1913–2000); see *Monks Pond*, 71–72, 108, 148–52, 222–26, 345.

17. See *Monks Pond*, 42–46, 63, 73, 108, 132–35, 340–44, 348.

Br. David: Could you read some of your poetry?

Merton: I don't have any [of my own], but I do have [some issues of] *Monks Pond*.

Coffee Break

Merton: I would like to tell you about a festival of the Apaches [that] I attended.[18] That's where I started [in New Mexico] on my way up here [to Redwoods]. [As with Pentecostalism] it's a manifestation of something happening. The Apache Indians were among those who got the most terrible treatment from the white people. This festival was near Christ of the Desert [Monastery] in New Mexico, and it was very significant. It was their fall festival to give thanks to the sun, and for the harvest. One of the things they do [during the festival] is have a relay race between two runners from two different clans in the Tribe; not so much in order to win, but to give back to the sun the energy you have been given in the corn. It's important who wins, because it determines what kind of weather there's going to be. Incidentally, it's going to be a wet winter, the way it turned out.

We got there the day before the race, and a great many things came out of it; very significant things. It took place way out in the country, and they were all out in these tents beside a lake. Outside each tent there were aspen boughs, and each family group was feasting under the aspen boughs. They invited their friends, and they feasted together. We went from booth to booth and shared in their feasting. I shared the feast of one of these families and got terribly sick. The weather was hot. And all the time, the preparatory day was going on, the sun was going down, and one could see two small groups on horses; three horses and a banner, just riding around. They were representing each one of these clans that were going to race.

The next day was the race. We got up there at about 10:00 in the morning and we were told that the race was going to be at 11:00. 11:00 came, and no race. You begin to get a whole new sense of time up there, and

18. Merton spent two days at the Jicarilla Apache Reservation, attending their September festival (*Other Side of the Mountain*, 177–78).

you begin to realize that this race is going to happen when it's going to happen, and when it's ready to happen. Instead of looking at your watch, you begin to feel when it's going to happen.

The way you begin to feel it is that, at each end of the field, there is a booth with this banner over the booth. You realize [that] the guys are in this booth and each is getting painted up and receiving instructions from the medicine man. You'd hear a "war cry" coming out—very exciting to hear—and you got a sense that a great thing was about to happen. It was like the whole earth was giving up this cry.

Then they come out. One starts at this end, and one at the other end, and one group comes out, slowly shuffling, each with a drum, very slowly down the path. It takes about an hour to do the whole thing. And when they meet in the middle, they begin throwing dust at each other; insulting each other. There was this old lady on the white banner's side throwing dust all over the other guys, running around, and everybody was laughing at her. This happened for about 15 or 20 minutes. Then they go back. And when they go back, you see that these two groups are utterly different.

The white flag group had sweatshirts, dirty sneakers. Instead of painting themselves up, most of them had painted their sweatshirts with a little paint on their foreheads. The other group was entirely painted up. They had a real good paint job on and [were] in racing shorts. One had two huge feathers and a mirror in front of his forehead. He was fabulous.

Then the race begins. Two old guys from each team who aren't really in the race start plodding down the course side by side with no competition. They look funny; side by side, smiling, and everybody's laughing. And then two of the same type come back from the other end. When these two guys come out, all of a sudden, it's like there's an explosion, and out comes this guy with the mirror, running like you never saw. One of the sweatshirt guys is plodding along—way behind—and you can see right away what is going to happen. You never saw people run like this. In about four or five laps the ["real" painted group] were already two laps ahead of the others. And then it starts to even out. These others are gasping and heaving—almost falling down.

Then, in the middle of the race, when these people have maintained this two-lap lead, a little kid comes out on the "real" side, and he's just even with this other big guy—full grown—and it seems like the other guy will [win], but this little kid—he just ran like a rabbit. The whole race was like this. Obviously, this group won, and the impression at the end of it was that they won because they knew they were really Indians—and took pride in it. They knew who they were and where they were, and that this was very important. These other guys only had [their identity] "written" on their sports shirts. This was what the whole thing really meant. The others knew they were Apache Indians on *their* reservation. They knew their identity.

There were Pueblo people there, and Navajo—it was a very serious thing. You knew something was going on. It was a real manifestation of birth and rebirth, of growth, and of life.

Comment: Something like the Black Power movement?

Merton: I think it's connected. There's an Indian Power movement. The Indians are aware of [their] power. From this we can learn to be open and to listen to what is happening. Actually, after the race, something did happen. A Black man did get into it, and he was running down the field with a shirt with "U.S.A." written across his chest. Apparently, he was a college football player who married an Apache girl, and this was his part in the tribe.

If we are thinking of opening this House of Prayer thing, I think it would be good to open it to the Indians; to know what is happening among them. Because this is real. There is something really important being built up now; a lot is going on.

Would you like me to read some poems now? I'll just read them, and we can talk about them, if you feel like it. This is from the third issue [of *Monks Pond*]. This picture was taken at Needle Rock—a beautiful tree.[19]

Merton ends by reading from his novel,
My Argument with the Gestapo.[20]

19. The remainder of Dardenne's notes include rough transcriptions of several poems Merton read from *Monks Pond*, including works by Lexington, Kentucky, poet Christopher Meatyard ("Inner Light No. 1"), as well as selected poems from the notebooks of Paul Klee, Theodore Enslin ("Dismissed without a Kiss"), Alfred Starr Hamilton ("Black Widow Spider"), and Finnish poet Anselm Hollo. Merton also mentions the Persian psychoanalyst, Reza Arasteh, who contributed an essay to *Monks Pond* ("The Art of Rebirth").

20. *My Argument with the Gestapo: A Macaronic Journal* (Garden City, NY: Doubleday, 1969). Merton wrote the novel in the summer of 1941, prior to his entrance into the Trappist Order.

Chapter Eighteen

Prayer and Time

Day Three: Morning Session

I'd like to talk about prayer and the experience of time.[1] We tend to approach this question of prayer and time in terms of time *for* prayer. This is a modern dilemma. The idea of time *for* anything tends to be misleading. Of course, there's not much you can do about it if you're in an environment where you have to make time for things—if I only confine myself to making certain gaps in the day for prayer, it may be better than nothing. But you can't really have a life of prayer on that basis. You make a hole in the day in the morning and another hole in the day at night, and you fill in each one with prayer. This is alright, but if we're going to be living in a House of Prayer, or [living] the contemplative life, I think the real thing is some other kind of approach. Can we make that approach? I don't know, but I'll give you some history of the possibilities and what may be involved.

The early monastic fathers came up with the idea that the whole point of monastic life is that it is a life of constant prayer—you pray all the time. This is, in many ways, a shattering concept. Take, for example, the two conferences on "constant prayer" in Cassian's *Conferences*,[2] which

1. This conference was issued commercially as *The Search for Wholeness: "3. Time and Prayer"* (Rockville, MD: Now You Know Media, 2013).
2. Conferences 9 and 10; see John Cassian, *The Conferences*, trans. Boniface Ramsey (New York: Newman Press, 1997), 323–87. On the theme of "unceasing prayer," see Columba Stewart, *Cassian the Monk* (Oxford: Oxford University Press, 1998), 100–113. For Merton's commentaries on Conferences 9 and 10, see *Cassian and the Fathers*, 231–55, and *Pre-Benedictine Monasticism*, 62–72.

approach constant prayer from two ways. One [approach] shifts from the dimension of prayer to the dimension of "purity of heart," which means an inner freedom, and puts it in a totally different context. [The other approach] shifts to the idea of constantly using some Scriptural phrase [for example] "God, make haste to help me," or "God, come to my assistance."[3] You use that, and then you're praying constantly, whether you're thinking about it or not. That is what I want talk about.

We need to recognize that for us, time is to be experienced in a different way. To live a life of constant prayer is to live a life in which time is experienced differently. And [ask] what are the possibilities of a different experience of time? This seldom occurs to us. We tend to think that there is only one possibility: taught time—that's the only time that there is. Let's begin by facing the fact that there is no "time." Time is something purely constructed by us. Time is simply a projection of our own inner condition, and our own inner adjustment; of course, we do have an evolving life—but time isn't "out there." For example, if "God is dead," why don't we get busy on something more important like time being "dead."

If modern man is said to experience God as "dead"; that is to say, conceptual knowledge of God is to him often irrelevant, it should be very easy for him to also experience time as non-existent. But he can't. Our society does not experience conceptual ideas of God as relevant, but for us, time is immensely relevant, because everything is built around it. If you got rid of all the clocks, the whole thing would collapse instantly. If nobody told you what time it was, we'd manage for about a day; but then suppose all the clocks suddenly vanished, and everything else was the same, and you couldn't count time anymore—it would be a disaster for our society. Everything would stop. You couldn't catch any planes. You couldn't go anywhere. You couldn't do anything.

There's nothing wrong with this particular concept of time. It works fine. But what we should realize is that it's not the only way to experience time. This is, in fact, an alienated experience of time, which doesn't have to be the one by which you live. In other words, it should be possible to take all this in one stride, and to be there on time when the plane's going, but not necessarily to think that is the whole [concept] of time. What I want to talk about is this experience of time, and the possibilities of different ways of experiencing time.

---

3. Psalm 70:1; see Cassian, Conference 10 (*Conferences*, 379).

When I was about 14 years old, I spent the summer in a little English town in the south of England, in a place called Rye, which is a very curious, unusual little town built up on top of the hill; an ancient town that everything stopped about 300 years ago. Nevertheless, it was a real grooving place in the sixteenth century. It was one of the five English ports, called the "Cinque Ports," which were naval bases [used] as defense against the Dutch, and other people. Protecting them all around the south border, out by Dover and around the corner there. This town had been abandoned by the sea. The sea used to come to the foot of the hill that the town was built on—it was now five miles away; it's moved out, so the town is left high and dry. This town still has the atmosphere of the sixteenth century, and I lived in a house that belonged to an Elizabethan dramatist, a fellow called John Fletcher,[4] who was a famous contemporary of Shakespeare. It was right by the parish church, and on the church was one of those little sixteenth-century clocks, with what they call "quarter boys"—two little statues—and each one would hit the bell at the quarter hour. It was fascinating. You waited for this to come around, and they would "bong, bong" on the bell.

And in the house, was a great big old clock. Over the top of the clock were written two Latin words, *eheu fugaces.* I was learning Latin, and I couldn't figure out what on earth *eheu fugaces* meant. I looked in the [*Latin*] *Grammar* and I couldn't find it, [because] actually, it doesn't mean anything. It's part of an opening line of one of Horace's *Odes*.[5] When I looked this up, I found out what it was: "The years are fleeting away." And so, in this little house here, we were living in this atmosphere of the Renaissance experience of time—which is, to some extent, on the way to ours—an experience rooted in the classical Latin and Greek background, a "classical" sense of time.

It has two levels—I'm going to relate it in a minute with Proustian time; it is the time of Proust.[6] This is a different experience of time than we have, but it's an intermediary one. On the surface, this experience of time is definitely an experience of time getting away from you. "The

4. John Fletcher (1579–1625), born in Rye, England, was one of the most influential dramatists of his time, rivaling Shakespeare in popularity.

5. *Odes*, 2.14.

6. Marcel Proust (1871–1922), noted French novelist. The work in question is Proust's *In Search of Lost Time* (1913–1927), originally published in seven volumes.

years are fleeting": time is going by and each quarter hour on the clock reminds you that you've got that much less [time] to have fun. And not in a bad way. It's the idea that life is getting away from you, and you have not really lived it yet. It's a good, serious concept of time, and because it's on a two-fold level, you also have the sense that it is there to be lived; that it is not merely a linear flank time, there is also always under it, an ever-present reality of life to be lived. What these very sophisticated and beautiful people of the Renaissance lived was really this twofold consciousness. A very sophisticated consciousness of time going by, and it going by rather gracefully.

This is actually a transitional state between two great concepts of time: the Renaissance concept of time, which is still very much in our European heritage. It's in the old Cistercian concept of life. It is at the same time, cyclical and linear, so that this produces a very special kind of consciousness. For [Indigenous] people, there is really no "time" in our sense at all; [instead] everything is cyclical. It's recurring: [rather than] the years getting away from you; everything is coming back. The seasons come back; the great feasts come back, and in the end, you are gathered to your fathers. You are gathered to the ancestors where everything is really paramount. So that [the Indigenous worldview] is permeated by a complete permanence, in which there is a cyclical movement, [where] you are finally gathered into the permanence of the ancestors who are there all the time.

Mother Myriam: Time as a matrix in which we live.

[Indigenous] man doesn't reflect on [time], he's just in it—in this world of myth and rites; he's completely involved in it. He's not too conscious of himself as being separate from the world. For [Indigenous] man, the world is completely sacred; he's completely in it and he's not separate from it at all.[7] Man is not conscious of himself as standing back from all this. Later, [time] appears to get away from him, and then he [begins] to

---

7. Merton's dated interpretation of Indigenous concepts of time most likely stems from Lévy-Bruhl's notion of "*participation mystique*"; the influence of which is also prevalent in the work of C. G. Jung (e.g., *Psychological Types* [Princeton: Princeton University Press, 1971], para. 781). Both instances necessitate a de-colonial revaluation of this concept.

float out of [the world]. This leads more and more to the kind of modern consciousness which we have: this sense of being isolated and alone, and ready to be dropped off the bus at any moment; feeling that we might just fall into the void, and nobody would ever know that we were there in the first place. This is the other end of it.

Of course, this cyclical thing is very basic in our nature, even though we've got this other [sense of linear time]. The idea of recurrence is very profound in man. It's profound in the child. You tell a child a story, and he wants you immediately to tell the same story again. And then he comes back the next day, "Tell me the same one again." It isn't that he wants to hear a new story. He wants to have the pleasure of something that he is familiar with recurring; coming back. This is a very profound thing; it's very profound in music. The basis of music is a recurrence of something that you have been led to expect.

What was happening in the poetry that we were talking about yesterday, was that it plays on this basic thing, but contradicts it. Instead of fulfilling an expectation, it deceives an expectation and gives you something else. Basically, it presupposes that you're expecting something. This, of course, is very important for our real experience of time, and in this sense, Proust is a very spiritual work—it's [also] a very individualistic work. [Throughout] this long novel, he's just concerned with himself. But still, it's this long novel about all these people that he knew, and all these situations that he got into and got out of. It is a kind of contemplation—[at least] on a low level. It isn't a religious contemplation, but it has special value, because he is quite aware of what he's doing. He knows precisely what is happening.

There are several incidents in this—one of which I remember being very struck by the first time I ever read him. There were several incidents in which Proust was very conscious of time lapsing and going away, [and] has a contemplative breakthrough into a sense of *present-ness* in this lapse of time. These are "intuitions," breakthroughs, that give a contemplative sense of reality. Usually, it is a *"déjà vu"* thing. This is an ordinary psychological experience; we all get these, and it is related to our sense of time; to our sense of contemplation—if we let it. You get the sense, "I have been here before," or, "I have seen this before," or "this is something that has happened before." Proust works on this kind of thing. He describes everything in minute detail. That's why it's very difficult to read Proust.

You just go on and on and on. You've got to have unlimited time to read Proust! You don't do anything else; [you] just sit down and read for six months. I've never done that; I just read one or two of the first ones and that was the end of it. You can't follow through to the end.

In the first one, he's riding in a carriage and they're leaving a town on a winding road, out into the country. He's sitting in one of these little carriages where you sit looking backwards—which of course is very significant—and they're going away from this town, and sometimes the trees hide the town, and then the [trees] part and show the town, and the spires of the church in town, in different relationship, and then *bang*, he has this intuition—of *everything*—this intuition of "being." It's like the same sort of basic intuition of being that many children have; the experience when a child suddenly realizes that he *is*—not just a part of the whole thing, but he suddenly realizes, "I'm me," or suddenly realizes that things *are*, or he just says a word, and suddenly realizes that it has meaning. Proust is talking about this sense of *this-ness*, and *present-ness*, that comes from this particular kind of reflection.

This is a good, modern thing; but again, pre-supposes a certain leisure. You have to be able to take time, reflectively, in order to see something like this. The question is: is this still possible? When you read Proust, you get the feeling of a "tempo" that is pre-World War I, a whole different tempo of life. Is it possible for us? I certainly think it is, but on the other hand, the official time that we live by now is not so easy in that regard, because it is moving awfully fast. We do tend now to be much more alienated—although Proust is writing about alienation. He's discussing the problem of alienation, which was already great at the end of the nineteenth century—but we're much more so. We don't even have time to reflect that we're alienated. We have to keep moving, just to keep from disappearing in the void.

So, what is our experience of time? Very often, "tomorrow" tends to be a great long line of gaps that are going to have to be filled. The average person has an appointment for 10:00, and then, "11:00, where do I have to be," and "Who am I going to see at 12:00?" Things are already filled up on paper; then you're going to have to make the reality meet what you've got lined up on paper already. You are going to check off what you have already planned to do, or what you are already forced to do. This gets us back into what? It gets us back into what we were talking about yesterday;

namely, death. We tend to experience time as infinite indebtedness. This is the way to experience time that doesn't help the life of prayer. If I am totally indebted, so that the future is entirely mortgaged, and I'm going have to pay [it] off—[then] this week isn't a week of freedom. I'm going to have to pay off Monday, Tuesday, Wednesday, Thursday, or Friday, and Saturday, as debt. They're going to be exacted from me.

You know what's going to happen to me this week? A whole day is going to disappear. Once I pass the international date line. For me, there's no Wednesday this week [laughter]. I leave San Francisco on Tuesday. I reach Bangkok on Wednesday night. But really, Wednesday will have disappeared. It'll still be Tuesday night where I started; it will be Wednesday night where I've arrived.

So, the great problem for us, is in experiencing time as indebtedness. We're becoming prisoners of a system of indebtedness. We have to be free enough, so that we don't think of our work in this sense of infinite indebtedness. It gets back to the liberation and the resurrection by which Christ has made us free. We are not "debtors to the flesh," in Paul's expression.[8] For Paul, what "the flesh" is, is not just "disordered pleasures"; it's a principle of indebtedness. And the thing to do is to live in the flesh in such a way that one is not indebted to the flesh, but is freed in the Spirit that has no debt but to love one another. What we saw yesterday; the answer is love: breaking through this indebtedness by being freed by loving. For example, in the monastery, no work should be alienating, because it should all be justified as a work of love. If it isn't, it should be changed. It should be either love, or not done. And if there comes a point where there is so much work that it is no longer possible to love, then it should stop.

But normally, a person should never have to feel that in her work she's doing anything else but "money." If it costs something, okay, that's fine; that's part of love. It's not [necessarily] part of alienation. But if it costs too much, then the shoe is on the other foot. So, what everybody has to do is to keep the thing balanced, in such a way that it is always love, and that they all agree that it's always love. So, we can all agree that what we are really doing is really love; then that liberates us.

Think of all the words that we now have, which have the prefix "over": over-work, overstimulation, overreaction, overcompensation, overproduction,

8. Romans 8:12.

and finally, the prize-winner, overkill, which is the result of all the others. It's the fruit of all the others. If you push, you start with overwork, and you go on to overstimulation, and overreaction—those of us who have allergies are living overreactions [laughter]. This is what allergy is: you overreact to certain foods and certain pollens and dusts. You're too healthy! [laughter] An allergy is a luxury. I've got too many of them. But that's what it is—you overreact to things. But all these things come from this sense of indebtedness. Why does a child overcompensate on some things? Because he's insecure and feels that if he doesn't express more love than he needs to express, he's going to be abandoned. So, a sense of debt, a sense of insecurity, a sense of being suspended over the abyss. That is our problem.

Yet, our asceticism consists in being free from this illusion of debt. It's useless, for example, to give up some small pleasure—even if it's a perfectly good pleasure, and there's nothing the matter with it, and it isn't hurting you; it isn't doing you a bit of harm. What one has to give up, is not that, but this sense of indebtedness: a wrong indebtedness in the sense of being dominated by imaginary claims, which society itself creates. We have to be in society without being dominated by imaginary claims; so that we can give instead of just being pushed. I think that's the whole key.

Biblical time is totally different from this. Biblical time isn't cyclical. That might have sounded like "encyclical" [laughter]—but it's not that. It is not cyclical, and it's not purely linear, either. It is a little bit of both. The real character of Biblical time is summarized in expressions like, "the fullness of time," or with Mary, when it says, "Her time has come to bring forth her first-born child." The time to bring forth a first-born child is not exactly on the clock. It's approximate within a certain area of possibility. It is not 10:15 on January the 15ᵗʰ. It is a special fullness, which is arrived at in a secret way, and which depends on every different person. The idea of [time in] the Bible is this fullness, which is arrived at by the inclusion of all sorts of elements that we don't understand. A fullness of which we can see a little bit, and the rest we don't see. What we see has to take into account what we don't see, and all these factors have to build up to this fullness willed by God, which will happen at His time, which is a *kairos*. What we have to do is keep this openness always existing; if we can do [that], then the *kairos* becomes evident to us at the right time.

The problem of the Jewish people [in the Gospels] was not knowing that the time had come. The time had come and they didn't see it, because they were not open to the unseen elements of preparation, or even to the visible ones: they didn't see John the Baptist, for example. Even their religious preoccupations tended to blind them to God's time, so that the pagans [the Greek gentiles], who had no particular religious preoccupations or expectations were more open. In certain terms, it was better not to have any religious expectations, because then the whole thing could really break through like a thunderbolt. [The Greeks] were so unready, that they were ready.

That is the idea of time in the Bible: a fullness, which develops. We experience a little bit of it, but we also experience the fact that most of it is unknown. That, I would say, should be our experience of time, because that is the experience of prayer. Prayer experiences time as something that we know we can do something about, amidst a whole lot that we don't know, but which is nevertheless leading us in the way that we are called to go. We are called into this way of development and growth, which is not—I don't like to use the word "plan," because if you say, "God is planning things for us ahead of time," you've got a completely false notion of the will of God. We used to run into this so much in the past in the novitiate, with people coming to you and saying, "What is God's will about my vocation?" and having in the back of their minds the idea that God has a file on them; in it is "The Plan" for Joe Smith: "Enter Gethsemani on January 5th, 1958."

The whole idea is that somehow, you're supposed to guess this. And in order to guess right, you have to get a lot of other magic agencies at work. The chief magic agencies of this question are the novice master and the abbot [laughter], because of the inside line. They do this on a slot machine. They come to you and put a nickel in the slot, and expect the answer: "God's will is . . . " The trouble is, that's exactly what we used to do. I didn't use to do it, but others in our place used to do this. At any time of the day or night, you could go to the abbot at Gethsemani and say, "What is God's will about my vocation?" He [gets] on the telephone and then, "His will is that you should stay" [laughter]. The thing that we have to realize, is that God's will in a vocation, or anything else like that, is something that is utterly free—it's something that's decided by us. It's the same thing that the Muslims were saying about monastic life. "If you want to be a monk, go ahead and be a monk. And once you've chosen, then be a monk and follow it along." But in no sense does [God] have a secret decision lined up for you, and then if you guess wrong, you come to your judgment day, and God says, "Hah, you guessed wrong, because you didn't have a vocation!"

People are always worried about this in a very wrong way. But if we're going to live our lives [from a place of] prayer, what we should do is experience ourselves as free from this infinite indebtedness of every possible kind—liberated from debt. Advancing in answer to a call, which draws us to an organic growth to fullness, which we don't completely understand, and which we don't see, but which we obscurely tend to. And to realize that there is much more in it than we understand, that is being taken care of for us by God, while we don't know. And to be open to this, and to go along with it.

I think I could illustrate all this. I don't know if I did this routine before. Did I do the thing on Faulkner's *The Sound and the Fury* when I was here last time? I don't think I did. I can run briefly [through it]. This is a very interesting book on time. Time is really the center of *The Sound and the Fury*, which is Faulkner's first really great novel. [9] William Faulkner is an American novelist of the South; he died about 10 years ago, and is really a very important, bizarre kind of religious novelist in his own way. It's so unreligious that it's religious in a lot of respects; he has really religious themes, treated in ways that shake you.

The Sound and the Fury is a novel about an idiot, but it's also about the whole family that is around this idiot. There are 4 or 5 main figures, and he gives each section of the novel to one of these figures. The first section of the novel is narrated by the idiot himself; therefore, you experience everything as he experiences it. Then you get another character, who was a student at Harvard, and you experience everything as he experiences it. Then you get the villain, Jason Compson, and you experience everything as he experiences it. Finally, you get Faulkner's great saint, Dilsey, who is the [Black] cook for the family. You see the whole thing through her eyes, and how she sums it all up. The last thing in the book,

---

9. Merton offered a series of novitiate conferences on the work of William Faulkner (1897–1962) throughout January–March 1967. For an expanded version of the material included here, see the transcription of Merton's March 1967 conference, "Time and the Unburdening and the Recollection of the Lamb: The Easter Service in Faulkner's *The Sound and the Fury*," in *The Literary Essays of Thomas Merton*, 497–514.

is where Dilsey takes Benjy, the idiot, to her church on Easter Sunday. The sermon is preached and the Gospel of the Resurrection is proclaimed very beautifully; then Dilsey has this illumination in which she sees everything. She sees the whole. She says, "I've seen the beginning and the end." It wraps it all up.

The thing that distinguishes all these people, is their experience of time. They all experience time in completely different ways. The idiot experiences time as there's no past, present, or future. Everything is jammed together. This is one of the things that makes the book very confusing, because you start off, and you don't know that he's experiencing past things as present. It's Easter day, his 33rd birthday, and he is thinking back to his childhood, and his growth through life. Everything is all mixed up together. Things that happened 30 years ago are represented in a simultaneous "now."

Benjy is very simple. He's an idiot. And the great thing in his life, was that he loved his sister very much—she ran away—and he misses his sister, Caddy. Caddy is one of the great characters in the novel; she disappears and then in another novel you find that she's off in France, married to a Nazi general. She's a completely scandalous character. But this whole thing revolves around the one reality of his life, which is his love for his sister. Most of the time, you think she's there, but she isn't. He is thinking in the past—he remembers her climbing a tree—and it's all as if it were present. So, you get this sense of timelessness. He's submerged in everything. He hasn't really been drawn out of this completely undifferentiated experience of time and existence.

Quentin Compson, the one at Harvard, is about to commit suicide. His idea of time is completely different. He is utterly obsessed with time. The first thing that he does, is he takes his watch off the dresser. It's a day for an examination at Harvard, and he's supposed to get up early and go the examination. He hears this watch ticking on the dresser, and he takes it off the dresser, and puts it in the drawer, and shuts the drawer and goes back to sleep. But he can't. He's absolutely hung up on time; he hears every[10]—he hears the bells ringing, and he's wandering the campus—he's obsessed with time. He's looking at the river, the waters—he's going to throw himself in the river eventually. So, Faulkner makes a terribly strong

---

10. At this moment, a monastery rooster crows loudly.

point: how this man was helpless against time. He has become completely overwhelmed by time. Faulkner has a lot of psychology underlining this; he ties it in with Quentin's family background, etc.

Now Jason, who's the real villain, is in complete control of time[11]—clock time. He's sending telegrams all the time; he's arranging things all the time. Jason's part of the story is that he's embezzling [Caddy's] money from his niece. This is Caddy's daughter. Caddy is sending back money to this girl, and Jason is taking it and keeping it for himself, and she steals it. She has broken into the closet on Easter, ripped up the floorboards and found the money, and has gone—ran off with a man from the circus. Jason's part of the action is where he plans to catch them. He's calling up the sheriff, and he's calling up people down the road. They're in a train and he's in a car—it's all very well-mapped out—and they get away.

The final one is this saint, Dilsey. Her part opens when she starts cooking breakfast on Easter Sunday morning for all these characters. She comes out of the kitchen, and the clock in the kitchen strikes 11:00. And she says, "Ah, 8:00." So, she's cooking breakfast for all these people, and there's all this mixed-up stuff. One of the things that happens to Benjy is that, whenever he thinks of his sister, he starts bellowing. So, he starts roaring and bellowing in the middle of breakfast, and everybody is thrown into turmoil by this as it happens.[12]

Finally, Dilsey takes him off to church. They get to church, and this [Black] preacher from St. Louis comes down and starts his sermon. The whole Easter sermon is a fantastic thing.[13] Faulkner himself read this sermon on tape, and it's very beautiful. It's something you should read in church. It's a very good, religious text. It's a fabulous text for reading in the liturgy. But this preacher comes in, and starts out preaching like a white man in a suburb, and the congregation is all looming around and sighing, fanning themselves. Then all of a sudden, he stops—and there's a long pause. All of a sudden, he says, "I got the revelation of the Blood of the Lamb," and then he starts this beautiful narration of salvation history, with a lot of

---

11. Again, the rooster crows loudly.

12. For additional summary of the above characters and their relationship to time, see Merton's "Time and the Unburdening and the Recollection of the Lamb" (*The Literary Essays of Thomas Merton*, 500–504).

13. See Merton's "Time and the Unburdening and the Recollection of the Lamb" for extended passages and commentary on Faulkner's Easter sermon (*The Literary Essays of Thomas Merton*, 505–15).

elements that really aren't strictly Biblical, [for example] a beautiful thing about the heavenly Father looking down and seeing what they're doing to His Son and saying, "Oh, what a shame this is. Why are they doing that? I'm going to shut my door against all these people for doing things like that to My Son." A completely different aspect from our redemptive theology. The Father as a kind of Mother, with compassion for what's going on. Then the Son dies and the doors are open and we're all saved.

And Dilsey is sitting there with tears streaming down her cheeks. She can't speak; she's just wrapped in ecstasy over this thing, until somebody says, "Dilsey, what are you crying for? Stop that." [She says] "I've seen the beginning and the end." This is the real revelation of Biblical time—the time of the New Testament, the time of the Kingdom. Although she's absolutely in the middle of this madhouse, of these crazy people—this utterly wacky southern family—still, in her, the Kingdom is present; the realization of the Kingdom is present. And the realization that everything is all sown up anyway; that all this milling around doesn't matter. This is the real central thing. It comes through in a very impressive way. You'll have to get ahold of *The Sound and the Fury* and read this. A friend of mine, a Baptist minister, Will Campbell,[14] did a beautiful service of different readings, in which he read this particular thing.

This is this Southern Baptist [minister] in Nashville, who said, "The guys you've got to convert are the [Ku Klux] Klan." So, he goes over to the Klan and says, "You've got to be reconciled with your Black brothers." And the Klan people say, "Who is this nut?" But they accept him. He knows the head of the Klan in North Carolina, and he goes and visits them. He brings his guitar. He's got a real crazy routine that he sings, which is very funny. And he sings this to the Klan; it's like an autobiography of himself, his last will and testament. He was a friend of Faulkner's. The thing to do would be to get him to come [to Redwoods] and to play the guitar.

To conclude, it seems to me that this shows us the variety of experiences of time that are open to us. The thing that is very important for us in a House of Prayer, is to realize the importance of experiencing time in some other way than simply having to be catching trains or catching planes all the time. When you have to catch a plane, you've got to catch the plane. There's nothing wrong with that. But we should be living in

---

14. Will Davis Campbell (1924–2013). For his unpublished correspondence with Merton, see: http://merton.org/Research/Correspondence/y1.aspx?id=274.

a dimension where you don't have to feel dominated by that kind of thing. You don't have to be dominated by the timetable. One shouldn't be obsessed with this whole business, as if the whole meaning of life were contained in that.

To conclude, I'll read something from Gary Snyder recently talking about "primitive" time. This is about Zazen. He says, "I think there is a plausible theory that Zen and Taoism go back to the Stone Age." This is really the carrying forward of a most ancient type of mentality of man. And he says—whether it's true or not, it's interesting—"I have a hunch how, at the beginning of Zazen, and all yoga practices, hunting, agricultural magic, and agricultural life produced ritual. Look what happens when you switch over from hunting to agriculture." He's saying agriculture is ritualistic and hunting is Zen-ish. "It's a completely different exercise of the intelligence. The hunter has to learn *samadhi*." That is to say, this unified, ecstatic, apprehension of reality. "He has to practice identification with his quarry. As somebody said, the only way you can ever get into the mind of another creature is by wanting to make love to it or wanting to kill it. The two are very close. The hunter learns to know his quarry like a lover. 'Hunting magic' is, as an [American] Indian friend of mine explained, not going out and hunting the animal, but making the animal want to come to you to be killed. A real hunter goes out and he sings his song, and he picks his place, and then the deer comes and he shoots it. Anyone who has ever hunted knows that what you have to do, is still your mind and sit still. Hunters have been able to sit still for hours. They have to go off for weeks at a time sometimes. There is a whole practice of mind and body which belongs to the late paleolithic period."[15]

Of course, when you talk about hunting, you're not just talking about killing. These Kentucky hunters now, it's a barbarous thing. They just go out and shoot everything that moves, and with all kinds of armament. Kentucky hunters with these huge guns, they shoot a little squirrel, and by the time they get the squirrel, there's nothing left of it. But the primitive hunter really had this ecological sense that you never killed more than you needed. There was an understanding with the animal species. You made reparation to the deer; there was this respect. This whole respect thing that you were talking about is very paleolithic.

15. Graham, *Conversations*, 77–78.

Br. David: You always make atonement in the Paleolithic period. The hunter makes atonement before they would shoot.

Part of the Indian's prayer before hunting is, "I am very sorry to have to kill a deer, but we have to eat," as this deer may be his vision person. Then you just kill one. Not more than you would need; whereas, we went in and killed thousands and thousands of bison. Just eliminated all the bison because the Indians were eating them—to starve the Indians—killing a whole species of animal. When you talk about sin, that's the kind of thing that's sin. People don't realize what they're doing when they do something like this, but this is a real expression of it. It is a sin with grave effects. It's more like this *kairos* concept. The things that were done to living beings a hundred years ago, two hundred years ago, are having their effect. And one of the results is that we treat the people of Vietnam as though they were Indians and bison—and make no distinction.

One last thing. I've got a beautiful text from Rabindranath Tagore here, so I thought I'd read this. It's a short little bit of a poem. We'll end it off with that, and discuss this, or anything else. This is a good concept of time that sums it all up in a way. It's really a nice little prayer. It's a short poem, about a dozen lines:

> Accept me, Lord, accept me for this while.
> Let those orphaned days that passed without thee be forgotten.
> Only spread this little moment wide across thy lap, holding it under thy light.
> I have wandered in pursuit of voices that drew me, yet led me nowhere.
> Now let me sit in peace and listen to thy words in the soul of my silence.
> Do not turn away thy face from my heart's dark secrets, but burn them till they are alight with thy fire.[16]

We could do a long commentary on that one. Here is the idea of time; the idea of the present: "Accept me for this while," which assumes an acceptance of non-finality. "This while" is not final. It's going to turn into something else, but I don't know what it's going to turn into, and that's not my business. But "this while" is the while where I encounter God—now—

---

16. From "Crossing," originally published in 1918.

in the present, which is all that I have. The past, that Proust was looking for, [Tagore] says, forget it: "Let those orphaned days that passed without thee be forgotten." Forget them—not to go over them and over them and keep bringing them back. "Only spread this little moment wide across thy lap, holding it under thy light." It's a very beautiful expression of prayer in the present. "Spread this little moment wide across thy lap, holding it under thy light." And then, "I have wandered in pursuit of voices that drew me, yet led me nowhere." Of course, we do that. "Now let me sit in peace and listen to thy words in the soul of my silence." And, "Do not turn away thy face from my heart's dark secrets"—this is the acceptance of the negative and the rebellious in ourselves. "But burn them till they are alight with thy fire." Transforming everything in us. The good and the evil, until they are nothing but one fire, through the fire of His love. There are many beautiful things here, and [Sr.] Veronique asked for it, so I'm going to leave it with you.

Mother Myriam: She will very much enjoy that one.

I think you all will. I'll leave that with you. I'll leave some other books with you, too. Use them well. Give them back or not; we'll see—whatever happens.[17] Does anybody have anything to add or any questions?

Br. David: There are a few things that have come up recurrently. One is that of prayer and rest. Somebody asked yesterday, "Should it be a House of Prayer, or should it be a 'house of rest'?" The other [thing] was prayer and ritual. Prayer vs. "saying your prayers"; what's the relationship between those two? And then the whole problem of duality; this pluralism that we have. For some of us, it's a problem [now]; whereas, for all of us, it will be a problem sooner or later. To whom are you praying? Who is praying in you, and to whom? Maybe if you could pick up some of those themes?

I think the idea really should be unifying: prayer is what should unify all of these things. A House of Prayer should be a "house of unification." Yes?

---

17. A number of these volumes remain in the library at Redwoods Monastery; a few inscribed by Merton.

Fr. Ed: I was interested in the hunting sequence that you were expressing. It seems to me that [Indigenous] people really feel so profoundly one with the whole process of the earth, and of nature, and the sky, and the animal life, that even the hunting was a part of becoming more identified with the rhythm of the whole. I think the concept is expressed so beautifully that nobody possesses the earth but God.

Faulkner develops that in "The Bear," too, which is a beautiful story. Underlying "The Bear" is the question of the present problems in the South, and "The Bear" is situated at a time where the last wilderness in Mississippi is being destroyed. The lumber companies are coming in. At the end of the story, the lumber companies move in, and are just about to cut down all the trees in this wilderness area, where years before this boy had seen this great bear who lived in the wilderness, and had a quasi-mystical encounter. He left his watch and compass behind, and went in unarmed into this thickest part of the wilderness, and the bear showed himself, and then disappeared. Underlying this is a long section of an argument between two of these characters about the fact that their ancestors, their grandfather and father, had tried to possess this land—that they bought it and owned it. And that the Indians never owned it, and never wanted to own it. So, one of these characters refuses his inheritance. He won't own the land.

It's a very interesting monastic question. It's treated as a monastic question. And it ends with a repudiation of monasticism by Faulkner, because in this "vow of poverty" that this man makes, it is not really enough. It's just a gesture. He renounces his land, but wants to live on the land and work as a carpenter, which he does. In the Faulkner saga, all these same people keep reappearing through these same families. It's all about one county in Mississippi. You get to know all these people, book after book. In a later book[18]—[set] in the 1930s—this man reappears and he comes up against a painful racial situation. His nephew is living with a [Black] woman, but won't marry her. And he runs into this, and he's on the wrong side. Although his heart has been in the right place; nevertheless, he can't face this thing. He falls down, and she rebukes him in the end, and says, "Old man, don't you understand anything about love?"

---

18. "The Bear" and this second story, "Delta Autumn," appear in Faulkner's 1942 volume, *Go Down Moses*.

This is a very interesting treatment. This idea of owning the land, and the statement that the Indians didn't own anything. We have to recover this sense, too, with regard to space and community. To what extent can we regard ourselves as owning property, and should we [even] own property? This is a great problem that comes up today. That will be an aspect of the House of Prayer—as I see it. This idea that we all own land; that the U.S.A. belongs to Americans. And that we're it. We're the Americans. We might be in the majority, but what does that have to say about [those who were here first]?

Fr. Ed: The whole concept of what the life of prayer, the life of seeking prayer, would be; whether it is really something done, or something lived, or a way of being toward [others], and being with [others].

To what extent is this a problem for others? How do you experience this problem? What would you say it would be?

Br. David: For me, to pray to a God who is somewhere "out there," and we are all against Him, isolated [is problematic]. The God of Scripture, it is the Holy Spirit who is God Himself that is created in us. So, it is God who prays; God is praying us. This is something that bridges the gap between, for instance, Buddhist prayer or meditation, and Christian prayer. Unfortunately, neither the Buddhists nor the Christians know it, but that is something which I think is worth talking about. The "God-is-dead" problem is really the same problem as the God who is over there, over and against us, who is dead, and was never alive.

On this point, I'm basically a Hindu, since the Hindus have no problem on this. For the Hindus, both are equally true. You've got the undifferentiated Godhead, of whom there is no explanation for; for whom there is no word, and to whom you cannot pray. And you also have *Ishvara*, which is God manifesting himself in a person. Now Ramakrishna, for example, this great person from the nineteenth century in India, had both.[19] Like most

19. Ramakrishna Paramahamsa (1836–1886). See the edited and redacted, *The Gospel of Sri Ramakrishna*, trans. Swami Nikhilananda (New York: Ramakrishna-Vivekananda Center, 1942). For a critical reading, see Jeffrey J. Kripal, *Kali's Child: The Mystical and the Erotic in the Life and Teachings of Ramakrishna* (Chicago: University of Chicago Press, 1998).

of these bhakti people, instead of concentrating on the undifferentiated God, he concentrated on the *Ishvara*, which happened to be Kali, which is God manifest as woman. This is something I want to find out about in Calcutta, which is the center of [Kali worship].[20] The strange thing about this is God as the avenging and destructive woman, who is nevertheless, secretly, the loving and merciful Mother. This is something, because now we are in the Kali Yuga, according to these people—we're in the age of Kali, the age of a destructive femininity, under which is mercy.[21] This is the typical Asian thing that gets to be terribly complicated, but really, it's quite simple.

What Ramakrishna was evidently doing, is he also had other gurus who moved him towards Advaita [Vedanta], which is undifferentiated oneness between the supreme God and us. But he maintained this devotion to Kali all his life. How a person could be emotionally devoted to a destructive mother and see her as a loving mother—you've got to have some special character for that. It certainly does inspire Jungian integration.[22] But for them, there's no problem. The very act of praying, conscious prayer, does establish a dichotomy: here I am and here's God. The only thing I would say about that, is that there is no problem.

Br. David: Ramakrishna always said that this dualism in which you pray to God is the beginning stage. As you said yesterday, leave it to the people, don't take the props away from them, but that more perfect next step, or last step—

Now you have dualism. This is how [Ramakrishna] overcomes the dualism, because it's not a step from less perfect to more perfect. The less perfect

---

20. See Merton's poem, written during his stay in Calcutta, "Songs of Experience: India, One / Poem and Prayer to Golden Expensive Mother Oberoi" (*Other Side of the Mountain,* 268).

21. Resources on Kali and Shakta Tantrism are vast; for an introduction, see David Kingsley, *The Sword and the Flute: Kali and Krsna: Dark Visions of the Terrible and the Sublime in Hindu Mythology* (Berkeley: University of California Press, 1975), and June McDaniel, *Offering Flowers, Feeding Skulls: Popular Goddess Worship in West Bengal* (Oxford: Oxford University Press, 2004).

22. For a Jungian interpretation of Kali as archetype of the loving and "terrible" mother, see Erich Neumann, *The Great Mother* (Princeton: Princeton University Press, 1963), 150. See also David M. Odorisio, "James Hillman's Tantric *Sadhana*: An Introduction to 'Notes on the Meaning of Kali Symbolism,'" *Jung Journal* 12.4 (2018): 62–72.

is also the more perfect. You see what I mean? Instead of saying, "Devotion to *Ishvara* is for the lower grade, uninitiated, non-mystic, and then there's a higher mystical path"; they say, "No, the lower is the higher, and there's really no distinction." Of course, this is the kind of Asian messing with things that we can't stand. But that is their logic, and existentially, it's perfectly true. Existentially, there is no difference, except conceptually—if you want to make a conceptual division out of it. But existentially, in our relationship with God, it doesn't matter how you go about it, as long as it expresses a view of right relationship. You've got all these strange ways in which the dualism arises. So, you accept relationship as an unreal thing, but you don't distinguish it from the Other. In the relationship is the Real, which is beyond relationship. Why do we accept that? Because we start from our experience, our empirical angle, which is what we have. We experience ourselves as separate, isolated beings, and you can't deny that experience.

What they do, is they don't deny it, or say that there is something more perfect, or more special. They just say that in this, and simultaneous with it, is the Other, which is beyond relationship. And I think that's what they would do with this. To me, "God-is-dead," is no problem whatsoever. So what? It doesn't mean anything. It's just trying to say, "You can't do this. You mustn't play this kind of baseball." I can play any kind of baseball I want.

Mother Myriam: To me, there is a kind of false god there.

Yes, that is the problem. Of course, the real problem is: this god has to be dead, and it has to be made quite clear that he never was alive. We all agree on this, I'm sure. This is the god of the theodicy manual, who loves nobody but himself, and who can't love anybody but himself; he's always pressing buttons: "More glory for me." He created this big "glory machine" and he threw all these people in it. And a lot of them are going to be sinners, and, "Boy, will those sinners go to hell if they don't give me glory," and [then] press the button: "god is great."

Comment: And then we make this "constructed Jesus" the justification for our [religious] life.

From the practical, every day plane for most religious, Jesus functions as an "idol."

And that's he's supposed to be the reason for why we're here—but it's a myth.

This is something we definitely have to get purified of. All these little "idol"-type images that we have made of Jesus, and of Mary, and of God the Father. In so far as they are obstacles, then there is this dualism; then there is this problem. It doesn't mean to say that you've got to get rid of all of these symbols. The kind of conclusion that some people jump to then, is, "Okay, no Jesus, no Mary, and no God the Father. Get them all out, because they're obstacles." No. You just simply see them in a totally different way; or, you just get the whole picture in a much simpler way.

I think where the trouble comes in is, we've got a heritage of choices that have been made in favor of a "Jesus figure"—and not the real Lord. What has happened is that people have repeatedly chosen [this figure] against real people, against love. They've chosen "rightness" against love—that there is a correct statement about this image, and if you haven't got the correct statement, then *pow*. We have conducted wars on this basis, and we've killed people on this basis for so long, that now we are really stuck with an idolatrous concept, which is dreadful. There is a real problem if we are affected with this. This we have to look out for, because this has got into religious literature, and into religious practice. I think you're perfectly right.[23]

23. A discussion ensues here regarding working through the machinations of the "institutional Church." Merton ends the discussion with: "There may be a chain of major consequences [involved]. But you're not defending yourself; [you're] defending the truth. You may be destroyed in it, but if you're defending [the] truth, you're indestructible."

Chapter Nineteen

Closing Discussion

Politics and Prayer

Day Three: Morning Session

There is an opening question on the topic of "prayer and rest," specifically related to medieval monastic spirituality.

It sounds like something from *The Cloud of Unknowing*.[1] There is no dichotomy between prayer and rest, because prayer is our true rest. The thing about the life of prayer is, once one comes to a realization that it is in prayer that we truly rest, and [realizes that] rest is a natural desire of the human heart, then we naturally seek to rest—but in a deep sense. Not that you simply sit down and relax, but that, in prayer, you are completely centered in a source from which there is infinite sustenance, so you are completely sustained in abandonment to God; that is, in total renunciation of all concern and all sense of indebtedness, so that you are completely at God's disposal in perfect rest—even though it can [include] action. The real rest is not just personal relaxation, but the relinquishment of everything [that is not God's will].

Where labor comes in, is in opposing God. The real labor is in fighting reality; fighting "what is." Real rest is in surrendering to "what is," so that there's no longer any struggle, and you're no longer defending yourself

---

1. Fourteenth-century treatise on contemplative prayer, authored by an anonymous English Carthusian monk; see James Walsh, ed., *The Cloud of Unknowing* (Mahwah, NJ: Paulist Press, 1981). For a brief discussion of *The Cloud of Unknowing*, see *Mystics and Zen Masters*, 137–40; see also Merton's foreword to William Johnston, *The Mysticism of the Cloud of Unknowing: A Modern Interpretation* (New York: Desclée, 1967), ix–xiv.

against God's will. Where most of the work goes on, is in trying to adjust two things that can't be adjusted: a refusal and an acceptance.

Comment: It would be like the phrase in Scripture, "Be still and know I am God."[2]

Yes, and also in Isaiah. The idea is [to] rest in God, and let Him take care of things. Don't enter into an alliance with the Assyrians; that's the context. There's a war going on, and "in silence and in hope shall your rest be."[3] Resting in total trust in God. There's where the real rest is. It's not just a temporary, physical relaxation—maybe that too—but the real rest is, you don't have to labor anymore because it's all in God's hands. You may have to do a great deal, but it is in Him, with Him, and for Him. He is sweeping you along with Him. So, it's rest.

Rest and action are really the same in this particular way, but because of our condition they alternate. There's an expansion and a contraction. But I think we should ultimately see that they're the same: that we rest in action and act in rest. Once this is understood on a transcendent level, this brings everything into a unity. Of course, this requires a long period of maturing, and what the House of Prayer should do, or what any contemplative life should do, would be to promote this process of growth, so that people would just naturally grow into this. Not that somebody would say, "I ought to be praying and resting and acting at the same time. How do we do this? What am I going to do about it?" Because then you just go around in circles. What I'm supposed to do, is not to get an idea of prayer and rest, and then try to put them together. It's just to pray.

Comment: What about "unknowing"? Do we have to even "know" that we have a spiritual life?

Better not to. One of the first things I want you to do is have no spiritual life.

Br. David: You know what the Zen masters say? The great Zen master is asked about Zen and he says, "Zen? What's that?" But they always stress

---

2. Psalm 46:10.

3. Isaiah 30:15, "In returning and rest you shall be saved; in quietness and in trust shall be your strength."

that first you have to go through a period of training before you can say that. If you say that as a beginner, it's ridiculous.

You have to want a spiritual life, and yet not want to see yourself have one. Let life live and don't put any words between you and it.

Comment: That's where I think you have to be careful in taking some of these things that you are saying as a "master." You may say you can't be conscious of prayer; you're not praying. But an artist has to go through a great many exercises and steps before he becomes unconscious of his art, doesn't he? Before he becomes an artist.

I don't know about these "masters" that you're talking about.

You're so delightfully free, but you must have paid a price for that.

[dramatically] Oh, how I've suffered so [raucous laughter]. I'll wait and do a book on it: *My Life in Suffering.* "I was officially appointed 'Spiritual Master' at Redwoods Monastery on October 13th at 10:15 a.m." [laughter]. I can't remember what your real question was [laughter].

Don't we have to go through some exercising in order to get to a freedom of doing it unconsciously, or subconsciously?

You have to propose ends, and then you have to show that they're really not ends that you're going to achieve by a certain orderly process. What's necessary, is a person has to be constantly willing to do whatever he has to do, and yet be completely detached from any sense of attaining a goal, because it isn't like that. If you find yourself attaining some goal and then resting in it in the wrong way, you're deceiving yourself. What happens is that then you stop willing in the way that you should. You have to be constantly forging ahead with your will in the direction of this unknown that God is calling you towards. You have to constantly respond to God with a "yes," with a consent, and to keep willing.

Of course, you've got to remember, the whole trouble when they talk about prayer is that actually none of us—these last couple of days—have really said much about God doing any of the work. He does all the work. It's been mentioned; it comes up once in a while, but He guides us, and what happens at every step is that He tells us what to do in a very obscure kind of way. Most obscure. But if you are attentive to it, you know that you have to do something along this particular line: "Come this way." Sometimes it gets to be terribly obscure and you don't know anything about anything. Alright, then wait. And if He says, "Wait," then I will to wait, and I may have to wait 20 years. But if He says, "Wait," [then] wait.

The whole life of prayer should be seen as a constant response to God. But the trouble is, then there's a dual way of expressing it, and Br. David brought this up, that really there is no dualism. Well, there is, and there isn't. Really, there isn't; but at the same time, there is, because there is also an apparent duality between my empirical self and my deeper self. This is the fun way of saying it, because really, they're one. But you have to experience them as two for a long time before it suddenly occurs to you that they're really not two. You have to experience your own will as different from God's will for a long time, because, in a way, it is. But in the end, they have to become one. Yes, Portia?

Portia: You don't wage a campaign on God by setting out a method of prayer, but you keep thinking you're discovered in God. You, yourself, all the time.

Yes.

You're talking about dualism. I was thinking, at some point—perhaps when you're a child, actually, because you're most aware of the central reality of Earth—you experience God as a substance in which you see yourself as you were, as you will become, as you've been held in His mind and conceived. And the day comes that you make the circle back to this point. You work your way through the activities [of life], the search, and you come back to discovering where you always were. Where you were before it all begins. Discovered in God.[4]

Exactly. There's no need of a campaign, except that sometimes you do feel very alienated, and you do feel very distant. And in proportion as you

---

4. Portia might as well be quoting T.S. Eliot's famous line from "Little Gidding," "We shall not cease from exploration / And the end of all our exploring / Will be to arrive where we started / And know the place for the first time" (*Four Quartets* [New York: Harcourt, Brace, Jovanovich, 1943], 59).

experience yourself as distant, then you have to experience yourself as getting close, although you're really there all the time. But the problem is that we do live on different levels. There are no levels, but we live on different levels anyway. We experience life on these different levels. And there are more than two. There are plenty of levels of experience on which one can operate. One of the levels is a total absence of anything, a complete automatic existence. But at the same time, the other levels are always potentially present, and they can always break through. You can always suddenly feel yourself on two of them. But really, there aren't any levels.

This is where the dualism is, in that you know that you are in God, because you always were, and your essential substance was there from the beginning, and it still is, and yet, you are still you before this God. It comes and it goes, back and forth. So, you're stuck with the dualism, and yet you have the unity, too, so it's a two-way street.

Yes, and what the Buddhists do with this, is they teach you to experience [this]. You don't at all deny your empirical self, and you don't deny anything at all about reality; you don't deny matter. You simply accept it and realize that there is no problem about everything being there anyway. We have gone about it too much in this divisive way: to get to God, get rid of matter, or get rid of self, and you get rid of everything. And then, when you've got rid of everything you look around and find you've got to start all over again, because all you've got is a pure abstraction.

What we have to do is simply live. The great thing is [in] the living and the growing. And you live your whole life—your eating is part of it, and your recreation is part of it, and your work is part of it, and everything is part of it. You just live all these things, without distinguishing too much between one and the other, in such a way that you begin to experience your life as a whole, just as it is, without any flim-flam, and no trimmings, and no explanations. But you experience it as redeemed in Christ, and as totally belonging to God in Christ, and as offered, and as thanksgiving. Then, even though there may be all kinds of dualities on the surface, underlying [it] there's complete unity. And this unity is in Christ, and it is received as a gift. The only real effort of will that we have to make—until it becomes so easy that you don't have to make it anymore—is to be constantly oriented towards a thankful openness. But this does require an act of will. Unless a person is naturally dumped in it from childhood.

Take somebody like Benedict Joseph Labre,[5] who was completely hung up in duality, and who experienced himself as always totally excluded from God, wandering along, going on pilgrimage to these different churches. It didn't make any difference; he was completely united with God anyway. He entered Sept-Fonts, the Trappist monastery in France. I think the reason they threw him out of Sept-Fonts, was that he insisted on spending the free time carrying a life-sized cross around the back of the garden. "I have to carry my cross." He went to the Carthusians and I don't think they even let him in. He spent the rest of his life as a pilgrim mostly around the churches of Rome and sleeping at the Colosseum. This is fine; but it's not for me. It is, however, perfectly comprehensible in Hindu terms. For a Hindu, there would be no problem. [They would see him as] a completely committed Advaita Hindu [and] would absolutely understand why Benedict Joseph Labre would have to go on pilgrimage from church to church, and from saint to saint, and to the Holy House of Loretto.[6]

But this whole thing of failure and non-failure, which is the thing that St. Therese understood so well, that they're really two sides of the same thing. My failure is not really a failure, because it is also God's success. Here, you have an apparent duality which is fused in this sense of mercy. Existentially, you have an experience of mercy, and forensically, you've got this problem of fault and forgiveness, and something to be regulated, but it's already regulated. And you can see it on either level. But what one must do, is not to say, "You can only see it on this level." If I experience myself as separated and alienated, what I must do is not repudiate that experience, but see through it. What we're hung up on in the West, is saying, "This is the right way to do it. This is the authentic experience—this one." And then, everybody gathers around that one and celebrates it for a while, and then somebody comes along, "No, pardon me, this is the one." Then, there's a mad rush over there. This is where we create problems.

---

5. Benedict Joseph Labre (1748–1783), Tertiary Franciscan and patron saint of the homeless. Merton refers to Labre in *New Seeds of Contemplation*, 105.

6. Merton does not complete his analogy here, but perhaps the reason why Hindu culture would accept Labre is because of the special accord placed on wandering renunciants, or *sannyasins*, in the Indian context.

Br. David: And yet, the language in which all this is expressed[7] presents a growing problem for us, because it's not just a matter of, "In the end, God blessing His people, and giving them all milk and honey," but He's tramping the enemies in the dust and making smithereens out of them. What are we to do with these texts? We have outgrown them, I think.

I don't agree with that. [Remember that] Ramakrishna accepts Kali as this menacing figure, and in Hindu mythology, you've got these dreadful [deities], and the Tibetans have got all of this talk about drinking blood out of skulls.[8] It's horrible. But I think that our rejection of the punishing Psalms is overcompensation. We're afraid. We're so scared to admit hostility in ourselves. We are terrified of hostility, but we're full of it. And what you have to do is get it out. Not in the wrong way, but the Scottish Presbyterians used to have an absolute love for these. They picked their own Psalms every Sunday, and every Sunday their enemies were cracked open like walnuts, and everybody was delighted. But if we exclude this, there again is dualism. It is horrible. It is a mess. But it has to come in somewhere.

But you are more than right in many respects, because so many people, for so many generations, have used this for the wrong purpose. "Therefore, we can go out and cut up Muslims into little pieces. God will be delighted with us for doing this." It's a dangerous thing all right.

This whole theology of revolution[9]—[psychologically speaking]—on the one hand, you have to see it in the light of a fear of violence, and a fear of violent expression in the Psalms, and as an overcompensation around that. [Today] you're getting these nice, quiet kids that were non-violent up until two weeks ago, and have suddenly decided now that the thing is revolution. They don't know one end of a gun from another; they don't have a gun, and they're not even likely to get a gun. [Yet] they are going out to start a revolution against people that are armed to the teeth, and who want to kill people; who'd be delighted to kill revolutionaries. I think there's something psychologically wrong with this kind of approach.

7. Brother David's response follows an extended comment by Fr. Ed on the language of the Psalms and Prophets.

8. See, e.g., the iconography of certain wrathful deities in Vajrayana Tantric Buddhism.

9. This is in response to a comment about how contemporary young people react to such violent biblical language.

Certainly, if I were a South American, I would be on the side of the revolutionaries, and there's no problem about that. I think the revolution in South America is justified, provided that it isn't going to be doomed to failure from the start. That's one of the things you have to take into account. But the possibility of a successful revolution in South America is something that people should envisage, because it may be the only way in which thousands of people can be prevented from starving to death. [However] if it's just somebody's myth, and if it's going to be ultimately self-destructive—because that's what I'm afraid they're all doing. They're going to get themselves destroyed for no good reason. Maybe I'm totally wrong, but it seems to me that this whole thing tends to be a masochistic myth, ultimately. This may be much too severe a judgment and totally wrong, but from some of the kids I know, that's the impression I get, because they are good kids, and they're real nice, gentle people. And they're the last ones in the world that are going to run an effective revolution. The first thing that they're doing is going [around] telling everybody about it [laughter].

Comment: Father, a while ago, when you said the great thing is to live your whole life without distinguishing too much one thing or not, and to experience it as a wholeness, and as redeemed in Christ, and that is the gift, and you do that in thankful openness. Is that another expression of what you would say is living God's will?

Sure. In the New Testament, there's so many texts saying, "be thankful," and "praise God all the time." Every [Pauline] Epistle ends with this kind of summing everything up in, "Just praise God. Thank Him that you are redeemed, and that you are in Christ."

Would you put the negative element that we discussed in that?

Sure. Thank God that we're sinners, and that we're violent, and that we're a mess, and that it doesn't matter.

And where we make mistakes and take the consequences . . .

Sure. We can thank God already for the hard times that we're bound to go through. We are going to go through a tough time. Things are going to be messed up, and rough, and bloody, but if we accept our location in Christ, and go through it in Christ, His good will come out of it; His kingdom will come out of it. Let's hope that the little people will come out of it with more hope.

How is this going to be? I don't know. Since the 1930s, I went sour on revolution in America anyway, because I saw what a complete mess the revolutionaries of that time made out of it by not really understanding at all what was going on. You've got to remember that those of us who were involved in this kind of thing in the '30s experienced these terrific traumatic sellouts that took place, especially when Stalin lined up with Hitler. Everybody thought that Russia stood for revolution and rooted for the underdog, and was going to help people. And then, we suddenly saw that the whole thing was completely opportunistic, and that they would sell anybody down the river immediately. For example, Stalin was selling guns to Italy, when Italy was fighting Ethiopia, and then condemning the Ethiopian War.

All of a sudden, this started coming through to us. We began to see what all this stuff really involved. And since that time, I'm very leery about any kind of thought about revolution, because it may look very nice—Che Guevara, very heroic, very nice, very romantic—but behind it, you always get some other power structure coming along that's going to pull some more iniquitous deal. So, I ended up always on the side of somebody like Camus, who's condemned by everybody, because he's in the middle, and he's saying I refuse to be either on the side of the victims, or the executioners. And when everybody said, "What side are you on?" he said, "I'm in the middle." And then something comes up like the Algerian conflict, and when he drew on his own experience as an Algerian to assess the thing, he assessed it in such a subtle way that nobody agreed with him, except a few Algerians.[10]

This is [what] we're up against today. I think all of us, who are more or less bound to be in the middle anyway, have to be careful about how we judge these situations. But we do have to line up, where lining up is easy

---

10. See Camus' essay, "Neither Victims nor Executioners," in Peter Meyer, ed., *The Pacifist Conscience* (New York: Holt, Rinehart & Winston, 1966), 423–39; quoted by Merton in *The Literary Essays of Thomas Merton*, ed. Patrick Hart (New York: New Directions, 1981), 238, 246.

and obvious. There are certain things that there should be no question about, for example, the race issue, the Vietnam War issue. I don't see that there's any argument. These things, we should all be very vocal about, at least expressing where we stand. But as to imagining that we can run a revolution—are the Sisters going to run a revolution in this country?

Comment: If you take your position, then we're both part of the problem and part of the solution; where we helped to cause it, but we can also help to correct it. In the middle position, in a renewal or transition time, we're hanging on to what's worthwhile from the past, while trying to account [for the future].

When you have revolutionary activity going on, you've got this activity, and you don't always know what it is. I assume that if these people are serious, which they definitely are, there is a pretty well-reasoned policy and tactic being carried out. This doesn't get through to us, and there's no reason why it should. But what gets through to us is that kind of message [that you are either part of the problem or part of the solution], which is what happens when there's a revolution going on. They're way ahead of you; you don't know what they're doing. They're out here somewhere. And what they're doing with regard to us is to get our sympathy; get us on their side in a general, political way.

[Therefore] what one has to have is some kind of knowledge of this whole hard-headed political thing that's going on, and to understand what it is, and evaluate the messages that come out to us from it. That is our real obligation. For that, we need much more information than we've got, and we need the kind of information that is rather hard to get, but we need to know what the score is. I would say this is important for all religious communities: to know the real score; because if you don't, you're constantly being used by somebody against your own intentions. And this is part of the game.

Br. David: How can we learn "the real score"?

You have to be in contact with people that know; somebody like ["Ping"] Ferry, who can keep you absolutely posted. He's right at the heart of this; because they get all these revolutionaries coming from universities in Europe, and they are very well-informed, and they know just what these kids are thinking. These kids came there. One of them ended up by saying, "What are you people going to do for the revolution." And obviously the Center [for the Study of Democratic Institutions] is not going to do anything.

It's getting close to time for Mass. This revolution topic is pretty much off the agenda, but it is important to know. Yes?

Comment: Father, this is again saying what I said the other day, but it's come up a few times. We were to go to Selma to march, and this opened up a question: you want to go to Selma because the race question is very, very pertinent, and you see what side you have to stay on, be on. But then, the realization came to me: what about all the other prejudices we have? And then, a whole world opened up, in which I realized, you just can't answer all these things. You're just one person. And perhaps, maybe we're even escaping larger issues, unless each one of us really is in peace in God. And that the only answer to all of these terribly big problems, is for each man to stand before God, and that this can only come, or the way it will come, is in prayer.

For a lot of people, Selma was a *kairos* moment and a decisive thing. [It informed] many people, [and] really crystallized a lot of things [regarding racism, prejudice, and human rights]. It [allowed many Christians to recognize] this *kairos* at that moment for them.

Where politics [comes in] when you're religious or contemplative, is that it should not be the kind of [activism] that leads into a whole chain reaction of commitments, in which you get more and more involved in the sticky part of politics—where you begin to be used by other people without knowing it. This is where we need information, and have to make the right kind of judgment. There is a definite Christian need in this century for a person to have come out, fair and square, on these issues, which really involve the Kingdom of God: race, war, and all this stuff—they definitely are religious questions. And a person has to have arrived at a formal Christian position and given witness to it in some way or other, somehow—even if it's just signing something.

But once you've done that, you have to also then consider another question. You may have a charismatic political vocation, but very few people have this, and the thing not to be, is an innocent and rather naïve person, who is used by conflicting forces. As Sisters, you are fair game for this. I'm not saying it's good or bad to get arrested, but get arrested if you think you should get arrested—and want to—but don't [get arrested], if you don't [think you should]. And don't get arrested because somebody else wants you to get arrested. That's the whole thing. In other words, keep your freedom, because you lose your value if you don't act as a free and independent witness.

When you talk of political judgments, you talk of a very particular, practical judgment. And we have to distinguish between a strictly political judgment, which is a practical thing in a special kind of a sphere, [with] a special kind of information. It may also have religious implications, but this is something that we have to know about. You have to have the information and the capacity to judge. That requires a great deal of political prudence, but this is another question; nevertheless, it's terribly important—and right now, it's crucial—because if you're going to have people running what they claim to be a Christian revolution, everybody's going to be involved in it. It could be the biggest mess that you ever saw, or it could be something really meaningful. But we have to judge.

I suppose it's about time [to end]. Thank you for everything. Let's go to church and thank the Lord for everything He's given us. I think it's been very fruitful; for me, anyway. I'm thankful for all of us.

Merton concludes with the following prayer:

Thank you, O Lord, for all these gifts You've given us during these few days. We realize more and more how much Your action and Your love is the most important thing. Help us to be open to that love, and open to one another, and to all whom You send to us. Help us to be men and women of prayer, without worrying about it, or knowing it, or wanting to see it.
Thank you, Father. Amen.

Bear Harbor, Pacific Coast, Sinkyone Wilderness

Bear Harbor, Creek and Beach, Sinkyone Wilderness

Bear Harbor, Jones House and Ranch, Sinkyone Wilderness

View from Old Logging Road between Bear Harbor and Needle Rock, Sinkyone Wilderness

Photographs by Thomas Merton used with permission of the Merton Legacy Trust and Thomas Merton Center at Bellarmine University

Part II

THE LETTERS

Saints Peter and Paul Church, Filbert Street, San Francisco
*Photograph by Thomas Merton used with permission of the Merton Legacy Trust and
Thomas Merton Center at Bellarmine University*

Chapter Twenty

The Thomas Merton-Myriam Dardenne Correspondence

December 12, 1962[1]

My Dear Mother Myriam:

I hope you are by now well settled in your new home. I have not heard any news from you or about you, but I presume you are well and that all the Sisters are very happy and busy, and that the Redwoods have lived up fully to your expectations.

The purpose of this letter is to enclose a copy of another letter I have just written to Graham Carey, the editor of a magazine called "Good Work" who will be interested in your projects. I hope he will write to you, and put you in touch with people who will be interested in your vestments. As time goes on, I will write to other people, but I presume there is no need for a furious rush right away. Let me know if there is anything you specially need, or if there are any questions I can answer.

Another letter I enclose is from a nun in a sanatorium (as nurse, not as patient) in Belgium. I presume you would not want to take her, though she might enter at Nazareth. I leave that to you. I know nothing about her of course.

It is quite cold here and there is snow on the ground. Christmas is near. It is a real Advent, cold and silent. Next week the novices will get Christmas trees, not too many I hope, and decorate the novitiate for the feast.

---

1. *School of Charity*, 159.

Are you making vestments yet? I am interested to know. I might perhaps ask Father Abbot if we could get a set from you for the novitiate chapel. Our white set is very shabby and does not fit properly.

We have not forgotten the joy of your visit with us. It was a grace to see in you the simplicity and good sense of the Cistercian tradition, so to speak incarnate. There is a great deal of talk about monastic tradition and monastic spirituality, but actually the reality of people who live the monastic life in simplicity is much more impressive than words about it. We do not have to have too many splendid programs and doctrines if we seek and find the Lord, and this we do not in ideals only but in the realities of life. Still, I am sure that one reason why you are all functioning well is that you have approached the life intelligently and with a little knowledge. Pray that we may do the same.

I will remember you and the Sisters at Mass during these last days of Advent. May the Lord bless you all at Christmas, and make your first Christmas in the new world a very happy one, filled with His light and His presence. I am sure that though everything is fine there, you will sometimes be lonely for Europe. However, the monastic life is intended to increase in us the sense of exile which is one of the basic realities of our life on earth, and it is a grace to feel this.

Best wishes to you all, and also to Fr. Roger. Pray for me please, and for the novices, who will all be praying for your community.

Most cordially and fraternally in Christ,

Fr. M. Louis

An Excerpt from Merton's Letter to Graham Carey:

December 12, 1962[2]

I think you will be interested in a foundation of Cistercian nuns that has been made out in California. They are from Belgium, and very superior types, with good sense and good taste in plenty. They intend to make vestments and do other things like that for a living, and the principles on which they intend to work are very sound. They are not going to strive for facile effects or for publicity, because they want to maintain a high level. They do not want to have to condescend to sham and compromise which would be inevitable in the event they got mixed up in commercialism.

Hence, they will need the support of discerning people and so I refer them to you. I do not know how well established they are as yet, but they will soon want to be in contact with people who will be interested in their work, and perhaps if you yourself go out that way, or if you know of anyone significant there who might drop in on them and get acquainted with them, that would be the obvious start. When they have something to show you, I think no more explanations will be needed.

January 2, 1963[3]

My Reverend Mother,

Thank you for your good letter. You have undoubtedly received three boxes of books which I sent you several days ago. Most of them are worth very little, but in the end there ought to be some which you will find useful. The others you can throw out. We have cleaned the house a bit to combine the two novitiates into one. Pray for us. I am happy to have the [lay] brothers together with the choir novices, and I believe it will be very important for everyone. It will be a blessing. And for me too.

---

2. *School of Charity*, 159–60.
3. Previously unpublished; original in French (translated by Michele Lamarche).

The surface of life is simple. The deeper aspects are too, in a sense. But all the same there is a sort of solitude, of exile, of confusion, which are painful. Especially in the depth of the soul. Sometimes I am very troubled by what is happening in the world around us, and, of course within our own selves too. One needs to be optimistic, but not naïve. This is very serious. The people around us live in great illusions, but they don't believe in them all that much. The great danger is a kind of nihilism and desperation, which hasn't yet erupted except among some of the youth.

I haven't yet done much to attract friends for you. Tell me if you have begun to make vestments for mass. And, I repeat, I would very much like to have a white vestment for the novitiate chapel. I haven't yet requested it of Dom James[4] but I believe he will permit it.

Thank you for your card. The four names of the <u>entire</u> community make things seem, after all, a bit desolate: like four people in a life raft in the middle of the ocean. But I know that you are very happy in the Lord, and full of the joy which only the Holy Spirit can give you. I bless you with all my friendship. Write to me all you want, and it goes without saying that you can mark the letter "conscience matter" if you wish.

I remain united to you in the Holy Spirit

Fr. M. Louis

March 6, 1965[5]

Dear Mother Myriam:

I received your letter the other day, and certainly there is nothing I would like better than to come to Redwoods and have a talk with you. A couple of years ago I asked permission to come out there for a rest, but naturally this was refused. Dom James certainly may have good reasons for not letting anyone go from here to preach a retreat. But at the same time, he is extraordinarily strict in the matter of traveling, and with no

---

4. James Fox, OCSO (1896–1987), Abbot of Our Lady of Gethsemani from 1948 to 1967.
5. *School of Charity*, 267–68.

one is he more strict than with me. So, by now I believe it is well known in the Order that he even refused to let me attend a meeting of novice masters unless the meeting was held here. This seems to me to be somewhat extreme, but after all one has to expect such things.

Since probably we are in about the same position with regard to travelling, and since perhaps it might be even easier for you than for me to get permission to travel, why not arrange to come here some time, if you can? Are there any more General Chapters coming, or any other occasions which would bring you in this direction? I think that if you put this matter before Dom Ignace[6] he <u>might</u> consider it, but I cannot offer much hope. What I want to say is that I would certainly be delighted to help you in any way I could, and it is up to you to find a way.

Actually, I have had little or no news of Redwoods since you founded it and I have little idea of how things might be going. How are you getting along with the American mentality??? This is a funny country, in many ways exasperating, yet I think one has to be thankful that there is as much good in it as there is. Generally, one has very little trouble with them, at least as novices. The big problems all center around their identity, I think. Once they are convinced that they are real, and that they don't have to do something at every minute to prove it to themselves, they settle down and are quite happy, except for those who must inevitably devise new plans for rebuilding everything, reforming everything and inventing five thousand new schemes for putting the Church at last in order. I find the naïve approach to these things a bit irritating at times, because in reality it seems to me that the problems of the Church and of our Order are quite serious and profound. The chief problem is that of freedom of the spirit, and allowing the Christian to develop and grow, rather than keeping him in a straightjacket forever. On the other hand, of course, so many people <u>desire</u> control and though they do not even admit this, they fear freedom and want to be told what to do all the time, provided that they can sometimes have the pleasure of resisting and attracting the attention of authority. And of criticizing others who do not absolutely conform.

I do not envy you your task as Superior, and I do think that people ought to let you have the help you desire, not from me especially, but

---

6. Ignace Gillet, OCSO (1901–1997), Abbot General of the Cistercian Order from 1964 to 1974.

from all kinds of good people. Does Dom Leclercq[7] get out there? You should work on Dom Eusebius[8] to see that a lot of good people come to your place and talk to the nuns.

For my part, I ask your prayers. It looks as if we are really going to develop an eremitical project. I am already much more in the hermitage since last fall and this is excellent. At least I find it so. I sleep here, and am learning to cook also. It is a good thing I like rice.

My best wishes and blessings to the Sisters, and to you above all. Do not hesitate to write if I can be of any use to you. I will try to remember to send you some things you may not have received. God bless your community: have courage and the Lord will provide such help as you may need.

Yours in the charity of Christ

March 12, 1968[9]

Dear Mother Myriam:

I am happy to say that with the improved situation here I have been able to obtain permission to come out and see you and spend some time with you in discussing our common aspirations and problems in the contemplative life. However, it will not be possible right away. I suggest that the best time might be in the middle of June, or after that. If the 17th of June is a good date, I could fly out then and spend six or seven days with you—or whatever you like. If you cannot have me there at that time, will you please suggest other dates after that. I could also come earlier, for instance about May 10th, but as I have a lot of work to finish, I think it would be better to put the trip off until later.

---

7. Jean Leclercq, OSB (1911–1993), influential scholar of medieval monasticism and regular correspondent and occasional visitor with Merton. Their correspondence is published as *Survival or Prophecy? The Letters of Thomas Merton and Jean Leclercq*, ed. Patrick Hart (New York: Farrar, Straus and Giroux, 2002).

8. Eusebius Wagner, OCSO, first Abbot of the Abbey of New Clairvaux in Vina, California, from 1959 to 1968.

9. *School of Charity*, 370.

Please let me know if June 17ᵗʰ is all right, and also give me some idea of some of the things you would like to discuss. For my own part, as I have been doing some work on Zen and Sufism, I think it might be useful to include some talks on them.

Needless to say, I hope to profit a little by the solitude and quiet of the Redwoods to make a quasi-retreat myself, while at the same time sharing whatever I can with you.

Let us hope that this will work out for the best interests of all. I look forward to hearing from you.

With cordial regards, in Christ,

Thomas Merton

March 19, 1968

Dear Father Louis:

Thank you for coming! The only problem is the question of dates. The reunion of Abbesses OCSO will take place in Citeaux from June 5 till June 16, but we are told that the meeting might be prolonged according to circumstances. Even if I am convinced that our discussions here on Zen, Sufism and the deep Christian monastic aspirations will be more useful than our meeting in France, I believe I should be present at the latter.

I will simply mention which dates might be best for us, with the agreement that if they do not fit you, we will make an effort to adjust ourselves to you.

From now on till April 8.

From April 28-29 till May 10.

After August 14 or even better after September 1.

Six or seven days are all right, whatever you will be able to give us. Also, you might stay longer, if your Abbot agrees, to enjoy the quiet as long as you wish. Six miles from here, the contrast between the Pacific Ocean and the rough Northern California vegetation is breath-taking. And most often the solitude is complete.

Several of us are interested in Zen. In any "approaches" to prayer, also, the media of contemplation, the nature of monasticism. We do not expect formal lectures; but we better leave you the leading.

Thank you again for coming. Gratefully, in Christ,

Myriam Dardenne
OCSO

❖   ❖   ❖

March 22, 1968[10]

Dear Mother Myriam:

Many thanks for your letter which came today. Strangely enough I am still not able to fit a full week into the periods you have named (at least the ones this spring which are best).

I could get away here on May 6th, or the evening of May 5th and work with you from May 7th on through the 10th or longer if you can arrange it. I'd very much like to stay with you or nearby in the woods or by the ocean for an extra day or two.

Hence, I propose that I fly out on the 6th of May and return the 14th or 15th. If I can get permission, I'll also try to stop off, on the way back, at Christ of the Desert monastery in New Mexico, where they have asked me to visit. I'll have to clear that first with Fr. Abbot.

Would you arrange for me to have a ticket from Louisville to the best airport for you on May 6th? The rest can be fixed up later when we know more about it.

I look forward with much anticipation to being with you, and will have lots of material to talk about with you. I'll send some recent articles we can also discuss. Pray that all may go well.

With cordial regards,
in the Lord,

Fr. Louis

❖   ❖   ❖

10. Previously unpublished.

March 29, 1968

Dear Father Louis,

Mother Myriam asked me to look into the flight possibilities for your Westbound trip, and here is the information obtained—considering that you would leave Louisville either on May 5ᵗʰ in the evening or on May 6ᵗʰ in the morning:

Louisville Lv	6:25pm	8:30am	(Delta, fl. 356)
Chicago Ar	6:41pm	8:30am	
Chicago Lv	8:25pm	9:55am	(United, fl. 123)
San Francisco A	10:45pm	12:10pm	
San Francisco L	7:30am	2:05pm	(Pacific, fl. 42)
Eureka	9:21am	2:55pm	

The first schedule—leaving in the evening—is rather impractical because of the long overlay in San Francisco and the prop flight SFO–Eureka . . . . May we therefore suggest, Father, that you take the 8:30am flight on May the 6ᵗʰ and that we meet you at Eureka airport at 2:55pm? The monastery is a 2:30 hrs. drive from there. Perhaps we could propose that unless we hear from you during the next week, we make reservations for you (leaving the return flight 'open') and send the tickets on to you from here . . .

All are looking forward to having you with us for a few days.

Gratefully,

Sr. Cecilia[11]
secretary

11. On Ascension Thursday 1968 (May 23), Merton wrote to Sr. Cecilia: "As I did not use the tickets between Albuquerque and Santa Fe either way, I am returning them so that you can get a refund. The trip back went well, and I had three good days at Christ in the Desert. The arid land of New Mexico is impressive but I must say I prefer Redwoods. I miss the community and the Pacific, and hope to get back. . . . Once again, I am most grateful for the hospitality shown me there. The days spent at Redwoods were a real joy for me. Also the care taken of me resulted in my putting on a few pounds!" (*School of Charity*, 381).

April 20, 1968[12]

Dear Mother Myriam:

At last, I think I am able to make more or less definite plans for the rest of my trip. I shall be able to accept the invitation to the Monastery of Christ of the Desert in New Mexico. So, I think it would be best if I went there, flying from San Francisco to Santa Fe on May 15th, the most convenient daytime flight. The drive to the monastery is several hours, as it is far away in the mountains. Then I will plan to fly from Santa Fe to Louisville on May 18th. Is that all right? I understand though that sometimes a change of date, for a weekend for instance, can affect a notable saving in the price of the ticket. If something like that would be convenient . . . for instance if it would be better for me to wait until Sunday 19th or Monday 20th for the Louisville flight, that would be possible.

In any event I hope to fly from Louisville to San Francisco and Eureka as suggested on May 6th and to Santa Fe on the 15th—with the hope of maybe a day of silence and retreat in the woods out there along the way.

I am looking forward very much to our meeting.

With warm regards, in the Lord,

Thomas Merton

April 28, 1968[13]

Dear Mother Myriam,

In just a week I hope to be with you. So now I am beginning to think a bit about what we might do. I intend to come prepared only in the sense of having a general line of thought to pursue: do not expect formal lectures or still less "sermons" (God forbid!)

What I'd like to do would be to have a couple of good sessions each day, mainly dialogue, seminar, or what you will. The subject I'd like to pursue, in a general way, is "the modern religious consciousness"—which

---

12. Previously unpublished.
13. *School of Charity*, 378–79.

means wondering if such a thing exists, or can exist, and if so what kind of shapes does it take on? This would be against the traditional backgrounds of religious consciousness in Zen, Sufism, the twelfth-century Cistercians, St. Benedict, Desert Fathers, etc., etc. In other words, I am coming not with answers but with questions, and I just hope the questions won't be too disturbing. But I really think it is imperative that we monks and nuns devote ourselves to some search in this area which is ours to explore. We cannot go on living by foregone conclusions.

In the context of these discussions, there will probably be plenty of room to take up the current practical questions of renewal, etc., but I wonder if already a lot of these questions have not reached an impasse, for lack of perspective, insight, depth, background, etc. Probably this is not true among you there, because you have background. But many American communities, it seems to me, have no background, no orientation, no perspective, and are just lost in the bushes trying to find themselves because they are not aware that anyone ever existed before them.

Well, pray that we may all have a fine profitable time, a real "happening."

One practical and mundane detail: I am furiously allergic to milk products and have for years been on a diet excluding them. Eggs and fish are all right. Don't bother too much about it: it's just that I don't live on milk and cheese as a good Cistercian should.

My very best to all of you,
in Christ,

Tom Merton

May 20, 1968[14]

Dear Sisters,

I am just leaving here to take the plane for Kentucky. This is a very isolated place in the mountains, in country full of traces of the Indians.

---

14. Handwritten from the Monastery of Christ in the Desert, Abiquiu, New Mexico (*School of Charity*, 380).

And many Indians around too. I have most happy memories of the Red-woods and of my stay with you—it is the best place of all, and I can find nowhere to compare with the solitude on the Pacific shore. I certainly hope I will be back with you some time. Thanks for your hospitality. I keep you in my prayers and will send some book and articles when I get to Kentucky. May God bless you and increase your love, and bring you always closer to Him. In His Spirit,

Tom

❖ ❖ ❖

June 29, 1968[15]

Dear Myriam:

Are you back alive? Prison? Bread and water? I have often thought much about you and prayed for you. How was the Chapter? Bearable? I hope some good came from it in some way.

I have taken the liberty of thinking and asking about a couple of things that might possibly be useful as sources of income. For one, the Georgia monks do well with stained glass. It requires very little capital and one or two are all they need to do the work. They could explain more about it and show you what to do. Frs. Methodius and Anselm at Conyers are the ones involved in this work.

Second—this is a bit worse—but I only suggest it as a vague possibility. You know that I am constantly being invited to that meeting in Monroe, Michigan.[16] I can't go. But I thought maybe if they were so terribly anx-

---

15. *School of Charity*, 386–87.

16. A reference to the Servants of the Immaculate Heart of Mary (IHM) at Saint Mary Convent, Monroe, Michigan. Merton first corresponded with Sr. Mary Immaculate, IHM, in an unpublished letter of August 30, 1967, and later with Mother Margaret (Benedicta) Brennan, IHM (see below), regarding their House of Prayer project, an attempt to infuse a more contemplative spirit into "active" religious orders. Merton describes the "Houses of Prayer" as "communities where people can go for more or less long retreats" (*Other Side of the Mountain*, 87).

ious to talk to me, a few of them might be willing to meet at Redwoods for a small seminar. It would have the advantage of being in the kind of place I think they are looking for. I have not proposed this to anyone, though I have vaguely mentioned the possibility. If you are very much in favor, you might suggest it . . . ? It would of course explicitly involve the nuns paying for their time there and getting there in the best way they could themselves.

Third, worse still: I got an invitation from the Esalen Institute[17] to speak in Big Sur, run a seminar, etc. I replied that I did not speak outside monasteries of our Order but suggested that a small group might meet at Redwoods. This would mean that any money paid to me would go to you (they offered me three hundred dollars). They would all get there on their own. And they would pay for accommodations.

All of this is merely suggestion and I have not involved you in any way. I made it quite clear that all would depend on the consent of all involved in it. But these are possibilities. In other words what I am saying is that once in a while, if I could do so, I could perhaps make a little money for you by giving a seminar there to a group of 15 or so. I would enjoy doing it and would hope to slip over to Needle Rock from time to time . . .

But if you think this is unacceptable, don't hesitate to say so at once and don't feel that you are in anyway bound to even think of this for a moment further.

Now for more practical affairs. First, Fr. Flavian is quite favorable to my spending some time on the shore and I want very much to do it.[18] Second, guess what (confidential)—I am to go to Indonesia and probably to the

---

17. The Esalen Institute was founded in 1962 by Michael Murphy and Richard Price on Murphy's family land along the southern edge of Big Sur on the California coast. It became a center of the Human Potential Movement in the 1960s and 1970s (for a history, see Jeffrey J. Kripal, *Esalen: America and the Religion of No Religion* [Chicago: University of Chicago Press, 2007]). See also Merton's journal entry of June 29, 1968: "More invitations. Yesterday the Esalen Institute—to conduct a seminar at Big Sur—and to speak in San Francisco. This is more attractive than most but I can't accept it either" (*Other Side of the Mountain*, 134; see also Merton's July 19 entry, p. 142).

18. Flavian Burns, OCSO (1931–2005), Abbot of Our Lady of Gethsemani from 1968 to 1973, granted Merton the permission to travel to Redwoods Monastery as well as New Mexico, Alaska, and Asia.

Bangkok meeting.[19] I am to preach a retreat at Rawa Seneng!![20] On the way out I hope to see you briefly (it would be in November). No more for the moment. Do tell me the news and what you think about the above. I hope I haven't been too wild. None of it may ever be realized anyway.

Best wishes—in XC [Christ]

Tom

❖ ❖ ❖

July 8, 1968

Dear Tom:

Thank you for your letters and your suggestions. You have been much with me both in thoughts and prayer during my trip to Europe.

Mauro was kind. . . . [H]e listened attentively to me before delivering a sermon. The Japanese abbesses saw the Pope, together with Fr. General and Dom Bernard, his Secretary. I didn't. However, there was a possibility to have a short memo on "the contemplative life" handed over to him personally. The same memo was given to Mauro as a synthesis of our talk.

The week with the Flemish "contemplatives" was much better than Citeaux; it was informative: Christology-formation-*groepsgesprektekniek*[21] (you are very good at guessing Dutch, aren't you . . .). A "*studium monasticum*" is planned in coordination with the Univ[ersity] of Louvain.

---

19. The Meeting of the Monastic Superiors in the Far East, held December 9 to 15, 1968, in Bangkok, Thailand.

20. See Merton's February 24 and July 9, 1968 letters to Dom Willibrord Van Dijk, OCSO (1903–1989), founder of the Cistercian monastery at Rawaseneng, Indonesia, regarding Merton's planned visit following the Bangkok Meeting (*School of Charity*, 367, 387–88). Due to Merton's untimely death, this opportunity never materialized. See also Merton's correspondence with Fransiskus ("Frans") Harjawiyata, OCSO (1931–2016), monk of Rawaseneng, who would serve as Abbot of the community from 1978 to 2006—the first native-born Abbot in Indonesia's history (*School of Charity*, 390). Merton journals about the proposed meeting in an entry of June 14, 1968 (*Other Side of the Mountain*, 129–30).

21. "Group process" or "group conversation technique."

Hausherr[22] was mentioned as [a] possible guest Professor. I was bold enough to suggest your [name] for one semester. After a full year of solitude at Needle Rock, this might be feasible. And my suggestion does not compromise you anyway.

Thank you for the thinking. Stained glass is excluded right now, because the whole wheat hosts take most of our work time and they are a reasonable source of income. Cecilia is in Spokane since the end of June. She has a job, a small apartment and takes help. She feels she is "faithful to life," she writes, in doing so.[23] We miss her much, as she misses the group. Shalome is doing much the same in San Francisco. So, the group is reduced to nine persons.

I was fool enough to accept to talk at the Monroe, Michigan meeting: the day before your letter came in, I even commit myself to develop something along the line of "the personal call to the contemplative vocation—its characteristics and implications." I love the idea of meeting at Redwoods with you and a few for a small seminar . . . But do you see a way out? May I openly mention your proposal to—f[or] ex[ample]—Sr. Benedicta Brennan?[24]

The Esalen seminar would be all right also, if not before late August or September. I smile at your imagination . . . : we are not sure we would accept all the money, but would be happy with a fair sharing.

Of course, we are delighted that San Francisco-Needle Rock is halfway to Indonesia. Yesterday [Christa]fora showed a five-minute 8mm film: most of it was taken at the Ocean. They all say: Ho . . . Tom should see this. Send it to him.

22. Irénée Hausherr, SJ (1881–1978), influential and foundational scholar of early Patristic and eastern Christian spirituality.

23. Sr. Cecilia Wilms (1932–1998) had been Redwoods' secretary. At the time of this letter she was on leave in Spokane, Washington, where she would remain an "urban hermit," becoming a consecrated virgin in the diocese, and living as a hermit until her death (see Paul A. Fredette and Karen Karper Fredette, *Consider the Ravens: On Contemporary Hermit Life* [Bloomington, IN: iUniverse, 2008, 2011]).

24. Mother Margaret (Benedicta) Brennan, IHM (d. 2016), corresponded with Merton in a number of unpublished letters from March and July 1968, first regarding an invitation to the Monroe meeting, and then in regards to Merton's proposed gathering at Redwoods Monastery.

Another thing: Basil Pennington[25] of Spencer speaks of publishing our Cisterc[ian] Fathers in English. He would ask you (mandate of U.S. OCSO region) to be Editor in Chief. He asks me if I would agree to represent the feminine branch as a member of the board of editors. I do not feel qualified. And as the group is small, I share in washing the dishes.

F[ather] Roger attends a few classes in Sacramental Theology with Piet Fransen[26] at U[niversity of] S[an] F[rancisco]. We thought it was not fair to invite you to be our Chaplain for three weeks; we have many guests in July. And they would eat you up. With hope. Till . . . ?

Love from all. In X [Christ]

Myriam

❖   ❖   ❖

July 11, 1968[27]

Dear Myriam:

The best way to reply to your letter is to enclose the letter I received from Sr. Benedicta. She knows of my idea and is eager to have a meeting at Redwoods. I think if you write to her about it, she will be glad to make some kind of arrangement that would allow you to substitute it for a talk at Monroe. We might make that (vocation to cont[emplative] life)[28] one of the themes of the meeting . . . ? Anyhow, the only thing for me would be the timing. I might have difficulty clearing it with Fr. Flavian before October. But in October I could make it part of the trip that is already

---

25. Basil Pennington, OCSO (1931–2005), an important twentieth-century author and teacher of contemplative spirituality who, along with Thomas Keating, OCSO (1923–2018) and William Meninger, OCSO (1932–2021), led the Centering Prayer movement, originating from Saint Joseph's Abbey in Spencer, Massachusetts.
26. Pieter Fransen, SJ (1913–1983), Belgian theologian and longtime faculty at the University of Louvain, Belgium.
27. *School of Charity*, 389–90. This letter includes a photograph taken by Merton of his hermitage. At the end of the letter he inserts, "This is my place in winter."
28. Handwritten and inserted at the top of the letter.

planned. I hope to fly to Asia Nov. 1ˢᵗ now, so October would be best for the meeting. Around the middle of the month would be best for me. Could you please return Sr. Benedicta's letter?

Fr. Flavian will visit you, he hopes, after the Vina election. He will hire a car and drive over, in the beginning of August. He is very interested in looking over possible places, as—this transpired recently—he is perhaps thinking of something more permanent, where two or three of us might settle down in a little hermit group, about a mile or two apart. Or closer if need be. Certainly, there is room for two or three spread out along the shore. I don't know what kind of arrangements he plans to make, and of course it is a long-term project anyway, far in the future. For my own part, I am looking forward to moving out to the shore on my return from Asia and getting a good taste of it. A year would not be a bad beginning . . . I don't know what the chances are.[29]

Let us keep praying. Meanwhile, if I get a chance, I'd like to look at some of the big wilderness reservations which are east and north of Garberville. One could not of course have anything permanent there but I guess one could spend long periods in a tent. The conditions would be very primitive, but ok for summer I'd think.

It was nice that you thought I could handle a course at Louvain! I don't know if ten years of Needle Rock would fit me for it. Actually, the more I see of solitude the less I want to teach courses in anything—except occasionally sharing something with a small congenial group like yours, entirely *en famille*. I do earnestly hope to stop being a public figure of

---

29. See Merton's journal entries of July 5, 1968: "[Fr. Flavian] is *very* interested in perhaps starting something out on the Coast. . . . When he goes out for the Vina election he will go over to Redwoods and look at the various places: Bear Harbor, Needle Rock, Ettersburg . . . " (*Other Side of the Mountain*, 139), as well as August 13: "[Fr. Flavian] came back from California Saturday evening and I saw him today. The California situation is not entirely satisfactory" (p. 153). Merton then lists a number of issues that arose during Fr. Flavian's visit: the problem of renting the entire ranch at Needle Rock; snakes at Bear Harbor ("Amazing descriptions of Fr. Roger kicking snakes aside right and left saying 'Oh! They're all harmless!' "); potential arson and burglary at Al Groth's house; and the increasing number of visitors ("Already full of hippies"). It is interesting to note that—as one door seems to close on the California coast—Merton mentions in the very next passage that an invitation has arrived from the Archbishop of Anchorage to preach a retreat to contemplative nuns in Alaska; thus opening the possibility of increased solitude in an alternate locale.

any sort (which is why I am having second thoughts about the Esalen Institute: but we'll see what they think).

I will be happy to share your news and ideas from Europe. And probably will have a few ideas of my own! I have refused the editorship of the Cist[ercian] translations and don't especially like the idea of the meeting of the board which is a sort of useless seminar rather than anything practical. Useless for me that is: others may certainly enjoy it, but I have had my fill of talks and discussions on academic topics.

After the meeting in Bangkok, I will probably be satiated with meetings for a good ten years. Will reserve some energies for the one in Africa in [19]69 if I am invited, which Dom Leclercq says I will be.

Best—love to all of you, in the Lord,

Tom

❖ ❖ ❖

July 16, 1968

Dear Tom:

The last Saturday evening "happening" was a meeting with a group of 30 hippies-gypsies type people. To meet them in word and silence was a little difficult because we were too many together. They live dispersed and rather isolated in the hills between Thorn and the Coast, Ettersburg, etc. . . . Some of them, going to Needle Rock met, they said, Mr. Jones and Stewart, the owners of both Needle Rock and Bear Harbor, who would be selling their land along the coast. And for this reason, they, the "gypsies" were not allowed to come to N[eedle] R[ock] any longer. Is this a trick to keep the people out off the place? A rumor?[30]

Don't you think you'd better check yourself with Mrs. Jones? And inquire perhaps, as soon as possible about the possibility of renting the place? This is only a suggestion. I do not want to interfere now; as Mrs.

---

30. See also Merton's journal entry of July 19 or 20, 1968: "A letter came from Mother Myriam. Jones, owner of Needle Rock, etc., has been chasing hippies, etc., off his property. . . . But if Fr. Flavian bought it we'd have to chase people off too??" (*Other Side of the Mountain*, 143).

Jones is fond of poets, you have a better chance to reach some kind of agreement yourself?

We will be happy to meet Father Flavian. To look at some of the big wilderness reservations, east and north from Garberville is a good idea, but if you have the choice between a trailer and a tent, would you not take the trailer? I will also contact Mrs. Barnum: a wealthy Lady from Eureka; she owns much land in this area. Is a widow. Her husband bought acres and acres of land in the twenties; he owned our place before Bob Usher purchased it from him. When we came over in [19]62 she <u>and her son</u> (there is a son . . .) gave us a few acres so that what we call now "the third field" (orchard) would be a natural geographic parcel till the Thompson Creek.

Thank you for sending M. Benedicta's letter. I doubt very much she will accept a seminar at Redwoods as a substitute for a talk at Monroe. She will probably take both. I made the proposal though.

When you come, I would like to speak of solitude and contacts. If our contacts, in monastic life, are more real than in the last 50 years, I believe our solitude also should be real and <u>important</u>.

Love and prayers: from all.
In C[hrist]

Myriam

July 20, 1968[31]

Dear Myriam:

It does not surprise me that Jones seems about to sell his land on the shore. I got that impression last spring. I wrote to him a couple of weeks ago, or perhaps less, saying that we were interested in getting some land out there and I hoped he would keep us in mind. I have not heard from him. My feeling is that the place will be split up into small lots, and that there will be a number of houses or cabins built out there.

---

31. *School of Charity*, 390–91.

Mrs. Barnum may have a good solution for us. I am thinking now of the project Fr. Flavian has in mind for the future. I told him that there might be a possibility with her.

Meanwhile, for myself next winter on my return from Asia—I'll look for something when I'm out there in October. Perhaps by then it will be too late for Needle Rock, etc. Or maybe even then they will let me spend part of the winter there. It will not be hard to find a temporary place of some sort, and certainly for a brief period of a few months, perhaps a trailer on your own grounds somewhere would be a good start—back in one of those valleys that don't have roads into them, perhaps up on a hill.

I am not sure they allow trailers in a wilderness area—certainly not for long periods anyway. That would all have to be looked into.

As things are now, I plan to reach Redwoods late in October. If Sr. Benedicta wants a meeting there, sometime between the 24th and the end of the month would be best for me. I must get going Nov. 1st. Things are shaping up well for Japan, I think.

Yes, I think the question of solitude is very important—naturally. We need a real solitude that will empty us out, help strip us of ourselves. There is a great deal of "vanity" (in the sense of Ecclesiastes)[32] even in a social life that is serious and good. One needs periods of real silence, isolation, lostness, in order to be deeply convinced and aware that God is All. Without experience of that, our prayer life is so thin. Certainly, I hope we will get a chance to talk of it—and live it. That is the one thing that preoccupies me now. The way Fr. Flavian is talking now, it is quite possible that I may move to California for good next year. I am certainly ready and anxious to do so!!! And I pray that God may show us the place He has in mind!

No more for the present. I enclose a new paper. More copies will be on the way. Love and prayers: peace in the Lord

Tom

The Esalen Institute is very pleased with the idea of a conference at Redwoods. But I would not plan it until next Spring. Still a bit in doubt myself. I'll tell them to contact you about it. We can talk about it when I come.[33]

---

32. "Vanity of vanities, says the Teacher, vanity of vanities! All is vanity" (Eccl 1:2).
33. Handwritten in the letter's margin.

July 22, 1968[34]

Dear Myriam:

This is just to say that my constantly changing plans have changed again. I have another important invitation in Asia—and have to be in India at the time when I hoped to be at Redwoods. However, I can still come by on my way out. I have to fly to Asia October 14th or 15th. I may get a couple of days with you before that. I don't know if it will be possible to plan a meeting with Sr. Benedicta, etc. at that time however. But if she can manage a couple of days around Columbus Day it might be possible. Or else, in a pinch, in September—but I may find it hard to get away from here then.

The Asian trip is shaping up famously, however, with India now on top of the rest. I don't expect to travel much in India but I may meet some very interesting and helpful people—even a chance I may meet the Dalai Lama,[35] which might mean an entrée to a lot of interesting monastic centers . . . I am beginning to think that my big trouble will be getting back from Asia at all!!! But I do hope to be back by February. If Sr. Benedicta could wait until then, it would be easier to arrange a meeting with more time. In October it will be quite a rush. But it can still be done, if necessary.

No more for the present. I enclose a couple of documents . . .

Love to all. In peace and prayer,

Tom

---

34. *School of Charity*, 391.

35. Merton would in fact meet with His Holiness the XIV Dalai Lama in Dharamsala, India, on three separate occasions: November 4, 6, and 8, 1968 (see *Other Side of the Mountain*, 250–52, 258–59, 266).

August 1, 1968[36]

Tom:

To receive God through "meditation," silent expectation, and "kenosis," don't we have this in common with the mystics of all religions?

As I am working on what I will say in Monroe, it appears to me over again—and this is a deep <u>joy</u>—that we should re-listen, today, to Jesus: the man who lived and died.

: witnessed as alive, present, after the Easter event, by the Apostles and the Primitive Church.[37]
: Jesus, our future.

With hope. Love from all of us.

We are waiting today for Fr. Flavian.

Myriam

P.S. I meant to say, you should come back to the States . . . Don't stay in Asia.
BUT WHO KNOWS!?

❖ ❖ ❖

August 5, 1968[38]

Dear Myriam:

Wishing you all luck at Monroe—whenever it is. Will you tell Sr. Benedicta that if she wants to meet at Redwoods I'll be available there Oct. 11 and 12 and part of 13? Will that be ok with you? I hope to get moving on the 14th on my big *pelerinage aux sources*. To the big overflowing confused sources of humanity. It was an Asian humanity that the Word chose . . .

---

36. Handwritten note.

37. Dardenne inserts above this line, "cf. [?] week spent with the Flemish contemplatives" (see her letter of July 8, 1968).

38. *School of Charity*, 393.

Ours is an Asian religion, basically. Though of course also non-Asian, beyond Asia.

I hope Fr. Flavian had a profitable visit with you. More than anything else, I hope his idea of starting something hidden and solitary out there somewhere will work out . . .

Of course, as you say, I may never get back from Asia. But don't let's talk about it!

In any event, yes, all the monastic traditions have this in common: total liberation and availability to "let go" and open up to the unspoken silence in which all is said: *qui erat et qui est et qui venturus est.*[39]

in the Lord

❖   ❖   ❖

August 28, 1968

Dear Tom:

Last Sunday, Mike the guitarist—do you remember the tape we listened to last May—played in the church, which he finds an ideal place to play the guitar. One hour before Compline, guests and several of us were simply there letting God's voice coming from the void. When it was time for Compline, Mike was still playing; Diane and Leslie prayed Ps[alms] 4 and 90, and Dominique who was hebdomadaria[40] said the *oratio*. No Salve, but Katreen danced accompanied by this strange, meditative, sober and yet colorful rhythm of Mike's guitar.

Would you think such an experience might be profitable to those who will meet with you at Redwoods in October? I talked to Mike: he is ready to come down from Spokane on October 11, or one of the following days if this is acceptable to you.

I returned from Monroe via Spokane. Cecilia is well. Interesting to know how she views our way of life in Whitethorn, now, from a distance

---

39. Latin for "who is, who was, and who is to come" (Rev 1:8).
40. A Latin term denoting the weekly, rotating role of leading the monastic choir.

. . . She is happy for the opportunity she will have to type your manuscript.[41] Thank you.

There was no time left to send you the talk prepared for the Monroe conference. I had my prejudices in going, but now, I regret that you were not present. The Spirit was speaking. To me, this genuine desire for prayer and the contemplative attitude in apostolic-"active" groups speaks worlds of newness for the Christian religious life of the future. HOW the "house of prayer" should come into existence, I do not see. Neither do I see that it is the single means—is it a means to an end???—of deepening the prayer life of those involved in the "mission" field.

At this point, Tom, it seems important that you offer your insight. I hope in the next days to reflect upon the Monroe happening, and will send you a few notes. Am sure the proceedings will be communicated to you. Do you see any possibility to be one day—or even more—earlier at Redwoods in October? I know your time with the Monroe people will be limited, but the whole movement of contemplative search is so important that the monastic tradition cannot be silent? And, forgive me for saying this, you are one of its most sane representatives . . .

On August 21, Fr. Hennessey, Mother Benedicta and a few others met, to think of what might be done or discussed with you in October. Have you any suggestion? However, I do not see much at this moment, I believe that the depth-dimension of such a movement should be investigated, and also the necessity of REAL solitude. At the other hand, how should we interiorize our experiences? What about the media of contemplation? Are there two ways, two disciplines of experiencing God? One—along the line of the Hindu tradition, starting from a method of concentration and deepening the center of our awareness . . . and another proper to our Western culture (American culture) starting from the experience of nature, life, events and men, discovering Christ born right there through a process of interiorization? Shouldn't the two ways meet? And how?

41. Sr. Cecilia had evidently volunteered during his May visit to Redwoods to type the manuscript of Merton's *The Climate of Monastic Prayer*, the inaugural volume of the Cistercian Studies series (subsequently published as *Contemplative Prayer* [New York: Herder & Herder, 1969]), a task which she completed while on leave from the Redwoods (*School of Charity*, 395, 399).

Mother Benedicta Brennan, Father Hennessey, Brother David of Mt. Savior, Sister Marie Goldstein, RSHM,[42] will come in October. Who else? Is it not best that Mother Benedicta and Fr. Hennessey contact you at Gethsemani? What do you think of having Sr. Corita with us then? I just heard yesterday by two of her personal friends that she tends to "withdraw." This expression was used to convey to me that she takes now much more time to contemplate and to pray.

Dom Columban invited Dom Leclercq to talk in Guadalupe Abbey,[43] as he will be on his way to Bangkok. Would you think he would be the right person to be invited also at the seminar???

Mike, Corita, Dom Leclercq: is this not too eclectic an approach? Mike and Corita might offer something like a contemplative experience, but for the rest, I wonder if it is not best to have you with the people interested in the house of prayer project. Am sure you will have better ideas.

We had lots of rain, which is exceptional in August. This might save us from a few forest fires in September though.

Love from all. Thank you for sending books and articles. We pray and hope for your Asia trip.

Yours in Christ,

Myriam

42. Marie Goldstein (Sr. M. Louis; d. 2011), Religious of the Sacred Heart of Mary (RSHM), taught for a time at Corvallis and Marymount High Schools in Los Angeles, California, where she might have formed a connection with Mother Myriam, perhaps through Sr. Corita.

43. Columban Hawkins, OCSO (1902–1982), Abbot of Our Lady of Guadalupe Abbey from 1955 to 1969. Guadalupe Abbey was founded in 1955 in the Willamette Valley, Oregon.

September 7, 1968[44]

Dear Myriam:

Since Dom Leclercq was coming here this weekend, I waited to answer your letter. I asked him where he would be Oct. 11, etc. He said he was tied up in Belgium then. He will go from here to Oregon, but will leave for Europe. However, he is coming back in November and can come to you then if you like. I leave the rest to you.

As to having Mike there—I leave all that to you also. Why not? Such things are good to loosen people up and break the hang ups with too much formal method. On the other hand, artistic spontaneity is not the whole story. A little of it surely does not hurt, but will do some good. As long as people do not get the idea that it is all you need.

I'll have something to say but I don't yet know quite what. A lot depends on the actual people there and I won't know until I meet them. Corita, sure, whoever wants to come. I leave that all to you, I am simply at your service to think aloud with you.

All I can give is the little that I have, which is certainly nothing. But I can think with you in terms of my own present development and—I won't say crisis because it is very smooth—but I am completely convinced that for some people the only thing is a solitary and "unattached" life. To simply go where the wind blows them, which is into various new deserts. With absolutely NO plans for any kind of structure, community, what to do, how to do it, but to simply seek the most desolate rock or the most abandoned island and sit there until the tourists move in, then to move on. I have NO ideal, NO program, and the last thing in the world I want is a disciple or anyone to listen or imitate. I'd rather warn everyone to do something else. For me the wind blows to Asia. . . . I don't know anything more after that, whether it blows for long or only for a week.

The Asians have this only: that for thousands of years they have worked on a very complex and complete mental discipline which is not so much aimed at separating matter from spirit, as identifying the true self and separating it from an illusion generated by society and by imaginary appetite. At the present moment this illusion has become law, even for Christians. The talk about the goodness of the world, etc. is largely justification of the illusion, though the world is certainly "good." But all the

44. *School of Charity*, 395–97.

Goodness of the World lingo seems to me to be vitiated by a Madison Avenue consumer-society approach which makes it utterly phony, and bespeaks nothing but the goodness of the market (see Erich Fromm, etc.). I don't intend to talk much about this. It is true that the yen for absolute solitude is often vitiated by pure narcissism, regression, immaturity, and is utterly sick. This does not alter the fact that there are vocations to solitude, and for these there remains only the question: when do I start? And how? Once artificial barriers are removed the question tends to answer itself.

I got a letter from Mrs. Jones. I can have Bear Harbor (to rent for a time if I want it, she says. She is eager to fix it up, etc.).[45] On the other hand, I don't want to bind myself to return from Asia before its necessary. I may run into some really extraordinary opportunities, as I am now in contact with the secretary of the Dalai Lama. There is so much openness there and great generosity to anyone who has a really serious interest. So, I probably won't be back before spring. (I have incidentally canceled the Esalen meeting for the same reason).

I might be at Bear Harbor for next summer, or someplace else. I have no way of knowing now what will turn up. It is all too far ahead.

This is all pretty much in confidence of course—I wouldn't want it to get outside your community.

Anyway, I'll try to get there a day or two early. I'll also want a little time on the shore myself, before the talks, which should be only the 11th, 12th, and 13th. The 14th I fly from Eureka to S[an] F[rancisco] on the morning plane and the 15th to Asia. Keep praying for me. The strong prayers of the Redwoods have done much for me so far! Keep them up!! And I pray for all of you too. We sometimes forget the real dimensions of our life. There must be long "dead" periods, they are necessary. But they may suddenly blossom out into unusual life, if we let them!

My love to all,

Tom

❖   ❖   ❖

45. See also Merton's journal entry of September 5, 1968: "A letter came, by surprise, from Mrs. Jones—wife of the owner of Needle Rock, Bear Harbor, etc. They have made their September arrangement . . . and I can have Bear Harbor if I want it. They all agree to fix the place up, etc." (*Other Side of the Mountain*, 164).

Eagle River
Alaska
September 20 [1968][46]

Dear Myriam:

Guess where I am now. Alaska!

I am doing a little work which—I hope—will earn me some money that will enable me to stay longer in India.

One of the things is a workshop with the Precious Blood nuns up here, and the superior, Sister Rita Mary, is very anxious to come also to the meeting in October.[47] I told her that she should write to you—maybe you could squeeze her in somewhere?

I hope to get there as planned on the 9th or 10th. Will let you know later, when I know definitely.

It is already cold here and snow falls nearby in the hills—of course there is perpetual snow on the mountains. And many glaciers. It is magnificent country!

My best—love to all of you

Tom

October 14 [1968][48]

Dear Myriam,

Thanks for the lovely and fruitful days at Redwoods. We arrived here safely and I am planning on a good rest before the flight tomorrow. Portia

---

46. Handwritten note. Previously unpublished.

47. Sisters Adorers of the Precious Blood in Eagle River, Alaska. These talks were included in *Thomas Merton in Alaska: The Alaskan Conferences, Journals, and Letters*, ed. Robert E. Daggy (New York: New Directions, 1988). Sr. Rita Mary Lang (d. 2008), Superior of the Precious Blood community, attended Merton's October Redwoods conferences. On Sr. Rita Mary and the Precious Blood Sisters' impressions of Merton, see Kathleen Tarr, *We Are All Poets Here: Thomas Merton's 1968 Journey to Alaska* (Anchorage, AK: VP&D House, 2018), 338–43.

48. Handwritten note on stationary from the Clift Hotel, San Francisco, California. Previously unpublished.

and I had lunch together today and I have my visa.[49] If you can possibly send on the habit (from Gethsemani) to India it would help to have two. Of course, send it <u>surface</u>. [Br.] Brendan may have ideas on that. To save expense.

My love to all—I enclose some pictures of fantastic beings.

In the Lord,

Tom

❖ ❖ ❖

Delhi [India]
October 29 [1968][50]

Dear Mother Myriam—

India has been so far a most rewarding experience—and disconcerting also. Great poverty and misery. Yet beautiful things and people everywhere. I met a marvelous old artist who does religious paintings of a sort of folk-ikon quality.[51] A friend will eventually bring you one of these paintings as a gift.[52] It is, I think, very simple and lovely. Love to all. Tom.

49. To Br. Patrick Hart, OCSO, Merton writes on the same date: "I've had a good day in San Francisco—with a Redwoods postulant! We went out to lunch at a fine seafood place on Fisherman's Wharf. She is entering in two weeks" (*School of Charity*, 404).

50. Handwritten postcard. *School of Charity*, 408.

51. On visiting the home of Calcutta artist Jamini Roy (1887–1972), Merton writes: "Walking barefoot on the cold tiles, through low quiet rooms filled with canvases of unattainable beauty: simple, formalized little icons with a marvelous sort of folk and Coptic quality, absolutely alive and full of charm, many Christian themes, the most lovely modern treatment of Christian subjects I have ever seen" (*Other Side of the Mountain*, 220). Merton describes Roy as, "a warm, saintly old man." He visited the artist's home with Amiya Chakravarty on October 21, 1968. Regarding the painting, Merton writes: "Amiya bought a Christ [painting] which he will take to the nuns at Redwoods." The painting hangs in the monastery church to this day.

52. Chakravarty personally delivered Roy's painting to Redwoods Monastery in the Spring of 1972 (see Chakravarty's "Epilogue" to Donald Grayston and Michael W. Higgins, eds., *Thomas Merton: Pilgrim in Process* [Toronto: Griffin House, 1983], 171–73, in which he relates the circumstances of purchasing the painting and bringing it to the Redwoods). See also Christine Bochen and Victor Kramer, "'A Journey into Wholeness': An Interview

❖ ❖ ❖

Dharmsala, India
November 7, 1968[53]

Dear Myriam—and all the Sisters,

I am finishing what is more or less a week's retreat in the Himalayas—in a cottage down the mountain from the Dalai Lama's residence. It has been a marvelous week—I have seen the Dalai Lama, in two long audiences, and am to see him again tomorrow before I leave. He is a most impressive and likeable person and we have got on very well—talking about Tibetan methods of meditation, etc. Also, I have met six or seven other Lamas who are reputed to be very great mystics and who are in fact very impressive. With all of them I have had really delightful and fruitful conversations (with a good interpreter) and it has been an amazing experience—like meeting monks of the time of St. Bernard. Much better than I anticipated. I have found all sorts of good directives for understanding Buddhism better. It seems to me Tibetan Buddhism is something quite special—and very interesting indeed—though some of it may appear bizarre. But the quality of these monks cannot be disputed. They are humble and profound human beings.

Tomorrow I return to Delhi, then I go to the other end of the Himalayas—for more monasteries. It has been a thrilling trip (this part of it). But also—the awful poverty and confusion of Calcutta is a shattering experience. We had two rather "shaking" experiences yesterday—two earthquakes. No damage, but real quakes!

Keep up your prayers—they are very helpful and necessary. I send you all my love. I wish you could share these experiences with me. It

---

about Thomas Merton with Myriam Dardenne at Redwoods Monastery," *The Merton Annual* 14 (2001): 50.

53. Handwritten note. *School of Charity*, 408–9. This letter includes a full-size greeting card printed on handmade paper of "A Family of Yak" with the Tibetan inscription and English translation, "*May you have a long life, free from illness, full of happiness and prosperity.*" The card is printed and published by Tibetan Craft Community, Dalhousie, Himachal Pradesh, India, which currently operates under the name Tibetan Refugee Handicraft Center and is actively seeking donations.

seems I must prolong my trip to Europe to see Tibetans who are setting up monasteries there—and other *"periti."*[54] Please pray that this may be acceptable to my good Fr. Flavian!!

Again, with all my best wishes, and love in our Lord,

Tom

Until Nov[ember] 25 I can still be reached c/o Mrs. Flanagan
USIS—7 Chowringhee
Calcutta[55]

54. Latin for "experts."

55. There is an additional page with the following note: "Myriam—When you have finished with this carbon copy, please send it and the original to Brother Patrick [Hart] to be <u>filed</u> with my unpublished MSS [manuscripts]. Thanks, Tom."

Chapter Twenty-One

Letters to Fellow Monastics, Acquaintances, and Friends

To W. H. "Ping" Ferry[1]

Selections

May 6, 1968 (on "friendly skies of United")[2]

I must admit drinking champagne over an entirely invisible South Dakota is something I find refreshing. Will be at Abbey of the Redwoods, White[t]horn, California, until May14.

May 24, 1968[3]

Here (over) is a spot on the Cal[ifornia] shore I am in love with. Certainly do hope to return. . . . Saw Ferlinghetti in S.F. and drank some espresso with visionaries. . . .

---

1. W. H. "Ping" Ferry (1910–1995), Merton's friend and host during his trip to Santa Barbara to speak at the Center for the Study of Democratic Institutions. In a number of journal passages, Merton mentions Ferry's desire and search for geographic solitude in Big Sur and along the California and Oregon coasts in general (June 16, July 19, August 5, 1968; *Other Side of the Mountain*, 131, 142, 150). On Merton's search for solitude along the California coast, see Paul Wilkes, "An Interview with W. H. (Ping) Ferry about Thomas Merton," ed. Paul M. Pearson, *The Merton Annual* 24 (2011): 51–52.

2. *Hidden Ground of Love*, 238.

3. *Hidden Ground of Love*, 238. Lawrence Ferlinghetti (1919–2021), influential American Beat poet and co-founder of City Lights Publishers and bookstore in San Francisco's North Beach neighborhood. Merton slept in the City Lights office the evening before his departure for New Mexico (*Other Side of the Mountain*, 102; see also Bill Morgan, *Thomas Merton, Lawrence Ferlinghetti, and the Protection of All Beings* [Temple, PA: Beatdom Press, 2022]).

June 1, 1968[4]

A wonderful idea to get a place on the Pacific—too bad you aren't further north, you c[oul]d buy Bear Harbor. But probably there are many equally fine places down at Big Sur—except I always wonder if that isn't too well known now. One very lovely place near the convent is obtainable, but lacks view of the sea. Very high up, lovely, well-protected little ranch. All around there, full of great places.

I am fully set on spending any time I can on that shore and wish I could move out for keeps.

June 16, 1968[5]

Well, I really do take seriously the idea of exploring the Pacific Coast with you. There is no question that I really need a top-secret hideout where nobody will know I am there and where I can be alone with a lot of wind and sea for long periods—perhaps indefinitely. . . .

It seems to me that the best thing would be for me to come out to Santa Barbara before my flight to the Indies and we could take a week or so to look at the Coast. Then perhaps when I come back I could hole in for that retreat I am hoping to make early next year. That's the way it seems to make sense at the moment and the way I think the Abbot would tolerate it.

July 20, 1968[6]

. . . my own idea would be to see as much of the actual coast as one leisurely can, probably following route 1 all the way up to Fort Bragg and then cutting over to get to Vina (near Redding).

For my part I'd like to spend some of the time just sitting around on a point meditating and listening to the waves: maybe we could stop here and there and you could watch birds meanwhile. But my main objective I guess is to explore around for a possible hideaway where I could get some real solitude someday, temporarily or permanently. In other words

---

4. *Hidden Ground of Love*, 238.
5. *Hidden Ground of Love*, 239.
6. *Hidden Ground of Love*, 240.

the Abbot—Fr. Flavian—is seriously thinking of setting something up out there one day. But he seems willing to let me move out there on my own quite soon. Even this winter, when I get back from Asia. I imagine it would mean being on land near the nuns at Redwoods, or else squatting on somebody else's territory. That is the real serious intent I have in mind. Probably I'll end up in the north near the nuns, as that is the most practical thing to do (re: food, etc.) but it would not hurt to look at the southern coast around Lucia-Big Sur, and also perhaps get back into the Zen place at Tassajara[7] spring and see other such places in those m[oun]t[ain]s.

July 28, 1968[8]

Will fly to Santa Barbara I hope on Sept. 30 and will let you know when my flying saucer touches down. . . . No plans need be made for meeting people, except maybe a poet or two in SF, and I may stop at the Esalen Inst. in Big Sur as they are hoping I'll give them a conference some time. I'll be slow to let any monasteries know I am around, but will have to stop here and there for Mass . . . Looking forward most eagerly!!

August 6, 1968[9]

Very glad Jo[10] will come and I think Rogue River [Oregon] is a great idea. The further north we get, the better for me. I'd think then if we get past San Francisco the second or third day and then slow down up on the Mendocino coast and reserve the best of dawdling for the north—unless you have some search to accomplish in the south: that w[oul]d be great.

---

7. Tassajara Zen Mountain Center, founded in 1967 by Shunryu Suzuki Roshi (1904–1971); located in the Ventana Wilderness area of the Los Padres National Forest in California's Coast Range.

8. *Hidden Ground of Love*, 241.

9. *Hidden Ground of Love*, 242.

10. Jolyne Marie Gillier, Ferry's wife at the time. In a letter of July 28, 1968, Merton adds, " . . . fine if your wife comes along. Addition of feminine wisdom will doubtless help find even better hideout" (*Hidden Ground of Love*, 241).

September 4, 1968[11]

. . . I don't think I'll hang around SF talking to anyone. Hate cities. Want to scram out after ten minutes. But will contact Milosz.[12] Maybe ought to go say Mass at SF Carmel the morning we get out of there.

Moving fast up coast fine with me. A couple of days around the ins and outs between Mendocino and Eureka good. I'm all for the desolate mists and the nords. Might be somebody in Eureka ready to give or lend an acre of sandbar or something. I'll find out, but it needs to be done with much discretion I guess, so's not to set off a great chain of firecrackers all over Cal[ifornia].

To Frank Jones

July 9, 1968[13]

Dear Mr. Jones:

I hesitated to write to you before there were any definite plans here. But now I have worked things out with the Abbot and we have reached the following conclusions.

1) I have the necessary permission to spend a couple of months at least somewhere on the Pacific shore in a remote place—Bear Harbor would be ideal for me. The time: sometime after next December.

2) As a more long-range project, he and I are interested in establishing a small permanent hermit colony of two or three, a kind of retreat area which would need to be cut off from the outside world as much as possible. Once again, your property there would offer the kind of thing we're looking for. Our little place could of course coexist with a small scattered

---

11. *Hidden Ground of Love*, 242.

12. Czeslaw Milosz (1911–2004), Polish-American poet and winner of the 1980 Nobel Prize in Literature. For Merton and Milosz's correspondence, see Robert Faggen, ed., *Striving Towards Being: The Letters of Thomas Merton and Czeslaw Milosz* (New York: Farrar, Straus and Giroux, 1996).

13. Previously unpublished. See Merton's journal entry of May 14, 1968, regarding his initial meeting with Frank Jones near Bear Harbor: "A red pick-up truck came up the dirt road. The owner of the land was in it with his wife and said he would be willing to rent me his house at Bear Harbor" (*Other Side of the Mountain*, 100).

community of other likeminded people, artists, etc., further along the shore. People who would respect our own need for isolation and quiet.

I also have a friend in Santa Barbara[14] who is interested in the same kind of thing and is going to look for a place on the shore. He might even look as far north as Bear Harbor.

I just wanted to inform you that we are very interested, and that I myself am definitely planning and hoping to spend two or three months at least in solitude out there somewhere, early next year. For my part all I need is a corner to put a trailer or a couple of rooms such as you have in your guest quarters. I'd be glad if you would keep us in mind and inform us if at any time your plans and ours might coincide. We'd be happy to work out something with you.

With my best regards,
Cordially yours

To Gracie Jones[15]

July 13, 1968

Dear Gracie:

This is a very inadequate reply to your two fine letters—and thanks for the pictures that remind me of that wonderful shore.

I just want to say that tomorrow my Mass will be offered for you and Ted and for the children. Enjoy your day at Vina! They are mad at me because I did not go there. I hope they understand that I had to get back fast and also didn't want to have too many know I was "out." I must write Fr. Bernard.[16]

Had a good letter from Mother Myriam after her return. Hope I'll see you all again one of these days.

Blessings and peace in the Lord

14. A reference to W. H. "Ping" Ferry.
15. No relation to Frank Jones. See the Introduction and Appendix. Previously unpublished.
16. Dom Bernard Johnson, OCSO (1925–2017), Abbot of Our Lady of New Clairvaux in Vina, California, from 1968 to 1970.

To Father Roger de Ganck, OCSO

Selections

April 1962[17]

When Rev. Dom Edward was here I did indeed speak to him about my interest in the Beguines in the Low Countries and their relation both to the Cistercians on the one hand and to the Rhenish mystics on the other. He advised me to write to you, but as I had little or no time to pursue the study further, I failed to do so.

But now it is a great pleasure to receive your letter . . . and then the splendid book . . . on the Beguines. . . . I am most grateful for your gift and deeply appreciate it. . . .

Certainly I will be very glad to send all the books that may be desired by the Sisters from Nazareth in their new foundation in California. . . . This foundation is very interesting, and I think it is fine that a foundation of Cistercian nuns should be made in America in the direct line of the great mystical communities of the Middle Ages in the Low Countries.

. . . I assure you of my prayers for the success of the new foundation. From what I hear of the site, it is very well chosen and will be most inspiring.

July 9, 1968[18]

Good news. First of all, Fr. Flavian has definitely granted me permission to make a retreat of two months or more on the shore out there somewhere. I would hope to do this sometime after the New Year—if possible, at Bear Harbor, Needle Rock, or somewhere in that area, overlooking the ocean.

I hope to be out there briefly in October or November on my way to Asia for the regional meeting of Abbots at Bangkok. I hope I can stop at Redwoods and perhaps make tentative plans for where I would stay in the winter on my return from Asia. . . .

I wrote to Mother Myrian recently, and spoke of a couple of ideas of a more active nature—possible meetings of people at Redwoods. But

17. *Witness to Freedom*, 49.
18. *School of Charity*, 388–89.

(in case she mentioned them to you) they are not the kind of thing I am really most interested in myself. They are however possibilities. What I am really looking for is to get away from activity and constant contacts such as I have here and settle down to a really prayerful life. In any case, I hope all is well at the Redwoods, and that Mother Myriam's experiences at the General Chapter were not too gruesome. I look forward to seeing you briefly in the fall, and being with you on my return from Asia. Please ask the prayers of the Sisters that all may go well, especially with the Asian project.

August 20, 1968[19]

I have decided to drop the Esalen conference. It turns out that I may be able to stay in Asia for a longer time than I expected, and I would be foolish to tie myself down to a specific date and thus be forced to return to this country. So, I am writing today to Michael Murphy that I cannot give the conference at Redwoods.

I think this is simpler for all concerned. It might be a bother for the convent, and I certainly do not want to get involved in this kind of thing myself. If I commit myself to this, it will mean destroying all hope of real solitude on the coast for me. It is much better to stay out of sight. . . .

I look forward to seeing you all in October—and though I know the news is out, I still hope to make my visit there relatively quiet and "unnoticed." And I hope to get a day or so on the shore!!

To Father Flavian Burns, OCSO

Selections

Redwoods
Whitethorn, Calif.
May 8, 1968[20]

This place here is ideal. You really must come here and see for yourself. Perfect for retreat. Complete isolation and silence. And the woods are magnificent. I have the whole day to myself until Vespers, after which I work for two hours in a long conference. . . . Yesterday I was more

19. *School of Charity*, 394.
20. *School of Charity*, 379–80.

entirely alone and in silence even than at Gethsemani for a good part of the day. It is much quieter here and much easier to go where you never see anyone.

I hope to finish the conferences Monday and then take two days of absolute solitude out by the Pacific where there is no one at all. . . .

The community here is very alive, very simple, and very real. I think you'd love this place as I do. Be sure not to miss it when you come to Vina!

Have to go to Mass now. Will write later if anything new comes up. The conferences are going well.

Whitethorn, Cal.
May 14, 1968[21]

Finished the talks to the nuns on Sunday and am now on retreat: which means the whole day in complete solitude over by the Pacific. Not a soul there, only seabirds and sheep.

This has been very good—also the days I had to myself before the official retreat—and I can see my situation in a new light. One thing is very clear: I am going to have to lead a less active life and be more solitary, less visits and contacts. I have some ideas I'll talk over, but the first thing is to try alternating periods of complete solitude with periods in which I see people, etc. on a limited basis. I'll try to take July and August for a more solitary period and see how it works.

I am quite definite and clear in my mind now about where I think I should go out. Only to things like this, which will contribute to my own monastic life while helping others. Definitely *not* as a *peritus* to big official meetings unless in a most exceptional case. But coming here has been excellent in every way.

Redwoods
October 9, 1968[22]

I borrowed Mother Myriam's Olivetti to write out my paper for Darjeeling (they wanted it written out in advance yet!) and so now I take advantage of the fact to write a few letters also. Thanks for your note

---

21. *School of Charity*, 380.
22. *School of Charity*, 402.

which reached me here after they had sent it on to Santa Barbara and it came back. I drove up with my friends the Ferrys and I can say without hesitation that the California coast is hopeless as regards solitude. Everywhere there is a land boom in progress and speculators are opening up new developments on every side. They can't lose, the population is increasing so fast people are going to have to build all over the place. Even at Bear Harbor which I liked so much last May, the bulldozers are active and they are opening up a lot of roads that will obviously be for housing sometime. It is just a question of time before this whole place will be spoiled.

To Dom Jacques Winandy[23]

Redwoods Monastery
October 11, 1968[24]

Mother Myriam wants me to say that if you wish to get away from Vancouver any time for a change and rest, you will be most welcome here. I am very fond of this place. It is a shame California is developing so much, for there are fine solitary places all around here. And even if developments continue, there are good places in the woods near the convent which could be well protected. I am seriously thinking of the possibility of settling near here and my new Abbot, would, I think be favorable. However (perhaps I told you this), I would myself be against the idea of a hermit colony, receiving postulants and disciples. If a man wants to be a hermit, I think he should do it more or less on his own or in conjunction with one or two other well-seasoned companions whom he knows in advance (not with people for whom he would have some assumed responsibility).

---

23. Jacques Winandy, OSB (1907–2002), monk and former abbot of Clervaux Abbey in Luxembourg, founded a colony of hermits on Vancouver Island, British Columbia, in 1964.
24. *School of Charity*, 403.

APPENDIX

4 Days with Merton

Encounter with noted priest-poet

By GRACIE M. JONES
(Special to The Monitor)

My being a Negro, you must know how I felt over the assassination of Dr. Martin Luther King Jr. I was deeply grieved and deeply hurt, for in Dr. King I saw real non-violent hope for a new way of life for Negroes in this country. I became more anguished as the days and weeks went by last April.

You have no idea what it feels like to have your white neighbors and your white friends telephone after such a tragedy and say: "Gracie, what can I do?" That phrase was asked of me so many times that it soon sounded like a broken record.

My husband was concerned about my mood and suggested that I go away for a few days and rest and seek peace within. That is when I telephoned Mother Myriam, the Abbess at Our Lady of the Redwoods in Whitethorn, the abbey of the Trappistine Nuns in the diocese of Santa Rosa.

SAID TO COME

I asked Mother if I could come up for a few days. At

THOMAS MERTON IN THE REDWOODS
... photographed by Mrs. Jones

ton the real Christian man. Not Thomas Merton a Trappist priest and monk or Thomas Merton a writer and poet, but Thomas Merton, my brother in Christ Jesus.

The next four days were to be the most exciting and

to come back for dinner at noon. So that first morning after Mass, I went to my room to clean it and get a book and began my retreat.

As I came out of my room, Father Tom suggested to me an area that was beu-

Time to see Christ in each other

ing along, a deer ran in front of the car. This I did not mind as I am used to deer. We have them in our backyard and in the summer they come in herds to eat up our front lawn. But all of a sudden I saw an oncoming car.

I tried not to appear frightened, but Fr. Tom took one glance and said, "Stop, and I will get out and ask the other driver if he will back up to an area large enough for us to pass." (Thanks be to God, I said to myself. I could never in this world back up on that winding one lane, unpaved road.)

We proceded until we came to a sheep ranch where we were to report to the owner that we would be at the beach and that we were from the Monastery. This beach was part of the ranch and we did not want to be mistaken for sheep thieves.

After Fr. Tom's brief talk to the rancher we started to the beach which was another five or six miles. As we left and I had driven a few hundred yards from the ranch, the car got stuck in a ditch and everytime I would put it either in drive or reverse the tires would go farther into the ditch.

PUSHED CAR

Photograph of Thomas Merton by Gracie Jones
The Monitor (San Rafael, California), January 2, 1969
Photograph of Thomas Merton used with permission of the Merton Legacy Trust and Thomas Merton Center at Bellarmine University

Chapter Twenty-Two

Four Days with Merton[1]

by Gracie M. Jones

My being a Negro, you must know how I felt over the assassination of Dr. Martin Luther King Jr. I was deeply grieved and deeply hurt, for in Dr. King I saw real non-violent hope for a new way of life for Negroes in this country. I became more anguished as the days and weeks went by last April. You have no idea what it feels like to have your white neighbors and your white friends telephone after such a tragedy and say: "Gracie, what can I do?" That phrase was asked of me so many times that it soon sounded like a broken record.

My husband was concerned about my mood and suggested that I go away for a few days and rest and seek peace within. That is when I telephoned Mother Myriam, the Abbess at Our Lady of the Redwoods in Whitethorn, the abbey of the Trappistine Nuns in the diocese of Santa Rosa. I asked Mother if I could come up for a few days. At first, she said I would not be able to come until after May 16. However, several hours later she telephoned me and said to come.

So it was that Wednesday, May 8, I left for the Redwoods where I was to stay through Sunday, May 12—Mother's Day. I arrived at the Abbey a little after 3 p.m. and was assigned a room in the first wing of guest rooms. One of the Sisters had given me a schedule. I noticed while unpacking that Vespers was at 3:35 and it was near that time. I hurriedly ran out of my room and approached my car as it is about an eight-minute walk from the guest area to the chapel.

---

1. This essay first appeared in the "A Personal Story" section of the San Rafael, California, newspaper, *The Monitor*, January 2, 1969.

As I went to get into the car, I noticed a man coming out of a room in the same building as my room. He asked if I had had a nice drive up. I mumbled something and drove off. (Never asking if he wanted a ride). At Vespers this same man came in and sat behind me. He was dressed in blue jeans and was wearing a grey sweatshirt. After Vespers one of the Sisters came out and said that Rev. Mother would like to see me in her office. I went to her office and Rev. Mother welcomed me to Our Lady of the Redwoods and informed me that during my stay that it would only be myself and Thomas Merton as guests. Well, I nearly fainted. I was speechless.

As I left her office and came outside, Thomas Merton was waiting to introduce himself to me. I was a little embarrassed for not having offered him a ride a half hour before. But you could never really feel embarrassed with Thomas Merton—he had a manner that once you became acquainted with him, you felt immediately at ease. You felt loved, you knew you would be remembered in his prayers, you knew he would be thoughtful of little things. So, this is how I met and began to know Thomas Merton the real Christian man. Not Thomas Merton a Trappist priest and monk or Thomas Merton a writer and poet, but Thomas Merton, my brother in Christ Jesus.

The next four days were to be the most exciting and happy, fun-filled and spiritual days of my life. There were times during the next four days that I thought for sure God was preparing me for death and was somehow in His goodness allowing me these unusual days. The first morning I overslept for ten minutes and had to dress in a hurry so as to make it to Lauds on time. As I came out of my room that early Thursday morning, Father Tom was already on the trail heading for the chapel and Lauds. He hollered to me: "Hurry Gracie, let's run so we will not be late." So, we ran in the brisk and foggy morning. With me assuring him that it was not raining but the wetness that comes with California fog.

The four Masses that I would be a part of during my stay were concelebrated by Father Tom and Father Roger, who is spiritual director for the Sisters at the abbey and their director. Thursday, Father Roger was the principal celebrant, and the nuns' new beautiful chapel is built in such a manner that as a retreatant you do not break the cloister. You do not feel isolated from the community but rather very much a part of it. Each day during the offertory of the Mass I would join the Sisters as we gathered near the altar. At this Thursday Mass, Father Roger gave the kiss of peace to Father Tom and he gave it to me and I passed it to the Sister standing next to me on the cloistered side of the chapel. Since I was making a retreat, I was able to receive Communion under both forms each day. And both priests as they gave me either the Body or the Blood of Christ, called me by my name. On that first day of the Eucharistic celebration, Fr. Tom said: "Gracie, the Blood of Christ."

At the Redwoods after Mass, you have the rest of the day free for your retreat until time for Vespers, except remembering to come back for dinner at noon. So, that first morning after Mass, I went to my room to clean it and get a book and began my retreat. As I came out of my room, Father Tom suggested to me an area that was beautiful if I liked hiking. Well, I would have liked anything to tell you the truth. We then went for a brief hike there on the grounds of the abbey. There were so many things I wanted to talk about. We talked about the death of Dr. King and I gave him my viewpoints on the struggle of the Negro as we discussed the role of the Church in civil rights. We also discussed the role of those in monastic life in relation to the world. Being that I had a close friend who had been in a Trappist monastery for almost a year at that time, I had many questions about the life of a Trappist and especially a novice Trappist. After the brief hike and chat, we each retired for silence.

That evening after supper and Compline we decided that on Friday morning after Mass we would go to the beach. Fr. Tom loved the seashore and I always found peace and calm by staying at the seaside. So, I was excited about this trip. Friday morning after breakfast and Mass, the Sisters had prepared a picnic lunch for us. They had packed our lunch in two airline hostess bags; one labeled "Fr. Tom" and the other "Gracie." Off we went. I had no idea that the road we would travel would be unpaved, one lane and the most winding road I had ever driven with real sharp curves. Suddenly, as we were riding along, a deer ran in front of the car. This I did not mind as I am used to deer. We have them in our backyard and in the summer, they come in herds to eat up our front lawn. But all of a sudden, I saw an oncoming car. I tried not to appear frightened, but Fr. Tom took one glance and said, "Stop, I will get out and ask the other driver if he will back up to an area large enough for us to pass." (Thanks be to God, I said to myself. I could never in this world back up on that winding one lane, unpaved road.) We proceeded until we came to a sheep ranch where we were to report to the owner that we would be at the beach and that we were from the Monastery. This beach was part of the ranch and we did not want to be mistaken for sheep thieves.

After Fr. Tom's brief talk to the rancher, we started to the beach, which was another five or six miles. As we left and I had driven a few hundred yards from the ranch, the car got stuck in a ditch and every time I would put it either in drive or reverse the tires would go farther into the ditch. Finally, Fr. Tom said he would try and lift and push the car and for me to put it in drive. This I did, and he lifted and pushed and got the tires out of the ditch and I raced some two or three hundred yards down the road with Fr. Tom left standing at the ditch. He ran to catch up with the car. I never knew until later that he had an injured back.

At last, we came to the ocean. All of a sudden, the sun was shining and the fog had disappeared. We ran like two children over one knoll and then another. We looked at the beautiful twisted trees that had become that way from the wind and the sea. Fr. Tom wanted me to see the black sand below at the seashore, so we hiked down and, oh, the beauty. We came back up to a knoll that had the most fantastic view of the beauty and splendor of the Pacific Ocean. He said: "I wonder how long it will be before someone discovers this beautiful area and spoils it with a development or a resort of some kind?" Since we had each brought a book along, we went our separate way to read, to meditate, to take in the beauty of God's own creation. I always make a habit of taking along a notebook with me wherever I go so as to jot down billboard ads or song titles or reflections that come to me. But this day I sat there on the knoll and wrote a letter to His Excellency, Archbishop McGucken,[2] to express my own personal feelings about some of the "Inner City" parishes, making suggestions to place priests who had special talents in working among the poor in these areas.

I somehow felt that the poor needed more than just special collections, but rather special priests to work with them and someone who would have a particular understanding of their needs. At lunch time there at the ocean, I shared this letter with Father Tom to get his reaction, as I wanted the letter to be specific but not harsh. Father Tom felt it was an honest and sincere letter, so it was that I mailed that letter to His Excellency from the Redwoods. We spent some five hours here in this beautiful area. Hours where we each had time alone and then hours together in real dialog. With Fr. Tom you felt that you had finally met your first "real priest"—your first "real Christian." His openness and sensitivity to the needs of the poor and those suffering from injustice were overwhelming. We returned to the monastery, late for Vespers but somehow filled to the

---

2. John Thomas McGucken (1902–1983), Archbishop of San Francisco, 1962–1977.

brim with the love of God. That evening after Compline he gave to me an unpublished article on "Dr. King and Gandhi."

By Saturday I was on Cloud Nine. I had asked Fr. Tom if I could share these days of my retreat with my Trappist novice friend. I told him how it was this priest who had baptized our whole family and it was he, who after our baptism, had started me to read books by Thomas Merton. Saturday was a day of real contemplation. I was drunk with the beauty of the love of the Sisters and the thoughtfulness of both Father Tom and Father Roger. However, the next day, Sunday, May 12, was to be a day that would outdo the previous days. It was also Mother's Day. After breakfast, there was some two-and-one-half hours before Mass, so Father Tom and I went for a walk down the highway, yet still on the property of the Monastery. Here we exchanged many ideas and really opened up to one another.

It was a time of seeing Christ present in each other and of being able to relate the Christ in you that was bubbling over. It was a time for me to discuss my feelings concerning the lily-white community I lived in, my role as a Negro woman in the Catholic Church. I told him of the struggle of the Olympic Club of 1966 and 1967 and the bitterness of Christians not willing to be sensitive to what is real to another. We discussed the Christian who is afraid to be himself. I later that morning took three pictures of him.

At Mass he was the principal celebrant. That was a great Mass and will be remembered by all of us there for years to come. It was a joyful Eucharist. We knew what the resurrection really means. We were "People of the Resurrection." "Real Easter People." That Mass was one in which all present felt the essence of the Mystical Body of Christ. Following our thanksgiving after Mass, Fr. Tom said: "I shall never forget this day and what it has meant to each of us." After dinner I knew I would have to leave in order to get home before dark. Father Tom had some mail he wanted me to drop off on my way home. He had picked a flower for me and gave it to me for Mother's Day. I left Our Lady of the Redwoods on Cloud Nine. I wanted to hurry and get home and share with my husband and our children all that the Lord had given to me. I wanted to hurry and spread all the love and insights of those precious days and hours and events.

Those days at the Redwoods were to be the last time I would ever see Thomas Merton alive, though I later received three letters from him. In June I received a letter thanking me for sending him copies of the pictures I had taken, especially the ones of the seashore. With this letter he also sent a copy of his Midsummer newsletter stating his reaction to the assassination of Senator Robert F. Kennedy and trying to answer the questions that had been asked by many concerning his good friends, Fathers Dan and Philip Berrigan, explaining why they had to take such extremes in order to shock people. On July 13, we received a second letter written on the 12th stating that he would celebrate and offer the Holy Sacrifice of the Mass for us on July 14, the day of our seventeenth wedding anniversary. In August we received a paper he had prepared called, "Notes on the Future of Monasticism."[3] We also received from him copies of the Summer, Fall, and Winter *Monks Pond*. And finally, a letter stating his going to be able to go abroad.

Father Tom had consented to write a preface of a book I told him I wanted to write regarding "The Negro and the Catholic Church." Because of the time it takes for research, I never really got started. Naturally, you think you will always have time, the person will always be there. I will however, get busy now and write that book.

I hope those of you who came to know Thomas Merton through his writings will somehow know him a little better as a Christian man by what I was able to share with him for a few days. I would like to sum up by quoting him from his book *Life and Holiness*:

> There is no charity without justice. Too often we think of charity as a kind of moral luxury, as something which we choose to practice, and which gives us merit in God's sight, at the same time satisfying a certain interior need to "do good."

> Such charity is immature and even in some cases completely unreal. True charity is love, and love implies deep concern for the needs of another. It is not a matter of moral self-indulgence, but of strict obligation.

> I am obliged by the law of Christ and of the Spirit to be concerned with my brother's need, above all with his greatest need, the need for love.[4]

---

3. Published posthumously in *Contemplation in a World of Action*, 232–39.

4. Thomas Merton, *Life and Holiness* (New York: Herder & Herder, 1963), 87–88.

Acknowledgments

The publication of *Thomas Merton in California* would not have been possible without the generous and prayerful support of Sr. Kathy DeVico, OCSO, and the Redwoods Monastery community. I remain humbled and extraordinarily grateful for the ongoing trust placed in me by Sr. Kathy and the Redwoods community to undertake this work. *Thank you.* Sharon Duggan has also been instrumental in this process, not only through her initiative to digitize the original reel-to-reel recordings, but also by accuracy-checking the entire manuscript against the original recordings, often making several editorial improvements.

The Merton Legacy Trust generously granted permission to publish this material, with special thanks to Peggy Fox. Scholarly work on Thomas Merton would not be possible without the support of Paul M. Pearson and Mark C. Meade of the Thomas Merton Center at Bellarmine University. Paul generously met with me, recommended sources I was not aware of (including the essay by Gracie Jones that appears in this volume), and was instrumental in selecting from over a hundred of Merton's California photographs to include in this volume.

Hans Christoffersen and the entire Liturgical Press staff have been exemplary in their professionalism, timely and helpful responses, and attention to detail. As a Saint John's University School of Theology alumnus, I could not be more thrilled to have this work come home to Collegeville.

Douglas Christie, a longtime friend of Redwoods Monastery, has been exceedingly generous in agreeing to compose the Preface for this volume. Brother David Steindl-Rast, OSB, lifelong witness to the fruits of contemplative practice and interreligious dialogue, and participant in the October 1968 Redwoods Conferences, wrote an endorsement that an author/editor could only dream of receiving. Brendan Collins generously shared his firsthand lived experience of monastic renewal in the 1960s, which provided helpful context for this work overall.

Vincent Pizzuto and the community of St. Columba's Episcopal Church and Retreat House, Inverness, California, invited me to join them as a visiting scholar in August 2022. There, I was able to compose the Introduction to this volume amidst the silence and expansive natural beauty of West Marin County. The peninsula of Point Reyes was one of Merton's last geographic "visions" before departing North America for Asia. The power of this wild and rugged place and that connection was not lost on me.

Patrick F. O'Connell, a living embodiment of the *Merton Encyclopedia*, generously read through the entirety of this manuscript, contributed dozens of additional references and line edits, and solved numerous outstanding historical and textual riddles, all of which have added significantly to this project, and greatly increased the integrity of the volume overall. Thank you, Pat, for all you continue to offer to the world of Merton Studies.

Patrick Walling (patrickwalling.com) generously and artistically "mapped" Merton in California as well as provided general cheer, gracious hospitality, and culinary delight. Amy Burke and Jamie Fortin have anchored me in my reality and contributed significantly to this project in unseen ways. My colleagues at Pacifica Graduate Institute have consistently inquired, supported, and cheered on this work, particularly Emily Lord-Kambitsch, Evans Lansing Smith, and Sondra Gatewood. My parents, Tony and Chris, have shown loving interest in my scholarly pursuits and particularly this volume, and deserve acknowledgment and thanks for encouraging such a wayward vocation.

My first pilgrimage behind the "redwood curtain" was co-authored alongside Robert K. Peach and Daniel DeForest London, introducing me to Redwoods Monastery and the Lost Coast over a decade ago. The seeds for this project were planted then and there; it only took the tending of sun, soil, and Spirit to bring it to life, and this was encouraged and witnessed firsthand by Joanna Walling, who midwifed and otherwise stood by me in ways seen and unseen. Thank you for your steadfast love and support throughout the completion of this work.

Lastly, to Jonathan Montaldo, for your friendship, mentoring, guidance, and laughter for over two decades. You saw the vision when I could not. Thank you for being the lighthouse.

David M. Odorisio
Santa Barbara, California

Permissions

Index